THE MAN FROM MONTICELLO

An Intimate Life of Thomas Jefferson

Also by Thomas Fleming

HISTORY

WEST POINT
The Men and Times of the United States Military Academy

AFFECTIONATELY YOURS, GEORGE WASHINGTON
A Self-Portrait in Letters of Friendship

ONE SMALL CANDLE
The Pilgrims' First Year in America

BEAT THE LAST DRUM

NOW WE ARE ENEMIES

FICTION

A CRY OF WHITENESS

KING OF THE HILL

THE GOD OF LOVE

ALL GOOD MEN

THE MAN FROM

Monticello

An Intimate Life of

Thomas Jefferson

BY

Thomas Fleming

William Morrow and Company, Inc., New York

1969

Published simultaneously in Canada by
George J. McLeod Limited, Toronto.

Printed and bound in the United States of America
by The Cornwall Press, Inc., New York, N.Y.

Designed by Paula Wiener.

Library of Congress Catalog Card Number 79–77220

Contents

PHOTOS APPEAR FOLLOWING PAGES 90 AND 250

BOOK ONE: Between Love and Liberty   1

BOOK TWO: Old World to Conquer   111

BOOK THREE: New World of Politics   163

BOOK FOUR: Birth of a Candidate   217

BOOK FIVE: Rebirth of a Nation   271

BOOK SIX: The Country Gentleman   345

A Jefferson Family Tree   387

Notes on Sources and Methods   388

Bibliography   391

Index   394

BOOK
ONE

*Between Love
and Liberty*

❧

Down a narrow, rutted dirt road, past fields where brown tobacco leaves mellowed in the sun, rode a rangy, rusty-haired man of twenty-seven on a big muscular bay horse. The man was in an exuberant mood. His blue-gray eyes devoured the vivid colors of the changing woods, in the rich fall sunshine. Other travelers on the road, whether white or black, got a cheerful good morning. Occasionally he would hum a song.

None of this was unusual. Thomas Jefferson was fond of saying: "There is not a sprig of grass that grows uninteresting to me." He could give without hesitation the ponderous botanical names for almost every tree and bush he passed. As a true-born Virginian, he was proud, too, of his courtesy. It did not matter if a fellow traveler was black, and a slave. He got the same gracious, soft-voiced greeting. As for humming songs, this long-limbed "straight-up" six-footer was always singing as he strode about his plantation.

Even more than most Virginians of his day, Thomas Jefferson loved music. A few feet behind the young lawyer rode his Negro slave, Jupiter, the guardian of his most precious possession—his violin. It may have been Jupiter who nine months before rode frantically into Charlottesville to bring Jefferson the worst possible news. His family home, Shadwell, had been completely destroyed by a wind-whipped fire. In anguish Jefferson asked if anything—above all his thousand-book library—had been rescued. "No, marster, all lost," was the reply, "but we save your fiddle."

Most of the melodies Tom Jefferson was humming on this journey in the fall of 1770 were love songs. The words were absurd, in the plaintive romantic tradition of the day.

Enraptured I gaze when my Delia is by
And drink the sweet poison of love from her eye;
I feel the soft passion pervade every part
And pleasures unusual play round my fond heart.

A few months ago this young man of the world would have laughed cynically at such bathos. But now he was on his way to make his first visit to a house called The Forest. A tall, rather ungainly wooden structure, it sat on a knoll overlooking the broad James River, the main highway of Virginia, that flowed serenely from Richmond to the sea. The great planters of the Old Dominion—the Carters, the Shirleys, the Randolphs—had far more magnificent houses, near-palaces of resplendent red brick. Only a mile and a half from The Forest was one of the finest, Shirley, where the agreeable and well-known Mr. Jefferson would have been equally welcome. But The Forest was his destination on this fine October day. There was someone waiting there who seemed to listen with a special attention to the young attorney's strenuous opinions on topics as various as slavery, architecture, the political rights of colonial Americans and the importance of scientific farming.

Her name was Martha Wayles Skelton and her hair was a rich auburn, her large eyes hazel. A fragile, delicately boned, diminutive beauty of twenty-two, she was the widow of Bathhurst Skelton, one of a lively group of young men with whom Tom Jefferson had shared his student days at the College of William and Mary in Williamsburg. He had probably met Martha Wayles then, along with a host of other girls whose names still twinkle in his youthful letters—Rebecca Burwell, Suzanna Potter, Alice Corbin, Nancy Randolph. Jefferson had spent the years between twenty and twenty-three adoring Rebecca, an orphan descended from some of the best families of Virginia. The heiress to a considerable fortune, she lived with the wealthy William Nelsons of Yorktown.

"Enthusiasm" was the word her contemporaries used to sum up Rebecca in later years. To the eighteenth century this meant a vivid, strongly emotional personality. For months Jefferson had carried with him in his watch a silhouette of her which she had cut out with her own hands—surely a sign that she did not treat his courtship with complete disdain. But this memento met a fate that might have made a more superstitious man suspect worse disasters to come. Visiting over the Christmas holidays with another set of friends, Jefferson put the watch containing "the dear picture," as he called it, on a table beside his bed. During the night it rained. Jefferson woke to find his watch "all afloat in water" let in by a leak in the roof. When he attempted to rescue Rebecca's image from the deluge, his "cursed fingers" gave it a rip that fatally mangled it.

For over two years the romance percolated but Jefferson could not seem to bring himself to ask the ultimate question. He rhapsodized in letters about "Belinda"—the romantic name he gave Rebecca, in the vain hope of disguising her identity among his friends, but he knew that marriage in eighteenth-century Virginia meant the end of youth, a sad farewell to the bachelor's freedom. For Jefferson it would also mean the extinction of his dream of traveling to that distant, fascinating old world of England, France and Italy, about which he had read so much. Once, alone with Rebecca in a garden, he had hinted strongly that if she would promise to wait a year or two he would begin his grand tour instantly. But the young lady's frown seemed to cast a shadow on this idea. The would-be lawyer returned to his struggles with "Old Coke," as he called Sir Edward Coke, the great British jurist whose commentaries on the laws of England were famed for their crabbed style and "uncouth but cunning learning." Retreating to Shadwell, he lamented that he was certain to spend his time thinking of Rebecca "too often, I fear, for my peace of mind, and too often, I am sure, to get through Old Cooke [Coke] this winter: for God knows I have not seen him since I packed him up in my trunk in Williamsburg."

A month later he was writing to his same friend, Page, asking plaintively, "How does RB do? What do you think of my affair, or what would you advise me to do? Had I better stay here and do nothing or go down and do less?" He decided on the first choice and spent his days and nights struggling with Coke and planning a voyage in an imaginary ship called *The Rebecca* in which he would visit "England, Holland, France, Spain, Italy (where I would buy me a good fiddle) and Egypt." Meanwhile, another college mate, Jacquelin Ambler, began visiting his unattainable damsel. All through the following spring and summer, Jefferson stayed home, philosophizing "If she consents I shall be happy; if she does not I must endeavor to be so as much as possible . . . Perfect happiness, I believe, was never intended by the Deity to be the lot of any one of his creatures in this world."

His friend Page, acting both as adviser and ambassador, warned Jefferson that Mr. Ambler was making ominous progress. So at last the philosophic lover bestirred himself, and came down to Williamsburg for the social season. He was soon giving Ambler strong competition. Then came a climactic night at Raleigh Tavern, the favorite gathering place of the young bloods and their belles. The tables were cleared and the ladies and gentlemen arrived for a ball. The ladies were dressed "in that gay and splendid" style that made Virginia famous, their hair "craped" high with rolls on each side, topped by caps of gauze and lace. The men looked almost as gorgeous in their clockwork silk stockings, lace ruffles, gold- and silver-laced cocked hats, and breeches and waistcoats of blue, green, scarlet or peach. The idea was to see and be seen, to charm and be charmed.

Jefferson had spent the hours before the dance composing a whole series of romantic compliments, witty remarks and bright observations. "I was prepared to say a great deal," he told his friend Page. "I had dressed up in my own mind such thoughts as occurred to me in as moving language as I knew how, and expected to have performed in a tolerably creditable manner."

But when the lover came face to face with Rebecca in all her finery: "Good God! . . . a few broken sentences uttered in great disorder and interrupted with pauses of uncommon length were the too visible marks of my strange confusion!"

"Last night," the vanquished suitor groaned, "I never could have thought the succeeding sun would have seen me so wretched as I now am!"

Behind and beneath the mask of the blithe bachelor, the engaging young lawyer, there was concealed a deeply sensitive, essentially shy scholar.

The following May, Rebecca married Jacquelin Ambler and Jefferson retired once more to philosophizing and making matches for his friends. He even proposed to Suckey Potter on behalf of his fellow lawyer William Fleming. A few lines later he was telling Will, "Many and great are the comforts of a single state, and neither of the reasons you urge can have any influence with an inhabitant and a young inhabitant too of Wmsburg." A few weeks later he was cheerfully reporting to Page the fate of their friend Warner Lewis. "Poor fellow, never did I see one more sincerely captivated in my life. He walked to Indian Camp with her yesterday, by which means he had an opportunity of giving her two or three love squeezes by the hand, and like a true Arcadian swain, has been so enraptured ever since that he is company for no one."

But such examples of romantic bliss did not impress Jefferson. After his narrow escape, he settled down to practicing law and enjoying life. He dated his Williamsburg letters "Devilsburgh" and needled friends such as Fleming for falling in love. The young lawyer even drifted in a direction more than one bachelor has taken and made wry comments on the matchmaking all around him. When William Bland won Betsey Yates, Jefferson wryly remarked: "Whether it was for money, beauty or principle, it will be so nice a dispute that no one will venture to pronounce."

Soon he was copying from his favorite books quotations which trace an equally familiar evolution of the bachelor's psychology.

> . . . Wed her?
> No! Were she all desire could wish, as fair
> As would the vainest of her sex be thought
> With wealth beyond what woman's pride could waste
> She should not cheat me of my freedom . . .

He placed more and more value on the company of his men friends, conveniently ignoring the fact that most of them had married. One day he was writing John Page about how much he enjoyed "the philosophical evenings" at Page's plantation, Rosewell. The next day he was copying: "I'd leave the world for him that hates a woman, woman the fountain of all human frailty."

The remarks about frailty may have special significance. Around this time the roving bachelor became involved in a flirtation that he was to regret bitterly in future years. One of his close friends in his native Albemarle County was Jack Walker. He had married a buxom miss named Betsey Moore and was living only a few miles from the Jeffersons' family seat, Shadwell. Young Walker was offered the job of clerk to a Virginia commission negotiating a treaty with the Indians at Fort Stanwix and he departed for this post beyond the Blue Ridge Mountains, leaving Betsey behind. Jefferson knew her, of course, and was a frequent visitor in their house, as he was in the houses of all his married friends. But for Betsey and him, the visits suddenly became more than casual meetings. It is—or was—the stuff of which popular fiction has long been made: the lonely bride and the lonelier bachelor, the unsuspecting absent husband. Before long a mixture of passion and calculation had the sophisticated bachelor using his college education to persuade Betsey that there was nothing whatsoever wrong with enjoying the delights of illicit love. To back him up he undoubtedly quoted poets and novelists by the yard. But Betsey, after hesitating long enough to send the bachelor into a frenzy of woman-hating, finally said no and Jefferson retreated with nothing to show for his efforts but a badly wounded ego.

Fortunately, there came into his lovelorn life a far more healthy influence. He had another boyhood friend from Albemarle—one much closer than Jack Walker. His name was Dabney Carr. Like Jefferson, he too was pursuing the law as a career and showed great promise. In 1765, Carr married Jefferson's younger sister Martha. Their happiness made a deep impression on bachelor Jefferson, and all but reversed his plunge into cynicism. Writing to his favorite correspondent, John Page, Jefferson told almost wonderingly how Carr "speaks, thinks and dreams of nothing but his young son. This friend of ours, Page, in a very small house, with a table, half a dozen chairs, and one or two servants, is the happiest man in the universe." Seeing Page himself happily married with two fine children and a wife who shared his fondness for books and good talk also impressed Jefferson. After a 1770 visit to Rosewell, the Page estate, he wrote: "I was always fond of philosophy even in its dryer forms, but from a ruby lip it comes with charms irresistible. Such a feast of sentiment must exhilarate life . . . at least as much as the feast of the sensualist shortens it."

Seven months after he wrote these words, the fast-fading bachelor was riding blissfully toward The Forest singing love songs. In Martha Wayles Skelton he had found a woman who totally routed the potential cynic in his nature. "Sweetness of temper" was the quality Jefferson put first in a list of wifely virtues he compiled for one of his numerous notebooks. This, Martha Wayles possessed to an extraordinary degree. Among her other qualities, two were especially attractive to a sophisticated young Virginian of 1770— "spriteliness and sensibility." In Virginia as in Europe there was a growing fondness for the romantic in contrast to the coldly classical formalism that had dominated literature and the arts for most of the eighteenth century. To be a person of sensibility, to react with strong emotions to the beauties and pleasures of life, to its joy and its sadness, was the newest style. One Virginia belle proudly reported to a friend her reaction to the latest work of the popular novelist, Lady Julia Mandeville: "I think I never cried more in my life reading a novel."

What delight it must have been for Jefferson when he discovered that he and Martha shared a common enthusiasm for *Tristram Shandy* by Laurence Sterne. This comic masterpiece was the black humor of its day, considered just a little naughty by the strait-laced, but fervently admired by the younger generation for the way it spoofed musty academic learning, windy doctors of medicine, boring old soldiers and a dozen other favorite satiric targets of the young, while pausing to bathe in pure sentiment such inevitabilities as true love and premature death. The philosophy of the book is clear in Sterne's dedication: "I live in a constant endeavor to fence against the infirmities of ill health and other evils of life by mirth; being firmly persuaded that every time a man smiles—but much more so when he laughs, that it adds something to this Fragment of Life."

Martha Skelton's fondness for *Tristram Shandy* was not her only recommendation. She also shared Jefferson's passion for music and played beautifully on the spinet and harpsichord. Add to these accomplishments a natural grace when walking and riding, a brilliant complexion, those large expressive eyes of the richest shade of hazel and that luxuriant hair of the finest tinge of auburn—and you know why Thomas Jefferson was wearing out his horseflesh on the road to The Forest.

He soon discovered there were other suitors. Martha was not only beautiful, she was rich. Her father was, in Jefferson's words, "a lawyer of much practice" who had amassed a handsome fortune, and she had inherited still more wealth from her two years of marriage with Bathhurst Skelton. Between her late husband, dead now two years, and her father, she would eventually own over 10,000 acres of prime Virginia land. Such a prize whetted the ardor of more than one young scion. But Jefferson soon forged ahead of the other eager visitors. At twenty-seven he was already a member of the House of Burgesses, Virginia's legislature, and a well-established lawyer making $3,000 a year from his practice at the bar and $2,000 from his 5,000 acres of good farmland. This was a substantial income in the days when a laborer could be hired for as little as $10 a month.

There is a tradition that her industrious father had trained Martha "to business" and this gave Mr. Jefferson another advantage. Martha was supposedly looking for a husband who could manage her substantial estate. A far wealthier Virginia widow, Martha Custis, had thus combined heart and head when she married Colonel George Washington in 1759. But there is no evidence of such a sensible if not inspiring explanation for Mr. Jefferson's success. On the contrary, there is far more evidence that between Martha Wayles Skelton and Thomas Jefferson the dominant emotion was deep, compelling love.

But as a woman of sensibility, and a true Virginia belle, Martha was not about to capitulate immediately to Mr. Jefferson. A girl in 1770 Virginia was expected to keep a suitor dangling for six or eight months at least. Martha did better than that, although it was not entirely her fault.

Twice before the year 1770 ended, Jefferson returned to The Forest, finally spending the Christmas holidays there. By the time he rode away, after sharing this jolliest of seasons on a Virginia plantation, he no longer had the slightest doubt that he and Martha were deeply in love. But he was confronted by an unexpected reluctance on the part of John Wayles to accept him as a son-in-law.

Just why is something of a mystery. Perhaps Wayles had higher social ambitions for his daughter. As a lawyer who was, in Jefferson's own words, "welcomed in every society," he may have envisioned a family alliance between his line and one of the aristocratic Virginia families whose great estates lined the banks of the lower James. Jefferson's lineage was good enough. His mother had been a Randolph, definitely one of the first families of the colony. But by 1770 the Randolphs had multiplied so prodigiously that a descent on the maternal side did not mean much. William Randolph of Turkey Island, who died in 1711, had been a man of vast wealth and energy. He had seven sons, and they in turn married and begat and acquired more wealth with all of their father's zest. By the end of the eighteenth century, so many people were involved in the Randolph line that despairing genealogists called William and his wife "the Adam and Eve of Virginia."

The Jeffersons, on the other hand, were much more obscure. They were descended from Thomas Jefferson I, who came to Virginia about 1679 and died in 1697. They never acquired vast swaths of prime Virginia land, as did the male Randolphs. They moved west, in search of cheaper land, in the manner of millions of Americans in generations to come, until they reached Albemarle County, where they achieved a sturdy prosperity, but, in 1770, Albemarle was still considered, if not the frontier, definitely back country, one of the less socially attractive parts of the state. In later years Jefferson was to refer acidly to the "cyphers of the aristocracy" who controlled Virginia in his youth—a hint that he may have more than once endured some painful comparisons with these elegant families. At any rate, on February 20, 1771, he was complaining to a friend about how the "unfeeling temper of a parent" could obstruct a marriage.

But he did not let this discourage him. Seldom did two weeks go by without seeing Mr. Jefferson and Jupiter ride up the hill to hand their horses over to the stable boys at The Forest. It was during one of these visits, family tradition tells us, that two other suitors arrived not long after Jefferson. They were preening themselves on the broad veranda, getting ready to make their entrance, when from inside the house there came the sound of a violin and a spinet playing a plaintive love song. For a long moment the two suitors stood there eying each other uneasily. Without a word they went down the steps, recalled their horses from the stables and rode away. Something about the duet made it clear that they were wasting their time.

Jefferson made no secret of his love. In August, 1771, he was telling another frequent visitor to The Forest, Robert Skipwith, who was courting Martha's younger sister Tabitha, to "offer prayers for me at that shrine to which though absent I pray continual devotions. In every scheme of happiness she is placed in the foreground of the picture, as the principal figure. Take that away, and it is no picture for me."

He was also singing Martha's praises in Williamsburg, as is evident from a letter he received in the spring of 1771 from an older woman friend, Mrs. Drummond. She was obviously still breathless from a word picture of Martha the capitulated bachelor had left with her. "Let me recollect your discription," she wrote, "which bars all the romantic poetical ones I ever read . . . Thou wonderful young man, indeed I shall think spirits of an higher order inhabits yr aerey mountains—or rather mountain, which I may contemplate but never can aspire too . . . Persevere, thou good young man, persevere—she has good sence, and good nature, and I hope will not refuse (the blessing shal' I say) why not as I think it,—of yr hand, if her heart's not ingagd allready."

The "aerey mountain" Mrs. Drummond mentioned with such admiration was a conical 857-foot peak little more than a mile outside Charlottesville, soaring in lonely splendor above the broad Piedmont Valley. When he was still in his teens, Jefferson and Dabney Carr used to ramble the slopes of this oddly isolated little mountain which was part of the Jefferson property. They would sit by the hour beneath the shade of a great oak, exchanging visionary plans of the future. Once in a sentimental moment they promised each other that if one died young, the survivor would see to it that he was buried here, beneath the brooding shadows of the great tree's sun-dappled branches. But Jefferson found the crest of the mountain more exhilarating and here, he impulsively told Carr one day, he planned to build a house. In eighteenth-century Virginia, with its all but nonexistent roads and dependence on river transportation, this was an idea almost as fanciful as flying.

The idea might have remained a boyish dream, if fire had not destroyed Shadwell. Earlier biographers had pictured this first home as a rude cabin in the wilderness. Recent archeological research on the site now makes it clear that Shadwell was a spacious country house, a rival, if not an equal, to The Forest and similar family estates. Shadwell's ruins revived Jefferson's dream of a more magnificent mansion on the nearby mountain. Soon he had workmen clearing and leveling the summit of the conical height.

Building was a slow business in the eighteenth century. After more than a year of work, all Jefferson was able to finish was a one-room brick cottage. But by now he was so much in love with his mountain that he moved into this tiny abode. In February, 1771, he was cheerfully writing to a friend that his one room, "like the cobbler's, serves me for parlour, for kitchen and hall, I may add for bed chamber and study too . . . I have hope, however, of getting more elbow room this summer."

This casual phrase was light-years away from the magnificent house Jefferson had already sketched and planned down to the precise proportions of every room. He was determined to create a house that blended the spirit of America and the architectural genius of Europe. Part of his motive was patriotic pride. He winced at most of the houses he saw in Virginia. The typical country house was usually constructed by the plantation owner himself, sometimes with the aid of a professional builder. The only architectural plans consulted, if any, were dull copies of English models. Except for a few great mansions such as Carter's Grove, near Williamsburg, most houses were unimaginative boxlike wooden squares or rectangles, with small ugly windows and low ceilings, their interiors haphazardly divided into smaller squares and rectangles. "It was impossible to devise things more ugly, [and] uncomfortable," Jefferson said. It cost nothing to add "symmetry and taste." But alas, there was "scarcely a model" in Virginia "sufficiently chaste to give an idea of them."

Already Jefferson had grasped the insight that was to make him the father of American architecture. In his college days, he had discovered the great Renaissance architect, Andrea Palladio, who had studied in detail the Roman ruins of Italy to learn the principles of his art. Jefferson instinctively responded to this classic tradition with its emphasis on clean chaste lines and carefully calculated symmetry. Not only did the style have "the approbation of thousands of years," but it was a perfect model for men struggling to bring order out of a chaotic wilderness. At the same time

Jefferson's American instincts set his house on a hill, where the eye could roam over miles of open country to the misty Blue Ridge Mountains, where the frontier began. The reconciliation of freedom and order—the theme that was to absorb Thomas Jefferson's life—was symbolized here, in its beginning years at Monticello.

American too was Jefferson's taste when it came to gardening. He liked contrast, mixture, in art, and envisioned his classic house surrounded by free-form gardens in the "Gothic" or natural style. His romantic state of mind obviously had something to do with this preference. In the summer of 1770, when he was urging his friend Skipwith to offer prayers for him at The Forest, he was sketching plans for a garden that included "a temple beside a spring" and a handy harp to add plaintive music.

In his woman-hating bachelor days, Jefferson had named his mountain "The Hermitage." Now, he began calling it "Monticello"—which means "little mountain" in Italian and is pronounced "Montichello." No doubt it came from his books on Palladio. But the chief appeal of the name was its sweetly romantic ring.

All this romantic staging meant little, unless Jefferson remembered Mrs. Drummond's advice to persevere. So he continued to pay frequent visits to The Forest. From England he ordered an expensive "forte-piano"—the very latest in musical improvements. He made a point of insisting "the workmanship of the whole [be] very handsome and worthy of the acceptance of a lady for whom I intend it." He also asked half humorously if his British agent would search the herald's office for the arms of the Jefferson family. "It is possible there may be none," he wrote. "If so, I would with your assistance become a purchaser, having Sterne's word for it that a coat of arms may be purchased as cheap as any other coat."

Jefferson was obviously straining to persuade someone—if not Martha, her father—that there was some worthwhile lineage on the Jefferson side of the argument too.

That he was making progress is evident from a letter written to him by Robert Skipwith in September of 1771. After thanking Jefferson for speaking affectionately of his "dearest Tibby," Skipwith expressed a wistful desire to "be neighbors to a couple so well calculated and disposed to communicate knowledge and pleasure. My sister Skelton, Jefferson I wish it were, has all the qualities which promise to assure you the greatest happiness mortals are capable of enjoying. May business and play musick and the merriments of your family companions lighten your hearts, soften your pillows and procure you health, long life and every human felicity!" Obviously, only the "unfeeling parent" needed to be worn down, to win the prize.

On November 11, 1771, if we interpret rightly the little pocket account book Jefferson kept, John Wayles finally agreed to surrender his daughter. The wedding date was set for January 1, little more than six weeks away, and proof of the couple's impatience. As the elated suitor departed for Monticello, he shared his joy with the Wayles's servants. Jefferson had always tipped them; it was the custom on Virginia plantations. But his amounts had been moderate, as befitted a sensible man who came and went regularly. Now he threw pounds and shillings right and left with an abandon that sent toasts to Mr. Jefferson echoing around The Forest's Negro quarter for the rest of the week.

What a ride back to Monticello Jupiter must have had, thundering over those atrocious roads in Jefferson's reckless wake. From boyhood Jefferson had been a fearless rider, always choosing the best blood horses, which he broke himself. Instead of letting Jupiter lead his horse across the Rivanna River, while he took a boat, Jefferson invariably plunged into this treacherous little stream, which he always had to cross on journeys to and from Monticello. Even when the river was swollen by spring rains and the horse had to swim for his life, Jefferson scorned the ferry.

Time was short and there was much to be done. Monticello had to be made as habitable as possible for the bride. In spite of the wintry weather, orders were issued to push hard on the construction of the main house, which had several rooms more or less completed. There were presents to be bought, guest lists to be drawn up, plans to be made for transporting Jefferson's mother, his four sisters and brother to the wedding.

On December 23, the all-but-ex-bachelor was back at The Forest to sign a very English-sounding wedding bond. His cosigner Francis Eppes was Martha's brother-in-law.

Know all men by these presents that we Thomas Jefferson and Francis Eppes are held and firmly bound to our Sovereign Lord the King, his heirs and successors in the sum of fifty pounds current money of Virginia . . . The condition of the above obligation is such that if there be no lawful cause to obstruct a marriage intended to be had and solemnized between the above bound Thomas Jefferson and Martha Skelton of the County of Charles City, widow, for which a license is desired, then this obligation is to be null and void; otherwise to remain in full force.

Jefferson paid the forty shillings for the marriage license and in the next eight days no "lawful cause" turned up to prevent the consummation of his dreams. No less than two ministers presided at the ceremony, each of whom Jefferson paid five pounds. There were fiddlers, also well paid by the bridegroom, and we can be certain that everyone devoured a sumptuous slice of a rich black wedding cake made with pounds of fruit, wine, brandy and dozens of eggs. The guests had traveled for days to enjoy the festivities, and enjoy them they did—for the next two and a half weeks. Not until January 18 did the newlyweds set out for Monticello, and even then they were in no hurry to get there.

On the way, Jefferson made a sentimental stop at Tuckahoe, the Randolph estate on the James a few miles above Richmond. The old white frame house with brick ends forming a letter H was rich in memories for him. For seven years, Tom Jefferson had lived there as a school boy, while his father, Peter Jefferson, had administered the estate and acted as guardian for the orphaned family of his friend and in-law William Randolph. Jefferson often said that his earliest memory was the day he was carried on a pillow by a mounted slave from Shadwell to Tuckahoe. Because William Randolph had stipulated in his will that his son, Thomas Mann Randolph, was to be taught by tutors, young Tom Jefferson also received his first schooling in a little house that still stands in the yard of Tuckahoe.

Jefferson made Martha laugh heartily with tales of those primitive school days. He loved to tell how once when he was desperate with hunger he repeated the Lord's Prayer in the hope of speeding the arrival of the dinner hour.

Tuckahoe also revived fond memories of Peter Jefferson, that giant of a man who had slept beneath Virginia's soil for almost fifteen years now. This huge pioneer, who had ventured into Albemarle when there were less that fifty white men living in the vicinity, was a kind of legend to Jefferson. He often told of the time his father was directing three able-bodied slaves to pull down a ruined shed with a rope. The Negroes hauled and sweated and nothing happened. Peter Jefferson seized the rope, slung it over one massive shoulder and gave a mighty heave. In an instant the shed was kindling on the ground. They still talked in Albemarle of his most fantastic feat, simultaneously "heading up" (raising from their sides to an upright position) two hogsheads of tobacco weighing nearly a thousand pounds apiece. As a surveyor Peter Jefferson had done as much as any man in Virginia to lay out the boundaries of the colony and construct a workable map. He had fought his way through the winter wilderness, leaving behind him a trail of assistants collapsed from starvation and fatigue, often living on the raw flesh of game and even on his own pack-train mules, sleeping in hollow trees while wolves and wildcats howled around him.

This same man went back to his plantation and read Addison, Swift, Pope and, above all, Shakespeare. Though he had died when Thomas was only fourteen, Peter Jefferson had already passed on to his son a vivid heritage. One of his favorite maxims was, "Never ask another to do for you what you can do for yourself." He made sure his son knew how to sit a horse, ford a swollen river, fire a gun, and fight his way up and down wooded hills in pursuit of deer and wild turkey. At the same time he insisted with ferocity on Jefferson obtaining the best possible education. He himself had had to snatch his learning whenever and wherever he could, in the course of a rugged life. Tom Jefferson had responded by becoming a student of almost incredible industry. It was not unusual for him to spend fifteen consecutive hours over his books. His friend John Page recalled in later years that Jefferson was the only one of their rollicking college group who could turn his back on a good time whenever he chose, and retreat for hours of studying. His love of books was nothing less than passionate. When his library went up with Shadwell's smoke, he remarked that it was worth 200 pounds —perhaps $5,000 in today's dollars. "I wish it had been the money," he said.

On went the newlyweds, with good wishes from Jefferson's old playmate, "Tuckahoe Tom" Randolph, through a landscape that grew more and more ghostly. Snow was falling in a way it seldom came down in Virginia. The Jeffersons dropped farther and farther behind schedule and finally the exhausted horses were literally plowing the light phaeton through drifts of three and four feet. Jefferson wisely turned off at Blenheim, one of the numerous Carter estates, seven or eight miles from Monticello. By now it was dark and the snow was falling faster and faster. The newlyweds could have easily taken advantage of the hospitality which was undoubtedly proffered by Blenheim's caretaker. But her husband had fired Martha's imagination with his rhapsodies about his mountain. He could restrain neither her nor himself in their determination to ignore the worst blizzard in decades, and push on. On horseback through the driving snow they slogged to the barely visible road that wound up Monticello's slope.

By now it was midnight and on the mountaintop there was not a sign of life. The white workmen and the Negro slaves had long since built up their fires against the howling storm and gone to bed. Trying to heat the few roofed rooms in the half-finished mansion house was out of the question, so Jefferson led Martha to the little one-room cottage he had built in those now laughable days when he pictured himself as the melancholy bachelor hermit, sardonically pondering the ways of the world from his lonely peak.

The place must have been brutally cold. While Martha shivered inside her cloak, the bridegroom constructed a fire with a skill he had learned from his frontiersman father. Soon a roaring blaze sent leaping waves of warmth and light against the walls of their little refuge, turning the wind's howls into a curiously comforting sound. They threw themselves before the blaze and shivered deliciously in each other's arms.

Suddenly Jefferson leaped up, remembering a hidden treasure. From behind a shelf of books he flourished with a whoop of triumph a half bottle of wine. Now the evening was complete. With bodies warmed and glasses full they lolled before the fire like a pair of Indian lovers, Martha's auburn head bent low, her hazel eyes shining over the sketches her husband spread out before her—brilliant promises of the magnificent house in which he vowed they would grow old together.

It was a night they both would remember for the rest of their lives. Neither thought, even for the tiniest moment, that there was anything ominous about that moaning winter wind, keening a kind of dirge around their little island of warmth and happiness. They did not stop to think how precious—and how rare—these moments were for human beings. They were young, life was young, and with such richness in their hearts and on their lips, how could promises fail? Mercifully, the future was as blank as the darkness that shrouded the windows.

II

The great world of Virginia—the courthouses, the plantation mansions—saw nothing of Thomas Jefferson for the next two months. The House of Burgesses met in its red brick capitol at Williamsburg without the young delegate from Albemarle. Fortunately the county had a second representative, Dr. Thomas Walker, so local needs were not neglected. Even that methodical recorder of Jefferson's goings and comings, his pocket account book, is silent until February 8. Not until April did the Jeffersons end their honeymoon and come down from their mountain for a journey to Williamsburg. They enjoyed the capital's highly social spring season, going to the theater regularly and riding out to visit friends such as the Pages at Rosewell. There was also a more significant visit—to a Dr. Brown. After a month's stopover at The Forest, they rode back to Monticello by easy stages, no longer able to conceal the happy expectation of an addition to the family.

On September 27, 1772, an hour after midnight, Martha gave birth to a daughter, whom Jefferson promptly named after her mother. The child was a thin, underweight baby and it did not seem to thrive. In an era when two out of every three children failed to survive the so-called childhood diseases, this was a bad omen. Someone, perhaps Jefferson, suggested allowing one of the Negro nurses to lend the baby her breast. The change was miraculous. In a matter of weeks the little girl was out of danger and the worried mother and father could smile once more.

Martha recovered very slowly from her pregnancy. On October 20 her father wrote plaintively to Jefferson using the family nickname, which her husband guarded jealously, even from his closest friends: "I have heard nothing about dear Patty since you left this place." It was the first faint hint of future sorrow.

But for a few more months there was only happiness at Monticello. By now the basic structure of the mansion was visible. It was organized around a spacious center room with an octagonal end, facing west, which Jefferson called the parlor. This was entered from a hall on the east side, through a classic, white pillared portico. Flanking the parlor was a smaller, square drawing room to the north, balanced by a matching square dining room to the south. These rooms in turn opened into small octagonal bow rooms, regaining the motif of the parlor. Off the hall was to be a large staircase to the roomy library, above the parlor. Balanced on either side of the library were two bedrooms. Off the parlor, on the west, was another handsome classic portico. The downstairs rooms were eighteen feet high—more than twice the height of the ordinary plantation house. The decorations on the porticos, on the mantels and indoor friezes were carefully selected from the various architectural "orders"—Doric, Ionic, Corinthian. It would, when finally finished, be a house that satisfied both the eye and the mind.

For Martha, perhaps the best proof of her husband's originality was his decision to put all the outbuildings that marred the appearance of so many Virginia plantations, below the ground under two L-shaped terraces that were to run from the bow rooms to their honeymoon cottage, and another matching cottage on the opposite side of the mountain. A kitchen, a laundry, a smoke room, a meal room, pantry, a dairy—there was room underground for everything in Jefferson's ingenious plan.

In the summer of 1773, Martha Jefferson was pregnant again. She and everyone else considered it good news. Women had to have a lot of babies if they hoped to raise even a few, and there was little or no thought of childbirth draining a woman's strength by inexorable degrees. Nature and its works were considered beneficent and health giving; women were supposed to blossom during pregnancy.

By now Jefferson had returned to the practice of law. But politics soon began absorbing more of his time and attention. As a member of the House of Burgesses, he experienced firsthand the prickly relationship gradually developing between the American colonies and the British government. The Burgesses reacted angrily when Parliament announced that henceforth any American who interfered with the operations of the British navy in its attempt to enforce laws against smuggling would be punished by death. Equally infuriating was the edict that the wrongdoer could be transported at the pleasure of His Majesty to any county in England for trial. This was not the first time Parliament indicated that it seemed committed to a policy of deliberately violating rights cherished by Americans in every colony. Agitation against British taxation had been going on since 1765, when young Jefferson, "yet a student of law in Williamsburg," stood in the door of the lobby of the House of Burgesses and heard a backwoods lawyer named Patrick Henry boom a warning that still echoes down American history. "Caesar had his Brutus—Charles I his Cromwell—and George III may profit by their example . . . if *this* be treason, make the most of it."

Jefferson and Henry were close friends, in spite of the widest possible divergence in their personalities, habits and tastes. Jefferson had a classical education and could read Homer in the original Greek and Horace in Latin; he had probed deeply into the roots and foundations of English law for over two years before he began to practice. Henry was almost totally uneducated and had become a lawyer almost on impulse, after his country store went bankrupt. He spent no more than six weeks paging through a few elementary textbooks. Jefferson's mentor, scholarly George Wythe, professor of law at William and Mary, was outraged when Henry was admitted to the bar.

Jefferson had first met Henry the year before the latter's admission to the bar, when they shared the Christmas celebrations at a neighboring plantation. "His manners had something of the coarseness of the society he had frequented," Jefferson recalled. "His passion was fiddling, dancing and pleasantry. He excelled in the last and it attached everyone to him." Although Jefferson was only seventeen at the time and Henry was already a married man, a friendship sprang up which continued through the next decade.

One reason, Jefferson said, "was the exact conformity of our political opinions." But equally important to the shy young intellectual was Henry's overwhelming personal charm and oratorical powers. "He appeared to me to speak as Homer wrote," Jefferson said. It was a gift Jefferson himself lacked. But he also saw that oratory was not enough. Henry "could not draw a bill on the most simple subject which would bear legal criticism or even the ordinary criticism which looks to correctness of style and ideas, for indeed there was no accuracy of idea in his head. His imagination was copious, poetical, sublime, but vague also. He said the strongest things in the finest language, but without logic, without arrangement . . ."

In 1773, Jefferson, Henry, Richard Henry Lee, Francis L. Lee and Dabney Carr, who was in his first term as a burgess, met in a private room at the Raleigh Tavern "to consult on the state of things." They were the young turks in an assembly dominated by older conservative members. They drew up a set of resolutions protesting rumors of parliamentary proceedings "tending to deprive them of their ancient legal and constitutional rights" and moved to create "a standing committee of correspondence and inquiry" to obtain the latest news on such matters from sister colonies. Jefferson had drawn up the resolutions, but with a generosity that was also a realistic estimate of his oratorical limitations, he suggested that his friend Dabney Carr submit them to the House. Already young Carr, practicing law in the same courts with Patrick Henry, had proven himself a formidable rival to the Virginia Demosthenes. Jefferson was eager to give his friend a chance to display his talents in the political arena. Carr performed magnificently and the motions passed without a dissenting vote. The Royal Governor, the Earl of Dunmore, promptly dissolved the House, indicating his august disapproval, but Jefferson and his friends, undaunted, retreated to the Raleigh and the Committee of Correspondence began functioning the very next day.

Back to Albemarle went Jefferson and Carr, for a common reason. Both their wives were pregnant, Carr's for the sixth time. There, on May 16, 1773, just thirty-five days after his brilliant debut in the House of Burgesses, Dabney Carr died in Charlottesville of "bilious fever"—a term doctors used in those days to describe a disease they could not identify. The illness was so swift and violent neither Jefferson, who seems to have been away on business, nor Mrs. Carr, just recovering from childbirth, reached him before he expired. When Jefferson returned home to hear the sorrowful news, Carr was already buried at Shadwell. Sadly, Jefferson remembered their boyhood promise and ordered some workmen to set out a graveyard beneath the great oak, where he and Dabney had spent so many happy hours. A few days later, the best friend of his Albemarle youth was reinterred there in the cool shade, and Jefferson himself wrote his epitaph, making clear that it was a tribute from "Thomas Jefferson, who of all men living loved him most." To his widow and six children, Jefferson and Martha opened their doors. Henceforth, Jefferson declared, he would regard the children as his own.

Two weeks later came more grim news. John Wayles was dead at The Forest. Martha's father was fifty-eight. His passing did not cause the kind of pain aroused by the death of Dabney Carr. But it meant a great deal more responsibility for Jefferson and his wife. The following year, when the estate was settled, they acquired more than 11,000 additional acres of land and 142 slaves, doubling the land and number of slaves they already owned. Unfortunately, the property came encumbered with a heavy debt—over 3,000 pounds—to British merchants. This was a nagging problem, not easily solved, because even when Jefferson sold 6,000 acres of Martha's land to pay it off, he could get only bonds—what we would call promissory notes—from his fellow Virginians and the English creditors refused to accept these. But this was not an immediate worry. More to the point was the rather overwhelming task of running this vast estate and simultaneously practicing law and politics.

Far from being trained to business, Martha was, if anything, completely dependent on Jefferson for almost every decision, and running a half dozen farms, with almost two hundred Negroes and several dozen white overseers and skilled workmen, required decisions constantly. She was also dependent in another sense. She lamented every day Jefferson spent away from her—and as a lawyer, he was inevitably forced to practice at distant county courthouses, as well as at Williamsburg.

At the same time, Jefferson was becoming disillusioned with the law. His $3,000 income was on paper. He rarely managed to collect more than half his fees from his cash-short clients. Letting bills glide on for years was an old Virginia tradition. In August, 1774, he turned over his entire practice to twenty-one-year-old Edmund Randolph, handsome son of John Randolph, the attorney general of Virginia, listing 132 active cases and surrendering to his cousin two thirds of the prospective fees.

Jefferson's tobacco fields still earned him a solid income. He went on adding to his library and his wine cellar, he pushed ahead on the construction of his house, and he picked up bits of land that interested him. In 1773, he exulted over the purchase of 120 acres in Bedford County, containing a unique piece of architecture today called the Natural Bridge. As a true son of Peter Jefferson, he had climbed to the top of this remarkable relic of another geological age. Here his nerve failed him and he yielded to the usual human reaction to that dizzying view. "You involuntarily fall on your hands and feet and creep to the parapet and peep over it," he wrote. "Looking down from this height for about a minute gave me a violent headache." If Jefferson found the view from the top "painful and intolerable," from below he found it "delightful in an equal extreme. It is impossible for the emotions arising from the sublime to be felt beyond what they are here; so beautiful an arch, so elevated, so light, and springing as it were up to heaven, the rapture of the spectator is really indescribable."

As Martha's pregnancy advanced, Jefferson spent more and more time at home. He cut winding paths that he called round-abouts through Monticello's forested slopes. Ultimately he had four of these for woodland wandering, connecting them by oblique roads. He planted fruit trees and a vegetable garden on the southeastern slope. In his garden book these vegetables suddenly began to blossom with exotic names: *aglio di Toscania* for garlic, *radicchio di Pistoia* for endive. The Italian names are the first evidence of Monticello's new neighbor, the Italian physician and political philosopher, Philip Mazzei. Banished from Italy for his revolutionary thinking, Mazzei had prospered as a wine merchant in London for a number of years. He had come to Virginia to plant vineyards and start a local wine industry, and was en route to the Shenandoah Valley, where his patron and traveling companion, the London merchant Thomas Adams, had property. The two men stopped overnight at Monticello. The household was asleep, but in the dawn Jefferson arose and greeted Mazzei, whom he took on a long walk around the neighborhood. Mazzei found himself amazed by the ease with which Jefferson discussed science, literature, politics, religion. Before the Italian knew what was happening, he was letting Jefferson persuade him to buy 400 acres of land adjoining Monticello to which Jefferson generously added 2,000 acres of his own land. Returning to Monticello for breakfast, they greeted Thomas Adams with obviously conspiratorial looks. "I see by your expression that you've taken him away from me," sighed Adams. "I knew you would do that."

In a matter of days, Jefferson had Mazzei's men and equipment transported to Monticello. The workmen, who had not heard a word of their native tongue since leaving Italy, burst into tears of joy when Jefferson greeted them in Italian—a language he had never heard spoken until he met Mazzei, but which he had taught himself to read fluently in his student days. Mazzei settled down to become an almost too fervent admirer. There were times when his nonstop conversation left Jefferson, no mean talker himself, wondering if the good doctor would ever run down.

By and large Jefferson was delighted with the success of his first venture into international friendship, and both he and Martha enjoyed the zest which the volatile Latin added to Monticello's Anglo-Saxon atmosphere. All they needed now, the Jeffersons fervently agreed, was a son. As Martha's second pregnancy reached its term in the spring of 1774, their hopes were high. But Martha gave birth to another daughter, whom they named Jane Randolph after Jefferson's mother. Again, Martha's recovery from the ordeal was slow. It was obvious that for her pregnancy was both an emotional and physical crisis. Her own mother had died in childbirth, and the memory was a perpetual threat to her peace of mind.

But Martha's very fragility only made her husband love her all the more. He nursed and fussed over her, and pronounced himself still the happiest of men. Two children safely born, his mansion house growing daily before his eyes, a cultivated neighbor to add some social spice to their daily round—life seemed quintessentially happy to Jefferson in that spring of 1774. He played with "Patsy," his private name for little Martha, toddling now at eighteen months, and began personally supervising the education of young Peter Carr, Dabney's oldest son. Together he and Martha worked in the vegetable garden. In the evening they would read aloud to each other—perhaps *Tristram Shandy* or Jefferson's other favorite, *The Poems of Ossian*, "translated" by James Macpherson. These were supposed to be the works of a Celtic Homer who flourished in the dawn of Scotch-Irish history, discovered by the learned Mr. Macpherson in the Scottish Highlands.

The Jeffersons, like thousands of other eighteenth-century readers, did not realize they were victims of one of the great literary hoaxes of all time. Macpherson had created Ossian in his own romantic imagination and when the poems became sensationally successful, did not have the nerve to admit that he, a failure as a poet under his own byline, was the actual author. Real or fake, the poems reveal the deeply romantic side of Jefferson's complex mind. Among the favorite passages heard before the firelight in Monticello's parlor was this one from "The Songs of Selma."

> Star of descending night!
> Fair is thy light in the west!
> Thou liftest thy unshorn head from thy cloud:
> Thy steps are stately on thy hill.
> What dost thou behold in the plain?
> The stormy winds are laid.
> The murmur of the torrent comes from afar.
> Roaring waves climb the distant rock.
> The flies of evening are on their feeble wings;
> The hum of their course is on the field.
> What dost thou behold, fair light?
> But thou dost smile and depart.
> The waves come with joy around thee:
> They bathe thy lovely hair.
> Farewell, thou silent beam!
> Let the light of Ossian's soul arise!

On Monticello's peak, Jefferson's mind soared off in every direction, the hours became an almost continuous enjoyment of beauty in books, in the woman he loved and the children she had given him, in the bountiful, blooming world of nature that fascinated both his eye and his mind. It is easy to see how this scholarly, reflective man began to treasure every hour he lived on this mountain and willingly would have spent the rest of his life there, yielding with reluctance the few days a year he was required to sit in the House of Burgesses.

But beyond the horizon of the world that Jefferson commanded from his hilltop events were about to force him to surrender that dream. Three and a half months before Jane Randolph Jefferson was born, a group of Bostonians disguised as Indians dumped 342 chests of British tea into the murky waters of the harbor, to underscore their refusal to pay the tax Parliament had placed on this favorite American brew. On April 22, another group of "Indians" performed a similar dumping operation in New York harbor. An angry Parliament retaliated by closing the port of Boston and ramming through a series of acts which all but annulled the Massachusetts charter. None of this bad news had reached Jefferson or his fellow burgesses, when they assembled in Williamsburg on May 5, 1774, in response to the summons of Governor Dunmore. On May 22, dust-covered express riders from the Boston Committee of Correspondence came pounding into the colonial capital with the news of Parliament's overbearing retaliation and a call from Massachusetts for aid from her sister colonies.

Jefferson, Patrick Henry, Edmund Randolph and the other young turks met in a private caucus to decide how to seize the political initiative and persuade the older conservatives to join in a public statement of solidarity with Massachusetts. Flowery resolutions would never win a majority vote, no matter how thunderingly Patrick Henry supported them. For the past two years, the people had been showing obvious signs of boredom with political fulminations. The colony was in a kind of "lethargy . . . as to passing events," Jefferson later recalled.

For the first time Jefferson revealed the intuitive judgment of the born political leader. The only thing that was likely to "alarm" the popular attention, he told Henry and the others, was a day of general fasting and prayer. Not since 1755, during a war with France, had "such a solemnity" been invoked. The beauty of the idea was instantly apparent. The group spent the rest of the night rummaging through old forms and proclamations and, in Jefferson's words, "we cooked up a resolution . . . for a day of fasting, humiliation, and prayer to implore heaven to avert from us the evils of civil war, to inspire us with firmness in support of our rights, and to turn the hearts of the King and Parliament to moderation and justice." The next day, the self-appointed revolutionary committee went to Robert Carter Nicholas, treasurer of the colony and one of the gravest and most religious members of the House of Burgesses, and asked him to introduce the resolution. It passed without a single dissenting vote and Lord Dunmore immediately dissolved the assembly.

Now it was easy for Jefferson and his fellow firebrands to lead a march to the Raleigh Tavern, where eighty-nine burgesses agreed to form a permanent association and ordered the Committee of Correspondence to inform committees in other colonies of Virginia's day of fast. The association also declared "that an attack made on one of our sister colonies is an attack made on all British America and threatens ruin to the rights of all." Most important was the call for all the colonies to meet in congress "at such place, annually, as should be convenient to direct from time to time the measures required by the general interest."

Jefferson did not stay in Williamsburg to march with his fellow burgesses to Bruton Church on June 1. He hurried home to Monticello and Martha. But he arranged for church services in his native Albemarle County and years later he recalled how "the effect of the day, through the whole colony, was like a shock of electricity, arousing every man and placing him erect and solidly on his center."

In August, Jefferson was back in Williamsburg, as Albemarle's representative at a "convention" of delegates which Lord Dunmore could not dissolve with a stroke of his royal pen. The county nominated Jefferson and John Walker to act for them at this meeting and the freeholders of the county also approved a series of resolutions which Jefferson had written. They called on Americans to stand fast against Parliament's invasion of their rights, and asserted that "no other legislature whatever" could exercise authority over Americans but those "duly constituted and appointed with their own consent"—the colonial assemblies. The resolutions also urged a boycott of all commodities on which Parliament placed a tax and demanded the repeal of parliamentary laws that blocked the growth of American manufacturing and restricted American trade. These ideas were far bolder than anything that emanated from other local Virginia conventions. The freeholders of Hanover County, Patrick Henry's bailiwick, only demanded "the privileges and immunities of their fellow subjects in England" and asked that they be permitted "to continue to live under the genuine unaltered constitution of England and be subjects in the true spirit of that constitution to His Majesty and his illustrious house." Burgess George Washington's Fairfax County conceded the right of Parliament to regulate American trade and commerce. "Such a power directed with wisdom and moderation seems necessary for the general good of that great body politic of which we are a part . . . Under this idea our ancestors submitted to it."

But Jefferson was prepared to be even bolder. He expanded the Albemarle resolutions into a vivid essay which he planned to submit to the Williamsburg convention as a "declaration of rights." This bristling document, twenty-three printed pages long, set forth Jefferson's contention that the colonists were subject to no laws but those of their own creation. "Our emigration from England to this country," he said, "gave her no more rights over us than the emigrations of the Danes and Saxons gave to the present authorities of the mother country over England." This was Jefferson, the legal scholar, speaking, and it did not in the least trouble him that he knew only one man who agreed with him—his old law-school mentor, George Wythe.

The declaration went on to denounce the "arbitrary measures" of both King and Parliament and condemned even more vigorously the use of "large bodies of armed forces not made up of the people here nor raised by the authority of our laws" to enforce them. "His Majesty has no right to land a single armed man on our shores," Jefferson declared. Finally, defending his bold tone, Jefferson said that "freedom of language and sentiment . . . becomes a free people, claiming their rights as derived from the laws of nature, not as the gift of their chief magistrate. Let those flatter who fear: it is not an American art."

This was more than bold, it was outrageously daring. In an age when kings were still approached with scraping bows and humble petitions, Jefferson lectured the British sovereign, head of a global empire that ranged from America through the West Indies to India. "Open your breast, Sire, to liberal and expanded thought. Let not the name of George III be a blot in the page of history."

Jefferson never got a chance to submit personally these burning words to the Virginia convention. On the road to Williamsburg he was stricken with an attack of dysentery and was forced to retreat to Monticello. He forwarded two copies of the declaration, one to Patrick Henry, the other to his cousin Peyton Randolph, who he knew would be the chairman of the convention. The copy sent to Henry vanished into the silence. "Whether Mr. Henry disapproved the ground taken or was too lazy to read it (for he was the laziest man in reading I ever knew) I never learned," Jefferson wrote later, "but he communicated it to nobody." Peyton Randolph laid the essay on the table for other members to read. The conservative majority thought it was "too bold for the present state of things." But Jefferson's friends in the convention, without bothering to ask his permission, had it printed in Williamsburg as "A Summary View of the Rights of British America." No doubt thinking to protect him, they did not list Jefferson by name as the author but simply said the pamphlet was "by a native and member of the House of Burgesses." The essay made its way to England where it was soon reprinted by Britishers sympathetic to the American cause.

Virginia's call for a continental congress had won a prompt response from Massachusetts, and other colonies quickly joined in a plan to gather in Philadelphia. The Virginia convention chose seven delegates to this momentous meeting. They included Peyton Randolph, whose massive corpulence exuded integrity and dignity; Benjamin Harrison, an equally huge but less mentally ponderous Virginia grandee; the firebrand Patrick Henry and Colonel George Washington, the colony's most distinguished soldier. These men were all a decade or more older than Jefferson. However ample the evidence of his maturity as a writer, he was a comparative newcomer to the Virginia establishment, and in no sense an acknowledged leader or persuader of men, such as Colonel Washington or Patrick Henry.

This fact did not disturb Jefferson in the least. He had no great desire to endure the long journey to Philadelphia, and the weeks, perhaps months, of separation from Martha which it would inevitably involve. He was perfectly content to be a distant spectator to the first congress and its decisions, which more or less followed the policy spelled out by the Virginia convention. The 56 delegates from 12 colonies issued a series of declarations which set forth the rights of the colonists, among them "to life, liberty and property." They named 13 parliamentary acts since 1763 which violated American rights and denounced particularly the so-called "coercive acts" against Massachusetts. Finally, they formed a continental association pledged to cease all imports from Great Britain after December 1. They also placed an embargo on all exports to Britain, Ireland and the West Indies beginning September 1, 1775. Then, with a conciliatory address to the King and the British and American peoples, congress adjourned. But they resolved to meet again on the 10th of May, 1775, if the crisis between the colonies and the mother country continued.

Jefferson wholeheartedly supported the nonimportation agreement, joining the association and persuading friends and relatives to sign up as well. In fact, he was so scrupulous he offered to destroy a shipment of sash windows which he had ordered from England before the association was created. The Committee of Safety at Norfolk was more lenient toward the author of "A Summary Declaration" than he was disposed to be toward himself, and permitted the forbidden window frames to proceed safely to their destination at Monticello. Bluff Ben Harrison was one of the committeemen and this hearty lover of good living was naturally inclined to make exceptions in deserving cases.

Events moved slowly in the eighteenth century, especially when the main actors were separated by 3,000 miles of ocean. For the next several months Jefferson stayed at Monticello pushing the work on his mansion house. Everything—nails, timber, bricks— had to be fabricated on the plantation and most of the skilled labor had to be trained on the job. How closely Jefferson supervised the work can be seen from his voluminous notebooks. He calculated precisely how many bricks he needed for the various parts of the house: "NE walls and partitions of parlor 77½ F. in length, to raise the story, 82,000 bricks. SE walls to raise the story, 40,000, whole, to raise second story, 63,000." Fifty thousand bricks were burned and laid in 1774 alone. By the end of the year Jefferson had completed what he called "the middle building" containing the parlor, the library, the drawing room and bedroom above it.

The well-trained Martha tried her utmost to please her methodical husband by keeping careful records in her domain. On the back of some of Jefferson's legal papers, in a beautifully delicate script, she wrote:

> February 10th.   Opened a barrel of Col. Harrison's flour
>   13   A mutton killed
>   17   Two pullets killed
>   27   A cask of small beer brewed, 15 gallon
>   cask

She inventoried her house linens too. Early in her marriage she counted:

> 6 diaper tablecloths, 10 ditto damask
> 12 diaper napkins marked TJ 71
> 12 ditto towels, TJ 71
> 6 pr. sheets, 15 pillow cases, TJ 71

Next came "a list of our clothes." Mr. Jefferson had:

> 9 ruffled shirts and 18 plain ditto
> 20 old cambrick stocks
> 15 old rags of pocket handkerchieves
> 3 pr. of English Cordied breeches
> 4 of Virginia ditto
> 6 Virginia cordied dimitied waistcoats
> 13 pair white silk stockings
> 5 red waistcoats, 2 buff, 1 white flannel ditto
> 1 green coat
> 1 black princes ditto

Among her own clothes she listed:

> 16 old shifts, 4 new ditto
> 6 old fine aprons
> 4 Virginia pettycoats
> 9 pr of silk stockings, 10 pr of old cotton
> 8 silk gowns
> 6 washing ditto old and 2 new to make up
> 2 suits of Brussels lace, 1 suit of worked muslin

On went the lists, noting the consumption of a goose, the slaughter of a beef cow, the eating of six hams and four shoulders. Beside these facts Martha Jefferson's pen would pause and sketch solemn little birds, perched on leafy twigs. Obviously, Martha yearned to escape such a dull routine—and it is easy to picture her doing just that, with a husband who was both doting and energetic. Always up before the sun, Jefferson had no trouble absorbing into his own hands all the business of the plantation, from the minute details of interior decoration (he even designed the curtains and chose the fabric) down to selecting the meat for tomorrow's dinner.

Elsewhere in Virginia, life continued its peaceful pleasant flow. Philip Fithian, a young New Jersey clergyman who was tutoring the children of Robert Carter at Nomminy Hall on the James, told of going to visit the nearby Lee plantation for a typical ball. The dinner, he reported, "was as elegant as could be well expected when so great an Assembly were to be kept for so long a time. For drink there were several sorts of wine, good lemon punch, toddy, cyder, porter &c." The young Presbyterian clergyman watched the ladies and gentlemen dancing in the ballroom and he noted how when dancing the ladies' "silks and brocades rustled and trailed behind them." He also noted that the men, in the privacy of the card rooms, were "toasting the sons of America; some singing 'liberty songs' as they called them, in which six, eight, ten or more would put their heads near together and roar . . ."

Like all Virginians, Jefferson kept in close touch with the political situation through the Virginia *Gazette,* and there he read in early February the report of the ominous speech which George III had made at the opening of Parliament. The King had grimly declared that he was determined to uphold "Parliament's supreme authority." The minority who tried to speak on behalf of the embattled Americans were ruthlessly voted down. The *Gazette* also reported a few weeks later that the King had received without comment the conciliatory petition of the Continental Congress.

In the middle of March, 1775, Jefferson departed from Monticello to still another Virginia convention, this time held in Richmond, to make sure that the colony's Royal Governor, Lord Dunmore, made no attempt to interfere with it. The Governor was growing increasingly restive about the almost total dissolution of his authority. En route to Richmond, Jefferson left Martha and the two girls at Elk Hill, one of the plantations they had inherited from John Wayles. The problems of caring for two small children in Monticello's unfinished mansion were obviously many, and Jefferson felt Martha would be far more comfortable, as well as nearer to him, at this fine old house overlooking a fertile island in the peaceful James.

The Virginia convention, largely the same delegates who had formed the previous one, met in white-walled St. John's Church in Richmond. Jefferson, Patrick Henry, Richard Henry Lee and the other young men were astonished to discover that in spite of the King's speech, a majority were against any and all measures that might tend to arouse popular emotions. After approving by unanimous vote the resolutions of the Continental Congress, the delegates sat back and listened to a petition to the King by the Jamaican assembly, supporting American rights. The mood of the majority was reflected in the resolution of thanks they forwarded to Jamaica, assuring the islanders that it was "the most ardent wish of this colony . . . to see a speedy return of those halcyon days, when we lived a free and happy people." Obviously most of the delegates were inclined to believe that a blizzard of respectful petitions from colonies around the world would change His Majesty's mind and persuade him to take back the dour words he had spoken to Parliament. This mood of moderate optimism was exploded by Patrick Henry.

Grimly the Hanover County orator, still self-consciously wearing his backwoods homespun in contrast to the satin and superfine broadcloth of the majority of the delegates, rose to introduce a call for an independent militia to put Virginia "into a posture of defense." Richard Henry Lee, a debater not quite as thunderous as Henry (Jefferson called him "frothy and rhetorical") but effective nonetheless, rose to second the resolution. Emphatically, the established leaders rose one by one to denounce the militia resolution. They insisted the King was showing signs of relenting and they questioned the wisdom of committing what could be construed by the British as an act of war. They reminded Henry that it was imperial Britain he was daring, an empire with an army and fleet second to none in the world.

Henry rose magnificently to the oratorical challenge. He insisted war was inevitable. The King, far from seeking reconciliation, was already using "the implements of war and subjugation"—armies and fleets—to cow Americans into surrender without a fight. "If we wish to be free—if we mean to preserve inviolate these inestimable privileges for which we have been so long contending . . . we must fight! I repeat it, sir, we must fight!" Already in the First Continental Congress Henry had declared he was no longer a Virginian, but an American. Now he used the idea to scoff at the argument that Virginia was too weak. It wasn't true, if Virginia considered herself part of an American union. "Three millions of people armed in the holy cause of liberty and in such a country as that which we possess are invincible by any force which our enemy can send against us," he thundered. ". . . the battle, sir, is not to the strong alone; it is to the vigilant, the active, the brave . . . I know not what course others may take, but as for me, give me liberty or give me death!"

Contrary to popular myth, Henry's speech by no means silenced the opposition. The debate raged on and Jefferson, as one of Henry's backers, made one of the few public speeches of his career, arguing "closely, profoundly and warmly" on behalf of preparedness. Finally, by a very close vote, the assembly agreed to appoint a militia committee to reorganize Virginia's armed forces. Jefferson was named a member of the 12-man committee which recommended that each county raise at least one 68-man company of infantry and one 30-man troop of cavalry, and see that both were trained and equipped with ammunition and weapons, including that native American invention, the tomahawk. This was hardly a formidable fighting force, even if all the companies could have been assembled quickly, which in a colony Virginia's size was clearly impossible. For all of Henry's bold words, the committee obviously, as Jefferson said in later years, "slackened our pace that our less ardent colleagues might keep up with us."

After approving this mild defensive posture, the delegates re-elected the same men to represent them at the second meeting of the Continental Congress in Philadelphia. Almost as an afterthought, Jefferson was elected as an alternate, in case Governor Dunmore called a meeting of the House of Burgesses and the delegation's leader, Peyton Randolph, was forced to return to Virginia to preside over this body.

Jefferson gathered his wife and two daughters from Elk Hill and returned to Monticello, where he plunged once more into his little world of building and farming. In distant Massachusetts the appeal to arms which Patrick Henry had declared inevitable became bloody reality when militiamen clashed with British regulars on Lexington green and at Concord bridge, and drove the startled British back to Boston in a day-long running battle.

Even before this news reached Virginia, the colony was aroused by a very rash move on the part of Lord Dunmore. On the moonlit night of April 20, Dunmore persuaded the captain of a British revenue cutter, the *Magdalene*, to spirit twenty barrels of powder out of the Williamsburg magazine. He was caught in the act and the entire colony rose in wrath against him. Patrick Henry placed himself at the head of the militia from Hanover County, and began marching for Williamsburg.

While the colony seethed, express riders from Massachusetts arrived with the news of Lexington. At Monticello, Jefferson heard it early in May. No matter how deeply he was committed to defending American rights, the bloodshed filled him with dismay, and made him sad to think that Parliament's folly might separate him from friends and loyalties which had for years been part of his life. On May 7, he wrote a touching letter to his old William and Mary professor, William Small, who was living in England. He sent him three dozen bottles of Madeira, "half of a present which I had laid by for you." Then he grimly recited the bloody news from Massachusetts. Others were denouncing it as British barbarism, but Jefferson called it "this accident" which "has cut off our last hope of reconciliation." After several more lines on the disintegrating relations between the colonies and the mother country, Jefferson broke off: "But I am getting into politics though I sat down only to ask your acceptance of the wine and express my constant wishes for your happiness." He was no war lover, this Jefferson.

On June 1, Jefferson was on his way to Williamsburg again in his durable phaeton. Governor Dunmore, for want of a better idea, had called a meeting of the House of Burgesses. Peyton Randolph hurried back to take his seat as speaker, and under his leadership the burgesses pressed the question of the stolen gunpowder so angrily that Dunmore panicked and retreated with his wife and family to the man-of-war *Fowey* off Yorktown. Peyton Randolph, meanwhile, showed the growing reliance of the older generation on young Jefferson's literary skills, by asking him to draft a reply to the Governor's message, calling on the assembly to consider the "alarming situation of the country." Jefferson composed a masterful document, calm and moderate in tone but unbending in spirit. Very significant was the clear declaration that the reply was offered "only as an individual part of the whole empire. Final determination we leave to the general Congress now sitting . . . To them also we refer the discovery of that proper method of representing our well-founded grievances . . . For ourselves we have exhausted every mode of application which our invention could suggest as proper and promising."

With Governor Dunmore all but abandoning the colony, the Virginians decided to stay in session and provide the state with a central government. This meant Peyton Randolph had to remain in Williamsburg. While one of the moderates, Archibald Cary, read Jefferson's coolly chiseled reply to Lord Dunmore's empty chair in the House of Burgesses, Jefferson jolted north in his phaeton toward Philadelphia and a rendezvous with world history. He went as a man deeply troubled about the state of his world and—equally important to him—with a nagging fear in the back of his mind that his wife was not strong enough to handle the heavy responsibilities he was leaving behind him. The mere fact of his absence would be a burden she had never borne easily—and now she had the added worry of seeing him involved in what looked more and more like a civil war.

III

The Philadelphia into which Jefferson rode after a leisurely ten-day journey was not an entirely new world to him. He had visited it ten years before, in 1765, to be inoculated for smallpox. But it was, nevertheless, a sharp contrast to the Virginia world he knew best. Williamsburg with its population of 2,000 was a village compared to this metropolis with paved and lighted streets and 34,000 inhabitants pursuing a dazzling variety of trades and professions. Moreover, the city was in the process of being transformed into an armed camp. Philadelphia Associaters, Quaker Blues, all sorts of companies drilled and practiced in factory yards and open fields. If Lexington was not yet a shot heard around the world, it had certainly echoed up and down the continent of North America.

The second Congress had already been in session six weeks when Jefferson arrived. Delegates were sitting in the red brick colonial State House, 65 men from all 13 of the colonies, although the member from Georgia was only a quasi-official personage. Virginia's substitute delegate quartered his horses with one Jacob Hiltzheimer, and found rooms with a cabinetmaker named Benjamin Randolph, a congenial name to Jefferson. That night Jefferson ate at the City Tavern with the Virginia delegates and a scattering of delegates from other colonies. The next morning, June 22, 1775, he presented his credentials to Congress and was seated as a duly certified member. His architect's eye undoubtedly appreciated the graceful proportion of the State House's white-paneled ground-floor chamber, lined on two sides with windows and surmounted by a handsome glass prism chandelier in the center. The heat of the room, with the doors and most of the windows closed to guarantee the secrecy of the deliberations, did not bother a Virginian as much as it wilted the New Yorkers and New Englanders.

Jefferson had already heard from his fellow delegates some shrewd estimates of the leaders from other states—the chief liberty men from Massachusetts, Samuel Adams, with his palsied hands and quavering voice, and his stumpy, solemn-faced, intensely serious cousin, John, learned in legal history and sharp tongued in debate; witty Caesar Rodney of Pennsylvania, by far the oddest-looking member of the Congress, tall, thin, pale, with a face not much bigger than a large apple; fiery Christopher Gadsen of South Carolina and the Rutledge brothers from the same state, strutting cavaliers. But the man Jefferson's eyes sought first was a newcomer to the Pennsylvania delegation—Benjamin Franklin, home from almost a decade in England where he had been America's spokesman. In his plain brown suit, the gray hair falling on his shoulders, the old man was a model of philosophic moderation.

Jefferson by no means slipped into Congress unnoticed or unheralded. He brought with him from Virginia the colony's reply to Parliament's so-called conciliatory proposals. The Old Dominion was the first of the colonies to answer this attempt to divide them, and Jefferson's firm unbending tone and well-tempered prose had a heartening impact on the weary delegates. Congress seemed to be getting nowhere. A moderate faction, led by wealthy John Dickinson of Pennsylvania, had clashed violently with the coalition of New Englanders and southerners who were in favor of a defiant stand. Over fierce protests from John Adams, Congress had voted unanimously to give Dickinson his way and present another humble petition to the King.

Shrewd politicking on the part of the Adamses had, it was true, produced one step forward—John Adams had nominated Virginia's favorite soldier, George Washington, to take command of the army of New Englanders besieging the British on the outskirts of Boston. On the next day, Friday, June 23, Jefferson probably rode out with most of the Congress when the new general departed. It was a festive, highly martial occasion, the Philadelphia Light Horse in white breeches and gleaming high-topped boots riding escort, and men, women and children lining the roads to give resounding cheers to the big Virginian, who never looked more like a leader of men than when he was sitting on a horse.

Little more than three hours after Washington had departed, a far less glittering horseman came thumping into Philadelphia with more bloody news from Massachusetts. On June 17, the very day Congress had chosen Washington to be general-in-chief, militiamen from Massachusetts, Connecticut, Rhode Island and New Hampshire had fought a stupendous battle with the best of the British army. The regulars had attacked the Americans in fortifications they had erected on Breed's and Bunkers hill, part of a neck of land known as Charlestown Heights, overlooking the city of Boston. Bunker Hill was no running skirmish, begun by some headstrong soldier's itchy trigger finger, as at Lexington, but a battle as formal and fierce as any fought against the traditional enemy, France, in Canada or in Europe. Four hundred Americans were dead or wounded. Twice, perhaps three times that number of attacking British regulars had fallen before the steadier guns of the American defenders. In Charlestown, across the harbor from Boston, perhaps 300 fine houses had been burned to the ground by hot shot fired from British warships. The Americans had been driven out of their entrenchments but they had fallen back to their siege lines around Boston, and were priming their guns for another British assault. This, Jefferson told his brother-in-law Francis Eppes two days later, meant "that the war is now heartily entered into, without a prospect of accommodation . . ."

The news jolted Congress into action. The next day a committee which had been appointed to prepare a declaration on the causes of taking up arms submitted a paper written by John Rutledge of South Carolina, which drew much critical fire. On the twenty-sixth it was recommitted and Jefferson and John Dickinson were added to the committee. When Congress adjourned that day, Jefferson approached another member of the committee, William Livingston of New York, and suggested that he do a draft of a revision. Livingston promptly excused himself and urged instead that Jefferson do it. Jefferson insisted Livingston was the better man.

"We are as yet but new acquaintances, sir," said Livingston, "why are you so earnest for my doing it?"

"Because," said Jefferson, "I have been informed that you drew the address to the people of Great Britain, a production certainly of the finest pen in America."

"On that," Livingston said, "perhaps, sir, you may not have been correctly informed," and went on to explain that thirty-year-old John Jay of New York, the only delegate younger than Jefferson, had done the writing.

The other member of the committee which drew up this final document of the first Congress had been Richard Henry Lee. The next morning Jefferson discovered firsthand the animosities which were taking root beneath the general air of unanimity. He saw Jay speaking vehemently to Lee, and then "leading him by the button of his coat" to confront Jefferson. "I understand, sir," said Jay, "that this gentleman informed you that Governor Livingston drew the address to the people of Great Britain."

The mortified Jefferson had to hastily assure him that he had received the information from another Virginian, not Lee. He vowed that "not a word had ever passed on the subject" between him and Lee.

The subject was dropped, but Jefferson had discovered the hard way what John Adams was writing home. Each delegate considered himself "a great man, an orator, a critic, a statesman" and was intensely jealous of his imaginary reputation. This natural hostility had been accentuated by what Jefferson called "some sparrings in debate" between the radical Lee and the moderate Jay.

In this acrimonious atmosphere Jefferson displayed for the first time another political gift—an ability to win and hold the friendship of remarkably opposite men, without compromising his own principles. Contentious John Adams wrote later that Jefferson "though a silent member in Congress . . . was so prompt, frank, explicit and decisive upon committees and in conversation—not even Samuel Adams was more so—that he soon seized upon my heart." But Jefferson was equally friendly with jolly Ben Harrison, whom the stiff-necked Adams described as "another Sir John Falstaff . . . his conversation disgusting to every man of delicacy or decorum."

During his first weeks in the Continental Congress, Jefferson demonstrated this tolerant spirit to an extraordinary degree. His draft of the declaration of the causes of taking up arms was strongly criticized by thin, cadaverous John Dickinson. "He still retained the hope of reconciliation with the mother country," Jefferson recalled later, "and was unwilling it should be lessened by offensive statements. He was so honest a man, and so able a one, that he was greatly indulged, even by those who could not feel his scruples. We therefore requested him to take the paper and put it into a form he could approve. He did so, preparing an entire new statement and preserving of the former only the last four paragraphs and half of the preceding one. We approved and reported it to Congress, who accepted it."

Here Jefferson learned a valuable political lesson—the power of a single individual to persuade intelligent men to vote against their inclinations. "Congress gave a signal proof of their indulgence of Mr. Dickinson . . . by permitting him to draw their second petition to the King according to his own ideas, and passing it with scarcely any amendment. The disgust against this humility was general; and Mr. Dickinson's delight at its passage was the only circumstance which reconciled them to it." Also involved was the

lesson Thomas Jefferson had already learned in Virginia, the necessity "not to go too fast for any respectable part of our body."

But there was no doubt that Jefferson glowed with carefully
concealed delight when Dickinson, rising to express his satisfaction
with the approval of his petition, said, "There is but one word, Mr.
President, in the paper which I disapprove, and that is the word
Congress." Up from his chair heaved massive Ben Harrison to
drawl, "There is but one word in the paper, Mr. President, of
which I approve, and that is the word Congress."

In a letter to Massachusetts, John Adams denounced the humble
petition. "Puerilities become not a great assembly like this the
representative of a great people." Finally he unleashed a personal
shaft at Dickinson. "A certain great fortune and piddling genius
whose fame has been trumpeted so loudly, has given a silly cast to
our whole doings." The letter was captured by the British and
published, converting Dickinson into one of Adams' permanent
enemies. In contrast, Jefferson refused to let the wranglings and
dawdlings of Congress disturb his essentially even disposition. He
declined to enter the debates and he became almost as famous for
his silence as Patrick Henry and John Adams for their oratory. But
in the long afternoon and evening hours of discussion with the
fellow members of his committee, and with other congressmen at
breakfasts and dinners, he continued to be the "prompt, frank,
explicit and decisive" spokesman of a tough though not yet revolutionary stand. Writing to the Virginia convention on behalf of
his fellow delegates, Jefferson said, "The present crisis is so full of
danger and incertainty that opinions here are various." He went on
to urge the convention to "reflect on the propriety of being prepared for the worst events and . . . to be guarded against probable evils at least" by doing everything in their power to achieve a
respectable military posture. Jefferson once more demonstrated
that, though no war lover, he was a realist. His study of history
had made it clear to him that force was the only answer to those
who tried to impose their politics at the point of a gun.

Jefferson's colleagues soon demonstrated that they still valued
his pen by making him a member of a committee to draw up an
answer to Lord North's so-called "Conciliatory Proposal." The
other members were Benjamin Franklin, John Adams and Richard

Henry Lee. Even the prestigious Franklin was sufficiently impressed with the reply Jefferson had written for the Virginia convention to ask him to do the writing. On July 31, 1775, Congress unanimously approved Jefferson's reply on their behalf to Lord North. The document substantially followed the one he had written for Virginia, but the tone was cooler and more dispassionate. Jefferson aimed at a more lofty dignity, befitting a continental congress. But the carefully controlled anger against British injustice could be seen smoldering beneath individual sentences such as, "We do not mean that our people shall be burthened with oppressive taxes, to provide cynosures for the idle or the wicked, under color of providing for a civil list." In the conclusion Jefferson achieved a sonorous, almost majestic defiance. "When it [the world] considers the great armaments with which they have invaded us, and the circumstances of cruelty with which these have commenced and prosecuted hostilities; when things, we say, are laid together, and attentively considered, can the world be deceived into an opinion that we are unreasonable, or can it hesitate to believe with us that nothing but our own exertions may defeat the ministerial sentence of death or abject submission?"

Two days later Congress adjourned. It really had no choice, since more than a few of the exhausted delegates had already departed and the Virginia delegation had announced they planned to follow them. Benjamin Harrison had wryly remarked, "I think it is high time there was an end of it. We have been too long together." The delegates could take some satisfaction in their accomplishments. They had created at least a semblance of an army and issued three million dollars' worth of bills of credit to equip and supply it.

They left George Washington outside of Boston, grappling with "discord and confusion" in the ranks. But this only reflected in the military order the lack of unanimity among the politicians. It was hardly surprising, when we consider the totally separate lives these men had lived, within their individual colonies, before they met to tackle the tremendous task of simultaneously forming a nation and fighting a war. Jefferson himself, for all his sophistication and scholarship, was a perfect example of provincial insularity. He wrote his brother-in-law about the death of the brilliant, handsome, young Massachusetts doctor-politician, Joseph Warren, at Bunker Hill, describing him as "a man who seems to have been immensely valued in the North." The growth of a nation was a slow process, and among the many lessons Jefferson learned at Philadelphia, perhaps the most important was patience.

Although he refused to retreat an inch from the principles he had already enunciated in his state papers, Jefferson still thought of his nation as the proud and triumphant British Empire into which he had been born. He showed this, as well as his gift for friendship, in response to a letter he received from John Randolph, not long after he returned to Virginia (sharing the road and his phaeton with genial Ben Harrison most of the way). Attorney General Randolph had decided that his loyalty to the King ran too deep to tolerate the revolutionary regime which had seized control of Virginia. He was going "home," as Virginians of his era called England, and he wrote to his young friend Jefferson, offering to sell him the violin about which they had written a lighthearted contract some years before.

The violin was a Cremona, made by Nicola Amati in 1660. The body bore the Amati trademark of brilliant amber varnish, the fingerboard and tailpiece were ebony, the string pegs, ivory. Jefferson and the attorney general had agreed in ponderous legal terms that when the older man died, Jefferson would get the violin. But if capricious fate decreed the reverse, Randolph was entitled to select from the late Mr. Jefferson's library books to the value of "one hundred pounds sterling."

Jefferson promptly accepted Randolph's new offer and added a personal note to the business paragraph, which revealed his inner thoughts on the crisis in the late summer of 1775. "I hope the returning wisdom of Great Britain will ere long put an end to this unnatural contest. There may be people to whose tempers and dispositions contention may be pleasing and who may therefore wish a continuance of confusion. But to me it is of all states, but one, the most horrid."

To this he added a statement which announced for the first (but not the last) time the deep reluctance with which this gentle man left his family for the brawling world of war and politics. "My first wish is a restoration of our just rights; my second, a return of the happy period when consistently with duty I may withdraw myself totally from the public stage and pass the rest of my days in domestic ease and tranquillity, banishing every desire of afterwards even hearing what passes in the world."

Behind these yearning words lay the harsh knowledge that he would soon he leaving Monticello again to perform once more on this public stage. Earlier in the month of August the Virginia convention had voted Jefferson third place in the seven-man Continental delegation, a flattering testimony to his growing esteem in the eyes of the men who knew him best.

Congress met on September 5. But Jefferson did not arrive until September 25. Little Jane Randolph Jefferson, eighteen months old, died in her weeping mother's arms, another victim of the child-raising hazards of a century that did not yet understand what germs even were, much less how they did their deadly work.

Jefferson left his grieving, disconsolate wife with Francis and Elizabeth Eppes. Losing children was common at the time, but in Martha Jefferson's emotional nature the impact of grief ran far deeper than in most women. She apparently sank into a depression, or a combination of a physical illness and depression, that left her too weak or listless to write her husband a letter. In Philadelphia, ensconced at Ben Randolph's house once more, Jefferson had set aside one day a week to write letters home. A month of wearying debate and committee work crept by and he got not a single answer. Finally, on November 7, he wrote to Francis Eppes in a tone that was nothing less than frantic. "I have never received a scrip of a pen from any mortal in Virginia since I left it, nor been able by any inquiries I could make to hear of my family . . . The suspense under which I am is too terrible to be endured. If any thing has happened, for God's sake let me know it." Eppes quickly reassured Jefferson that Martha was not seriously ill. But he wanted to hear the words from her own hand. Meanwhile Lord Dunmore, the Royal Governor gave Jefferson something else to worry about—the menace of civil and racial war in Virginia. Dunmore established a base at Norfolk and began recruiting a loyalist army. Early in November he took an even more ominous step, declaring he would give every Negro who joined his banner immediate freedom. A slave uprising was always a lurking dread in the back of every

Virginian's mind and this gesture made the awful reality more than a figment. Jefferson wrote another anxious letter to Martha, recommending that she retreat to their plantation at Poplar Forest in Bedford County, deep in the interior of the state, where Dunmore was unlikely to penetrate. To this too he received nothing but silence.

Congress, meanwhile, did little but watch the steady drift on both sides to all-out war. On November 9, they learned that George III had refused to receive Dickinson's olive-branch petition and on the 23rd of August, 1775, had proclaimed the colonies to be in open rebellion. Parliament received the petition on November 7 and voted it down, 83 to 33. But it was the King's contemptuous rejection that most affected Americans like Thomas Jefferson. On November 29, he wrote another letter to his friend John Randolph. The ostensible reason was to report to him the melancholy news of the death of his brother, Peyton Randolph, who succumbed to a stroke on the 22nd of November. Jefferson quickly expanded the letter into a discussion of the crisis.

Although Jefferson had spoken boldly and firmly to the King in the declarations and addresses he had already written, he had, like most Americans, still retained the hopeful opinion that the quarrel was between America and the greedy politicians in Parliament, and not with George III himself. The King's words and conduct had steadily eroded this fragile optimism and now Jefferson wrote: "It is an immense misfortune to the whole empire to have a King of such a disposition at such a time. We are told and everything proves it true, that he is the bitterest enemy we have . . . To undo his empire there is but one truth more to learn, that after colonies have drawn the sword there is but one step more they can take. That step is now pressed upon us by the measures adopted as if they were afraid we would not take it."

Jefferson meant independence. "Believe me, dear sir," he wrote, "there is not in the British Empire a man who more cordially loves a union with Gr. Britain than I do. But by the God that made me, I will cease to exist before I yield to a connection on such terms as the British Parliament propose and in this I think I speak the sentiments of America."

In the last week in December, Jefferson abruptly abandoned

Congress and Philadelphia, and headed back to Virginia. There were political reasons for the move. Delegates came and went frequently; each colony only had a single vote so no one felt any need to maintain the delegations at full strength at all times. Also Jefferson had been appointed a member of the Committee of Safety for the colony of Virginia, as well as commander of the militia for his home county of Albemarle. With Lord Dunmore making more and more threatening noises, he may well have felt he was needed at home. But the paramount motive was his continuing anxiety about Martha.

For the next four months he remained at Monticello, pushing ahead with the building of the mansion house, taking on his own shoulders more and more of the housekeeping details. His wife was not Jefferson's only worry during these private months. On March 31 he recorded in his account books the loss of his mother, who died suddenly at the age of fifty-seven. We know little about Jane Randolph except that she was born in London in the parish of Shadwell and brought that musical name with her to christen the plantation on which she gave birth to six daughters and four sons. Only a family tradition tells us that she was a cheerful, outgoing person who, for a woman of her time, was unusually fond of writing and who composed lively, highly readable letters.

Shortly after her death Jefferson experienced a blinding, debilitating pain that coursed from his temples through his entire head, and throbbed relentlessly day and night for the next five weeks. It was his first recorded attack of what he called "the head ach." Today we would call it migraine, and it is the best possible proof that Jefferson was under a terrible personal strain during these months at Monticello. His mother's death may have contributed to this mental burden. But she was fifty-seven, considered old age in the eighteenth century, and all her children were grown. Almost certainly the migraine points to a more profound and continuing worry—Martha. Jefferson had planned to leave for Philadelphia at the end of March; one might almost think that the attack was brought on by an unconscious desire to find some excuse, no matter how torturous, to delay his departure.

A fellow delegate, Thomas Nelson, Jr., had brought his wife to Philadelphia with him, and he wrote to Jefferson, urging him to

bring Martha along too. But eighteenth-century cities were unhealthy places and in spite of Nelson's assurance that his wife
would "take all possible care of her" (which also hints that Martha's delicate health was common knowledge), Jefferson rejected
the idea. Early in May, he reluctantly left Monticello and, accompanied only by Jupiter, began the seven-day journey to the metropolis. He arrived on May 13, to find both the political and
military aspects of the crisis on the brink of climax. The war news
was both good and bad. Washington had driven the British out of
Boston and they had retreated to Halifax. But the understaffed,
undersupplied American army which had fought a winter campaign to bring Canada into the union had been all but destroyed by
disease and a stubborn British defense. They were now in alarming
retreat before a revived and reinforced British Army of the North.

On the political front, a new author had exploded into print
with "Common Sense," a pamphlet that had changed many minds
about independence. Jefferson had read it long before he had arrived in Philadelphia. A fellow delegate had sent him a copy early
in February. The author was Tom Paine, a rough, blunt, English-
born freethinker who wasted no words. He called George III a
brute and boldly summoned America to a rendezvous with history
as a nation in her own right. The obvious determination of the King
and his ministers to suppress American resistance with force made
the advice of this muscular pamphleteer doubly persuasive. In Philadelphia Jefferson found a letter from his best friend, John Page,
written a month before. "For God's sake declare the colonies independent at once and save us from ruin." This was but a single
rivulet in what an exultant John Adams called "the torrent" for
independence that rolled in upon the Congress every day.

But those who hoped, however dimly, for some kind of reconciliation as an alternative to all-out war, still had strong voices in Congress. Only three short months before, an important committee
had declared that independence was most emphatically not America's goal. Everyone in Philadelphia knew that the real decision
would be made, not in the Pennsylvania State House, but in Williamsburg, where the Virginia convention was meeting on May 15.
Though Massachusetts may have struck the spark that sent the
Revolution flaming, the New England personality was too abrasive

to bring the colonies together under her leadership. Virginia had taken the lead in almost every significant step since George III had closed the port of Boston.

All Jefferson could do was wait patiently for instructions from "his country," as he still called Virginia. What was uppermost in his mind is evident in his May 16 letter to Thomas Nelson, Jr. "I am here in the same uneasy, anxious state in which I was the last fall without Mrs. Jefferson who could not come with me." As for independence, his opinion on the subject certainly did not equal the vehemence of Richard Henry Lee, who was writing Patrick Henry: "Ages yet unborn and millions existing at present must rue or bless that assembly [of Virginia] on which their happiness or misery will so eminently depend." Jefferson merely noted that in the upper counties, such as Albemarle, he had taken "great pains to inquire into the sentiment of the people" and found "nine out of ten are for it."

If Virginia voted for independence, Jefferson hoped "respect will be expressed to the right of opinion in other colonies who may happen to differ from them." He was, in fact, much more concerned about the possibility that the Virginia convention, once it voted to break the bond with England, would immediately take up the problems of forming a new government, and this made him wish he was not three hundred miles away in Philadelphia. "It is," he said, "a work of the most interesting nature and such as every individual would wish to have his voice in." He even suggested to Nelson that it might be a good idea to recall the Virginia delegation, except for "one or two to give information to Congress" and let them join in the work of government building, which was, he said, "the whole object of the present controversy; for should a bad government be instituted for us in the future it had been as well to accept at first the bad one offered to us from beyond the water without the risk and expence of contest."

Jefferson rushed to Speaker Edmund Pendleton a draft of the sort of constitution he thought Virginia should have. It was a remarkable document, especially when we consider that it was written in great haste. It called for wider democracy—anyone with twenty-five acres of farmland or a quarter of an acre of town land could vote—and it explicitly guaranteed religious freedom, freedom of the press, and abolished the antiquated inheritance laws which Virginia had brought from England. It was much too radical for the conservative majority in the Virginia Assembly. All they adopted from Jefferson's draft was his preamble, which was a burning recital of the wrongs England had committed against Virginia, thus justifying the formation of a new and independent government.

Not long after Jefferson fired off this revolutionary constitution, his anxiety over Martha became overwhelming, and he wrote two letters which came close to canceling his rendezvous with world history. The first was to his friend Dr. George Gilmer, who was representing Albemarle in the Virginia convention, and the second was to Edmund Pendleton, the chairman of the convention. The letters are lost, but we know from references to them that he asked the assembly not to re-elect him to the Continental Congress, and requested permission to come home as soon as possible. Gilmer was unable to attend on the day the convention elected delegates for Philadelphia and he passed the chore of getting Jefferson excused on to another friend, Edmund Randolph, who "urged it in decent terms." All he got for his effort was a "swarm of wasps about my ears who seemed suspicious that I designed to prejudice you." Jefferson's letter to Pendleton had not arrived and after a half hour's debate, the assembly rejected Jefferson's plea and elected him and four other delegates for another year's service in Philadelphia. Thus, with an irony which often seems to be history's favorite sport, Jefferson remained at his post, bemoaning his fate and fretting over every post rider who arrived from Virginia without a letter from Martha.

On June 7, 1776, in the humid State House, where Jefferson sat with his fellow congressmen each day, Richard Henry Lee, in obedience to instructions from Virginia, laid before the house a historic resolution.

That these united colonies are and of right ought to be, free and independent states, that they are absolved from all allegiance to the British crown, and that all political connections between them and the State of Great Britain is, and ought to be, totally dissolved.

That it is expedient forthwith to take the most effectual measures for forming foreign alliances.

That a plan of confederation be prepared and transmitted to the respective colonies for their consideration and approbation.

Pugnacious John Adams leaped to his feet and seconded the motion. If he and Lee had any hopes that they could force the issue to an immediate vote, they were soon dashed. The moderates made a motion to postpone debate for a day. On June 8, Saturday, Lee, Adams and George Wythe debated ferociously with James Wilson and John Dickinson of Pennsylvania, Robert R. Livingston of New York, and Edward Rutledge of South Carolina. Jefferson did not say a single word all day, or on the following Monday, when the war of words was renewed with rising ferocity. But he was keenly aware of the momentous nature of the occasion, and he sat in his seat, taking more voluminous notes than anyone else, even Charles Thomson, the secretary of Congress.

Basically the moderates argued against the timing of the declaration. They pointed out that the people of the middle colonies (Maryland, Delaware, Pennsylvania, New Jersey and New York) were undecided about independence. It would be better to wait for them to ripen, lest they secede and weaken the union. Adams, Lee and their supporters argued that the declaration was merely the statement of an already existing fact. They asserted that "the people wait for us to lead the way," and argued that a majority, even in the middle colonies, were for the measure even though their local representatives hesitated to approve it. Above all they argued that it "would be vain to wait either weeks or months for perfect unanimity since it was impossible that all men should ever become of one sentiment on any question."

On and on the orators rumbled until President John Hancock's gavel fell, adjourning the house once more with no agreement in sight. The next day, when the undaunted moderates rose to renew the battle, the independence men decided to admit temporary defeat. As Jefferson said later, it was clear that New York, New Jersey, Pennsylvania, Delaware, Maryland and even South Carolina were "not yet matured for falling from the parent stem."

Both sides agreed to postpone further debate for three weeks. This would give the uncertain colonies time to write home to their local assemblies for instructions. Meanwhile, there was no reason why a committee should not be appointed to draw up a possible declaration of independence. Everyone agreed on the vital importance of such a document; it was not something that should be thrown together hurriedly in a few brief days. Nominations were accepted for a committee, and in a matter of minutes Secretary Charles Thomson was inscribing in the minutes: *The members chosen: Mr. Jefferson, Mr. J. Adams, Mr. Franklin, Mr. Sherman, and Mr. R. R. Livingston.*

Ben Franklin was incapacitated by an attack of gout. Ten days after the committee was formed, he wrote to Washington that it had kept him "from Congress and company almost ever since you left us, so that I know little of what has pass'd there, except that a declaration of independence is preparing . . ."

Neither Sherman nor Livingston had any literary reputation, and the question of who was to draft the declaration descended to a choice between John Adams and Thomas Jefferson. Years later Adams recalled that Jefferson had offered the job to Adams, who promptly replied: "I will not."

"You should do it!"

"Oh! No."

"Why will you not? You ought to do it."

"I will not."

"Why?"

"Reasons enough."

"What can be your reasons?"

"Reason first—you are a Virginian, and a Virginian ought to appear at the head of this business. Reason second—I am obnoxious, suspected and unpopular. You are very much otherwise. Reason third—you can write ten times better than I can."

"Well, if you are decided, I will do as well as I can."

"Very well, when you have drawn it up, we will have a meeting."

Jefferson went to work. He had recently moved from Ben Randolph's house to new quarters in a fine brick house, three stories high, on the southwest corner of Market and Seventh streets. It belonged to a bricklayer named Graff, and Jefferson had taken two rooms on the second floor—a bedroom and a parlor, separated by a stairs between them. Before he left cabinetmaker

Randolph, he purchased a piece of his handiwork made to Jefferson's specifications—a portable desk, which he later described as "plain, neat, convenient and taking no more room on the writing table than a moderate quarto volume, and yet displays itself sufficiently for any writing." In Mr. Graff's sunny second-floor parlor he set up this self-designed "writing box" on a convenient table beside a supply of paper, ink and pens.

Years later Jefferson recalled that he consulted "neither book nor pamphlet." He had no desire to find out "new principles or new arguments never before thought of." His purpose was to "place before mankind the common sense of the subject in terms so plain and firm as to command their assent." He did not even aim at "originality of principle or sentiment," in the individual sense of these terms. The declaration "was intended to be an expression of the American mind and to give to that expression the proper tone and spirit called for by the occasion."

But there were other more personal emotions fermenting in Jefferson's mind. One was the lurking sense that he was risking—perhaps even sacrificing—his beloved Martha to this cause. "Every letter brings me such an account of her health, that it is with great pain I can stay here," he had recently written to John Page. Another more visible worry was the rumor that he was somehow being downgraded by the politicians of his home state because his distaste for violent political conflict had inclined him to be friendly to men on both sides of the widening conservative-radical gulf. To his friend Will Fleming he wrote: "It is a painful situation to be 300 miles from one's country and thereby open to secret assassination without a possibility of self-defense. I am willing to hope nothing of this kind has been done in my case, and yet I cannot be easy. If any doubt has arisen as to me, my country will have my political creed in the form of a declaration &c., which I was lately directed to draw." It is clear that along with an intention to express the "American mind," Jefferson poured deep personal anguish and burning personal conviction into the declaration.

Even if we did not know these things, the emotion is visible in the dramatic cadences of the declaration itself. All we have to do is compare it to the style of Jefferson's preamble to the Virginia constitution. This began with a legal "whereas" and then listed grievances singly, beginning each one with a clumsy participle. Two examples are enough.

By putting his negative on laws the most wholesome & necessary for the public good.

By denying his governors permission to pass laws of the most immediate and pressing importance.

This was Jefferson, the lawyer, speaking. When he bent his head over Ben Randolph's writing box on those hot mornings in mid-June in Philadelphia, he was no lawyer drawing a brief for an interested client, he was an anguished, deeply involved human being who felt the momentous nature of the document he was writing, both for his personal and public self. The rhythms of the opening paragraph throb with a deeper, richer timbre than anything Jefferson ever wrote.

When in the course of human events it becomes necessary for one people to dissolve the political bands which have connected them with another, and to assume among the powers of the earth a separate and equal station to which the laws of nature and of nature's God entitle them, a decent respect to the opinions of mankind requires that they should declare the causes which impel them to this separation.

But Jefferson did not let his emotion interfere with conscious literary craftsmanship. How hard he worked on the declaration in the first days of composition has only recently been discovered. A fragment of one of his early drafts, which Jefferson had ripped up and used to take notes on another matter, was not found among the mass of his papers until 1943. On this, the earliest existing (though incomplete) draft of the declaration, no less than 43 of the 156 words were additions or substitutions for words and phrases that had been deleted. In the text that was for almost two centuries considered "the rough draft" all these changes appear intact. Thus we now know that the rough draft was close to a final copy. But even then Jefferson continued to polish it.

The final changes we see him make on this so-called rough draft are by no means insignificant. The opening lines first read: "When in the course of human events it becomes necessary for a people to advance from that subordination in which they have hitherto remained." The sentence ended with "change" instead of "separation."

In the next paragraph he first wrote: "We hold these truths to be sacred & undeniable that all men are created equal & independent, that from that equal creation they derive rights inherent and inalienable, among which are the preservation of life, and liberty and the pursuit of happiness."

How much better is the final effort. "We hold these truths to be self-evident; that all men are created equal; that they are endowed by their creator with certain inalienable rights."

What were these rights? In a line that he never had to change, Jefferson summed them up in words that are forever linked with his name—"Life, liberty and the pursuit of happiness." The idea, of course, was not original with him. As early as 1770 Pennsylvanian James Wilson, in a pamphlet on the legislative authority of the British Parliament, wrote: "The consequence is that the happiness of the society is the first law of every government." Jefferson's fellow Virginian, George Mason, had drafted a bill of rights which was adopted by the Virginia Assembly. In it he wrote that men had certain inherent rights—"the enjoyment of life and liberty, with the means of acquiring and possessing property, and pursuing and obtaining happiness and safety." How much more concise, and at the same time more majestic, is Jefferson's phrase.

Almost as famous are the words Jefferson wrote next. "That to secure these rights governments are instituted among men, deriving their just powers from the consent of the governed." Again the idea can be traced to a dozen writers, the English philosopher John Locke, James Wilson, George Mason. But Wilson wrote: "All lawful government is founded on the consent of those who are subject to it." Mason wrote: "All power is vested in and consequently derived from the people." Again Jefferson created a more compact and memorable statement of the basic idea. He was earning a rich dividend on his youthful struggles with "Old Coke," who taught him, he once said, "never to use two words where one would do."

In the third clause of his bill of rights, Mason wrote:

Government is or ought to be instituted for the common benefit, protection and security of the people, nation or community; of all the various modes and forms of government that is best which is capable of producing the greatest degree of happiness and safety, and is most effectually secured against the danger of mal-administration; and that when any government shall be found inadequate or contrary to these purposes, a majority of the community has the undubitable, unalienable right to reform, alter, or abolish it, in such manner as shall be judged most conducive to the public weal.

See what Jefferson does to this pedestrian statement of a great ideal:

Whenever any form of government becomes destructive of these ends, it is the right of the people to alter or to abolish it, & to institute new government, laying its foundation on such principles and organizing its powers in such form, as to them shall seem most likely to effect their safety and happiness.

This magnificent statement of the rights of man has been the heart of the declaration's immortality. But to Jefferson and his audience, by far the most important part of the document was the indictment of George III for creating the crisis. Instead of beginning the list of the King's crimes with a weak participle, he used again and again the words "He has."

He has refused his assent to laws the most wholesome and necessary for the public good;
He has forbidden his governors to pass laws of immediate and pressing importance . . .
He has dissolved representative houses repeatedly and continually, for opposing with manly firmness his invasions of the rights of the people . . .
He has made our judges dependent on his will alone . . .

No less than nineteen times Jefferson repeated this "He has" until it became a mournful but meaningful bell tolling the death of American affection for George III.

As a climax—and for Jefferson the most significant item in this grim bill of particulars—Jefferson wrote a paragraph that tells us more about himself, personally, than anything else in the declaration.

He has waged cruel war against human nature itself, violating its most sacred rights of life and liberty in the persons of a distant people who never offended him, captivating and carrying them into slavery in another hemisphere, or to incur miserable death in their transportation thither. This piratical warfare, the opprobrium of infidel powers, is the warfare of the Christian King of Great Britain. Determined to keep open a market where Men should be bought and sold, he has prostituted his negative for suppressing every legislative attempt to prohibit or to restrain this execrable commerce and that this assemblage of horrors might want no fact of distinguished dye, he is now exciting those very people to rise in arms among us, and to purchase that liberty of which *he* has deprived them, by murdering the people upon whom *he* also obtruded them; thus paying off former crimes committed against the *liberties* of one people, with crimes which he urges them to commit against the *lives* of another.

Thus Jefferson declared to the world his passionate loathing of slavery. Among his earliest legal cases—one for which he waived a fee—he had pleaded for the liberty of a mulatto grandson of a white woman and a Negro slave by boldly arguing that slavery was a violation of a man's natural right to freedom. One of the reasons he so desperately wanted to join his fellow Virginians in their constitutional convention was his wish to lead a fight for the gradual abolition of slavery in his "country." His draft constitution, which the convention ignored, had contained an explicit provision for such a measure.

Now Jefferson turned to another question which loomed large in the minds of his fellow Americans—their relation with the British people, as distinguished from the British Parliament. Jefferson showed his boldness by writing a fierce indictment of them as well. Then, in a sonorous closing paragraph, Jefferson declared "these colonies to be free and independent states." Finally, third in the roll call of his immortal phrases, came the sentence: "And for the support of this declaration we mutually pledge to each other our lives, our fortunes and our sacred honor."

Jefferson showed a rough draft of the declaration to John Adams, Roger Sherman and Robert Livingston. They suggested a few word changes and one or two minor additions. This is evident from a recently discovered letter from Jefferson to Benjamin Franklin, probably written Friday morning, June 21. "The enclosed paper has been read and with some small alterations approved of by the committee," Jefferson wrote. "Will Doctr. Franklyn be so good as to peruse it and suggest such alterations as his more enlarged view of the subject will dictate?"

Franklin had only a few word changes to suggest. Some scholars feel it was he, not Jefferson, who changed "sacred and undeniable" to self-evident. Jefferson made what he called "a fair copy" of the declaration and with the approval of the full committee, submitted it to Congress on June 28, 1776. Congress ordered it to "lie on the table," undiscussed and unvoted upon, for the next two days. We can be sure, however, that it was not unread. John Adams had already made a copy and Jefferson had made several. Almost certainly there were others. But for a moment the document was in limbo. Congress had yet to make the crucial decision which would bring it to life, or consign it to oblivion. July 1 was the fateful day on which Congress was to reconsider Richard Henry Lee's resolution for independence.

The day dawned hot and clear and from their lodgings around Philadelphia, the delegates walked to the State House in a saturnine mood. Independence and anti-independence men formed on opposite sides of the room; the conservatives' leader, John Dickinson, was lean and pale in a plum-colored coat and breeches. On the independence side the ranks were thin. Richard Henry Lee and George Wythe were still in Virginia. New representatives from New Jersey, which John Adams had predicted would "vote plump" for independence, had not yet arrived. Nor had new instructions for the Maryland delegates, which Samuel Chase had vowed to send from Annapolis. Delaware, with two delegates present, was temporarily a cipher, because one was for, the other against independence. None of these states had deserted the cause. Their leaders had gone home to fight for it, but distances were great, travel slow and local assemblies were as divided about independence as the Congress.

At noon John Hancock stepped down from the president's chair, thereby signaling that Congress was resolving itself into a committee of the whole, in which debate and vote would be unofficial. Benjamin Harrison, his hearty good nature cloaked in official seriousness, took his seat as chairman for the committee of the whole and the debate began.

John Dickinson spoke first. A grimly earnest, deeply sincere man, he proclaimed his indifference to personal popularity. It was the survival of the nation that was at stake, he insisted. To abandon the protection of Great Britain by declaring independence now, Dickinson vowed, "would be like destroying our house in winter and exposing a growing family before we have got another shelter." As he spoke the doorman gave John Adams an envelope postmarked Annapolis. Adams tore it open and read: "I am this moment from the House with an unan: vote of our convention for independence . . . Your friend, S. Chase."

John Adams rose to answer Dickinson. Out of a passion as deep and personal as Jefferson himself felt for the cause, Adams gave the greatest speech of his career. In later years Jefferson said it had "a power of thought and expression that moved us from our seats." Nature, meanwhile, added to the drama. The smiling summer sky above the State House had slowly changed to an ominous black. Thunder rumbled and crashed, shaking the windows; lightning streaked the gloom. Candles were lit, and Adams spoke on, outroaring the storm. He was still on his feet when into the chamber stalked three rainsoaked delegates from New Jersey, with instructions to declare for independence.

Harrison called for a vote. The four New England states, Virginia, North Carolina and Georgia were for separation. But New York had specific instructions against voting for independence, although their delegates lamely explained that personally they favored it. Delaware was divided, and Pennsylvania and South Carolina voted nay. The worst fears of many Congressmen seemed on the brink of coming true. Four states, almost a third of the thirteen colonies, were against independence. Instead of unifying the colonies, the Declaration threatened to become the issue that divided and destroyed them.

Quickly, Edward Rutledge rose and suggested postponing an official vote until the following day. The idea was gratefully accepted, and Benjamin Harrison's gavel fell, dissolving the committee of the whole.

A night of frantic negotiation and desperate action began. An express rider was rushed to Dover, Delaware, to summon Caesar Rodney, to rescue his state with his pro-independence vote. Rutledge was lectured on the dangers of disunity. John Dickinson was bluntly told that his attitude was not shared by the majority if his fellow Pennsylvanians, and the recent elections to the Pennsylvania assembly, where pro-independence men had won handily, were offered as proof.

The next morning, Tuesday, July 2, President Hancock took his seat and called for an official vote "in full congress assembled." Caesar Rodney, splattered with mud and water, was in his seat from Delaware, after an eighty-mile all-night ride through pelting rain. Edward Rutledge, "for the sake of unanimity," had changed South Carolina's mind. John Dickinson and his friend Robert Morris stayed home, giving Pennsylvania a three-to-two majority in favor of independence. So the momentous vote was recorded, twelve states for independence and New York abstaining only because new instructions had not yet arrived from her assembly. (They would take another thirteen days to reach Philadelphia.) The torrent for independence had become a flood. To his wife Abigail, John Adams wrote: "The 2nd day of July, 1776, will be the most memorable epocha in the history of America. I am apt to believe that it will be celebrated by succeeding generations as the great anniversary festival."

That was a wholly sincere, perfectly logical prophecy from a man immersed in the moment-to-moment drama of independence. But John Adams' great speech vanished without a man recording a single word of it. Thomas Jefferson's declaration, which Congress now undertook to consider in detail, was to be published and republished around the world. That was why July 4, when the declaration was approved, and not July 2, when independence was voted, became America's Independence Day. It is a testimony to the enormous power of the written word.

The next two days were not happy ones for Jefferson. No author likes to see his work edited, and Jefferson now had to sit there and endure the criticism of not one but a squadron of editors. The declaration was scrutinized, word by word, line by line, paragraph by paragraph, with Congress sitting once more as a committee of the whole. Before Jefferson's shocked eyes and ears, whole paragraphs were ripped out of the document he had labored so hard to perfect. His comments, made years later, still reflect the pain of the author who is seeing his efforts mauled by men whose purposes were decidedly unliterary.

"The pusillanimous idea that we had friends in England worth keeping terms with, still haunted the minds of many. For this reason, those passages which conveyed censures on the people of England were struck out, lest they should give them offense." Next, from north as well as south, came objections to the paragraph Jefferson felt was among the most important in the document—the slashing attack on the slave trade. Gentlemen from South Carolina and Georgia proclaimed themselves angrily in favor of continuing to import slaves. "Our northern brethren," Jefferson wrote, "also I believe felt a little tender over those censures; for though their people had very few slaves themselves, yet they had been pretty considerable carriers of them to others."

None of these changes were accomplished without vigorous debate and John Adams was in the forefront with his usual blunt ferocity, "fighting fearlessly for every word," Jefferson testified later. If Jefferson had already "touched" Adams' heart with his forthrightness, now it was the stumpy New Englander's turn to forge on his side a debt of friendship which Jefferson never forgot. But unity was the vital necessity in 1776, and Adams and his supporters got nowhere with their protests. Let South Carolina and Georgia have their slave trade, the majority decided. After the war was won, if a nation was formed, then would be time enough to do something about slavery. If, on the other hand, the colonies decided to pursue independent courses (at this point no one was entirely certain), then slavery was their own dirty business. So Jefferson could only sit in obvious misery, and watch Benjamin Harrison, once more presiding over the committee as a whole, draw his official pen through the fiery phrases.

Sympathetic though any writer must be with Jefferson's anguish over these "mutilations," an objective reading of the declaration makes it clear that on the whole Congress improved the finished product. They added one of the more resounding final phrases, "with a firm reliance on the protection of Divine Providence." Even their surgery, for motives wholly political, had a healthy literary effect. The final result was a leaner, harder-hitting document. The best way to see at a glance the changes Congress made is in the following copy of the declaration. The parts omitted by Congress are crossed out and the parts added are interlined in italics.

A Declaration by the Representatives of the
UNITED STATES OF AMERICA
in General Congress assembled.

When in the course of human events it becomes necessary for one
people to dissolve the political bands which have connected them with
another, and to assume among the powers of the earth the separate and
equal station to which the laws of nature and of nature's god entitle
them, a decent respect to the opinions of mankind requires that they
should declare the causes which impel them to the separation.

We hold these truths to be self-evident; that all men are created
                                                    certain un-
equal; that they are endowed by their Creator with ~~inherent and~~ ∧in-
alienable rights; that among these are life, liberty, and the pursuit of
happiness; that to secure these rights, governments are instituted among
men, deriving their just powers from the consent of the governed; that
whenever any form of government becomes destructive of these ends,
it is the right of the people to alter or to abolish it, and to institute new
government, laying its foundation on such principles, and organizing
its powers in such form as to them shall seem most likely to effect their
safety and happiness. prudence indeed will dictate that governments
long established should not be changed for light & transient causes; and
accordingly all experience hath shewn that mankind are more disposed
to suffer, while evils are sufferable, than to right themselves by abolishing the forms to which they are accustomed. but when a long train of
abuses and usurpations, ~~begun at a distinguished period &~~ pursuing invariably the same object, evinces a design to reduce them under absolute despotism, it is their right, it is their duty, to throw off such
government, & to provide new guards for their future security. such
has been the patient sufferance of these colonies, & such is now the
                                                    alter
necessity which constrains them to ~~expunge~~∧their former systems of
government. the history of the present king of Great Britain is a his-
                    repeated
tory of ~~unremitting~~∧injuries and usurpations, ~~among which appears no~~
                                                    having
~~solitary fact to contradict the uniform tenor of the rest, but all have~~∧in
direct object the establishment of an absolute tyranny over these states.
to prove this let facts be submitted to a candid world, ~~for the truth of~~
~~which we pledge a faith yet unsullied by falsehood.~~
He has refused his assent to laws of the most wholesome and necessary
    for the public good.

he has forbidden his governors to pass laws of immediate & pressing
importance, unless suspended in their operation till his assent should
utterly
be obtained; and when so suspended he has ₍neglected ~~utterly~~ to
attend to them.

he has refused to pass other laws for the accommodation of large districts of people, unless those people would relinquish the right of
representation in the legislature; a right inestimable to them, & formidable to tyrants only.

he has called together legislative bodies at places unusual, uncomfortable, & distant from the depository of their public records, for the
sole purpose of fatiguing them into compliance with his measures.

he has dissolved Representative houses repeatedly ~~& continually,~~ for
opposing with manly firmness his invasions on the rights of the
people.

he has refused for a long time after such dissolutions to cause others to
be elected whereby the legislative powers, incapable of annihilation,
have returned to the people at large for their exercise, the state remaining in the meantime exposed to all the dangers of invasion from
without, & convulsions within.

he has endeavored to prevent the population of these states; for that
purpose obstructing the laws for naturalization of foreigners; refusing to pass others to encourage their migrations hither; & raising
the conditions of new appropriations of lands.

obstructed
he has ~~suffered,~~₍the administration of justice ~~totally to cease in some of~~
by
~~these states~~ refusing his assent to laws for establishing judiciary
powers.

he has made our judges dependent on his will alone, for the tenure of
their offices, and the amount & paiment of their salaries.

he has erected a multitude of new offices ~~by a self assumed power,~~ &
~~sent hither swarms of officers to harass our people, and eat out their~~
substance.

he has kept among us, in times of peace, standing armies ~~and ships of~~
~~war,~~ without the consent of our legislatures.

he has affected to render the military independent of, & superior to, the
civil power.

he has combined with others to subject us to a jurisdiction foreign to
our constitutions and unacknowledged by our laws; giving his assent

to their acts of pretended legislation for quartering large bodies of
armed troops among us;

    for protecting them by a mock-trial from punishment for any
       murders which they should commit on the inhabitants of these
       states;

    for cutting off our trade with all parts of the world;

    for imposing taxes on us without our consent;

          in many cases

    for depriving us˄of the benefits of trial by jury;

    for transporting us beyond seas to be tried for pretended offenses;

    for abolishing the free system of English laws in a neighboring
       province, establishing therein an arbitrary government, and en-
       larging its boundaries so as to render it at once an example & fit
       instrument for introducing the same absolute rule into these
       states;

    for taking away our charters, abolishing our most valuable laws,
       and altering fundamentally the forms of our governments;

    for suspending our own legislatures, & declaring themselves in-
       vested with power to legislate for us in all cases whatsoever.

                                                by

he has abdicated government here, ~~withdrawing his governors~~ &˄de-

                    and waging war against us

claring us out of ~~his allegiance and~~ protection˄.

he has plundered our seas, ravaged our coasts, burnt our towns, & destroyed the lives of our people.

he is at this time transporting large armies of foreign mercenaries, to
compleat the works of death, desolation & tyranny, already begun

          scarcely paralleled in the most barbarous ages and totally

with circumstances of cruelty & perfidy˄unworthy the head of a
civilized nation.

    excited domestic insurrection amongst us and has

he has˄endeavored to bring on the inhabitants of our frontiers the
merciless Indian savages, whose known rule of warfare is an undis-
tinguished destruction of all ages, sexes, & conditions ~~of existence.~~

he has incited treasonable insurrections of our fellow citizens, with the
allurements of forfeiture & confiscation of property.

      our fellow citizens

he has constrained˄~~others~~ taken captives on the high seas to bear arms
against their country, to become the executioners of their friends &
brethren, or to fall themselves by their hands.

~~he has waged cruel war against human nature itself, violating its most~~
~~sacred rights of life & liberty in the persons of a distant people, who~~
~~never offended him, captivating and carrying them into slavery in~~
~~another hemisphere, or to incur miserable death in their transporta-~~
~~tion thither, this piratical warfare, the opprobrium of *infidel* powers,~~
~~is the warfare of the *Christian* king of Great Britain. determined to~~
~~keep open a market where MEN should be bought & sold, he has~~
~~prostituted his negative for suppressing every legislative attempt to~~
~~prohibit or to restrain this execrable commerce: and that this assem-~~
~~blage of horrors might want no fact of distinguished dye, he is now~~
~~exciting those very people to rise in arms among us, and to purchase~~
~~that liberty of which *he* has deprived them, by murdering the people~~
~~upon whom *he* also obtruded them: thus paying off former crimes~~
~~committed against the *liberties* of one people, with crimes which he~~
~~urges them to commit against the *lives* of another.~~

In every stage of these oppressions, we have petitioned for redress in
the most humble terms; our repeated petitions have been answered
only by repeated injury. a prince whose character is thus marked by
                                                              free
every act which may define a tyrant, is unfit to be the ruler of a people
~~who mean to be free. future ages will scarce believe that the hardiness~~
~~of one man adventured within the short compass of twelve years only~~
~~to build a foundation, so broad and undisguised, for tyranny over a~~
~~people fostered and fixed in principles of freedom.~~

Nor have we been wanting in attentions to our British brethren.
we have warned them from time to time of attempts by their legislature
         an unwarrantable   *us.*
to extend a jurisdiction over ~~these our states.~~ we have reminded them
of the circumstances of our emigration and settlement here, ~~no one of~~
~~which could warrant so strange a pretension: that these were effected~~
~~at the expence of our own blood and treasure, unassisted by the wealth~~
~~or the strength of Great Britain: that in constituting indeed our several~~
~~forms of government, we had adopted one common king, thereby lay-~~
~~ing a foundation for perpetual league and amity with them: but that~~
~~submission to their parliament was no part of our constitution, nor ever~~
                                                              have
~~in idea, if history may be credited: and~~ we appealed to their native
                        and we have conjured them by
justice & magnanimity, ~~as well as to~~ the tyes of our common kindred,
                                would inevitably
to disavow these usurpations, which ~~were likely to~~ interrupt our con-

                    s
nection~& correspondence. they too have been deaf to the voice of
justice and of consanguinity; ~~and when occasions have been given~~
~~them, by the regular course of their laws, of removing from their~~
~~councils the disturbers of our harmony, they have by their free election~~
~~re-established them in power. at this very time too, they are permitting~~
~~their chief magistrate to send over not only soldiers of our common~~
~~blood, but Scotch and foreign mercenaries to invade and destroy us.~~
~~these facts have given the last stab to agonizing affection; and manly~~
                                                        therefore
~~spirit bids us to renounce forever these unfeeling brethren.~~ we must~en-
~~deavor to forget our former love for them, and to hold them as we~~
~~hold the rest of mankind, enemies in war, in peace friends. we might~~
~~have been a free & a great people together, but a communication of~~
~~grandeur and of freedom, it seems, is below their dignity. be it so,~~
~~since they will have it the road to happiness and to glory is open to~~
~~us too; we will climb it apart from them and~~ acquiesce in the necessity
and hold them, as we hold the rest of mankind, enemies in war, in
which denounces our ~~eternal~~ separation.~
peace friends.

   We therefore the Representatives of the United States of America
appealing to the supreme judge of the world for the rectitude of our
in General Congress assembled,~do, in the name & by authority of
intentions   colonies, solemnly publish and declare, that these
the good people of these~~~states, reject and renounce all allegiance and~~
united colonies are and of right ought to be free and independent
~~subjection to the kings of Great Britain, & all others who may hereafter~~
states; that they are absolved from all allegiance to the British Crown,
and that
~~claim by, through, or under them; we utterly dissolve~~ all political con-
                                                them   state
nection ~~which may heretofore have subsisted~~ between ~~us~~~and the~~~peo-~
                        is & ought to be totally dissolved;
~~ple or parliament~~ of Great Britain; ~~and finally we do assert and declare~~
~~these colonies to be free and independent states,~~ & that as free & independent states, they have full power to levy war, conclude peace, contract alliances, establish commerce, & to do all other acts and things
which independent states may of right do. And for the support of this
with a firm reliance on the protection of divine providence,
declaration,~we mutually pledge to each other our lives, our fortunes,
and our sacred honor.

   In spite of this heavy editing, the declaration was still Jefferson's creation. As one historian summed it up, "His pen had written it, his spirit brooded over it, giving light to the whole . . ." But the author did not feel that way on July 4, 1776, when the final version was read aloud to a satisfied Congress. John Hancock took the president's chair once more and Congress voted its official approval. Whether the members present signed it then, or later in the month, is a subject which historians have been debating for almost a hundred years. According to Jefferson, a copy was signed on July 4. An "engrossed" or parchment copy was signed on July 19.

Benjamin Franklin and other friends tried to console him, but Jefferson's pain over the amputation of so many of his favorite phrases and clauses remained acute. When he sent copies of the final declaration to his friends in Virginia, he made a point of enclosing a copy of his original draft as well. A few, such as Edmund Pendleton, were gentlemanly enough to assure him that Congress had "altered it much for the worse." Richard Henry Lee flattered him unctuously, assuring him that though the manuscript had been "mangled" it was nevertheless "wonderful . . . the thing is in its nature so good that no cookery can spoil the dish for the palates of free men." Only his old friend John Page had the good sense to ignore the implied comparison and simply tell Jefferson, "I am highly pleased with your declaration."

Meanwhile, Jefferson's thoughts were already returning to Monticello. On July 4 he bought no less than seven pairs of gloves, and a number of other items of feminine finery for Martha. Throughout the month of July, while Congress held melancholy hearings on the disastrous retreat of the American army that had hoped to conquer Canada, and debated Articles of Confederation, Jefferson's anxiety about Martha's health continued to mount. On July 15 he wrote to Francis Eppes. "I wish I could be better satisfied on the point of Patty's recovery. I had not heard from her at all for two posts before, and no letter from herself now." On July 23 he was again writing to Eppes. "I have received no letter this week, which lays me under great anxiety."

Meanwhile, the declaration was circulating throughout the colonies and was being proclaimed, in accordance with the orders of President John Hancock, "in such a mode that the people may be universally informed of it." Philadelphia saw the first proclamation on July 8. Some forty congressmen, no doubt including Jefferson, watched while it was read from a scaffold in the State House yard to a huge crowd of people. "Three cheers rendered the welkin," John Adams said. "The battalions paraded on the Common . . . the bells rang all day and almost all night." On July 9, George Washington had it read before the army at New York, and reported to Congress that "the measure seems to have their most hearty assent; the expressions and behavior of both officers and men testifying their warmest approbation of it." On the Battery, civilian New Yorkers pulled down the leaden statue of George III and melted it into bullets.

Providence, Rhode Island, celebrated the publication with thirteen volleys from the ships in the harbor. In Baltimore, patriots carted an effigy of George III through the town and then it was "committed to the flames amidst the acclamations of many hundreds—the just reward of a tyrant." It soon became evident that the declaration had done more to unite the colonies than any other single pronouncement of Congress. As time passed, men also realized that Jefferson's magnificent phrasing was the vital factor in its electrifying impact on hesitant and divided minds.

But for the moment, Jefferson's authorship was known only to a small handful of his friends and fellow congressmen. In July, 1776, everyone was keenly aware that the declaration was nothing less than an act of treason. Elias Dayton of New Jersey summed up the prevailing state of mind when he wrote, "As to my title, I know not whether it will be honorable or dishonorable: the issue of war must settle it. Perhaps our Congress will be exalted on a high gallows." For another eight months, Congress kept even the names of the signers a closely guarded secret. But knowledge of Jefferson's authorship slowly filtered down to the common man, who read those opening phrases about equality and the pursuit of happiness as a promise of a better future, and began to admire both the words and the man who wrote them.

I V

For the moment, however, Jefferson remained an obscure, harassed delegate to a Congress that bickered through the sweltering heat of August over what he called "the minutia of the confederation." Jefferson's thoughts were in Virginia. Martha had sent him a letter, plaintively begging him to come home. Impulsively, Jefferson had promised her he would be at her side by the middle of August.

Then, to his mounting distress, the older members of the Virginia delegation found various excuses to absent themselves, until only he and Carter Braxton were left. Next Braxton too anticipated Jefferson's desire, by announcing on July 20 that he was going home within two days. This left Jefferson the only guardian of Virginia's vote in Congress, and thus made it impossible for him to leave. He had already written to Richard Henry Lee, begging him to return to Philadelphia to relieve him. On the twenty-first, Lee had written casually that he would be on his way on the 3rd of September. This answer drew from Jefferson a cry of anguish. "For God's sake, for your country's sake and for my sake, come," he begged. "I receive by every post such accounts of the state of Mrs. Jefferson's health that it will be impossible for me to disappoint her expectation of seeing me at the time I have promised." At the end of the letter, after a few more hurried sentences about Congressional business, he added one more plea. "I pray you to come. I am under a sacred obligation to go home."

But Lee could not be hurried, and Jefferson had to spend the rest of the broiling month of August in Philadelphia, where he dutifully served on several committees, none of which involved matters that could justify his absence from home when he was so badly needed. He recommended a seal for the United States of America (his motto, "*e pluribus unum*," was later adopted, but not his artwork), debated with Pennsylvanians and others the conflicting claims the various states had to western lands, wrote a long report on gold and silver coins full of tables which are models of scientific exactitude. Though he did not realize it, the report was a major step toward one of his least recognized achievements, the creation of the American monetary system. He also corresponded with Edmund Pendleton about revising the laws of Virginia. But his mind and heart were at The Forest where Patty was staying with Francis Eppes and his wife.

Jefferson had rushed a letter to her, forbidding her to journey to Monticello and become involved in the plantation's responsibilities without him. In another letter, his anxiety had impelled him to write Edmund Pendleton that he hoped he could retire completely from politics. The alarmed elder statesman, who had just finished telling Jefferson how badly he was needed to help create a new government for Virginia, urged him in reply to "get cured of your wish to retire so early in life from the memory of man, and exercise your talents for the nurture of our new constitution." Finally, on September 1, Jefferson could stand it no longer and even though Lee had not yet arrived, he settled his various accounts, bought some hats and guitar strings and on September 3, 1776, set out for Monticello. He picked up Martha en route and for a few all too brief weeks they enjoyed the autumn beauty of their mountain.

In later years a visitor to Monticello left a vivid description of this season of the year at Monticello. It was a paean of praise to the way "the imperial mantle of forest, wrought into brilliant dyes by the frost and sunshine, seemed in the soft haze to float down the graceful slope." But the beauties of nature, the joy with which little "Patsy" and Martha greeted him could not disguise the fact that his wife was seriously ill. Some physicians who have studied the scanty evidence believe that Martha Jefferson was suffering from diabetes. Others think that she was simply a fragile, emotionally dependent person who became depressed when she was separated from her husband and this in turn had a disastrous effect on her physical health.

Certainly Jefferson seemed to feel that his presence was literally vital to her well-being. On October 20, he took her to a doctor for an examination, and she was pronounced well enough to go with him to Williamsburg, where the Virginia convention was meeting. His old mentor, George Wythe, was in Philadelphia serving out his term as a delegate, and the Jeffersons persuaded him with no difficulty to lend them his handsome brick house on the west side of the Palace green in Williamsburg. "Make use of the house and furniture. I shall be happy if anything of mine can contribute to make your and Mrs. Jefferson's residence in Williamsburg comfortable," wrote this kindly man.

The house and grounds were a plantation in miniature. Vegetables in abundance were available from the garden and Jefferson undoubtedly made sure that Martha's diet was as healthy as the knowledge of the day could make it. He himself was passionately fond of vegetables and fruit, and so little interested in meat he was almost a vegetarian. Behind the house was a pleasure garden, where Martha and her husband, with their enthusiasm for growing things, spent many an hour strolling the brick and marl paths lined with tree-box topiary.

The Jeffersons were just beginning to enjoy the Wythe house when a letter from Philadelphia came swirling in by special express, throwing both husband and wife into new turmoil. Congress had nominated Jefferson as one of three commissioners to go to France and negotiate a treaty of alliance. It was a striking testimony to how deeply Jefferson had impressed his fellow congressmen. The other commissioners were Benjamin Franklin and Silas Deane, who was already in France and had established important contacts with the French court.

Moreover, the words of President John Hancock's letter made it clear that Congress was very much aware of the honor and the importance of the mission. "It is with particular pleasure I congratulate you on the occasion," Hancock wrote. In an accompanying letter, Richard Henry Lee was even more explicit, describing the treaty as "this all-important business." He added that "the great abilities and unshaken virtue, necessary for the execution of what the safety of America does so capitally rest upon, has directed the Congress in their choice . . . In my judgment the most eminent services that the greatest of her sons can do America will not more essentially serve her and honor themselves than a successful negotiation with France."

Here, thrust upon Jefferson as a gift—more than a gift—a high honor—was the opportunity to fulfill that youthful dream of seeing the Old World—seeing it moreover as a man of importance, not a mere student counting his pennies and scratching for introductions to minor dignitaries. Congress was even stretching its slender resources to the utmost to accommodate him. "If it is your pleasure, one of our armed vessels will meet you in any river in Virginia that you choose," wrote Richard Henry Lee.

For three days Jefferson was a man in torment, trying to make a decision. Take Martha with him? A look at her wan face, the way she leaned invalid fashion on his strong arm when they strolled in Wythe's garden, scotched that idea. Only someone in the very best physical health could be expected to endure six to eight weeks on the Atlantic in late autumn, eating stale ship's food, confined to a cramped, sunless cabin by heavy weather. Go alone? Martha Jefferson was not the sort of woman who would use her illness as a weapon in an argument. It was not necessary. The pain in her eyes at the mere proposal that she could bear a separation of perhaps a year, even two years, silenced Jefferson's tongue.

Finally, on the third day, Jefferson sat down in George Wythe's book-lined study and wrote one of the most mournful letters of his life. "No cares of my own person, nor yet for my private affairs would have induced one moment's hesitation to accept the charge," he said. "But circumstances very peculiar in the situation of my family, such as neither permit me to leave nor to carry it, compel me to ask leave to decline a service so honorable and at the same time so important to the American cause. The necessity under which I labor, and the conflict I have undergone for three days, during which I could not determine to dismiss your messenger, will I hope plead my pardon with Congress . . ."

Jefferson was too embarrassed even to reply to Richard Henry Lee. That acerbic gentleman declined to show the least understanding of Jefferson's agonizing position. From Philadelphia he wrote: "As I have received no answer to the letter I wrote you by the express from Congress, I conclude it has miscarried. I heard with much regret that you had declined both the voyage and your seat in Congress. No man feels more deeply than I do, the love of, and the loss of, private enjoyment; but let attention to these be universal, and we are gone beyond redemption, lost in the deep perdition of slavery."

Jefferson's dilemma was literally insoluble. He could not admit, even to himself, that his wife was seriously ill. Even if he could admit it, an instinctive reticence about his private life made him shrink from blurting out the news in starkly sentimental terms. Thus the private torment, the worry about Martha's health, became a public embarrassment, making Jefferson seem a hypocrite who wrote glowing phrases but was not willing to shoulder the burden of turning his lofty ideas into realities.

This sense of public censure drove Jefferson to throw all his energy into his work as a delegate to the Virginia Assembly. He was also deeply convinced that the state's laws had many "vicious points which urgently required reformation" as holdovers from Virginia's royal past. Still another reason for the importance he attached to this work was the position of Virginia, as the largest, most populous state in the new union. Where she led, others would inevitably follow. So Jefferson felt that he was legislating both for his native state and for the American nation.

Within a few days after taking his seat as a delegate, he introduced a series of bills aimed at removing the aristocratic bias from Virginia society. The base of the aristocracy's power was two inheritance laws—entail and primogeniture. Thanks to entail, the head of a great estate, such as Landon Carter, could literally forbid his descendants to break it up, in order to settle family arguments or reward favorite sons and daughters. The goal was the preservation of the Carter name and influence, beyond the uncertainties of a particular generation's talents or intelligence. If Landon Carter, III, turned out to be an idiot, and Landon Carter, IV, a genius, the great estate would still be there, more or less intact for him to build upon. Primogeniture had a similar aristocratic purpose. If a man died without a will, his inheritance automatically went to the eldest son.

In this same crowded period, Jefferson collided with Virginia aristocrats over still another matter crucial to the future development of the American nation. For several decades, settlers had been drifting over the Blue Ridge Mountains into an area vaguely known as Kentucky. In this same uncharted west, the great landholders of Virginia had laid claims to huge tracts which they had purchased on credit or procured by influence with the crown. The pioneers and these speculative land companies were soon in a state of semiwarfare, with the settlers angrily refusing to surrender land that they had cleared and farmed at the risk of their lives, merely because some traveling representative of a land company flourished a piece of paper and asserted ownership.

The biggest of these companies, set up by one Richard Henderson of North Carolina, with the backing of a number of prominent Virginians, actually attempted to create a state of Transylvania, and sent a delegate to the Continental Congress in the hope of winning recognition. Jefferson wrecked this scheme by sponsoring a bill dividing the area into three counties and giving the western, anti-aristocratic portion of Virginia six new representatives. The bill also specified that no one could be made a civil or military officer in these new counties if he had taken an oath of office "to the pretended government of Richard Henderson, Gent. & Company."

These bills won Jefferson the enmity of some of the most powerful men in Virginia. In an explosive letter to George Washington about the bill abolishing entails, Landon Carter compared Jefferson to "a midday drunkard." (He also gave grudging credit to Jefferson's growing reputation by sneering at "the famous T. J—n!") But to Jefferson it was all part of a fight to "make an opening for the aristocracy of virtue and talent . . . essential to a well ordered republic." It was in his view the gentlest and most civilized of revolutions. "No violence was necessary, no deprivation of natural right, but rather an enlargement of it . . ."

Against him, as the chief spokesman of the "ancient establishments," was Edmund Pendleton, whom Jefferson called "the ablest man in debate I have ever met with . . . cool, smooth and persuasive." A veteran parliamentarian, Pendleton was as tenacious as he was skillful. "If he lost the main battle, he returned upon you," Jefferson said, "and regained so much of it as to make it a drawn one by dexterous maneuvers, skirmishes in detail and the recovery of small advantages which, little singly, were important all together. You never knew when you were clear of him . . ." But again, in his recollections of the often feverish debates that raged over these bills during the autumn of 1776 in Williamsburg, the young Jefferson revealed his gift for opposing men in principle without personal rancor. Pendleton was, he says, "one of the most virtuous and benevolent of men, the kindest friend, the most amiable and pleasant of companions."

Jefferson won his fight on primogeniture and entails. But when he tackled another holdover from the days of royalty, he was rocked back on his heels. This was the "establishment" of the Church of England in Virginia. Under the law, Anglicanism was the official religion of the colony, and every citizen, no matter what his religious belief, had to contribute to the support of the parish church in his vicinity. Theoretically, at least, he was also liable to prosecution for dissenting beliefs.

Jefferson wanted to abolish this system totally, and sever all connection between the state and the church. But he soon found himself involved in what he later called "the severest contests in which I have ever been engaged." A bill exempting dissenters from contributing to the established church finally passed. But Pendleton and his allies returned to the fray with a suggestion for a general tax, to be distributed to all the churches on a percentage basis. The debate on this and other amendments made it clear that a great many Virginians were determined to maintain some form of religious establishment. The best Jefferson and his supporters could do was fight off the general tax, and the main issue was left for future decision.

In these bruising battles Jefferson found a new and most welcome ally, a diminutive, scholarly representative from Orange County named James Madison. He was seven years younger than Jefferson but the two found, almost from the moment they met, that they shared an intuitive union of mind and feeling about politics. Jefferson found himself deeply impressed by Madison's voluminous learning and his ability to apply it successfully to practical matters. He was also delighted by the little man's rather ribald wit and fund of droll stories. Above all he admired Madison's habit of "never wandering from his subject into vain declamation, but pursuing it closely in language pure, classical, and copious, soothing always the feelings of his adversaries by civilities and softness of expression . . ."

While Virginians fought a war of words among themselves, George Washington was fighting a war of bullets with the British in New York. It is hard for the twentieth-century reader, accustomed to the idea of total war, in which a nation presses every ablebodied man and woman into service, to understand the eighteenthcentury attitude toward war. It was a compartmentalized approach, a belief that those who had the talent and inclination to be soldiers would and should do the fighting, while politicians continued to politick and businessmen continued to trade. But grim news from the battlefront made more than one man wonder if this was not a dubious assumption. Harassed by orders from Congress that forced him to fight where defeat was almost a certainty, relying on an army that was half untrained militia who ran at the first shot, Washington was driven out of New York and into New Jersey, where his army dwindled to a ragged fragment that fled across the Delaware one jump ahead of the pursuing British.

Letters poured in to the Virginia debaters, abruptly reminding them that the government they were trying to perfect might be stillborn if they failed to support Washington and his desperate men. Jefferson, back at Monticello in mid-December, received a letter from Governor Patrick Henry, appointing him the county collector of blankets and rugs for the freezing soldiers. The message was in itself an ironic comment on the woeful lack of American resources. Like most of his fellow Americans, Jefferson had optimistically pictured the war as a single campaign, perhaps two or three battles fought in the summer and early fall. Washington temporarily rescued the situation from total disaster by slashing across the Delaware on Christmas night, 1776, to capture 900 crack German troops at Trenton. A few days later, a brilliant flank march carried him around the overconfident enemy and enabled him to repeat this success against startled British regiments at Princeton. The war settled into a winter stalemate. By now it was grimly evident to both sides that it was not going to end quickly.

Jefferson spent the winter of 1777 battling the elements and worrying over Martha's health. She was pregnant again. The weather was unbelievably severe for Virginia—the coldest winter in the memory of anyone living. Jefferson's wells went dry, and he was forced to devote hundreds of man-hours to dragging water up the winding road to his mountaintop.

Blocked in the legislature, Jefferson now tried a flank attack on Virginia's religious establishment. He accepted membership on a committee to undertake a general revision of the laws. He himself had proposed the idea, and he willingly shouldered much of the enormous burden. For two years he toiled on this task, interrupting it only for meetings of the legislature.

In mid-March, 1777, Jefferson returned hastily from one of these sessions to be at Martha's side for a now familiar ordeal. For six days he waited and worried in her bedroom, half nurse, half husband. On May 28, his friend Dr. George Gilmer and his sister, Martha Carr, resolutely showed him the door and he paced the floor of his still unfinished mansion, while Martha writhed and gasped in labor. Then the door burst open and George Gilmer stood beaming at him, holding in his arms a tiny red body swathed in blankets. It was a boy. Thomas Jefferson was at last the father of a son!

The whole plantation rejoiced. Nothing was more precious to a Virginian, with his deep sense of family pride, than a son. Seventeen days later, the words of joy became the ashen taste of sorrow on everyone's lips. Mournfully on the night of June 14, 1777, Jefferson wrote in his little pocket diary: "Our son died 10 H. 20 M. P.M."

Monticello's wells remained dry for the rest of the year, a kind of symbol of the Jeffersons' spiritual desolation. Work on the mansion house dragged. Letters drifted in from his friends in Congress. John Adams wrote: "We want your industry and abilities here extremely." Adams added a soft rebuke: "Your country is not yet, quite secure enough, to excuse your retreat to the delights of domestic life."

Not until late August did Jefferson answer this letter, which Adams wrote to him two days before the birth of the lost son. Richard Henry Lee was more sarcastic, writing, "It will not perhaps be disagreeable to you in your retirement, sometimes to hear the events of war, and how in other respects we proceed in the arduous business we are engaged in."

To neither of these friends did Jefferson attempt to explain the real reason for his retirement. He could only hint at it in a wistful letter to Benjamin Franklin, written in mid-August. "I wish my domestic situation had rendered it possible for me to have joined you in the very honorable charge confided to you . . ."

In the North the war thundered on with the same depressing alternation of victory and defeat. Washington lost two desperate battles before Philadelphia, and the British occupied the American capital, sending Congress scurrying westward to York. At Saratoga, another British army led by John Burgoyne blundered into defeat and finally surrendered to the British-born general, Horatio Gates. Jefferson watched hopefully from afar and tried to bury his personal grief in work on the revision of Virginia's laws. His reluctance to leave Martha was evident, even in October, when he was ten days late taking his seat at the fall meeting of the Virginia Assembly. He may not have planned to come at all, but no less than fifty members had absented themselves and the speaker of the house was forced to order the sergeant at arms to summon the delinquents under threat of arrest for contempt.

For the next eighteen months, while the war stumbled along in the same dreary stalemate, Jefferson gave almost all his time to assembly politics and the immense scholarly effort involved in revising the laws. He played a leading role in whipping through the Virginia legislature a prompt approval of the Articles of Confederation, which created at least a semblance of national unity. But a continental vision was not enough, in the opinion of the man who was bearing the heaviest burden of the war. In the winter of 1778–79, George Washington wrote to Benjamin Harrison to lament the second-rate men that all the states, including Virginia, were sending to Congress. "Where is Mason, Wythe, Jefferson, Nicholas, Pendleton, Nelson and another I could name?" (Meaning Harrison himself.) A few months later Washington pleaded with George Mason: "Let this voice . . . call upon you, Jefferson and others," he said.

For Jefferson, the explanation still lay in the fragile figure who stood in the foreground of his vision of the future at Monticello. On August 1, 1778, he recorded in his notebook, "Our third daughter is born." It had been a repetition of all Martha's previous births, anxiety over her condition before, and even more anxiety over both mother and child after the event. Jefferson did not take his seat in the assembly that year until the fall session was almost over. He stayed at Monticello until he was certain that both Martha and the newcomer, whom he named Mary, were out of danger.

In February, 1779, Jefferson met George Wythe and Edmund Pendleton, his two fellow law revisers, at Williamsburg. "Day by day," he said, "we examined critically our several parts, sentence by sentence, scrutinizing and amending until we had agreed on the whole. We then returned home, had fair copies made of our several parts which were reported to the General Assembly on June 18th, 1779." The magnitude of the effort is best summed up by Jefferson's own words. "We had in this work brought so much of the Common Law as it was thought necessary to alter, all the British statutes from Magna Charta to the present day and all the laws of Virginia from the establishment of our legislature . . . to the present time which we thought should be retained, within the compass of 126 bills, making a printed folio of ninety pages only." James Madison later called it "the most severe of his [Jefferson's] public labours." It was, Madison said, "a model of statutory composition, containing not a single superfluous word."

Jefferson's main motive in undertaking this huge job surfaced in his bills on religion and education. Both were bold and sweeping visions of how a free society should organize itself, in order to encourage the "natural aristocracy of talent and virtue." To the end of his life, Jefferson believed that his "Bill for Establishing Religious Freedom" was, with the possible exception of the Declaration of Independence, the most important thing he ever wrote. The preamble contains some of his finest, least-known phrases.

Well aware that the opinions and belief of men depend not on their own will, but follow involuntarily the evidence proposed to their minds;

that Almighty God hath created the mind free, and manifested his supreme will that free it shall remain by making it altogether insusceptible of restraint;

that all atempts to influence it by temporal punishments or burthens, or by civil incapacitations, tend only to beget habits of hypocrisy and meanness, and are a departure from the plan of the holy author of our religion, who being lord both of body and mind chose not to propagate it by coercions on either . . . as was in his Almighty power to do, but to exalt its influence on reason alone;

that the impious presumption of legislators and rulers, civil as well as ecclesiastical, who being themselves but fallible and uninspired men, have assumed dominion over the faith of others, setting up their own opinions and modes of thinking as the only true and infallible and as such endeavoring to impose them on others, hath established and maintained false religions over the greatest part of the world through all time;

that to compel a man to furnish contributions of money for the propagation of opinions which he disbelieves and abhors is sinful and tyrannical;

that even forcing him to support this or that teacher of his own religious persuasion is depriving him of the comfortable liberty of giving his contributions to the particular pastor whose morals he would make his pattern, and whose powers he feels most persuasive to righteousness; and is withdrawing from the ministry those temporary rewards, which proceeding from an approbation of their personal conduct are an additional increment to earnest and unremitting labors for the instruction of mankind;

that our civil rights have no dependence on our religious opinions, any more than our opinions in physics or geometry;

that therefore the proscribing any citizen as unworthy of the public confidence by laying upon him an incapacity of being called to offices of trust and emolument, unless he profess or renounce this or that religious opinion, is depriving him injudiciously of those privileges and advantages to which in common with his fellow citizens he has a natural right;

that it tends also to corrupt the principles of that very religion it is meant to encourage by bribing with a monopoly of worldly honors and emoluments, those who will externally profess and conform to it; that though those indeed are criminal who do not withstand such temptation, yet neither are those innocent who lay the bait in their way;

that the opinions of men are not the object of civil government nor under its jurisdiction;

that to suffer the civil magistrate to intrude his powers into the field of opinion and to restrain the profession or propagation of principles on supposition of their ill tendency is a dangerous fallacy, which at once destroys all religious liberty because he being of course judge of that tendency will make his opinions the rule of judgment and approve or condemn the sentiments of others only as they shall square with or differ from his own;

that it is time enough for the rightful purposes of civil government for its officers to interfere when principles break out into overt acts against peace and good order;

and finally, that truth is great and will prevail if left to herself;

that she is the proper and sufficient antagonist to error and has nothing to fear from the conflict unless by human interposition disarmed of her natural weapons, free argument and debate; errors ceasing to be dangerous when it is permitted freely to contradict them.

Then came the statute itself, a prime example of Jefferson's distaste for the superfluous in language, as well as in architecture.

We the General Assembly of Virginia do enact that no man shall be compelled to frequent or support any religious worship, place or ministry whatsoever, nor shall be enforced, restrained, molested, or burthened in his body or goods, or shall otherwise suffer, on account of his religious opinions or belief; but that all men shall be free to profess, and by argument to maintain, their opinions in matters of religion, and that the same shall in no wise diminish, enlarge or affect their civil capacities.

With this declaration of spiritual independence Jefferson coupled his "Bill for the More General Diffusion of Knowledge" which aimed at buttressing this freedom with an informed, educated electorate. It not only called on Virginia to set up a public school system, but planned it in detail. Jefferson proposed dividing each county into "hundreds"—small neighborhood school districts for the primary level. Above these the better students would move on to "grammar" schools where a much smaller number of young men of genuine ability would be educated at public expense and, finally, twenty students from these schools would be selected to go on to the College of William and Mary on public scholarships. Those able to afford an education would, Jefferson expected, send their children to these schools at their own expense.

Jefferson regarded these two bills—and the abolition of entail and primogeniture—as the heart of his program for Virginia. "The restoration of the rights of conscience relieved the people from taxation for the support of a religion not theirs; for the establishment was truly of the religion of the rich," he said. The bill for education would enable them to "understand their rights, to maintain them, and to exercise with intelligence their parts in self-government; and all this," Jefferson triumphantly concluded, "would be effected without the violation of a single natural right of any one individual citizen."

Jefferson's vision was too advanced for his contemporaries. The declaration of religious freedom caused such a furor in the assembly practically nothing else was discussed. Nor was it possible to settle the matter for years to come. The education bill was considered too burdensome for Virginia's strapped finances, and not for another eighteen years would even part of it be enacted into law. But Jefferson had created what James Madison called "a mine of legislative wealth" on which he and other Virginians would draw for the next two decades.

V

During the first months of 1779, when he was completing the revisions of the laws, the war suddenly became much less distant for Jefferson. Over four thousand British and German officers and their troops, captured at Saratoga, were marched into Albemarle County where Congress thought there would be more food and less chance of their escaping. Congress was supposed to have barracks built and ample food ready for these men when they arrived. Instead, the prisoners found the barracks half finished and most of the food spoiled.

The addition of so many hungry mouths put a severe strain on the resources of thinly populated Albemarle, and soon there was talk among Governor Patrick Henry and his council, no doubt prompted by more than a few complaining letters, that the troops should be moved elsewhere. The moment Jefferson heard about this idea, he wrote a long letter to Henry, protesting violently "as an American" and "a citizen of Virginia." He especially denounced the plan to separate the officers and men, which would be a direct violation of the surrender terms signed at Saratoga. This, he declared, "would be a breach of public faith." The plan was dropped and the troops went to work, finished the barracks themselves, planted gardens and were soon established in moderate comfort.

For the German and British officers, Jefferson threw open the doors of Monticello, inviting them to dinner, joining them in duets on the violin and discussing philosophy and science with those who were interested. One young English captain named Bibby later recalled how he and his friends would visit Monticello and almost invariably find themselves pressed into an impromptu musicale, those who could play performing on instruments and others joining in the singing. Bibby said that Jefferson was one of the best amateur violinists he ever heard. To a studious young German officer named De Unger, Jefferson wrote: "When the course of events shall have removed you to distant scenes of action, where laurels not moistened with the blood of my country may be gathered, I shall urge my sincere prayers for your obtaining every honor and preferment which may gladden the heart of a soldier. On the other hand, should your fondness for philosophy resume its merited ascendancy, is it impossible to hope that this unexplored country may tempt your residence, by holding out materials wherewith to build a fame, founded on the happiness, but not on the calamities of human nature?"

With the two commanding officers, plump Major General William Philips and stocky, red-faced Baron de Riedesel, Jefferson was on equally intimate terms, entertaining back and forth at dinner. Riedesel and his Amazonian wife rented the house of Philip Mazzei, who had returned to Italy. General Philips was so touched by Jefferson's liberal spirit, he wrote him a note of gratitude, to which Jefferson replied: "The great cause which divides our countries is not to be decided by individual animosities . . . to contribute by neighborly intercourse an intention to make others happy is the shortest and surest way of being happy ourselves."

While Jefferson charmed these former enemies, the war seemed to be stumbling along at the same stalemated pace. Most Americans felt time was in their favor. Congress, on February 15, read a report from a committee, proposing peace terms. France had entered the war on the American side, and Spain was making threatening noises toward Great Britain too, all of which seemed to point toward only one conclusion—Britain, convinced that victory was impossible, would give up the struggle. Only in the south was there some contradictory evidence. A British army had come rampaging up from Florida, to capture Savannah and almost totally subdue Georgia. This new strategy lay like a small but ominous cloud on Virginia's horizon, when Jefferson received what was, for him, even more alarming news. His friends were nominating him for Governor.

VI

Jefferson's instinctive reaction was refusal. He could barely perform the duties of an assemblyman, meeting for a few brief weeks twice a year. A governor was on duty day in, day out for his entire term. But this time his friends were adamant. Edmund

Pendleton told him, "You are too young to ask that happy quietus from the public, and should at least postpone it till you have taught the rising generation the forms as well as the substantial principles of legislation."

Over his protests, Pendleton and others proceeded to put his name in nomination. His chief opponent, ironically, turned out to be his friend John Page, who had served as lieutenant governor under the outgoing executive, Patrick Henry. Page wanted the job even less than Jefferson. His friends, largely followers of Henry, who was already drifting farther and farther away from Jefferson's ideas, put him forward, and after a rather brisk contest in the assembly (which chose the Governor under the new constitution), Jefferson won by a mere six votes. The two friends promptly exchanged cheerful notes assuring each other that there was not an iota of hard feelings on either side.

Six days after Jefferson took office, he was writing to William Fleming, who was serving as a delegate to the Continental Congress in Philadelphia, asking him if there was any truth to the rumor that the British were willing to make peace, but Congress was dragging its feet on negotiation. "It would surely be better to carry on a ten years war sometime hence," Jefferson said, "than to continue the present an unnecessary moment."

Even a cursory look at Virginia's situation made it clear to Jefferson that disaster was imminent. A runaway inflation was on its way to making the paper money issued by the Continental Congress, Virginia and other states a bitter joke. Jefferson's salary was a princely 375 pounds a month—close to $9,000 in contemporary money. But its purchasing power was another matter. During the first months of his term he was paying 5 pounds for some pens and 36 pounds for a bonnet for Martha. In Philadelphia, it took 50 Continental dollars to buy two pairs of shoes.

The galloping inflation was a personal as well as a public disaster for Jefferson. The signers of the bonds he had accepted as payment for the Wayles's debt were able to pay him off in the worthless paper at about two cents on the dollar, and he found himself faced with paying the debt all over again. The British creditors, who had refused to accept the bonds in the first place, were of course hardly inclined to settle for the depreciated American dollars.

At least as ominous as her finances was the condition of Virginia's defenses. Two months before Jefferson became Governor, a British fleet had dropped anchor in the Chesapeake and sent ashore 2,000 men who captured with almost ridiculous ease a supposedly reliable seacoast fort, burned the town of Suffolk and cut a swath of fiery destruction across several dozen square miles of Virginia's Tidewater, without losing a man. The ease with which this exploratory raid had been conducted, made it almost certain that the British would return.

Simultaneously, Jefferson had to worry about an even more bitter and barbarous war on Virginia's western borders. More than a year before, he and two other assemblymen had been appointed by Governor Patrick Henry to advise a valiant frontier fighter named George Rogers Clark on his plans to combat British-led Indian forays in the Ohio River Valley. The rough frontiersman found in the polished Virginia intellectual a companion spirit, when it came to a vision of American expansion westward. It was Jefferson more than anyone else who encouraged Clark to assemble the small, compact force honed for frontier warfare that routed the British from the Northwest Territory and created a legitimate American claim to this vast virgin land. But the redcoats were far from beaten. Clark was back in Virginia soon after Jefferson became Governor, begging him for more money and munitions. Simultaneously, Congress called on Virginia for more men to fill her Continental battalions, and for more money to bolster the sagging Continental treasury. Governor Jefferson was swamped.

Worst of all were the severe limitations on the Governor's authority. Elected by the legislature, surrounded by his council, he was little more than the echo of many voices. The framers of the Virginia constitution had been so nervous about potential dictators, they had hedged the executive office with dozens of crippling restrictions. He was not expected to initiate policy, only execute what the legislature decreed, and then he had to have the approval of his council for his interpretation. This made for maddeningly slow government when the harsh exigencies of war might demand the utmost speed. Jefferson had no power to stop the state from printing more and more paper money. He could not tighten the lax militia law, which enabled men to give almost any excuse and avoid a call to arms. He had no power to requisition horses and supplies, if the individuals refused to surrender them.

There was also Martha's health to worry about. Jefferson did not bring her to hot, feverish Williamsburg during the first summer of his governorship, but left her in the cool, familiar shade of The Forest, where he visited her at every opportunity. In the fall, Martha and her two daughters moved into the handsome red brick Governor's Palace. There Jefferson no doubt entertained her with reminiscences of his college days, when he had been a frequent dinner guest of the cultured Royal Governor, Francis Faquier. But the overwhelming amount of work to be done gave the harassed Governor little time for his family. He met daily for hours with his council, which fortunately included his new friend James Madison, his old friend John Page, and his still older friend from Albemarle, John Walker. There was little they could do but watch the lengthening shadow of war move closer to them. In February, 1780, a British fleet and army descended upon Charleston, South Carolina, and trapped a 5,000-man Continental army inside the city. Many of these irreplaceable troops were Virginians and when the British settled down to a siege, it soon became evident that their capture was only a matter of time.

Charleston fell in May, 1780, and the British then moved swiftly to subjugate the rest of South Carolina. On May 29, British cavalry under Lieutenant Colonel Banastre Tarleton, a name that was to haunt Jefferson, wrecked another Virginia regiment at Waxhaws Creek. Virginians shuddered at these blows, which destroyed the cream of their fighting men, and swept away tens of thousands of dollars of irreplaceable military equipment. Carping voices began to wonder about the wisdom of letting Virginians fight and die to defend other states, when their own shores were all but naked to the enemy. But Governor Jefferson more than proved his vision of the Revolution was continental—no matter how much time he had spent in Virginia.

When Major General Horatio Gates marched south to challenge the British grip on Georgia and South Carolina, Jefferson manfully called out the best of Virginia's militia and committed 800 of these part-time soldiers to bolster Gates' slender 1200-man force of Continentals. They blundered into the worst disaster of the war.

Weakened by bad food and exhausted by an all-night march, the Americans collided with Charles, Lord Cornwallis, near Camden, South Carolina, and were routed by a British bayonet charge. Most of the Virginia and North Carolina militia fled without firing a shot. Gates, on the fastest horse he could find, did not stop retreating until he reached Charlotte, North Carolina, sixty miles away. The Continentals were wiped out almost to the last man and those militia who were not killed or captured in the pursuit were unlikely ever to volunteer again.

Jefferson could only grit his teeth, apologize for the disgraceful performance of the Virginia militia, and grimly send word to Gates that he was calling on 2,000 more men to join him in North Carolina by the 25th of September. He noted the futility of this brave gesture in the same sentence, with the words, "We have not Arms to put into the hands of these men."

To multiply Jefferson's worries, Martha was pregnant again. The threat of British invasions had inspired the assembly to take a suggestion Jefferson had made in 1776; they finally moved the capital from coastal Williamsburg to Richmond. There Jefferson rented a small wooden house from a relative, and set up housekeeping once more with Martha and the two little girls. In the middle of November, Martha gave birth to another daughter, Lucy Elizabeth, and the usual atmosphere of crisis prevailed. But the little girl seemed to thrive, and Governor Jefferson was soon back at his desk, engulfed in the swirling problems of trying to run a war without money.

During these same frantic months, he nevertheless found time to demonstrate his capacity for friendship. James Monroe was a twenty-two-year-old Virginian who had fought with skill and bravery under Washington at Trenton and other battles. Returning to Virginia, he seemed to have experienced one of those crises which many young men of other generations have gone through after fighting a war. He drifted aimlessly, unable to decide on a career until he met Jefferson in 1780. With all that he had to do, Jefferson not only recommended a legal career for Monroe, but worked out a course of study for the young ex-soldier which he personally supervised.

During the crisis created by the defeat of Gates, Jefferson

commissioned Monroe a lieutenant colonel and sent him south to make a personal report on the situation in the southern army. The result of this attention is a seldom-quoted but memorable letter, which is one of the finest tributes to Jefferson ever written.

. . . A variety of disappointments with respect to the prospects of my private fortune previous to my acquaintance with Your Excellency, upon which I had built as on ground which could not deceive me and which failed in a manner which could not have been expected . . . nearly destroyed me. In this situation had I not formed a connection with you I should most certainly have retir'd from society with a resolution never to have enter'd on the stage again . . . Believe me I feel that whatever I am at present in the opinion of others or whatever I may be in future has greatly arose from your friendship. My plan of life is now fixed, has a certain object for its view and does not depend on either chance or circumstance further than the same events may affect the public at large.

Meanwhile, Jefferson's troubles as Governor were just beginning. In early January he was at work at his desk, when a message arrived from the coast, which had unaccountably taken two full days to reach him. A British fleet was in the Chesapeake!

Jefferson had no way of knowing that he was about to become the first American to confront Brigadier General Benedict Arnold of the British army. Having failed in his plot to surrender West Point in the fall of 1780, Arnold had escaped to British-held New York, where he was given a general's commission and promptly sent south with 1600 troops. One of the boldest commanders on either side in the entire war, Arnold wasted no time starting up the James River with his army in captured American ships.

Desperately Governor Jefferson tried to assemble some militia to oppose him, but everything went wrong. In wild haste, Jefferson had to pile his wife and children into a carriage and send them to Tuckahoe. He himself stayed at Richmond until the last possible moment, directing the removal of public records and stores. That night when everything possible had been done in the deserted capital, Jefferson rode to Tuckahoe and decided the plantation was too close to Richmond for safety. In the early dawn he took Martha and the three girls across the river and sent them on to another plantation, eight miles farther inland. Martha could hardly have recovered from her pregnancy, and little Lucy was only two months old. Neither was in a condition to become a refugee in the worst of winter.

Jefferson, though he must have been almost sick with anxiety for Martha and the children, turned his horse in the other direction and rode furiously down to Manchester, directly across the river from Richmond. Except for three or four hours' rest snatched at Tuckahoe, he had been in the saddle for most of the previous thirty-six hours, and just before he reached Manchester his horse collapsed and died on the road. Jefferson had to carry his saddle and bridle on his back until he reached a farmhouse and borrowed an unbroken colt. He rode on, to arrive in Manchester in time to see Arnold's red-coated battalions marching down Richmond's main street. Two hundred Virginia militia could only retreat at top speed before the formidable royal force. Jefferson watched in helpless frustration from the other side of the river while Arnold burned the public buildings, tobacco warehouses and other property. The traitor marched a detachment upriver to Westham, where they burned the foundry, magazine and artificer's shops in which Virginia made its muskets, and incidentally destroyed most of the public papers, which had been left there by some confused wagoneers.

In the midst of his troubles, the public person remained the essential Jefferson. One day, driving hard along a narrow road, he passed a soldier with a huge pack on his back. The footsore infantryman begged Jefferson to give him a lift in his phaeton. Jefferson's mind flashed ahead, warning him that the road was probably full of soldiers, and if he gave them all rides, his already gasping horse might collapse. He said no and drove on, but before he had gone a quarter of a mile, his conscience troubled him so badly that he turned around and rode back in search of the man. But the soldier had turned down a side road and Jefferson never found him. The memory of this small incident troubled him for years.

On January 7, Benedict Arnold boldly marched his men 25 miles back to his ships, waiting for him on the James at Westover, and sailed back down the river, troubled by nothing but a minor skirmish with a detachment led by George Rogers Clark. The turncoat general occupied Portsmouth and set up what looked ominously like a permanent base. In March, 1781, he was reinforced by 2,000 more men under Major General William Philips, Jefferson's erstwhile Monticello neighbor, who had been exchanged.

Against these 3,000 tough professionals, the distracted Jefferson had nothing but a handful of green Continentals, and whatever militia he could induce to risk their lives in such an unlikely contest. At the same time, pleas for aid from west, north and south continued to bombard the harassed Governor. A new American commander in the Carolinas, Nathanael Greene, begged him for men and material. George Rogers Clark and other westerners warned of impending disaster along the border. Washington needed men if he ever hoped to dislodge the British from their main base in New York.

With all these worries, Jefferson had to endure another wrenching personal loss. At 10 A.M. on raw, rainy April 15, five-month-old Lucy Elizabeth died in the rented house in Richmond. Martha was so stricken, Jefferson did not even dare to leave her to walk the few yards from his residence to the brick house where his council met. He sent a note to David Jameson, a member of the council, "The day is so very bad that I hardly expect a council, and there being nothing that I know of pressing, and Mrs. Jefferson in a situation in which I would not wish to leave her, I shall not attend today."

Two weeks later, Jefferson must have shuddered to learn that the British were on the James once more, this time with an army of 2,500 men. Jefferson's only hope was word from Washington that the Marquis de Lafayette was marching south with 1,200 Continentals. The British landed near Williamsburg, routed a body of militia there, and burned a state shipyard on the Chickahominy River. Landing again at City Point, where the Appomattox met the James, the British fought a brief battle with a thousand militia, led by Baron Johann von Steuben, drove these amateur soldiers and their commander over the Appomattox and then leisurely destroyed huge quantities of tobacco and other stores and burned a number of ships. Another division marched to Chesterfield Courthouse and burned barracks and military stores there. At the same

The Gilbert Stuart portrait of Jefferson, the best painting of him in mature middle age. This was the man Americans chose as their third president, in one of the bitterest, most slander-filled elections of all time. *Culver Pictures, Inc.*

Know all men by these presents that we Thomas Jefferson and Francis Eppes are held and firmly bound to our sovereign lord the king his heirs and successors in the sum of fifty pounds current money of Virginia, to the paiment of which well and truly to be made we bind ourselves jointly and severally, our joint and several heirs executors and administrators in witness whereof we have hereto set our hands and seals this twenty third day of December in the year of our lord one thousand seven hundred and seventy one The condition of the above obligation is such that if there be no lawful cause to obstruct a marriage intended to be had and solemnized between the abovebound Thomas Jefferson and Martha Skelton of the county of Charles city, widow, for which a license is desired, then this obligation is to be null and void; otherwise to remain in full force.

Th: Jefferson

Francis Eppes

FAC-SIMILE OF JEFFERSON'S
MARRIAGE-LICENSE BOND.

Jefferson's marriage bond, in which he vowed his fealty to the King, as the good British subject he was at the time. Like George Washington, he married a widow. *The Bettmann Archive.*

The Governor's Palace in Colonial Williamsburg was familiar to Jefferson from his student days at William and Mary, when he often dined with the cultured Royal Governor, Francis Faquier. Later, Jefferson presided there as a harried governor himself during the Revolution. *Culver Pictures, Inc.*

One of the few portraits of the young James Madison. His political skills first impressed Jefferson, older by seven years, in the Virginia Assembly. He was also delighted by the smaller man's wit and fund of droll stories, which made Jefferson laugh until the tears rolled down his cheeks. *The Bettmann Archive.*

Revolutionists at work. In this imaginary recreation Jefferson, Patrick Henry and other young Turks in the Virginia Assembly plot defiance of Great Britain, in a room at the Raleigh Tavern in Williamsburg. *Culver Pictures, Inc.*

The house in Philadelphia, at Seventh and Market Streets, where Jefferson wrote the Declaration of Independence. He consulted "neither book nor pamphlet." His purpose was to place before mankind "the common sense of the subject in terms so plain and firm as to command their assent." *Culver Pictures, Inc.*

Thanks to Jefferson, British officers captured at Saratoga led a pleasant prisoner's life. They lived in the vicinity of Monticello, and he regularly invited them to his mansion for dinner and impromptu musicales. In this imaginary rendition, Jefferson himself is performing. One Briton pronounced him the finest amateur violinist he had ever heard. *Culver Pictures, Inc.*

Jefferson at 43, painted in London in 1786, for his friend, John Adams. His face still shows traces of deep depression that racked him after his wife's death in 1782. *The Bettmann Archive.*

Paris as Ambassador Jefferson knew it, in the last days of the *ancien régime*. He thought Louis XVI was "a good man" and urged moderation upon the French Revolutionaries. *Culver Pictures, Inc.*

The Grand Trianon was one of the pleasures at Versailles during the years of Jefferson's ambassadorship. He preferred the less crowded gardens and walks of other royal palaces, in the hills around the city. *Culver Pictures, Inc.*

The Halle au Blé, the Parisian market, considered one of the architectural marvels of its time. Ambassador Jefferson went to admire it, and found himself paying far more attention to the beautiful Maria Cosway. *Culver Pictures, Inc.*

Maria Cosway, the 'beautiful Anglo-Italian painter and musician with whom Jefferson fell deeply in love during his years as ambassador to France. When she left him, he stumbled back to his embassy "more dead than alive." *Culver Pictures, Inc.*

Jean Antoine Houdon's bust of Jefferson, done in 1789, shows him reinvigorated, about to leave France for America and a turbulent career in the politics of the new republic. *Culver Pictures, Inc.*

A view of the not yet finished White House in 1799, the year before Jefferson won the Presidency. It is easy to see why Washington, D.C., was called "the Federal village." *Culver Pictures, Inc.*

A contemporary cartoon, satirizing President Jefferson on his efforts to avoid war, in spite of the abusive and arrogant way the two superpowers of the era, France and England, were treating the United States. *Culver Pictures, Inc.*

Martha Jefferson, his oldest daughter, in later life. Tall and red-haired, she was often described as a "delicate" edition of her father. Of Jefferson's six children, she alone survived him. *The Bettmann Archive.*

This "life mask," taken at Monticello when Jefferson was 82, is probably the most nearly accurate portrait of Jefferson as an old man. *Culver Pictures, Inc.*

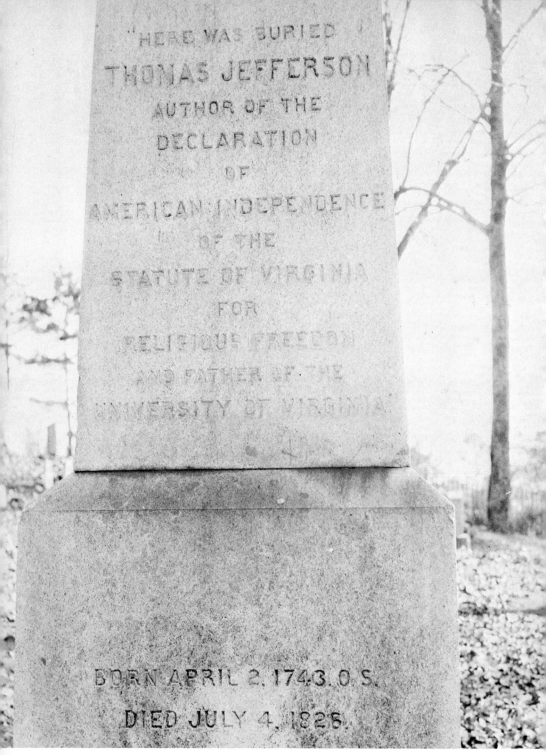

"HERE WAS BURIED
THOMAS JEFFERSON
AUTHOR OF THE
DECLARATION
OF
AMERICAN INDEPENDENCE
OF THE
STATUTE OF VIRGINIA
FOR
RELIGIOUS FREEDOM
AND FATHER OF THE
UNIVERSITY OF VIRGINIA

BORN APRIL 2, 1743, O.S.
DIED JULY 4, 1826.

Jefferson wrote his own epitaph, selecting the three achievements he considered the most important of his long life. These, he said, were the things he had given to the people. All his offices, from Virginia Assemblyman to President, were things the people had given to him, and were therefore omitted. *The Bettmann Archive.*

time Arnold was out on the James, smashing a small flotilla of river boats with which the desperate Virginians attempted to halt his progress up the river. James Monroe, under intense British fire, risked his life to burn several abandoned American ships, rather than have them fall into British hands. This last fight took place at Osborne's, only a few miles below Richmond.

For Jefferson the defeat had nerve-wracking personal meaning. He had sent Martha and the two remaining little girls fleeing into the country again, with orders to await him at Elk Hill. Now the British breakthrough exposed them to capture or worse. There was nothing to stop the enemy from cruising up the James to land at the plantation, whose lush farmlands would immediately catch their marauding eyes. Martha and the girls tried to get across the river (no doubt on Jefferson's advice) and retreat to Tuckahoe, but found themselves trapped by an order which had collected all the canoes and boats in the neighborhood to carry grain to the militia army.

His family's plight may have been an added reason why Governor Jefferson resolved to make a stand at Richmond. He was also loath to abandon the considerable amount of tobacco and public stores which had been again collected in the town. His military advisers heartily concurred and they had concentrated every militiaman they could muster in the little village.

On April 29 these unreliable soldiers were bolstered by the arrival of the Marquis de Lafayette, at the head of a dusty advance column of 900 Continentals. It was the first time the homely, engaging, young Frenchman and Jefferson had met, though they had been corresponding since Lafayette began his march south. It was the best possible way to begin a friendship. The marquis' battle-toughened regulars saved Jefferson from the humiliation of another headlong flight. The next day the British appeared at Manchester across the river, and after looking at the determined American array on the Richmond bluffs decided it was the better part of valor to retire down the river and attack more tobacco instead.

But Governor Jefferson's troubles were still far from over. Benedict Arnold sailed back to New York, and Major General Philips died of a bilious fever. They were replaced by the toughest, most aggressive British general in the war, Charles Cornwallis. He had been fighting Nathanael Greene up and down North Carolina and finally decided that chasing the elusive American was a futile game as long as Greene was able to replenish his battered army with men and supplies from Virginia. The solution to the problem—possibly the solution to the entire war, Cornwallis decided —was an all-out campaign to smash Virginia's spiritual and material resources. He brought with him from the Carolinas enough troops to swell the British army in Virginia to almost 9,000 men—a force that made Lafayette and his puny 1,200 Continentals almost laughable. Lafayette mournfully wrote to Washington on the 24th of May, "I am not strong enough even to get beaten."

The last weeks of Jefferson's governorship were trickling away in an atmosphere of almost total despair and futility. The assembly, having been driven out of Richmond twice, decided to transfer the capital to Charlottesville, which seemed beyond reach of Cornwallis' vengeance. Jefferson sent Martha and the two children back to Monticello and prepared to join them there. The mortified Governor could only write one last despairing letter to Washington, begging him for his "personal aid." If Washington came to Virginia, Jefferson was convinced that the militia would rise en masse and drive the British into the Chesapeake.

But Washington replied that he was committed for the time being to an assault on New York, which he hoped would force the British to withdraw most of the army in Virginia to reinforce that key bastion. Jefferson's only consolation was the last paragraph of Washington's letter which was testimony from the best possible witness that the weary Governor had done his utmost to support the war on a continental scale, even at the risk of weakening Virginia. "Allow me . . . to express the obligations I am under for the readiness and zeal with which you have always forwarded and supported every measure which I have had occasion to recommend through you," Washington wrote.

Long before Jefferson received this letter the British were on the march again. Lafayette could only retreat before Cornwallis, hoping to wear him down, or catch him at a moment when he could strike a damaging, if not a decisive blow. Burning, destroying and plundering as he went, Cornwallis rumbled through the Virginia countryside, while Lafayette and Jefferson watched in helpless dismay.

Virginia's morale dwindled to the vanishing point. Even Jefferson's friend John Page was reduced to despairing gloom. Page told another friend that the British invasions had sunk Virginia "so low in the eyes of the world that no illustrious foreigner can ever visit her or any historian mention her but with contempt and derision . . . I am ashamed and ever shall be to call myself a Virginian."

Jefferson returned to Charlottesville to prepare for the meeting of the assembly while Lafayette wrote desperate pleas to Major General Anthony Wayne, who was mustering reinforcements at York, Pennsylvania. The assembly met on May 24, 1781, and voted Jefferson and his council special war powers which should have been granted to them months before. It was much too late now to rally the prostrate state. For the last three days of Jefferson's term as governor, he and William Fleming, the only member of his council who bothered to attend, met, formally recognized that the governor and his council were in session, and adjourned.

June 2 was the last day of Jefferson's term. But the British were not inclined to let him enjoy his retirement. At dawn on June 4, 1781, a fantastic figure in a scarlet coat, military hat and plume, came racing up Monticello's winding road on an exhausted horse. Jefferson and several members of the assembly, who were staying at Monticello, were routed from their beds to hear wild words tumble from the eccentric messenger's lips—Tarleton was coming! The horseman was Jack Jouett, Virginia's Paul Revere. At 11 o'clock on the previous evening he had been enjoying a drink in a roadside tavern when up to the doors thundered 180 green-coated British dragoons, and 70 red-coated mounted infantry, led by Banastre Tarleton himself, Cornwallis' commander of cavalry. Guessing where Tarleton was going, Jouett slipped out a back door, leaped on his horse and while the British cavalryman allowed his men three hours' rest, Jouett pounded down side roads and over back trails to beat him to Charlottesville.

Jefferson took the news calmly. He summoned a carriage, awakened Martha and the children and ordered his favorite riding horse taken to Monticello's blacksmith to be shod. The Jeffersons and their guests then had a leisurely breakfast and the assemblymen rode down to Charlottesville to spread the alarm. Everyone mistakenly thought that Tarleton's heavily armed troopers could not possibly equal Jouett's pace on the road and that they had several hours to spare. They were wrong. Riding all night, Tarleton paused only to burn a few wagons and steal a breakfast from Dr. Thomas Walker, where he also scooped up a member of the Continental Congress. The assembly had barely adjourned, after resolving to meet again at Staunton, farther inland, and many of them were still dallying in town when the green-coated dragoons were upon them. The legislators fled in all directions, but seven of them did not move fast enough, and they too became captives.

Meanwhile, underscoring his desire to bag Jefferson, Tarleton had taken the risk of dividing his small force, sending Captain Kenneth McLeod with a detachment thundering up the road from Charlottesville to Monticello. Jefferson, Martha and the children were still in the house when a patriotic Virginian named Hudson came pounding breathlessly up to the door to tell him that the British were almost to the foot of the mountain. A wild scramble ensued. Martha and the children were piled into the carriage, along with several servants and a young Virginian who volunteered to serve as escort, and told to head pell-mell for nearby Blenheim.

It was the third flight in three months for Martha Jefferson, and by far the most frenetic. As she said good-by to Jefferson she had no way of knowing if she would ever see him or Monticello again. A hundred possibilities must have swirled through her mind. If the British caught him, they might hang him on the spot. Or send him in irons to London, to be tried for high treason, with the verdict a foregone conclusion. Would they burn Monticello? It was all too possible. What if she herself and the little girls were caught on the road by Tarleton's troopers, infamous for their brutality? No matter how calm her husband was, how soothing his reassurances, this was an hour of terrible anguish for Martha Jefferson.

As soon as his wife and children had disappeared down the road Jefferson rushed back into the house, told two of his servants to hide the silver and any other valuables they had time to grab, and ordered his horse to be brought from the smith's to a point in the road between Monticello and nearby Carter's Mountain. He then left the house on foot and disappeared into the woods, cutting across his own property to Carter's. He picked up his horse, and began walking it up the neighboring mountain, where he paused and used a telescope he had brought along to study the situation in

Charlottesville. He saw not a sign of cavalry and decided that Hudson's alarm had been premature. He started back down the mountain, intending to return to Monticello, to see if he could get some of his private papers out of the house, lest the British burn it. He had gone only a few steps when he noticed that in kneeling down to sight his telescope, he had lost a small dress sword he was carrying at his waist. He went back to search for it and decided, after finding it, to have another look at Charlottesville. In the round eye of the telescope the main street of Charlottesville was swarming with Tarleton's green dragoons. Jefferson promptly sprang on his horse and cantered into the woods on Carter's Mountain.

The lost sword saved Jefferson's life. Five minutes after he left the house, Captain McLeod and his detachment of dragoons had swarmed up the mountain and were already in possession of Monticello. As the dragoons came up the road, two of Jefferson's slaves, Martin and Caesar, were busy hiding the silver plate and other valuables under the floor of the front portico. At the sound of the British hoof beats, Martin slammed down the planks and trapped Caesar in the dank darkness underneath the porch. He stayed there for eighteen hours without food or water, a testimony to his devotion to Jefferson. Martin, the other slave, was equally loyal. One dragoon shoved a pistol into his chest, cocked it and ordered him to tell where Jefferson was or he would fire.

"Fire away then," snarled Martin. The dragoon retreated.

For eighteen hours the British remained in possession of Monticello. But they touched nothing except a few bottles of wine in the cellar. Tarleton had given McLeod strict orders to damage no property and the command was scrupulously obeyed. The British captain even locked the door of Jefferson's study and gave the key to the slave Martin.

Jefferson, meanwhile, had ridden over Carter's Mountain and joined his family for midday dinner at Blenheim. Later he sent them to another plantation, nine miles away, and finally took them another seventy miles to Poplar Forest in Bedford County.

Jefferson had escaped British depredation at Monticello, but he was not so lucky elsewhere. While Tarleton drove the Governor and the legislators into headlong flight, Cornwallis advanced up the

James to the Point of Fork and occupied Jefferson's plantation at Elk Hill. This was richer and more abundant farm land than Monticello; it was probably the most valuable of all Jefferson's lands. Here in Jefferson's own words is what Cornwallis did to the place. "He destroyed all my growing crops of corn and tobacco; he burned all my barns, containing the same articles of the last year; having first taken what corn he wanted; he used, as was to be expected, all my stock of cattle, sheep and hogs for the sustenance of his army, and carried off all the horses capable of service; of those too young for service he cut the throat; and he burned all the fences on the plantation, so as to leave it an absolute waste." It cost him, he later said, more than the entire 3,700 pounds he owed to his father-in-law's English creditors.

A less scrupulous man might have written off the debt as twice paid. But Jefferson instead wrote the English businessmen a letter, reiterating his intention to pay the money as soon as possible. He was too honest to transfer his own losses to individual Englishmen who had nothing to do with the vicious policy of their government.

At Poplar Forest, meanwhile, Jefferson's misfortunes continued to multiply. One morning as he cantered out for a ride on his favorite horse Caractacus, the high-spirited animal reared and pitched his master out of the saddle, leaving him crumpled in the dust with a broken left wrist. Jefferson was so badly shaken up, he was housebound for the next six weeks. In this same period of unremitting gloom, he continued to fret over Martha's health. But what seemed like the capstone to his troubles was a report from Staunton, where the Virginia Assembly had managed to scrape together little more than a quorum of forty members. A motion had been made and carried recommending an investigation of his governorship.

The motion had been sponsored by one George Nicholas, a very young member of the assembly, son of Robert Carter Nicholas, the austere and influential ex-treasurer who had introduced Jefferson's fast-day resolution. The family owned land in Albemarle and had always been friendly to Jefferson. He had no doubt that the man behind young Nicholas was Patrick Henry, who was already beginning to see and think in purely political terms, and was not above attempting to destroy, at the first sign of weakness, a rival as potentially powerful as Jefferson. Like a good lawyer, Jefferson demanded a specification of the charges. Nicholas hastily denied that he was making any charges. He was merely asking questions that were on everyone's mind, he claimed, questions that ought to be answered if the people were ever again to have any confidence in their government. Most of the questions which young Nicholas proceeded to scribble off the top of his somewhat empty head concerned the preparation—or lack of it—for Arnold's first raid. The assembly, meanwhile, adjourned until fall, leaving Jefferson dangling between guilt and innocence.

At this point, Congress added another burden to Jefferson's already harassed mind. They once more offered him a post in the American diplomatic mission in France, this time to participate in the much-rumored but not yet definite peace negotiations. The idea must have seemed a little ludicrous to a man who had just felt the hot breath of Tarleton's dragoons. But it was a serious offer, and Jefferson once more had to undergo the pain of refusing his long-cherished opportunity to see Europe, for the same mournful reason. After six months of refugeeing, it would have been madness to suggest that Martha Jefferson could survive a sea voyage in which the chances of capture by blockading British warships would have doubled the dangers of confinement and stale food. Lafayette, through whom the offer passed, did his utmost to persuade Jefferson by dangling promises of introductions to every personage of note in France. Jefferson could only reply that it had given him "more mortification than almost any occurrence in my life" to say no.

VII

Partly because of his broken wrist, and partly to take his mind off his own misery, Jefferson spent the summer of 1781 writing a book. A member of the French legation in Philadelphia, the Marquis François de Barbé-Marbois, had sent him a set of 23 questions about the state of Virginia. Jefferson began writing his answers during the six weeks of the summer of 1781 when he was confined to his house by the fall from his horse, and before he stopped he had a 200-page book, which eventually came to be called *Notes on Virginia*. It was an amazing accomplishment for a man who had spent the previous 12 years of his life deeply involved in politics, running a half dozen plantations, building a mansion on a mountain, and worrying over an ailing wife.

Jefferson was candid enough to admit later that he did not simply sit down and dash off so many pages crammed with facts and information relying on what he had in his head. Just as he took careful notes on every aspect of his farming operations, whenever he noticed a particularly interesting fact about any other aspect of life, he was in the habit of jotting it down on a piece of paper. "These memoranda," he said, were "bundled up without order" and difficult to find when he needed one. He decided that Marbois' queries were a perfect opportunity to put them in order and elevate them to the dignity of literature. The result was a unique book, the most complete and thorough study of America up to that time, and the only one done with an artist's sensitivity, a philosopher's perspective and a scientist's exactitude. The *Notes* made Jefferson's reputation as a universal scholar and pioneer American scientist. What other American could discourse in such amazing detail on fauna, flora, geology, natural history, meteorology, Indians, Negroes, farming, manufacturing and government?

Notes on Virginia also glows with Jefferson's love of his country, and his deep appreciation of its natural beauty and abundance. Again and again the artist obscures the scientist. The Ohio was for him "the most beautiful river on earth; its current gentle, waters clear and bosom smooth and unbroken." He became even more lyrical describing the junction of the Potomac and Shenandoah rivers at Harpers Ferry. This was, he said, "one of the most stupendous scenes in nature." Looking down on the "wild and tremendous" clash of waters, breaking through the Blue Ridge on their rush to the sea, the eye through the cleft in the mountain finds "a small patch of smooth blue horizon at an infinite distance in the plain country, inviting you, as it were, from the riot and tumult roaring around to pass through the breach and participate in the calm below." This scene alone, Jefferson declared, was worth "a voyage across the Atlantic."

Intermingled with this proud praise were hundreds of useful

facts. The Missouri was "remarkably cold, rapid and muddy. Its overflowings are considerable . . . During the months of June and July a bateau passes from the mouth of the Ohio to the mouth of the Mississippi in three weeks and takes two to three months getting up again. From the mouth of the Ohio to Santa Fe the journey takes forty days."

His most dazzling display of learning was his discussion of Virginia's natural resources. Dividing trees, plants and fruits into medicinal, edible, ornamental and useful, he listed two dozen in the first category, three dozen in the second, four dozen in the third and 27 in the fourth. In this section of the book, Jefferson found an opportunity to combine science and spirited pride in his native country. The leading European naturalists, all followers of the Frenchman, Comte Georges de Buffon, who had published a massive series of books on natural history, maintained that "a degenerative" process was at work in North America, which made animals and men smaller and punier in size and vitality (and by implication in intelligence as well). Jefferson, the part-time scientist, demolished Buffon by carefully comparing the largest known weights of animals found on both continents. The American elk outweighed his European brother by almost 300 pounds. The American cow was almost 2000 pounds heftier and even the little otter beat out his European relative by 2.3 pounds.

Buffon, determined to prove his degenerative theory, also cast aspersions on the American Indian. The Frenchman's prejudice inspired Jefferson to an eloquent defense of the red man. He was brave, "he will defend himself against a host of enemies, always choosing to be killed rather than surrender." He was "affectionate to his children" and his friendships were "strong and faithful to the uttermost extremity." His "vivacity and activity of mind was fully equal to a white man." To prove this, Jefferson reported the speech of Logan, a Mingo chief, in which the proud old warrior defiantly declared that he had taken up the hatchet because treacherous white men had murdered his entire family. Jefferson, overstating the case a little, declared that no orator in the entire history of Europe, including Demosthenes and Cicero, could equal Logan's eloquence.

When he reached the subject of the Negro, Jefferson began with a dispassionate, very scientific discussion of his racial characteristics and origins. As a good scientist, limiting himself to his observations, he expressed his doubts about whether the black man was equal in intelligence to the white man or the red man. But he admitted that he had only had an opportunity to study the black man in the degraded condition of the slave.

The mention of this grim subject brought some of Jefferson's deepest feelings rushing into his prose. He bluntly stated that he favored emancipating all slaves born after a certain date, as he had previously suggested to the Virginia legislature. His picture of slavery was nothing less than devastating. "The whole commerce between master and slave is a perpetual exercise of the most boisterous passions, the most unremitting despotism on the one part and degrading submission on the other . . . The man must be a prodigy who can retain his manners and morals undepraved by such circumstances." For Jefferson the effect of slavery on the white man was as ruinous as its effect on the Negro. "With the morals of the people, their industry also is destroyed. For in a warm climate, no man will labor for himself who can make another labor for him." Above all, Jefferson was convinced that slavery threatened the very foundation of American freedom. "Can the liberties of a nation be thought secure when we have removed their only firm basis, a conviction in the minds of the people that these liberties are the gift of God? That they are not to be violated but by His wrath? Indeed I tremble for my country when I reflect that God is just; that His justice cannot sleep forever."

Those last words had a very contemporary meaning for Jefferson. The summer of 1781 had dwindled to a close, with little apparent change in the military situation in Virginia. Cornwallis had fallen back to the coast, where he began fortifying the small tobacco port of Yorktown, at the end of the long peninsula which juts down toward the Chesapeake from Williamsburg. Lafayette, with an army still barely one-third the size of the enemy, could do little but maintain a sort of sentinel duty at Williamsburg. It seemed clear that the British were planning to make Yorktown a permanent base from which they could renew their cruel raiding whenever they chose.

In Europe, Russia had offered to mediate the war, and the great

powers were making preliminary arrangements for a peace conference, at which England was prepared to claim all the territory in
North America over which she could show the British flag with
impunity. This would undoubtedly include Georgia, the Carolinas,
much of New York, most of Maine and the vast Ohio River
Valley, and now, possibly, Virginia.

On August 29, 1781, arrived a personage who transformed this
doleful scene as dramatically as if he had been an archangel with a
fiery sword. A 6'2" Provençal sailor named François Tilly, Comte
de Grasse, came booming into the Chesapeake, with 29 ships of the
line, and 3,000 troops from the West Indies. The troops swiftly
debarked and joined Lafayette's meager regiments, while the warships took up a grim blockade at the mouth of the York River,
their tiers of guns frowning down on the startled British at Yorktown. Meanwhile, around New York, George Washington and
another aggressive Frenchman, Comte de Rochambeau, were bom-
barding the overcautious British commander in chief, Sir Henry
Clinton, with a barrage of false intelligence that befuddled him into
letting them head south with 6,500 crack troops. Horsemen bearing messages direct from Washington himself pounded through
Maryland, calling out every available militiaman, while Jefferson's
successor as governor, Thomas Nelson, Jr., made equally vigorous
efforts in Virginia.

By September 28, an amazing concentration of men and guns
had been achieved at Williamsburg. With 20,000 men and over a
hundred cannon, Washington rumbled down the peninsula to
besiege Cornwallis behind his incomplete fortifications at Yorktown. After little more than seven days and seven nights of intense
bombardment, the fighting earl was forced to surrender the best
British army in North America. Jefferson watched the great event
from a distance, learning some of the details from James Monroe.
A flash of his feelings about the victory can be glimpsed in his
answer to Monroe's remark that Washington ought to have dis-
charged the militia since he had more than enough regulars to do
the job. "I think with you," Jefferson wrote, "that the present
force of regulars before York might admit of the discharge of the
militia with safety. Yet did it depend on me, perhaps I might not
discharge them. As an American, as a Virginian, I should covet as

large a share of the honor in accomplishing so great an event as a superior proportion of numbers could give." There were, counting sailors, some 28,000 Frenchmen at Yorktown, and only about 10,000 Americans. It was a piece of arithmetic that Thomas Jefferson never forgot.

A few weeks later Jefferson wrote a revealing letter to George Washington. He would have come in person to congratulate the commander in chief on his victory at Yorktown, he said, "notwithstanding the decrepitude to which I am unfortunately reduced." But he felt that Washington had better things to do than make small talk with "a private individual." This decrepitude could hardly be blamed on a broken wrist, which had healed by midsummer. A glance at the original manuscript of this letter suggests another possibility. The draft is crossed out and interlined to an extraordinary degree, suggesting that Jefferson could not concentrate, even to the point of writing a simple letter of congratulation. It is a letter written by a man whose mind was burdened with almost overwhelming anxiety.

Martha Jefferson was pregnant again. After so many years of slow but visible decline in which every pregnancy was a grave crisis, the news must have sent a shiver of foreboding through Jefferson. He also brooded about the so-called charges that had been preferred against his governorship. These were so trifling, no man in a normal frame of mind would have taken them seriously. In his morbid mood, Jefferson magnified the charges into a fantastic grievance which gave him an excuse to withdraw from public life without confessing either to himself or his friends the real reason. To Edmund Randolph he wrote: "I have returned to my farm, my family and books, from which I think nothing will ever more separate me."

His friends were utterly astounded by this declaration, and Randolph, serving in Congress in Philadelphia, replied with the first of many remonstrances. "If you can justify this resolution to yourself, I am confident that you cannot to the world."

When the legislature met later in the fall, their attitude made clear the emotional disproportion in Jefferson's view of the charges. When he rose in his seat on December 19 and declared himself ready to meet any and all inquiries, not a word was spoken against him. His accuser, George Nicholas, discreetly absented himself from the chamber. Jefferson then read the list of charges Nicholas had sent him, and his own answers to them, and the House of Delegates unanimously passed a resolution declaring their high opinion of Jefferson's "ability, rectitude and integrity as chief magistrate of this Commonwealth."

The moment that the assembly voted this exoneration, Jefferson departed for Monticello. Even before he returned, he was again telling friends of his determination never to leave it. "My future plan of life scarcely admits the hope of my having the pleasure of seeing you at your seat," he wrote Horatio Gates, in reply to an invitation to visit that discomfited general at his plantation in Berkeley County. In his desperation, Jefferson almost seemed to believe that his mere presence would be a kind of magic that would give Martha the strength she needed so badly to survive.

He spent the next six months at Monticello, once more half nurse and half companion. Sporadically, he revised his *Notes on Virginia*, expanding the sections on natural history. Early in the spring of 1782, a handsome Frenchman, Major General Marquis de Chastellux, one of the commanders of the French army at Yorktown, visited Monticello and found Jefferson still working on the book. It was the first time Chastellux and Jefferson had met, although they had corresponded. The Frenchman's experience was to be repeated by almost everyone who met Jefferson. "I found his first appearance serious, nay even cold," Chastellux said. "But before I had been two hours with him, we were as intimate as if we had passed our whole lives together." Jefferson was not a hail-fellow-well-met, a political backslapper. A man had to prove himself a kindred spirit, worthy of genuine friendship. Once that was decided, there was nothing he would not do for him. The four days Chastellux spent at Monticello passed, the French aristocrat said, "like so many minutes."

Chastellux gave us one of the few descriptions of Jefferson's house at this point in his life. The ground floor, the Frenchman said, "consists chiefly of a very large lofty saloon [salon] which is to be decorated entirely in the antique style. Above it is a library of the same form. Two small wings with only a ground floor and attic story are joined to this pavilion and communicate with the kitchen, offices, etc., which will form a kind of basement story over which runs a terrace." These words make it clear that Jefferson had not yet entirely completed his mansion, but he had done enough to convince Chastellux that "Mr. Jefferson is the first American who has consulted the fine arts to know how he should shelter himself from the weather." Summing up his host, Chastellux called him "an American who without ever having quitted his home country is at once a musician, skilled in drawing, a geometrician, an astronomer, a natural philosopher, legislator and statesman . . . It seemed as if from his youth he had placed his mind, as he had done his house, on an elevated situation from which he might contemplate the universe."

Chastellux barely mentioned Martha Jefferson, and it is evident that he saw little of her. By now she was far advanced in her pregnancy, and one evening he noted that she retired early, leaving Jefferson and his guest to discover a mutual enthusiasm for Ossian. With a bowl of punch at their side, they proceeded to read favorite passages from the rude bard of the north to each other until "the night far advanced imperceptibly upon us." Surely this was an experience that Martha Jefferson, with her love of literature, would not have missed if she had been in good health. When Chastellux departed, Jefferson persuaded him to ride eighty miles farther into Virginia to see the Natural Bridge. But he accompanied the Frenchman only to the ford of the Mechum River, sixteen miles away, because, as Chastellux put it, "his wife [was] expected every moment to lie in."

A few days after the Frenchman departed, Martha Jefferson gave birth to a very large baby girl; tradition places the weight at sixteen pounds. Undoubtedly at her request (and it is a sign of how deeply she grieved over her losses), the baby was named Lucy Elizabeth, after the little girl who had died during the refugeeing months around Richmond.

Now began the four most terrible months of Jefferson's life. Martha simply did not rally after this last exhausting birth. Day by day she became weaker and more wasted, her steady decline in anguishing contrast to the blooming spring and summer outside her bedroom windows.

Two days before the birth, Jefferson abruptly declined his seat in the House of Delegates, to which the citizens of Albemarle County had elected him. James Monroe, who had been elected a delegate from another county, wrote him as a friend, to let him know that the assembly was strongly critical of his decision. Again no one knew the real reason because once more Jefferson could not bear to state it, even to himself.

The Speaker of the House of Delegates, John Tyler, added a more impersonal and sharper note warning Jefferson that the house "may insist upon you to give attendance" and added a warning about the "censure of being seized." It was within the power of the House of Delegates to send a sergeant at arms to Monticello and drag Jefferson to Richmond under arrest.

By now Jefferson was in such a state of anxiety, he was almost incoherent. He wrote Monroe a long passionate letter, arguing his right to refuse the position, and referring in bitter terms once more to the temporary censure which the House of Delegates had cast on his governorship. The experience had inflicted on him injuries, he vowed, which would only be cured "by the all-healing grave." At the end of this wild diatribe Jefferson remarked, almost as if it was an afterthought, "Mrs. Jefferson has added another daughter to our family. She has been ever since and still continues very dangerously ill."

Monroe, in his reply, proved himself a discerning friend. He ignored Jefferson's disquisition on his right to refuse public service and replied with a touching letter, telling him he was "much distressed" to hear of Martha's illness. He referred to her affectionately as "our amiable friend"—Martha had been very kind to the lonely young ex-soldier on his visits to Monticello. He assured Jefferson "that nothing will give me so much pleasure" as to hear of Martha's recovery. Only in a postscript did he tell Jefferson news that was very important to Monroe personally—he had been elected to the Governor's council, quite an honor for so young a "parliamentary man." He hoped that Jefferson, "as soon as circumstances will permit you," would let him seek his advice "upon every subject of consequence."

Jefferson did not even answer this letter, written at the end of June, 1782. He spent the rest of the summer in a torment of soul, watching Martha slowly waste away. His sister Martha

Carr and Martha's sister, Elizabeth Eppes, were in the house, but Jefferson did most of the nursing himself. For hours he sat by her bedside reading to her from their favorite books and when she slept he retreated to a small room, just outside the bedroom, where he drove himself to forgetfulness by working on his revisions of the *Notes on Virginia*. Years later, his daughter Martha, who was ten at the time, recalled that Jefferson was "never out of calling" during the four mournful months that Martha lingered.

These two deeply intelligent, sensitive human beings could not conceal from each other, no matter how hard they tried, that each knew what was happening. One day, toward the end, Martha could not bear the truth unspoken any longer. She took a pen from her bedside, and wrote on a piece of paper words from their favorite book, *Tristram Shandy*, which the author, Laurence Sterne, himself a dying man, had written to someone he loved.

> Time wastes too fast: every letter
> I trace tells me with what rapidity
> Life follows my pen. The days and hours
> Of it are flying over our heads
> Like clouds of windy day, never to return—
> More everything presses on—

This was as far as her strength could take her. Her faltering handwriting ends with these words. But she knew the rest of the passage as well as Jefferson. Perhaps only a few hours later he took the paper and completed it in his stronger, bolder hand.

> —and every
> Time I kiss thy hand to bid adieu,
> Every absence which follows it, are preludes to
> that eternal separation
> Which we are shortly to make!

On September 6, 1782, Martha Jefferson slowly slipped away from her husband's desperate grasp. In the last anguished hours, she made an emotional request, a compound of love and old fear. She asked Jefferson to promise her that he would never marry again. More than death, she dreaded the thought of her three little girls being raised by a stepmother. To Martha that word was synonymous with unhappiness. Her own father had married soon after her mother's death, and her girlhood had apparently been troubled by the hostility of a woman who had no love to give a child of a previous wife.

Jefferson, of course, agreed. But he begged her not to say such things. She was not dying. She could not be. Even now he was unable to face the terrible truth. As Martha sank into a coma and her breath became the shallow, labored gasps of the dying, Jefferson blacked out. He would have toppled to the floor beside her bed, if his alert sister, Mrs. Carr, had not caught him. With the help of Martha's sister, Elizabeth Eppes, Jefferson was half carried, half dragged into the library, where he lost consciousness completely.

For a while the agitated women thought he too was dying. It took the better part of an hour to revive him and then his grief was so terrifying, fear of death was replaced by fear of madness. For three weeks he did not come out of the library. Up and down, up and down, he paced hour after hour, collapsing only, as his daughter put it in her recollection, "when nature was completely exhausted." Occasionally little Martha would tiptoe into the room, obviously sent by her aunts in the hope that she would remind Jefferson that life had to go on, he still had responsibilities. But the sight of the little girl at first only brought on even wilder paroxysms of grief. Writing fifty years later, Martha Jefferson said, "The violence of his emotion . . . to this day I do not trust myself to describe."

Jefferson's sensitivity, his devotion to Martha, explain in part this almost incredible grief. But it seems necessary to add one more factor which has run like a dark thread through the years of his married life—guilt over the time he gave to pursuing a reputation as a public and political man—the fear, the dread even, that the long separations, the frantic flights from British raiders to which he had exposed her, were the real reasons for Martha's death. He had sacrificed her to the Revolution, and for what? All he had gotten in return was a blotted name for his supposed failures as a war governor. It was this tangle of grief and guilt that drove Jefferson to the brink of insanity.

After three weeks, he finally emerged from the library. But he was still a haunted, driven man. All he could do was ride hour by hour around the countryside, always taking the least frequented roads, and as often leaving these to blunder through the woods. It was in these weeks that ten-year-old Martha Jefferson became a woman. She reached out to this reeling, incoherent man, this stranger, and offered herself as a wordless companion on these rambling, aimless rides. It was the beginning of a bond between father and daughter that was stronger and more meaningful to both than a marriage.

On October 3, Jefferson wrote a letter to Elizabeth Eppes, who had returned to her home. He told of Patsy (Martha) riding with him five and six miles a day and asking his permission to accompany him on horseback when he went to visit Elk Hill. "When that may be, however, I cannot tell; finding myself absolutely unable to attend to anything like business," Jefferson said. Then his grief burst uncontrollably onto the page. "This miserable kind of existence is really too burthensome to be borne and were it not for the infidelity of deserting the sacred charge left me, I could not wish its continuance a moment. For what could it be wished?" He did not write another letter for almost eight weeks.

Martha Jefferson was buried beneath the great oak on the side of the mountain, near Jefferson's friend Dabney Carr and the bodies of her lost children. Over her grave, on a plain horizontal slab of white marble, Jefferson placed the following inscription:

To the memory of
Martha Jefferson,
Daughter of John Wayles;
Born October 19th, 1748, O. S.
Intermarried with
Thomas Jefferson
January 1st, 1772;
Torn from him by death
September 6th, 1782;
This monument of his love is inscribed.

Beneath these words he placed a quotation, in Greek, from the *Iliad*.

If in the house of Hades men forget their dead
Yet will I even there remember you, dear companion.

The most deeply felt dream of Jefferson's life was over. The figure who stood "always in the forefront" of his vision of happiness was dead. It is easy to understand why he embraced this vision. It is harder, but necessary, to pronounce it an essentially selfish dream. It would have resolved the warfare that flickered in Jefferson's personality between the scholar and the man of action, the theorist and the realist, in favor of the pale life of the mind.

Jefferson like all men needed a personal vision to give order and direction to his life. It had to be a vision that satisfied his equally demanding head and heart. Could he find one that would replace what he had lost? Wandering the Albemarle hills, pacing Monticello's cheerless rooms, he simply did not know. It would take almost a decade for him to realize that the words he had written in Philadelphia about the pursuit of happiness by free men required constant defense and interpretation, if they were to become the guiding spirit of a new nation. Even then, he would only begin to realize that these words must be *lived*, spelled out act by act in the harsh harassing world of politics, if they were to have meaning to men. Gradually, as Jefferson learned these things, these words would become a new, more generous vision that would ultimately fill—and fulfill—his life.

For now, all he knew was what the words had cost him. Thomas Jefferson was sightless, a man blinded by pain.

BOOK
TWO

Old World
to Conquer

❦

THOMAS JEFFERSON might have moldered at Monticello, savoring his grief and guilt until he became an eccentric recluse. But he now reaped the first of many rewards for the care with which he cultivated friendships. James Madison was serving as a delegate to the Continental Congress at Philadelphia. He heard tales of Jefferson's extraordinary grief, and it became plain to the diminutive man with the large mind and generous heart that it was imperative to get his friend back into public life as soon as possible.

Madison briskly went to work and suggested that Jefferson be reappointed as a peace commissioner, this time for a peace conference that was very definitely on its way to convening. Congress concurred with a unanimous vote. Madison showed that he knew how to handle Jefferson by writing to Edmund Randolph in Virginia, "The resolution passed a few minutes ago . . . You will let it be known to Mr. Jefferson as quickly as secrecy will admit. An official notification will follow . . . This will prepare him for it." Then he added, knowing that Jefferson's "wounds" over his governorship still needed balm, "It passed unanimously, and without a single remark adverse to it."

The news reached Jefferson at a nearby plantation, where he had taken his three daughters to be inoculated against the smallpox. By now Jefferson was, as he told the Marquis de Chastellux in a letter, "a little emerging from that stupor of mind which had rendered me as dead to the world as she was whose loss occasioned it."

Monticello had lost its charm for Jefferson, that was clear. What better way to escape painful memories of lost happiness which his house on the hilltop evoked? On the same day that he wrote to Chastellux, he wrote to Madison and to the President of Congress, accepting the appointment.

Leaving his daughters with Francis and Elizabeth Eppes, Jefferson journeyed first to Philadelphia, and then to Baltimore, braving mud, snow and freezing weather. He spent three and one half months in Baltimore, waiting for the French frigate on which he was booked to sail. First winter storms, then British blockaders frustrated him. Finally came news from Europe that the peace negotiations were almost over—a preliminary treaty had been signed—and it was foolish to waste money on sending another diplomat.

Aside from keeping him away from Monticello—good medicine in his present frame of mind—about the only thing these wasted months produced was a correspondence between Jefferson and George Washington, which deepened the already strong friendship between the two men. Jefferson's admiration for the leader of the Revolution shines through a letter he wrote to him from Philadelphia late in January, 1783, in which he told Washington he could not leave the country without offering his "individual tribute" for all Washington had "effected for us." He hesitated, he told Washington, to indulge in "warm effusions" because even the "appearance of adulation" was "foreign to my nature." Washington replied in equally warm terms, saying he was "flattered" by Jefferson's remembering him and declaring that winning the approval of "good and virtuous men" such as Jefferson was all the payment he sought for his long toils and hardships.

When Congress withdrew his commission, Jefferson went home to Monticello. He was scarcely settled there when he learned that the Virginia Assembly had appointed him a delegate to the Continental Congress, with orders to present himself to that body on the first of the following November. He spent the summer at Monticello, cataloguing his 2640-book library and serving as schoolmaster to eleven-year-old Martha and the six children of Dabney Carr. He fretted over Martha's education, writing to his friend François Barbé-Marbois in Paris to find her a French tutor and a list of good books in that language. It was extremely important to give Martha the best possible education, he explained to Marbois, because schools in Virginia ranged from scarce to nonexistent and "the chance that in marriage she will draw a blockhead I calculate at about 14 to 1." This meant that the education of her family would "rest on her own ideas and direction without assistance." He already had Martha reading *Gil Blas* and *Don Quixote* and was planning a future course for her "in the graver sciences."

When he departed for Philadelphia in the fall, Jefferson took Martha with him. It may have been on this journey that an incident occurred which Martha Jefferson often described in her later years. They came to a ferry where two boatmen were having a violent quarrel. The antagonists took Jefferson and Martha on board and rowed into the middle of the stream where the argument exploded again. They completely abandoned their oars and let the boat drift with the current toward some dangerous rapids. At first Jefferson spoke to them calmly, and then sternly, but they paid no attention to him. Suddenly Jefferson leaped to his feet with, in Martha's words, "a face like a lion," grabbed each boatman by the back of the neck and ordered them "in tones of thunder" to row for their lives or he would pitch them into the river. They seized the oars and rowed like madmen, occasionally glancing up at the snarling man who stood over them until they reached the opposite shore.

All his life, Jefferson consciously cultivated a serene, civilized good humor. Many people who knew him well said they never saw an expression of anger or impatience on his face. But Martha never forgot the sudden apparition of the frontiersman's son she saw that day on the river.

Behind him in Virginia, Jefferson left with James Madison a draft of a new constitution for his state. He thought he foresaw the possibility of a constitutional convention and he wanted to make sure his friends had some ammunition. He was wrong about the convention. Patrick Henry, becoming more conservative every day, decided he preferred the status quo. But Jefferson's document was nevertheless significant, in terms of the future. It divided the powers of government into three equal and independent departments—executive, legislative and judicial—and it gave all free male citizens the right to vote. It guaranteed religious freedom, trial by jury, and freedom of the press and made the military clearly subordinate to civil power. Finally, it contained one more of Jefferson's tireless efforts to abolish slavery, forbidding further importation of slaves or the enslavement of any individuals born after December 31, 1800. Madison wrote a long, careful critique of this document in which he added some valuable thoughts of his own. Jefferson had suggested that a governor should be elected by both houses of the legislature. Madison disagreed and argued that "an election by the people at large" freed the executive of "improper obligation" to the legislature. Since nothing immediate came of the project, the subject was dropped with Jefferson's remark that the draft constitution might prove useful to Madison "in some future situation."

When Jefferson got to Philadelphia, he found that Congress had adjourned to Princeton to escape the demands of mutinous unpaid Revolutionary soldiers. That town proved to be no sanctuary and the national assembly decamped to Annapolis, Maryland. He left Martha in Philadelphia, with the family of Francis Hopkinson, gifted musician and fellow signer of the declaration, who assured him that they would follow Jefferson's carefully worked-out plan of education. Sadly he begged his daughter to consider Mrs. Hopkinson as "your mother," and in a rather stern letter laid out a formidable schedule for the youngster. "From 8 to 10, practice music. From 10 to 1, dance one day and draw another. From 1 to 2, draw on the day you dance and write a letter next day. From 3 to 4, read French. From 4 to 5, exercise yourself in music. From 5 till bedtime, read English, write, etc."

Finally catching up with Congress in Annapolis, Jefferson was dismayed by what he found there. Not until the 13th of December were they able to scrape together delegates from seven states. This permitted them to discuss only minor business and there was soon laid on the table the most important major business imaginable— the treaty of peace. Moreover, most of the delegates were utterly lacking in the stature of the men who had launched the great experiment in 1776. Many were young fops, who looked on the job as an excuse for a trip away from home; others were crusty old country squires who had never read anything more mind-expanding than their local gazette. Most, Jefferson said later, were "afflicted with the morbid rage of debate." In such a group, it was almost inevitable that Jefferson would become the natural leader.

He was appalled to discover that the treaty of peace stipulated that it had to be signed within six months. It was a generous treaty;

the British yielded much western territory, agreed to hand over border forts, and made numerous other concessions which were a tribute to the brilliant negotiating powers of Benjamin Franklin, John Adams and John Jay. Some of the delegates wanted to ratify the document immediately, even though the Articles of Confederation clearly stated that foreign treaties required the approval of nine states. Jefferson violently objected to this slapdash way of doing business, which would have given Great Britain a perfect excuse to abrogate the treaty if she chose. Finally, the President of Congress managed to round up delegates from New Jersey and New Hampshire, and the statement of ratification, prepared by Jefferson, was legally voted. Thus the man whose resounding words declared America's independence wrote the more matter-of-fact sentences that transformed the hope into a reality. Congress issued a proclamation announcing the news, but only in a few states were there any significant celebrations.

Another episode in which Jefferson played a prominent role was George Washington's retirement as commander-in-chief. He was in charge of the committee which worked out the ceremony at which Washington resigned his commission. It was a deeply significant moment for those who participated in it. Here was the man who could at a word have made himself a king or dictator, handing over his power to the President of Congress, and retiring to his Virginia farm as a plain citizen once more. The pathetically thin ranks of congressmen sat with their hats on, symbolizing the sovereignty of the nation. The other spectators in the Maryland assembly chamber stood with their hats off, while Washington with shaking hands read a brief address announcing his departure from "the great theater of action" and bidding Congress "an affectionate farewell." At one point Washington's voice broke and he almost wept. Spectators and congressmen were already weeping. Jefferson called it "an affecting scene."

Thereafter, Congress devoted itself to wasting day after day, Jefferson said, on "the most unimportant questions." Another distraction was the social life of Annapolis. Congressmen were invited to an endless round of balls and parties by the sociable, affluent ladies and gentlemen of Maryland. Jefferson, however, took no part in these pleasures. He complained in numerous letters of bad health, although it did not prevent him from working harder than anyone else in Congress. Obviously he was still deeply depressed by Martha's death. In March, 1784, he struck up a friendship with a young Dutchman, Count Gijsbert Karel van Hogendorp, a relative of the Netherlands' minister to the United States. Though he was only twenty-one, Hogendorp was a sensitive, perceptive man, who was deeply impressed by Jefferson. "He indulges in no amusements," the young Dutchman wrote a friend. "The bad state of his health, he has often said to me, is the reason for his retirement; but it seems to me, rather, that accustomed to the agreeable society of an amiable wife, he is not attracted to ordinary society now that she is gone."

Hogendorp spent hours with Jefferson, who became very much attached to him. They discussed science and literature, and Jefferson gave him a copy of his *Notes on Virginia*. But Jefferson's manner remained cool and reserved and the young Dutchman began to wonder if he had any feelings to express. One evening as they talked, Hogendorp abruptly shifted the conversation to love. Then he saw a different Jefferson, a still tormented man frankly confessing his grief and regrets. In a letter to Hogendorp, Jefferson admitted the "gloom" in which he lived. "I have been happy and cheerful," he wrote. "I have had many causes of gratitude to Heaven; but I have also experienced its rigors. I have known what it is to lose every species of connection which is dear to the human heart."

The day-to-day life of a congressman was not likely to raise Jefferson's spirits. So lean were the delegations, when a single congressman came down with gout, he reduced the number of voting states to six and Congress to helplessness. Seven of the nine states there had only two representatives each, and on any of the really important issues—such as authorizing foreign ministers, disposing of western territory, Indian treaties and the currency—it required nine affirmative states. As Jefferson pointed out to the Governor of Virginia, any one of these fourteen gentlemen "differing from the rest stops our proceeding." To James Madison he wrote, "We have not sat above three days, I believe, in as many weeks." Yet he drove himself relentlessly, writing no less than thirty-one committee reports in five months.

Far and away the most important of these documents was the Ordinance of 1784. To help pay the Federal Revolutionary War debt, Virginia had joined New York in ceding all claims to the vast western lands. North Carolina, Connecticut and Pennsylvania and other states with similar claims followed this lead. The plan was to sell the land to the thousands of settlers who would soon be flocking into the territory. This prospect in turn produced more problems. What sort of government was to be established among these people? They could not be left in a state of nature. Congress found itself faced with the task of providing a plan for orderly growth in this enormous region, stretching from the Great Lakes almost to the Gulf if Mexico, between the Appalachians and the Mississippi. Congress turned to Thomas Jefferson.

They were asking for nothing less than a colonial policy for the United States. The federal union of states seems so natural now, it is hard to imagine other alternatives. But in 1784, there were many men who were by no means convinced that the thirteen original colonies should grow beyond that number. Power was balanced delicately between New England, the Middle States and the South, and many thought Congress ought to keep any new territories in a kind of colonial dependency to the original thirteen.

Jefferson, true as always to his instinct for freedom, went in the opposite direction. His committee report boldly set up the principle that new states would be formed out of the western territories, and any other territory acquired by the United States. Jefferson even drew a rough map, laying out possible boundaries for fourteen new states, and suggesting names for some of them. After the states acquired 20,000 free inhabitants, they were to petition Congress for the right to call a convention to establish a permanent constitution and government for themselves. But that government had to be "republican" in form, and would be "subject to the government of the United States and Congress assembled" in the same degree as the thirteen original states. Then came the most important clause, one that could have changed the history of the nation. After the year 1800, Jefferson suggested, there would be "neither slavery nor involuntary servitude" permitted in any of these states.

Once more Jefferson was attacking America's worst social

cancer and once more the opposition was fierce. Southern delegates demanded that the report be sent back to the committee but Jefferson was chairman of the committee, and he saw to it that when it was once more brought to the floor the antislavery clause was still there. A motion was made to strike it out. By now ten of the thirteen states had managed to send delegates. As a shrewd parliamentarian, Jefferson had the question put in the affirmative: "Should the slavery clause be allowed to stand?" New Hampshire, Massachusetts, Rhode Island, Connecticut, New York, Pennsylvania voted yes. Maryland and South Carolina voted no. The two North Carolina delegates split. New Jersey voted yes, but there was only one delegate present and the rules of Congress required two in order for a state to register a vote. Two Virginia delegates, to Jefferson's mortification, voted no, overwhelming the chairman's yes. Seven affirmatives were needed, and the clause had received only six. Except for the illness of the single New Jersey delegate, it would have passed, and slavery would have been confined to the four original southern states, where Jefferson was sure it would have withered away.

Jefferson's last large job as a congressman was a report on the nation's monetary system. He took over much preliminary research from Robert Morris, Financier of Congress, and transformed it from a theoretical exercise—Morris had suggested a coin representing 1/1440 of a dollar—into the decimal system substantially as we know it today, using the Spanish silver dollar as the base because it was well known and used throughout all the colonies.

When Morris proved stubborn about giving up some of his ideas, Jefferson demolished him with an irrefutably realistic argument. "The bulk of mankind are schoolboys through life. Certainly in all cases where we are free to choose between the easy and difficult modes of operation, it is most rational to choose the easy."

For his untiring efforts on what Jefferson called "the laboring oar," Congress finally gave him a reward. Early in May, 1784, the delegates took up the question of commercial treaties with other nations. In the colonial era, almost all of America's trade had gone to England. Unless treaties were worked out with other countries, lowering the prohibitive tariffs each nation used to control imports,

the trade of the infant United States would continue to flow to the
mother country, for want of any place else to go, and independence could soon become a mere political fiction. John Adams and
Benjamin Franklin were already in Europe, working on this problem. But Congress felt that these two men should have a southerner
on their team, because the trading needs of each section of a
continental nation were drastically different. What better man
than the southern delegation's most distinguished spokesman—
Thomas Jefferson? Thus, after three false starts, Jefferson was
given one more chance to see the Europe he had been hungering to
visit since his student days.

II

He seized it eagerly. Letters whizzed out to friends making all
the necessary arrangements. James Madison was asked to take
charge of continuing the education of Peter Carr, and his younger
brother, Dabney, Jr. Neighbors were asked to superintend his
Virginia farmlands. Martha, still with the Hopkinsons in Philadelphia, was told the news with an exciting extra fillip—she was
coming along. It was an ideal opportunity for her to acquire an
education she could never get in America and it gave Jefferson the
comfortable feeling that he was taking his family with him. Little
Mary, or "Polly," as Jefferson was fond of calling her, and little
"Lu," as he called Lucy Elizabeth, would have to be left with Aunt
Elizabeth Eppes, where they were staying already, so there was no
need to disturb them. For a secretary he scooped up another
promising young Virginian whom he was educating to become a
public man—twenty-five-year-old William Short. The official or
"general" secretaryship Congress had given to one of Washington's ex-aides, Colonel David Humphreys, so Jefferson could offer
Short only the job of personal secretary, which offered "no other
advantage than a bed & board free." But he added, "I am also able
to assure you I shall give you very little trouble."

Within three days, Jefferson had settled all these complicated
matters, paid his bills and cleared out of Annapolis for Philadelphia.
There he picked up Patsy, paused to marvel at a balloon ascension
and bought a panther skin to take to Europe, where he planned to

display it personally to Comte de Buffon, as one more proof that nature in the New World was not degenerative. On to New England and Boston, where he paused for some dining with old friends from the Continental Congress, and then he was aboard a stout Newburyport merchantman that fairly skimmed across the Atlantic on balmy spring winds to dock in England in nineteen days.

By August 6 he was in Paris, having experienced along the way some of the customs of the country that persist to the present day. "It is amazing to see how they cheat the strangers," Martha Jefferson wrote to a friend in Philadelphia. "It cost Poppa as much to have the baggage brought from the shore to the house, which was about half a square, as for bringing it from Philadelphia to Boston." For those who have been scorned by French cab drivers for mispronouncing their sacred language, it may be comforting to know that Jefferson, although he read French fluently, floundered when he tried to speak it debarking from the Channel boat at Le Havre. "I fear we should have fared . . . badly," Martha wrote, "if an Irish gentleman, an entire stranger to us, who seeing our embarrassment, had not been so good as to conduct us to a house and was of great service to us."

They also got a premature insight into still another aspect of France. Everywhere their carriage halted on the road to Paris they were surrounded by beggars. "One day I counted no less than nine when we stopped to change horses," Martha Jefferson wrote.

As a Virginia aristocrat, Jefferson saw at a glance that his clothes were out of the current Parisian mode, and he instantly ordered a tailor to his hotel to whip up an entire new outfit. Shirts, a hat, a sword, a belt, knee buckles were also lavishly acquired. Thirteen-year-old Martha was by no means ignored. "I'm sure you would have laughed," she told her friend in Philadelphia. "We were obliged to send immediately for the staymaker, the mantillamaker, the milliner and even a shoemaker before I could go out." A *friseur* also arrived to tease her hair, but Martha demonstrated her American independence with this gentleman. "I soon got rid of him and turned my hair down in spite of all they could say." Thereafter, she avoided this three- or four-hour ordeal because "I think it always too soon to suffer."

Getting his daughter settled was among Jefferson's first concerns. After setting up temporary quarters, he carefully investigated the available schools, and selected the Abbaye de Panthemont, a convent school within the city limits, where Protestant diplomats felt free to send their children because the education was excellent and the abbess was "a woman of the world"—it was understood that the controversial aspects of religion were omitted. Martha, growing into a loose-limbed, redheaded teen-ager with a remarkable resemblance to her father, was not in the least fazed by being unable to speak a word of French when she found herself ensconced with some sixty girls who spoke not a word of English. As Mr. Berlitz has since demonstrated to his profit, this was an ideal way to learn a foreign language, and Martha was soon chattering away *en français* with the best of them. She reported to her correspondents in America that her classmates called her "Jeffy" and she liked everything about the school, including the crimson uniform, "made like a frock, laced behind" with muslin cuffs and tuckers.

Even while he was settling Martha, Jefferson was journeying out to the village of Passy, where the ailing sage, Benjamin Franklin, was living. Afflicted with bladder stone, Franklin was too feeble to enjoy any longer the frenetic social life of Paris. He preferred the quiet little village and the company of the select group of French men and women who were personally devoted to him, and through him to America. The other member of the American diplomatic team, John Adams, was living less than a mile away, in the village of Auteil, and the three men met regularly at Franklin's house in conferences that recalled the heady days when they pondered Jefferson's draft of the Declaration of Independence. Now the problem was how to make that independence a reality to European nations, many of whom looked on the upstart republic with attitudes that ranged from contempt to outright hostility.

In the early months of that first summer and fall in Paris, Jefferson was more concerned with enjoying—and at the same time trying to judge—what he called "the vaunted scene"—this dazzling, sophisticated Europe which he had so long yearned to see. Franklin's immense popularity opened all sorts of doors to him, and the Marquis de Lafayette's charming wife Adrienne, whose family, the Noialleses, was one of the most powerful in France, was equally helpful. The marquis himself was on another of his American visits, but he soon returned to place his exuberant personality and wide popularity at Jefferson's service.

With John Adams and his wife Abigail, Jefferson felt particularly at home. Arthur Lee, brother of Richard Henry Lee, and a specialist at making trouble, had written a nasty letter to Adams about Jefferson. "His genius is mediocre, his application great, his affectation greater, his vanity greater than all." But Adams had sternly replied to this busybody that Jefferson was "an old friend and coadjutor whose character I studied nine or ten years ago [in the Continental Congress] and which I do not perceive to be altered." Jefferson's "industry, integrity and talents" were still visible and admirable, and the Adamses warmly welcomed him into their household.

Jefferson was always fond of young people, and the Adamses had brought with them their oldest son, John Quincy, and their oldest daughter, Abigail, known as "Nabby." Jefferson's relaxed, cheerful manner soon wove a spell around these young people. To solemn young John Quincy, who at seventeen had already absorbed a grown man's share of diplomacy from a year as his father's private secretary, Jefferson almost became a second father. John Adams disliked Paris' "putrid streets" but Jefferson found the city fascinating, and he often took young John with him on his rambles. They discussed science and literature, politics and law, went to the opera and to concerts at the Tuileries, and ogled the celebrities.

More surprising was the way Jefferson charmed Abigail Adams. This brisk, sharp-eyed lady could spot a flaw in a person's character at a glance, and describe it in vivid, acid terms that made her one of the century's great letter writers. Even more than her husband, she was the quintessence of New England pride and reserve, looking down her aquiline nose at everyone and everything with a suspicion which, she would be quick to maintain, was frequently justified from experience. But it was hard to look down on this tall, engaging Virginian, who always had a funny story to tell or a witty observation to make. His courtesy came naturally to him, and his instinctive southern gallantry made him pay far more attention to a woman than the crusty males of Massachusetts. No doubt to her own amazement, Abigail was soon telling her sister back home that Mr. Jefferson was "one of the choice ones of the earth."

Jefferson wasted no time, once he got to France, in joining combat with Comte Georges de Buffon about his theories on the degeneracy of North American animals. Introduced to the naturalist by Chastellux, Jefferson unpacked his panther skin and presented it as proof that this animal was certainly larger than his European relations. Confronted by visible proof, Buffon did the handsome thing and admitted he was wrong. But when Jefferson claimed that American deer and moose were much larger than their Old World counterparts, Buffon scoffed. When Jefferson claimed that a European reindeer could actually walk head up under the belly of an American moose, Buffon guffawed.

Infuriated, Jefferson dashed off a letter to Governor John Sullivan of New Hampshire, telling him to spare no expense to find a moose big enough to silence Buffon permanently. American honor was at stake, and Governor Sullivan, who had been a major general under George Washington, received Jefferson's request as a military command. Summoning the best trappers and hunters in New Hampshire, he sent a veritable army snowshoeing through the winter woods to find a super moose. They succeeded in shooting a giant. But he was so big, ten men together could not carry him out of the forest primeval in which they had slain him. Undaunted, Sullivan summoned ax men and cut a twenty-mile road into the woods to haul the monster out by sleigh. Stuffing, dressing and shipping him to the seacoast was another major operation.

When the beast finally arrived on Jefferson's doorstep, it was not in the best of condition—most of the hair had fallen off and the bill had become almost as big as the moose: 46 pounds sterling, almost $1,000 in today's money. Jefferson gasped with pain; he was having trouble meeting his current expenses in Paris. But he manfully saw the business through, sending the specimen on to Buffon, and receiving from that opinionated gentleman the assurance that he would revise his theories about animal life in North America for the next edition of his natural history. But he died a few months later and Jefferson never did have the satisfaction of seeing the great French naturalist eat his words in public.

True to his nature, Jefferson made new French friends slowly. A surprising number of them were women. As a Virginian, he found himself especially delighted by the French woman's instinct for femininity, with which she often combined an acute, penetrating intelligence. Among his favorites was Madame de Tesse, who was around Jefferson's age, although Lafayette called her "Aunt." She shared Jefferson's enthusiasm for painting, architecture and music. Closer to Jefferson, on a personal level, was pretty, gay Madame de Corny, who often joined him for walks in the Bois de Boulogne. Her husband was one of Lafayette's closest friends. More distant was the aged Comtesse de la Rochefoucauld, immensely dignified and sarcastic, but with an amazing enthusiasm for Americans. Some of the brightest and most liberal spirits in France gathered regularly at her Normandy chateau. Her son, the Duke de la Rochefoucauld, was the same age as Jefferson, and shared his enthusiasm for the sciences and liberty. At the palatial Hôtel de la Rochefoucauld in Paris he also met the Marquis de Condorcet, one of the most brilliant of the *philosophes*, the apostles of "enlightenment," who were seeking to transform French society.

But much as he enjoyed these polished and intelligent people, the art, the spectacles, plays and concerts of Paris, for the first year Jefferson found it impossible to shake off the depression that shrouded his normally sanguine spirits. In November he wrote his young Dutch friend van Hogendorp that he had "relapsed into that state of ill health in which you saw me in Annapolis, but more severe. I have had few hours wherein I could do anything."

In January came a devastating letter. Little "Lu" Jefferson was dead—"a martyr to the complicated evils of teething, worms and hooping cough." The youngest Eppes child had died in the same epidemic. Jefferson was in no condition to stand the blow, and he relapsed into almost total gloom. He was sure that his "sun of happiness [had] clouded over, never again to brighten." The rest of the winter his health continued to be poor. He was probably dogged by his migraine, plus poor digestion, colds and other minor illnesses which depression often inflicts on the body. In one of her letters Abigail Adams described him as "very weak and feeble" and in March, Jefferson himself told Monroe that he had been "confined the greater part" of the winter.

When spring sunshine finally appeared—"my Almighty physician," Jefferson called it—his physical recovery was swift. By April he was walking "six or eight miles a day . . . regularly." But the melancholy persisted. He complained about the wet gloomy climate. Not until he had been in France a full year did he note in his little book of weather observations a completely cloudless day.

To a cultivated Virginia friend he wrote, "You are perhaps curious to know how this new scene has struck a savage of the mountains of America. Not advantageously, I assure you." Too much of Paris was "empty bustle" to him. At the same time, his keen eye was dissecting French society, and his conclusions reveal an intense pride in his American origins. "The great mass of people were suffering under physical and moral oppression" and even the nobility did not possess the happiness "which is enjoyed in America by every class of people." The trouble, as Jefferson saw it, was twofold. "Intrigues of love occupy the younger and those of ambition the elder part of the great . . . Conjugal love having no existence among them, domestic happiness . . . is utterly unknown." He contrasted this to the American ideal of the happy marriage.

On another level Jefferson found much to admire in the French people. They were so polite, he wrote one friend, "that it seems as if one might glide through a whole life among them without a jostle." He liked their temperance, declaring nine months after he arrived, "I have never yet seen a man drunk in France." He deeply admired their achievements in architecture, sculpture, painting and music. "In these arts they shine." Their music, Jefferson confessed, "is the only thing which from my heart I envy them."

One thing he did not admire was the Gallic sense of humor. His secretary, William Short, recalled in later years that Jefferson "blushed like a boy" when one of his French friends made an off-color remark in his presence. But he was also a man of the world and he never seems to have disapproved of Franklin's great and good friend Madame Helvetius, who shocked Abigail Adams by sprawling nonchalantly on the sage's couch at Passy, "showing more than her feet."

French food, on the other hand, sent Jefferson into raptures. He had never been fond of the American habit of eating huge quantities of meat, preferring vegetables and grain. When he tasted French bread for the first time, and discovered what they could do to ordinary peas, spinach, potatoes, he fell in love with the country all over again. Even French meat, cooked for hours in their ragouts and stews with wine sauces, became ambrosia to Jefferson's palate. He immediately paid out several hundred dollars to bring James Hemings, one of his brightest slaves, from Monticello to learn the chef's art under the instruction of Adrien Petit, the *maître* who ran his Paris house.

The longer Jefferson stayed in Paris the more he valued the experience. He urged his friends Madison and Monroe to join him for the summer, telling them that the trip back and forth might cost them two hundred guineas but it would be more than worth it. Madison declined because he did not feel he could risk his delicate health on a sea voyage, and Monroe could not afford it. But Jefferson, with that effortless generosity which was so natural to him, made sure that as much of France as possible came to them. To Madison particularly Jefferson shipped books by the dozens, including some thirty-seven volumes of the *Encyclopédie Méthodique*, which Madison called "a complete scientific library." Books on politics, history, Voltaire's memoirs, journals from France, Holland and England made Madison, in the words of one historian, "the most cosmopolitan statesman never to have quit American shores." Madison reciprocated by sending Jefferson long informative letters that kept him in close touch with political developments in America.

Late in 1786 came news of the first, and some think the richest, fruit of this unique friendship. Marshaling votes with a master hand, Madison had won approval of Jefferson's bill for religious freedom without a single change in the enacting clauses. Proudly he wrote to Jefferson on January 22, 1786, that Virginia had "extinguished forever the ambitious hope of making laws for the human mind." Jefferson was equally delighted, and rushed to spread the word among his French friends. Some months later he was able to write to Madison, "The Virginia act for religious freedom has been received with infinite approbation in Europe and propagated with enthusiasm. I do not mean by the governments, but by the individuals which compose them. It has been translated into French and Italian, has been sent to most of the courts of Europe . . . It is inserted in the new Encyclopédie." Jefferson made it clear that much of the credit belonged to his friend, the modest Mr. Madison, who had unfortunately resisted his invitation to visit Europe. A year later, Jefferson's secretary, William Short, told Madison his name was inextricably linked with "the philosophical legislation of Virginia" and was "in the mouths of all the learned of this place."

Jefferson repaid this debt of gratitude to his "country," Virginia, by acting as the state's cultural agent abroad. When the assembly decided they wanted a statue of George Washington, they asked Jefferson to select the artist. He chose the greatest sculptor of his age, Jean Antoine Houdon. After months of negotiation Jefferson finally persuaded the artist to risk the sea voyage he dreaded, and execute the great work, which stands today in Richmond. Next the Virginians decided they wanted a suitably handsome capitol building, and asked Jefferson to select an architect. This was like asking Leonardo da Vinci to select an artist. Jefferson instantly appointed himself. "I shall send them [designs] taken from the best morsel of ancient architecture now remaining," he told Madison. "It will be superior in beauty to anything in America, and not inferior to anything in the world. It is very simple."

Jefferson was talking about the Maison Carrée, an exquisitely proportioned temple built by the Romans at Nîmes in southern France, and restored by Louis XIV. It was considered, Jefferson said, "the most perfect example of cubic architecture, as the Pantheon in Rome is of the spherical." Jefferson had long since decided that the public buildings of America should be modeled on the classic architecture of Rome. Not only did classicism's balance and restraint have the same symbolic value vis-à-vis the wilderness that had attracted Jefferson to it at Monticello—in public buildings it would also educate the taste of the people by teaching them in stone the vital principles of great art. Equally important to Jefferson's American pride, it was new, a break with the prevailing baroque tradition in England, which Jefferson had pronounced "the most wretched style I ever saw."

With Madison providing the leadership at home, Jefferson's designs were accepted, and the capitol of Virginia became, in the words of one architectural historian, "the first monument to the classical renaissance in the United States, and one might add, in the world." The style was to dominate American public buildings for the next fifty years.

Gradually Jefferson became more at home in Paris. He rented a house on a corner of the Champs-Elysées and furnished it with more elegance than he could afford—as he complained mightily to friends in America. A few months later he moved to a more sumptuous home on what is today the Rue Napoleon, on the left bank of the Seine. It was only a few doors away from the Rochefoucaulds' residence. The house, Martha Jefferson recalled later, was "a very elegant one even for Paris with an extensive garden court, outbuildings, in the handsomest style."

Jefferson chose this residence not because he was in love with elegance (though as a true Virginian he always believed in living with style) but because a year had made a significant alteration in his diplomatic status. John and Abigail Adams had departed for England, where he had been named America's first ambassador. Franklin had at last persuaded Congress to recall him, and for once Congress had done the sensible thing and appointed Jefferson ambassador to France. Although he was paying many of his expenses out of his own pocket, Jefferson felt he owed it to the new American nation to live in a mode that at least won the respect of the style-conscious Parisians.

His more sumptuous style probably also reflected Jefferson's clear realization that following the enormously popular Franklin in this important post was no easy task. One French admirer of the sage reportedly asked Jefferson, with just a tinge of contempt in his voice, if he was "replacing" Franklin. Jefferson rose to the challenge by replying: "Sir, I am succeeding Dr. Franklin. No one can replace him."

Jefferson had no illusions about his new role. The American ambassador was "among the lowest of the diplomatic tribe." The enthusiasm for Americans that had swept Europe in 1783, when they had done the seemingly impossible and humbled imperial Britain into granting them independence, had long since cooled. Soon after he became ambassador, Jefferson wrote that he had not "been able to discover the smallest token of respect toward the United States in any part of Europe." For this he blamed "the torrent of lies published unremittingly in every day's London paper."

Jefferson got a firsthand look at England's hostility early in 1786, when he rushed to London at the behest of John Adams. The New Englander thought the English were inclined to negotiate a commercial treaty, but he was much too optimistic. He and Jefferson cooled their heels endlessly in various outer offices and were treated with barely civil politeness, and a great deal of implied insolence, whenever they managed to wangle an interview with one of the King's ministers. When Jefferson went to Buckingham Palace and was introduced to George III, that dumpy personage, already in the market for what Jefferson called "a straitwastecoat," abruptly turned his back on the author of the Declaration of Independence, without saying a word.

Jefferson toured the countryside with Adams, and came away enormously impressed with English gardening, and little else. His detestation of John Bull, which had been implanted by Cornwallis' fire-and-sword tactics in Virginia, was in full bloom by the time he returned to Paris. The contrast between England and France had, on the other hand, a directly opposite impact on John Adams and his wife, Abigail, who found everything in the mother country more to their taste, except, of course, the studied contempt for America.

His country's lowly status was not entirely England's doing. Jefferson discovered this harsh truth when he tried to persuade the European nations to form a league against the Barbary corsairs who preyed on Mediterranean shipping along the coasts of Africa. Most European nations found it expedient to pay a tribute to these "lawless pirates," as Jefferson called them, but this outraged the American minister's pride as well as his empty purse. When two American ships were seized, he labored tirelessly to concoct an international naval force to smack down the outlaws once and for all. He lined up several smaller nations and even persuaded France to agree. But when he asked Congress to contribute at least a frigate to the allied armada, he learned to his chagrin that this nebulous body was now so "openly neglected by the several states" that it was useless to enter into a contract which they would never have the money to fulfill.

Such humiliations may have been part of the reason why Jefferson's melancholy occasionally returned to haunt him. "I am burning the candle of life without present pleasure or future object," he told an American friend. ". . . I take all the fault on myself, as it is impossible to be among people who wish more to make one happy."

III

Lurking just around a bend in time was a cure for this gloom. She appeared one late summer day in 1786, on the arm of the American painter, John Trumbull. Her name was Maria Cosway. She combined a modest reputation as a painter and musician with a beauty that had been the rage of fashionable London for several seasons. A great mass of golden curls crowned an oval face and almost too pretty rosebud lips. Liquid blue eyes and a fluttery, dependent manner completed a style that was more meltingly feminine than the brittle French could manage. Maria had been born in Italy of English parents and she spoke her mother tongue with a piquant Italian accent. Left penniless by the death of her father, she had made a marriage of convenience with Richard Cosway, who was the foremost miniature painter of his time. Unfortunately, he was a miniature himself, a wrinkled, gnomelike little man who resembled a chimpanzee, and was almost as famous for his "macaroni" styles (mulberry silk coats embroidered with scarlet strawberries, for example). He was about Jefferson's age, but temperamentally and physically the two men could not have been more different. Cosway made no attempt to conceal his amours with other women, and he seems to have treated Maria with a mixture of indifference and condescension.

Jefferson, of course, knew none of this when he first met the Cosways beneath the magnificent dome of the Halle aux Blés, the recently completed Parisian market. Ten minutes of listening to Mrs. Cosway's lilting conversation, in a mélange of five or six languages, while his eyes wandered over her exquisite figure and lost themselves in that mass of golden hair, and Jefferson transformed what was to be nothing more than a casual chat into a daylong expedition.

This was Mrs. Cosway's first visit to Paris? He would lend her his eyes and ears, and show her the sights that enchanted him most, if she in turn would lend him her artist's eyes and help him to better appreciate the paintings, statuary, and music, with which the city abounded. Mr. and Mrs. Cosway were already committed to other social engagements throughout the day? So was Ambassador Jefferson. He was dining with a duchess himself. But such obstacles were no problem to a man of the world. Before the bewildered Cosways and Trumbull knew what was happening, they were sending messengers to make excuses for them to the various lords and ladies they had expected to visit, while Jefferson rushed another courier to his duchess, solemnly informing her that "urgent dispatches" from America had just arrived that demanded replies by the next boat.

There, wasn't that simple? The Cosways were forthwith bundled into the ambassador's carriage and they rattled off to the beautiful royal park of St.-Cloud with its long sun-dappled green lanes and magnificent fountains. There they dined and strolled through the famous gallery of the Royal Palace with its magnificent mythological murals and pictures of the royal chateaux.

Back to Paris in the autumn dusk, while the ambassador racked his fevered brain to find some excuse for prolonging the pleasure of Mrs. Cosway's company. It was too early to say goodnight. To the Rue St.-Lazare to see the *Spectacle Pyrrhique des Sieurs Ruggieri?* All Paris was talking about the delights of this huge pleasure garden, created by two ingenious Italians whose specialty was "pantomimes" and fireworks. Nothing could have pleased the Italianate Maria more. She cried out with pleasure as the rockets and bombs exploded against the darkening sky, creating a vision of Vulcan toiling at his forge, another of Mars, the god of war, in combat.

Now surely it was time to go home. But again the bedazzled ambassador looked down at those golden curls and found the thought appalling. Back to his dull empty house with his dispatches and their ponderous discussions of exports and imports, whale oil and tobacco? No. Maria had told him in her deliciously different English that her favorite musical instrument was the harp. She played it, and composed music for it. Then she must meet and hear the greatest living teacher-composer for the harp and his wife, the most gifted harpist in Europe. Her andante movement, the critics said, was "so irresistibly pathetic" that it "caressed the soul." Back into the carriage, and through the darkened streets to the home of Johann Baptiste Krumpholtz. This good-natured gentleman and his young wife, Julie, agreed to give them a concert, and they sat for another hour, listening to Julie play her husband's delicate music and discussing a number of improvements he had made in the design of the harp.

At last, alas, goodnight became inevitable. But the ambassador was in no mood to say good-by. The price of parting was a promise from Mrs. Cosway to join the ambassador in similar expeditions. They had only begun to sample the beauties of Paris.

Day after day for the next month, Jefferson's carriage stopped before the Cosways' house in the early morning and they whirled away on another six- or seven-hour trip. Mr. Cosway soon dropped out. He was busy painting miniatures of the noble Orléans family. John Trumbull was the next to go. He went back to London to work on his soon-to-be-famous painting, "Signing of the Declaration of Independence." But the loss of these chaperones did not seem to trouble Maria and Jefferson in the least. For a golden, glowing month they continued to see each other almost daily.

Typical of these trips was the one they made on the 5th of September. They stopped first at the Bagatelle, a park containing gardens and the elegant casino built by the Comte d'Artois, brother of Louis XVI, near the Bois de Boulogne. The gardens were both magnificent and amusing. Maria laughed with delight as her knowing escort ridiculed the attempt to re-create the wilds of America, complete with stockades, which the French imagined were necessary to prevent the traveler from being devoured by savage beasts. Deeper in the gardens was a "natural thicket" filled with rare exotic plants. In still another secluded glade was a lovely statue of Diana. Next came an Egyptian obelisk, then a small Gothic-style philosopher's retreat. It was a place where lovers could commune with each other, and with whatever kind of beauty suited their mood.

From the Bagatelle they journeyed on to Madrid, a magnificent chateau built by Francis I. A semicircle of huge trees stood like somber sentinels before the building whose varnished terra-cotta decorations sparkled in the sunlight like precious jewels. From the esplanade of Madrid, Jefferson could say to Maria, "Behold Paris!" Beneath them the great city spread along both banks of its guardian river.

Two days later they crossed the Pont de Neuilly, a bridge that excited all of Jefferson's architectural fervor, and threaded through the wooded hills above the Seine to the village of St.-Germain. Again there were superb views of the Seine and Paris, and an intriguing pleasure garden laid out by one of Lafayette's Noailles relatives, but above all the great machines which pumped water from the Seine into a reservoir in the distant hills. Four hundred huge wheels drove 225 pumps to force up 8,000 tons of water every 24 hours. The actual course of the Seine had been changed for six miles to make this waterworks—which supplied the fountains and gardens of several royal palaces. The machines were a spectacle in themselves, casting up brilliant rainbows in the sunlight, as they churned the river's waters.

Next, Maria and Jefferson turned back to visit Marly-le-Roi, the favorite palace of Louis XIV. The superb central pavilion was guarded by six small pavilions on each side leading up to it. All around them on the grounds were literally hundreds of statues of gods and demigods. On the top of the hill stood the reservoir which received the water from the machines in the Seine. From the reservoir water cascaded into a channel down which swans floated. At intervals fountains sent jets of sparkling water leaping high into the sunlight. Between the small pavilions of the palace were walks covered by bowers of jasmine and honeysuckle. The place was literally dreamlike in its beauty.

Nearby in a small inn there was a cold supper laid out for the wanderers by Petit, Jefferson's *maître*. Wine, cold chicken, ham and more conversation tête-à-tête. It was a time for exchanging confidences, and Maria poured out to Jefferson the story of her life. Her convent education in Italy had left her deeply religious, and after her father's death, only her mother's firm objections had prevented her from taking the veil. She was repelled as Jefferson was by London's dampness and smoke—and even more repelled by the realization that she was an object for which wealthy lords and sons of East India merchants were supposed to bid. For three years she remained indifferent to numerous offers, until once more her mother exerted her authority and all but forced her into marriage with Richard Cosway.

Much as she enjoyed the brilliant society that gathered in her husband's house, and welcomed the opportunity to display her not inconsiderable talents as a painter and musician, there were times when she was overwhelmed by a strange sadness, and fled the world of idle fops and leering ladies for the simplicity and quiet of the country. She yearned to do something more important with her life. How she envied Jefferson, who had already created a nation, written new laws and set new goals for a continent.

Everything about this woman—her sense, her sensibility— echoed something in Jefferson's own self. No wonder he fell help- lessly, totally in love with her. But at the same time, the cooler, intellectual portions of Jefferson's brain were sending him ominous warnings. There was no hope, no future to this infatuation. The lady was married, and too religious to commit adultery. She was really half woman, half child. There was an innocence about her that made her Latin-flavored coquetry seem harmless, even when it was wreaking havoc on his emotions. What to do? Never since his dancing days at the Raleigh Tavern, when he had botched his well- rehearsed gallantries to the fair Rebecca, had Jefferson been in such a state.

Ignoring all the warnings of prudence and conscience, he con- tinued the intimate day-long journeys. The climax came on the 16th of September, when they traveled beyond St.-Germain to the Désert de Retz, a fantastic garden in what was then called English- Chinese style. A wealthy French engineer had created it, and it abounded in wildly romantic curiosities. There were no less than 26 buildings inside the grounds, including a ruined Gothic church, a temple of Pan, an unbelievably delicate Chinese mansion, a Temple of Repose and an Island of Happiness. Most marvelous of all was a ruined column sixty-five feet in diameter, with a spiral staircase circling through four floors, the interior decorated in the exquisite style of Louis XVI. Jefferson found the column almost as exciting in its grandeur as his own Natural Bridge, and it inspired him to give Maria a vivid description of this and other wonders that nature, not man, had provided for the eye in America. For both the charming Maria and the entranced, not quite middle-aged ambassador, it was an unforgettable day.

Two days later, they were out again, promenading along the Seine. By now the ambassador had completely forgotten his age and the dignity supposedly incumbent upon his station. He was a coltish college boy again, his high spirits bubbling in his head and heart like champagne. Not far from the Place de la Concorde this animal energy sent him hurtling to disaster. Perhaps Maria was bantering with her "American savage," as he liked to call himself, about the natural superiority he boasted for the men and animals of his native country. See those French boys jumping that little fence? Could he do that? Perhaps Jefferson was describing to Maria that special thrill of the hunt, the soaring leap over fence or hedge, the crunching contact with earth on the other side. Perhaps it was the sheer exhilaration of the lady's company. At any rate, Jefferson forgot that a Virginian, all but born on horseback, was by no means as agile on his own feet.

Away went the ambassador to bound over the little fence and come crashing to earth, flat on his face, on the other side. When he staggered to his feet, his right hand dangled uselessly. He was in agonizing pain. But he made light of the whole matter. It was nothing at all, he assured Maria. They finished their walk chatting cheerfully as before. Only when he reached his own house did he tell her that the wrist was undoubtedly dislocated and he had better send her home in his carriage and call a surgeon.

By the time the doctor arrived, the wrist was badly swollen and the medical man had great trouble setting it properly. Jefferson spent days and nights in sleepless agony, while Maria sent him sympathetic notes. On the way home from dinner with the Duchess of Kingston, she insisted that her husband stop their carriage at Jefferson's house, but the invalid had already gone to bed and all the windows were dark. The next day she tried to tempt him out to dinner where she promised to "serve you and help you . . . and divert your pain after with good musik." But the ambassador was in too much pain to accept. Not until almost two weeks later, on October 4, did he venture out with Maria again, though she no doubt visited him several times in the interim.

It was her last day in Paris, and she begged Jefferson to share it with her. Jefferson took the risk, and they set out for one more look at some of their favorite places. But the jouncing carriage turned this trip into another disaster. The poorly set wrist was dislocated again and Jefferson spent another night in sleepless torture. He sent a note to Maria telling her that instead of seeing her off as he had promised he would be forced "to relinquish her charming company for that of the surgeon." Maria sent back a mournful missive, by the same messenger. "Why would you go," she cried,"and why was I not more friendly to you and less to myself by preventing you of giving me the pleasure of your company?" Mr. Cosway had promised to bring her back to Paris in April, and Maria closed her note sighing, "I . . . shall long for next spring."

This inspired Jefferson to rise from his bed of pain. Summoning a French friend, M. Danquerville, to help him with possible language difficulties, he rushed to Maria's house in time to find the Cosways still packing. They rode together down the broad, tree-lined avenue that led to the Port St.-Denis, and down to the little village of the same name. There they had a last meal together and then Jefferson handed Maria into the carriage that was to take her to Antwerp. As he said good-by, he was overwhelmed by emotions he never felt before in his life, a longing for this beautiful woman that was also the last cry of youth, the last echo of that carefree college gallant who had pursued in vain the fair Belinda in the gardens of Virginia. He turned away, unable to speak a word, stumbled to his carriage and all but fled back to Paris and the refuge of his lonely house.

There he sat down and composed, with his left hand (he had trained himself in his two-week convalescence to write with it), the most revealing letter of his letter-filled life.

He began by telling Maria how, after he had performed "the last sad office" of handing her into her carriage at the Pavilion St.-Denis, he had walked "more dead than alive" to the opposite door where his own carriage was awaiting him. He and M. Danquerville had ridden back to Paris "like recruits for the Bastille," without even "soul enough to give orders to the coachman." Finally at home, "solitary and sad" beside his fireside the following dialogue took place between his head and heart.

Head: Well, friend, you seem to be in a pretty trim.

Heart: I am indeed the most wretched of all earthly beings. Overwhelmed with grief, every fiber of my frame distended beyond its natural powers to bear, I would willingly meet whatever catastrophe should leave me no more to feel or to fear.

Head: These are the eternal consequences of your warmth and precipitation. This is one of the scrapes into which you are ever leading us. You confess your follies indeed: but still you hug and cherish them, and no reformation can be hoped where there is no repentance.

Heart: Oh, my friend, this is no moment to upbraid my foibles. I am rent into fragments by the force of my grief! If you have any balm, pour it into my wounds; if none, do not harrow them by new torments. Spare me in this awful moment! At any other I will attend with patience to your admonitions.

Head: On the contrary, I never found that the moment of triumph with you was the moment of attention to my admonitions. While suffering under your follies you may perhaps be made sensible of them, but the paroxysm over, you fancy it can never return. Harsh, therefore, as the medicine may be, it is my office to administer it. You will be pleased to remember, that when our friend Trumbull used to be telling us of the merits and talents of these good people, I never ceased whispering to you that we had no occasion for new acquaintances; that the greater their merits and talents, the more dangerous their friendship to our tranquility, because the regret at parting would be greater.

Heart: Accordingly, sir, this acquaintance was not the consequence of my doings. It was one of your projects, which threw us in the way of it . . . I never trouble myself with domes or arches. The Halle aux Blés might have rotted down before I should have gone to see it. But you, forsooth, who are eternally getting us to sleep with your diagrams and crotchets, must go and examine this wonderful piece of architecture; then when you had seen it, oh! it was the most superb thing on earth! What you had seen there was worth all you had yet seen in Paris! I thought so too. But I meant it of the lady and gentleman to whom we had been presented; and not of a parcel of sticks and chips put together in pens. You then, sir, and not I have been the cause of the present distress.

Head: It would have been happy for you if my diagrams and crotchets had gotten you to sleep on that day, as you are pleased to say they eternally do. My visit to Legrand and Molinos [architects of the Halle aux Blés] had a public utility for its object. A market is to be built in Richmond. What a commodious plan is that of Legrand and

Molinos: especially if we put on it the noble dome of the Halle aux Blés . . . While I was occupied with these objects, you were dilating with your new acquaintances, and contriving how to prevent a separation from them . . . Every soul of you had an engagement for the day. Yet all these were to be sacrificed, that you might dine together. Lying messengers were to be dispatched into every quarter of the city with apologies for your breach of engagement . . .

Heart: Oh! My dear friend, how you have revived me by recalling to my mind the transactions of that day; how well I remember them all, and that when I came home at night, and looked back to the morning, it seemed to have been a month agone. Go on then, like a kind comforter, and paint to me the day we went to St.-Germain. How beautiful was every object! The Pont de Neuilly, the hills along the Seine, the rainbow of the machine of Marly, the terras of St.-Germain, the chateaux, the gardens, the statues of Marly . . . Recollect too *Madrid, Bagatelle,* the king's garden, the *Desert.* How grand the idea excited by the remains of such a column! The spiral staircase too was beautiful. Every moment was filled with something agreeable. The wheels of time moved on with a rapidity of which those of our carriage gave but a faint idea. And yet in the evening when one took a retrospect of the day, what a mass of happiness had we traveled over! Retrace all those scenes to me, my good companion, and I will forgive the unkindness with which you were chiding me. The day we went to St.-Germain was a little too warm, I think, was it not?

Head: Thou art the most incorrigible of all the beings that ever sinned! I reminded you of the follies of the first day, intending to deduce from them some useful lessons for you; but instead of listening to these, you kindle at the recollection, you retrace the whole series with a fondness which shows you want nothing but the opportunity to act it over again. I often told you during the course that you were imprudently engaging your affections under circumstances that must cost you a great deal of pain: that the persons indeed were of the greatest merit, possessing good sense, good humor, honest hearts, honest manners, and eminence in a lovely art: that the lady had moreover qualities and accomplishments belonging to her sex, which might form a chapter apart for her; such as music, modesty, beauty and that softness of disposition, which is the ornament of her sex and charm of ours. But that all these considerations would increase the pang of separation; that their stay here was to be short; that you wrack our whole system when you are parted from those you love, complaining that such a separation is worse than death, inasmuch as this ends our sufferings whereas that only begins them: and that the separation would in this instance be the more severe as you would probably never see them again . . .

The head and the heart continued this debate for many more pages. The heart argued that the Cosways would return. (Jefferson, in an era when letters were often opened, was careful to guard himself and Maria from scandal by talking about both husband and wife. But we can be sure Maria had no trouble deciphering the real message.) The heart even maintained that some day the Cosways might come to America. "Especially the lady, who paints landscapes so inimitably. She wants only subjects worthy of immortality to render her pencil immortal. The falling spring, the cascade of Niagara, the passage of the Potomac thro the Blue Mountains, the Natural Bridge. It is worth a voyage across the Atlantic to see these objects; much more to paint, and make them, and thereby ourselves, known to all ages. And our own dear Monticello, where has nature spread so rich a mantle unto the eye! Mountains, forests, rocks and rivers. With what majesty do we there ride above the storms! How sublime to look down into the workhouse of nature, to see a cloud, hail, snow, rain, thunder, all fabricated at our feet!"

If Maria became a sorrowing widow, Jefferson made it clear there would be someone waiting for her in America. "I hope in God no circumstances may ever make either seek an asylum from grief! With what sincere sympathy I would open every cell of my composition to receive the effusion of their woes; I would pour my tears into their wounds; and if a drop of balm could be found . . . at the remotest sources of the Missouri, I would go thither myself to seek and to bring it. Deeply practiced in the school of affliction, the human heart knows no joy which I have not lost, no sorrow of which I have not drank; fortune can present no grief of unknown form to me! Who then can so softly bind up the wound of another as he who has felt the same wound himself?"

The words make it clear how much of his inner self Jefferson had already shared with Maria. He ended this passionate literary explosion with a promise that his future letters would not be so long. But he begged Maria not to be brief with him. "If your letters are as long as the Bible, they will appear short to me." He asked her only to make them "brim full of affection." Then he would read them like a lover who when he wrote the words, *je t'aime*, "wished that the whole alphabet had entered into their composition."

Maria replied with a brief note, in Italian. She expressed her detestation of London and added a little sighing sentence Jefferson was well disposed to hear. "In the company of pleasant friends, practicing the fine arts, one can hope to escape sadness, even if something is lacking to perfect happiness . . ."

Jefferson hurried off a note, containing a love song from a popular opera. The song's title, "The Happy Days," summed up the sender's feelings once more. Maria replied by sending him a series of love songs that she had written in Italian, all lamenting parted lovers and unrequited love. For the next year, they corresponded regularly, Maria never failing to scold Jefferson if his letters were too short or too infrequent. When he left Paris for a long sight-seeing trip, she demanded, "as though by right, that you will write me as many pages as the days you are absent . . ." But as the months of separation lingered, Jefferson's head gradually regained control over his rebellious heart. His letters, while still full of expressions of affection, became less ardent.

The following summer Maria returned to Paris without her husband, and spent four months there. But by this time the beauty's emotions too seemed to have cooled. She surrounded herself with dozens of friends, and made it practically impossible for Jefferson to see her alone. Then, with feminine inconsistency, she pouted and complained that Jefferson was ignoring her. His answer was a note of mild complaint that with her clouds of company, they could not "unpremeditatedly mount into my phaeton and hie away to the Bois de Boulogne, St.-Cloud, Marly, St.-Germain . . ." But not even that litany of happier days persuaded Maria to change her style.

IV

Another reason for this victory of head over heart may have been the robustly masculine society of Jefferson's Paris household. It is one more example of Jefferson's amazing diversity, that he could be at home with intellectual French ladies, the clinging Maria Cosway, and such high livers as William Smith, one of Washington's doughtier army colonels. Smith had a soldier's sense of humor and manner, yet he and Jefferson hit it off instantly. Jefferson, describing him to Madison, compared Smith to Monroe. Both men had a blunt, tough honesty that Jefferson admired. "You could turn his soul inside out and not find a speck on it," he said.

Both the ambassador and Smith enjoyed poking fun at the legation secretary, pompous David Humphreys, another ex-Washington aide. Humphreys was always delivering gaseous opinions at great length on matters military and political. Abigail Adams was appalled at his lack of polish, and her daughter Nabby was baffled by his "stiffness of manner."

Humphreys was perpetually defending American virtues—but he apparently was not able to defend his own from one of Paris' oldest charms. Smith and Jefferson joined forces to break up the liaison. In his letters, Smith referred to their strutting friend as "Hump." Not too seriously, Smith told Jefferson that "Hump" was "converted" and had promised him never again to form such a "connection." Wryly, Smith tells Jefferson, "You'll never see him again at your breakfast table with his blue and white and red surtout." The only thing left to reform was Hump's "boundless appetite." But short of pulling his teeth, Smith did not know how to solve this problem. "If he should get a sight of this part of the letter I imagine he would immediately return and challenge me," chortled the hearty colonel.

Several months later, Colonel Smith married Nabby Adams in London. Jefferson was delighted. "May your nights and days be many and full of joy!" he wrote. "May their fruits be such as to make you feel the sweet union of parent and lover, but not so many as that you may feel their weight! May they be handsome and good as their mother, wise and honest as their father, but more milky! For your old age I will compose a prayer 30 years hence."

Jefferson constantly opened his doors to American travelers, especially young men who needed help in finding their way around Europe. William Smith sent him one—Thomas L. Shippen of Philadelphia, who had a definite predilection for meeting royalty. "I expect to see him on his return either a remarkable, amiable, improved gentleman or a sensible coxcomb who has seen the world," Smith said. He asked Jefferson to do his best to avoid the second possibility.

Jefferson had young Shippen to dinner twice a week, and the young man was soon calling him "my best friend." Jefferson took him to Versailles, where he gravely introduced the surprised tourist as "nephew of the President of Congress." This, Jefferson explained, was his title (accurate enough). Without some kind of title, a person could not get near the royal personage. After touring the palace apartments and meeting the Queen and many other members of the royal family and making enough bows to "tire a Scotchman," they at last reached the King.

He was just pulling on his coat [young Shippen wrote home]. His servant was tying his hair on which there was no powder, while one of his attendants was arranging his sword belt, and when the file of ambassadors, envoys, &c. in full dress, representatives of monarchs mightier than himself and the republics more great because more virtuous were prostrating themselves before him emulous of each other in demonstrating their obsequious adulation, he hitched on his sword and hobbled from one side of the room to the other, spoke three words to a few of the ambassadors and two to a German prince, who was presented with me, and left the room. I revolted at the insufferable arrogance of the King but I was more mortified at the suppleness and base complaisance of his attendants.

I observed that although Mr. Jefferson was the plainest man in the room and the most destitute of ribbands, crosses and other insignia of rank, that he was most courted and most attended to (even by the courtiers themselves) of the whole diplomatic corps.

In another letter a few days later, Shippen, obviously cured of his title fever, wrote his father: "Mr. Jefferson is in my opinion without exception the wisest and most amiable man I have seen in Europe. He has supplied to me the want of you better than I thought it could have been supplied."

Several visiting beauties may have also helped fill the void Maria's departure temporarily created. Most noteworthy was Anne Bingham. She had come to Paris with her wealthy Philadelphia husband, who hoped to spend his way into an ambassadorship. Mrs. Bingham was only twenty, but she was a remarkable person. Abigail Adams, after declaring her "too young to come abroad without a pilot" and overmuch inclined "to the follies of this country [France]," was soon admitting that she was "possessed of more ease and politeness . . . than any person I have seen." Her "excellencies," as Abigail called them, overbalanced her love for gay life which Abigail was woman enough to admit was hardly cause for wonder, with so much to be gay about. Jefferson very much enjoyed Mrs. Bingham's company, and she and her husband were often dinner guests at his house. Tête-à-tête with her one evening, he made her a bet that when she had been home twelve months she would find "the tranquil pleasures of America preferable to the empty bustle of Paris."

"For what does that bustle tend?" he asked her, and proceeded to skewer the foibles of the fashionable Parisienne with a skill that a gossip columnist might envy.

At eleven o'clock it is day, chez madame. The curtains are drawn. Propped on bolsters and pillows and her head scratched into a little order, the bulletins of the sick are read, and the billets of the well. She writes to some of her acquaintances, and receives the visits of others. If the morning is not very thronged, she is able to get out and hobble around the cage of the Palais Royal; but she must hobble quickly, for the coiffeur's turn is come; and a tremendous turn it is! Happy if he does not make her arrive when dinner is half over. The torpitude of dinner a little past, she flutters for half an hour through the streets, by way of paying visits and then to the spectacles. These finished, another half hour is devoted to dodging in and out of doors of her very sincere friends, and away to supper. After supper, cards; and after cards, bed— to rise at noon the next day, and to tread like a mill horse the same trodden circle over again. Thus the days of life are consumed, one by one, without an object beyond the present moment; ever flying from the ennui of that, yet carrying it with us; eternally in pursuit of happiness, which keeps eternally before us. If death or bankruptcy happen to trip us out of the circle, it is matter for the buzz of the evening, and is completely forgotten by the next morning.

Compare, Jefferson asked Mrs. Bingham, this futility with life in America, where "children, the arrangements of the house, the improvements of the grounds fill every moment with a useful and healthy activity . . . The intervals of leisure are filled by the society of real friends, whose affections are not thinned to cobweb, by being spread over a thousand objects."

"If we do not concur this year, we shall the next," Jefferson avowed. "Or if not then, in a year or two more. You see I am determined not to suppose myself mistaken."

Mrs. Bingham protested that Jefferson's portrait was rather overcharged. She made a spirited defense of French women, praising their accomplishments and social understanding. "We are irresistibly pleased with them because they possess the happy art of making us pleased with ourselves . . . I have the pleasure of knowing you too well," she assured Jefferson, "to doubt of your subscribing to this opinion."

The ambassador made no attempt to counter this *touché*.

Equally charming was the beautiful Angelica Church, born Schuyler in Albany, who had eloped with a wealthy Englishman. She was friendly with Maria Cosway, who wrote to Jefferson, introducing her. "If I did not love her so much I would fear her rivalship. But no, I give you free permission to love her with all your heart." Jefferson was soon telling Maria that he found in Angelica "all the good the world has given her credit for." His only complaint was that he had "seen too little of her." That Angelica was the sister-in-law of a New York lawyer named Alexander Hamilton meant little or nothing to the charmed ambassador, for the moment.

About this time Jefferson became involved in intricate negotiations with another woman in his life. Six-year-old Polly Jefferson, he decided, must join him in Europe. This would complete the family circle, and relieve him from the dread of receiving a message announcing she had followed little Lu into the shadows. But Jefferson was the very antithesis of the stern father. Miss Polly was to be persuaded, not ordered, to come. This turned out to be a challenge which taxed all Jefferson's formidable rhetorical powers. His first letter, in which he promised her as many French dolls and playthings as she wanted for herself, or to send to her Eppes cousins at their new home Eppington, plus the opportunity to learn to play the harpsichord, to draw, to dance, to read and talk French, received the following reply:

Dear Papa—I long to see you, and hope that you and sister Patsy are well; give my love to her and tell her that I long to see her and hope that you and she will come very soon to see us. I hope that you will send me a doll. I am very sorry that you have sent for me. I don't want to go to France, I had rather stay with Aunt Eppes . . .

> Your most happy and dutiful daughter,
> Polly Jefferson

Further strenuous paternal persuasion only produced similar replies.

Dear Papa—I should be very happy to see you, but I cannot go to France, and hope that you and sister Patsy are well.

> Mary Jefferson

Dear Papa—I want to see you and sister Patsy, but you must come to Uncle Eppes's house.

> Polly Jefferson

The baffled father finally had to resort to outright deception. A ship was chosen, passage was booked, and Polly and her Eppes cousins were brought aboard for several days before it sailed, and allowed to romp merrily above and below decks. On the day of departure, Polly was allowed to play so long, she finally crept into a cabin and fell asleep. When she awoke she was at sea. With her was Sally Hemings, a pretty mulatto slave girl of fourteen, who was pressed into service at the last moment when an older, reliable nurse became ill and could not make the voyage.

Temperamentally, as well as physically, Polly was the image of her dead mother—which adds charm as well as interest to her behavior. She became the pet of the ship, and grew so attached to the captain and crew that by the time the voyage ended, there was more trouble trying to pry her off the vessel. The captain took her to London, and handed her over to Abigail Adams. He wrote Jefferson a very unsalty letter, telling him how Polly "seldom parts with me without tears—and indeed I am almost the same way with her." Three weeks with Mrs. Adams produced more complications. Polly revived all the maternal feelings of that acidulous lady, who had just lost her only daughter in marriage. Abigail was soon writing Jefferson that Polly was "a child of the quickest sensibility and the maturest understanding that I have ever met with for her years . . . I never felt so attached to a child in my life on so short an acquaintance."

Jefferson, no doubt feeling a little swamped by all this feminine emotion, decided to send his *maître*, Petit, to collect Polly. This proved to be a blunder. The little girl declined even to go near the swarthy stranger, who spoke to her in such atrocious English. Polly clung to Abigail, and for a while it looked as if the Adamses might yet gain a second daughter. (Abigail had already written jestingly to Jefferson, offering to trade one of her three sons for Martha, as a gesture toward "strengthening the federal union.") Petit finally gave up all attempts to persuasion, and appeared with stagecoach tickets in hand, and literally tore a weeping Polly away from a tearful Mrs. Adams.

Although she barely recognized her father when she reached Paris, and did not know her fifteen-year-old sister at all, Jefferson was soon as ecstatic with this Virginia charmer as everyone else. He wrote delightedly to Abigail Adams of how "she flushed, she whitened, she flushed again" when she received a letter from her. To Elizabeth Eppes, Jefferson declared "everlasting obligation" for the affection and attention she had lavished on Polly with such good results. After a week of holidaying with him, Jefferson placed Polly in the convent school with Patsy where, he reported proudly to Mrs. Eppes, she had already become "a universal favorite with the young ladies and the mistresses."

V

Jefferson had been away from Paris during the four months before Polly's arrival. He had taken a trip through the south of France and then down into northern Italy, which had given him a new insight into both the magnificences and the weaknesses of France. He was enchanted by the sun, the brilliant colors, the Roman ruins of Languedoc. He made numerous notes on farming, bridges, boats, canal locks and wine. At Nîmes, he rhapsodized to his friends in Paris over the perfect proportions of the Maison Carrée.

In Italy he made elaborate notes on making Parmesan cheese, spending an entire day in a dairy to observe the process. He was unimpressed by the churches of Italy, calling the cathedral of Milan "among the rarest instances of the misuse of money." If the Italians had spent on engineering what they had spent on their churches, he said, they would have been able to throw the Apennines into the Adriatic and "render it terra firma from Leghorn to Constantinople."

On this and other trips that he made, Jefferson was constantly making observations that he did not confide to his letters or notebooks. He talked as well as he could in his halting French to the people of France, knocking on their doors, and buying lunch from them in their kitchens, asking them about the hours they worked, the money they made, the taxes they paid, their feelings about their country and their government. He returned to Paris with a knowledge of the common people which far surpassed that of any other foreign ambassador, and was more profound than that of many leading Frenchmen.

Once, strolling near the royal chateau of Fontainebleau, Jefferson met a poor ragged woman trudging along the road, and struck up a conversation. Did she work? Yes, she was a day laborer. How much did she earn? Eight sous (about 8 cents) a day, she replied. She had two children to support, and the rent for her house was 600 sous a year—75 days' wages. This was bad enough, but often there was no work. What then? No bread. They starved.

"We walked together near a mile and she had . . . served me as a guide," Jefferson said. "I gave her on parting 24 sous. She burst into tears of gratitude which I could perceive was unfeigned because she was unable to utter a word."

To Lafayette, who had the best interests of the people at heart, Jefferson addressed a significant letter in the midst of his southern journey, urging him to make a similar trip. "To do it most effectually you must be absolutely incognito," he wrote. "You must ferret the people out of their hovels as I have done, look into their kettles, eat their bread, loll on their beds under the pretense of resting yourself, but in fact to find if they are soft. You will feel a sublime pleasure in the course of this investigation, and a sublimer one hereafter, when you shall be able to apply your knowledge to the softening of their beds, or the throwing of a morsel of meat into their kettle of vegetables."

This was not casual or general advice Jefferson gave his old friend. It was very specific, and designed to be applied to the crisis of the French nation, in which Lafayette found himself playing a central role. Early in 1787, the King and his ministers had confessed the bankruptcy of both the exchequer and their policies by summoning a Committee of Notables from all parts of France to advise the crown on how to solve its multiple dilemmas. Jefferson attended the first meeting of this assembly, which had not been called since 1626. He was particularly pleased by the inclusion of his friend Lafayette, toward whom King Louis XVI (who was a good man, Jefferson said) was "favorably disposed." Much as Jefferson liked the young marquis personally, he was realistic about his political abilities, which he felt were weakened by a "canine appetite" for fame.

Along with advising Lafayette to find out the real needs of the common people, Jefferson, drawing on his experience in America, emphasized that evolution, not revolution, was the best hope of reforming society. He urged Lafayette to keep "the good model of your neighboring country"—Great Britain—"before your eyes" and proceed "step by step towards a good constitution." Even if every advance had to be purchased from the bankrupt King, "it will be gold well employed."

Although the Assembly of Notables did little but wrangle, for a long time Jefferson persisted in being optimistic about this first fateful step in what became the French Revolution. As late as August, 1788, he was writing to friends in America, "I am in hopes her internal affairs will be arranged without blood. None has been shed yet." Even a year later he was telling James Monroe, "This country will, within two or three years, be in the enjoyment of a tolerably free constitution, and that without its having cost them a drop of blood . . ."

But by then he was realistic enough to have some doubts about the Estates General, which the King was finally forced to summon in May, 1789. This immense conclave of nobility, clergy and commons was, Jefferson thought, simply too huge to function efficiently. "Twelve hundred persons of any rank and of any nation assembled together, would with difficulty be prevented from tumult and confusion," Jefferson said in another letter home. "But when they are to compose an assembly for which no rules of debate or proceeding have yet been formed, in whom no habits of order have yet been established, and to consist, moreover, of

Frenchmen, among whom there are always more speakers than listeners, I confess to you that I apprehend some danger."

Jefferson attended the flamboyant opening of the Estates General on the 5th of May, 1789. "Had it been enlightened with lamps and chandeliers it would have been almost as brilliant as the opera," he said. But the delegates made little progress; they could not even agree on how they should vote. Lafayette introduced on the 10th of July a Bill of Rights, which he had first submitted to Jefferson. It drew heavily on Jefferson's Declaration of Independence and his proposed constitution for Virginia. By now the third estate, representing the common people, had declared itself the National Assembly. When the King attempted to disperse them, they retreated to the famous indoor tennis court at Versailles where they took an oath, binding themselves never to separate until they had created a constitution for France. The nobility around the weak and bewildered King began summoning foreign troops from all parts of the nation and forced the resignation of the King's ministers who were disposed toward compromise.

I was quite alarmed at this state of things [Jefferson wrote later] . . . I considered a successful reformation of government in France as insuring a general reformation through Europe and the resurrection to a new life of their people now ground to dust by the abuses of the governing powers. I was much acquainted with the leading patriots of the Assembly. Being from a country which had successfully passed through a similar reformation, they were disposed to my acquaintance and had some confidence in me. I urged most strenuously an immediate compromise to secure what the government was now ready to yield . . . It was well understood that the King would grant at this time, one, freedom of the person by habeas corpus; two, freedom of conscience; three, freedom of the press; four, trial by jury; five, a representative legislature; six, annual meetings; seven, the origination of laws; eight, the exclusive right of taxation and appropriation; and, nine, the responsibility of ministers.

This, Jefferson said, reiterating the advice he had given to Lafayette, was more than enough for the first step, and would have satisfied all but the lunatic fringe of extremists on both the right and the left. But Lafayette's dominant Patriot Party, Jefferson added in a mournful postscript, "thought otherwise."

Events now moved swiftly. The French Army revolted and the Paris mob became more and more uncontrollable. The Bastille was stormed, and its governor and lieutenant governor were executed. Lafayette became commander in chief of the Paris militia and led a march on Versailles. The King allowed himself to be led to Paris as a virtual captive, and became, in Jefferson's words, "a passive machine in the hands of the National Assembly."

Once more Jefferson saw a superb opportunity to resolve the crisis. The King, he said, "would have willingly acquiesced in whatever they should devise as best for the nation." Jefferson urged on the patriots the formation of "a wise constitution along the British model with the King guaranteed his hereditary title, with powers so large as to enable him to do all the good of his station and so limited as to restrain him from its abuse."

But the National Assembly could not agree on a constitution. In their perplexity, they turned to Jefferson, assuring him that they would not regard his advice as a violation of his diplomatic status. "There are no foreigners (for us) where the happiness of man is at stake." Jefferson politely declined the invitation but within the week he found himself deeply involved in constitution making on a more clandestine level. Lafayette, despairing of any kind of rational debate while the assembly was in session, asked Jefferson for the use of his house and table to bring six or eight of the more important members together, in the hope of achieving a consensus.

Jefferson agreed, and from 4 o'clock in the afternoon until 10 o'clock in the evening the eight leaders, many of them destined to lose their heads in the forthcoming Reign of Terror, debated the nation's future. As a "silent witness" Jefferson said later he found himself admiring the "coolness and candor of argument, unusual in the conflicts of political opinion." Looking back in later years, he declared that the "logical reasoning, and chaste eloquence" he heard from these high-souled men was "truly worthy of being placed in parallel with the finest dialogues of antiquity handed to us by Plato and Cicero."

The next morning, Jefferson, like a good diplomat, told the French foreign minister, Comte Montmorin, about the conference, and hastened to assure him that he himself had done his utmost to maintain a strictly neutral role in the discussion. The count calmly assured Jefferson that he knew all about the meeting, and instead of reprimanding him, he urged him to attend future conferences. He was sure that Jefferson's cool head would do much to moderate the "warmer spirits."

Jefferson's voice of moderation was soon lost in the mounting revolutionary upheaval. He became more and more gloomy about the outcome of the crisis. On September 19, 1789, he wrote to John Jay, "The Assembly proceeds slowly in forming their constitution. The original vice of their numbers causes this as well as a tumultuous manner of doing business." The result, he noted grimly, was "sensible injury to the public cause. The patience of the people, who have less of that quality than any other nation in the world, has worn threadbare." Comparing the two revolutions, the American and the French, Jefferson saw a striking dissimilarity. In France, "the King and aristocracy together have not been a sufficient resistance to hoop the patriots in a compact body." George III and his minions, on the other hand, had been so relentlessly hostile to America and so resolute in seeking vengeance, that he had literally forced them to maintain at least a semblance of unity. In France, the assembly soon split into four distinct parties. "Civil war," Jefferson said, "is much talked of and expected."

VI

This was Jefferson's last eyewitness comment on the French Revolution. After almost five years in Europe, he was going home. One reason was his daughters. They were growing older and Jefferson felt if they stayed much longer in France they would be aliens in their own country when they returned, with no friends to warm their mature years. A warning sign in this direction was a letter from Patsy announcing to Jefferson that she wished to become a Roman Catholic. Jefferson did not waste a moment. He went directly to Panthemont, had a long and reportedly friendly conversation with the abbess, and that was the end of Patsy's and Polly's convent education. Thereafter, they lived with Jefferson and he personally supervised the rest of their French schooling.

Jefferson was also homesick. Europe, he wrote to John Adams in May, 1789, "would be a prison to me were it ten times as big."

There were other equally pressing reasons to return. After five years the income from his neglected farms had dwindled to the vanishing point. English creditors were pressing him for old pre-war debts, part of them his own, and part of them connected with the estate of his late father-in-law. Finally there was a natural desire to meet and talk with the men who had, during the same tumultuous years that France began to tear herself apart, met in convention and formed a new constitutional government for the United States of America.

Thanks to his continuing correspondence with James Madison, Jefferson had been in close touch with the making of the Constitution and the fight to ratify it. He knew that Madison had emerged at the Constitutional Convention as one of the master thinkers of the era. Jefferson no doubt glowed with pride at the descriptions sent to him by other friends of "the great little Madison" standing up to Patrick Henry's torrential tirades against the Constitution in the Virginia Convention, beating down the self-styled Tribune of the People with quiet, relentless logic, and winning the crucial ratification by a handful of votes.

In the Constitution's separation of powers and the careful attempt to strike a balance between a strong executive and a popular legislative government, Madison obviously drew on many of Jefferson's ideas. Thus it was not surprising that Jefferson approved the final document—except for two points to which he at first objected with considerable vehemence. The first was the omission of a bill of rights. The second was the lack of the principle of rotation in office, particularly in the case of the President. Jefferson was sure that the strength of the President's office guaranteed him re-election for a lifetime unless the Constitution expressly prohibited it. Madison, knowing that Washington would be the first President, professed himself to be unworried about the possibilities of a dictatorship, but he agreed with the need for a bill of rights.

The correspondence of the two men blended their differing experiences during their years of separation. Jefferson saw the chief danger in centralized tyranny which divided people into two classes, wolves and sheep. Madison, who had watched local legislatures upsetting contracts, issuing cheap money, and fulminating against property rights, was more inclined to worry about the tyranny of the majority over the rights of the minority. Madison reacted with alarm when a group of Massachusetts farmers under the leadership of ex-Revolutionary soldier Daniel Shays revolted against low farm prices and high taxation. Jefferson took a far more tolerant view. "God forbid we should ever be twenty years without such a rebellion . . . The tree of liberty must be refreshed from time to time with the blood of patriots and tyrants."

There is no doubt that Jefferson at this point in his life was deeply influenced by the events he witnessed in France, but when a Frenchman asked Jefferson a question which had an American ring—what exactly did he mean by "government by the people"? —his realistic thinking on politics reasserted itself. He told his inquiring friend that in America it was the policy "to introduce the people into every department of government, as far as they are capable of exercising it." The extent of this capability Jefferson then proceeded to clearly define. "One, they are not qualified to exercise themselves the Executive Department, but they are qualified to name the person who shall exercise it . . . Two, they are not qualified to legislate. With us, therefore, they only choose the legislators. Three, they are not qualified to judge questions of law, but they are very capable of judging questions of fact. In the form of juries, therefore, they determine all matters of fact, leaving to the permanent judges to decide the law resulting from those facts."

Such practical insights, based on careful observation, were lost on the French. They tended to think in Utopian terms. Jefferson's politics was that of the careful gardener, as one French thinker of this century has ruefully admitted. He knew that nations could not be freed by decree. They had to mature slowly, gaining the strength which alone enables a people to use freedom without allowing it to degenerate into license.

VII

When he sailed for home on October 22, 1789, Thomas Jefferson did not think he was leaving France permanently. Once he settled his daughters in Virginia and spent four or five months putting his farms in order, he planned to return. He felt, with considerable justification, that no one except Benjamin Franklin, who was on his deathbed in Philadelphia, could do more to cement good relations between the emerging French revolutionary government and the United States. He was also deeply committed to the cause of freedom in France, and believed that he could still exercise a healthy influence on its orderly development.

In the light of these strong convictions, it is easy to imagine Jefferson's consternation when he landed in Virginia after a pleasant twenty-nine-day voyage and discovered in the newspapers very strong rumors that President George Washington had appointed him Secretary of State. These rumors were confirmed a few days later, when Jefferson reached Eppington and his Eppes relatives handed him a letter from the President. In it Washington said that "private regard" as well as "public propriety" had prompted him to nominate Jefferson for this important post which "involves many of the most interesting objects of the executive authority." At the same time Washington made it clear that he was "desirous to accommodate to your wishes" and he had refrained from nominating any successor to Jefferson in Paris.

Behind the scenes, meanwhile, the President was showing some of the talent for handling men which had made him a successful leader of a revolution. Before he wrote to Jefferson he had conferred at length with James Madison on Jefferson's probable reaction to the appointment. Madison had discreetly sounded out Jefferson in a letter sent to Europe, and Jefferson had emphatically declared in favor of remaining as ambassador to France. But Madison had drawn his own conclusions about the importance of Jefferson's presence in the new government. So the cool-headed little man in black had told the President to go ahead and nominate Jefferson, and he, Madison, would pay him a visit in Virginia and see what he could do about talking him into it.

Even before Madison went to work on him, Jefferson's reply to Washington revealed once more the deep personal devotion Jefferson felt for the President. Jefferson frankly said that he would rather stay in his present post, but he added, "You are to marshal us as may best be for the public good: and it is only in the case of its being indifferent to you that I would avail myself of the option you have so kindly offered in your letter." If Washington wanted him in New York, "my chief comfort will be to work under your eye, my only shelter the authority of your name, and the wisdom of measures to be dictated by you, and implicitly executed by me."

A few days later, Madison, as he later told the President, "took a ride to Monticello." He listened patiently while Jefferson poured out to him all his fears and hesitations about the appointment. He dreaded the thought that he would inevitably come under fire from critics for his performance on the job. Moreover, he would be involved in running an executive department, handing out political jobs, buried in a thousand and one nit-picking details that had driven him to the brink of insanity when he was Governor of Virginia.

Madison calmly reassured him that the domestic part would be "very trifling." Then his little friend gave Jefferson a very candid analysis of the new government and how vitally it needed his influence. He discussed its numerous enemies, especially in the pivotal states of New York and Virginia, where ratification had been won by mere handfuls of votes. He also discussed the strong antidemocratic currents flowing in the minds of many influential men who supported the government. In the opening session of Congress, Madison had been forced to lead a fierce fight in the House of Representatives to bar the use of titles. Vice President John Adams had wanted to call Washington "His Highness the President of the United States and Protector of our Liberties." Thanks to Madison, Congress had settled for "The President." Washington, with the advice of the still pompous David Humphreys and others aristocratically inclined, had instituted weekly "levees" full of formal bows and announced entrances that bore alarming similarities to a royal audience.

If Jefferson wanted to see freedom triumph around the world, there was no place more important than here in America. The policies of the new government could play a vital role in the destiny of the French Revolution. Would it not be better, Madison argued, with his usual brilliance, to be a creator of these policies rather than a mere executor? Besides, Jefferson was too complacent if he thought the fight for freedom and order was already won here in America. A good deal of light would have to be shed in the "councils of our country" before the truths that Jefferson could see with his philosopher's eye became visible to "the ordinary politician."

Madison departed to report to President Washington. The chances were good, he said, that the hopes of Jefferson's friends for his acceptance "will not, in the final event, be disappointed."

Not long after Madison made this optimistic report, a delegation of Albemarle citizens arrived on Monticello's hilltop to present a welcoming address to their esteemed neighbor. It is highly probable that the instigator of this visit was Madison, practicing one more in his very large bag of political wiles on his reluctant friend.

After reciting in the warmest and most flowery terms their praise for Jefferson's previous service to their common country, the men of Albemarle concluded: "If we consulted the particular benefits of our county . . . we should feel anxious that you would for the future remain with us. But America has still occasion for your services, and we are too warmly attached to the common interest of our country, and entertain too high a respect for your merit, not to unite with the general voice that you continue in her councils."

Next came a letter from Washington, making it clear that he was anxious to "marshal" the ambassador into his cabinet. Jefferson, his defenses completely overrun, capitulated and became America's first Secretary of State.

VIII

Jefferson did not let the shadow of this momentous decision disturb the solid happiness of his return to Monticello. The years in France had healed the raw memory of Martha's death, and his primary love of his mountain and his mansion flooded him once more. The mood of the plantation itself was a perfect counterpoint to his feelings. The sight of the Jeffersons had touched off a wild celebration. As their carriage passed Shadwell, where the burnt-out remains of Jefferson's boyhood home still moldered, all of Monticello's Negroes came shouting and whooping down the road. They were wearing their brightest, gayest Sunday clothes and they swirled around the carriage in a veritable Mardi Gras of joy. Ignoring Jefferson's protests, they unhitched the horses and proceeded to drag and push the heavy vehicle up the steepest part of the mountain. Then came the most amazing moment of all. "When the door of the carriage was opened," Martha Jefferson said, "they received him in their arms and bore him to the house, crowding around and kissing his hands and feet, some blubbering and crying—others laughing. It seemed impossible to satisfy their anxiety to touch and kiss the very earth which bore him." Jefferson's protests were lost in the wild uproar and he could only submit to this outburst of affection with the best dignity he could muster.

Just before the end of the year, Monticello had a visitor who soon became another cause for joy. He was a tall, swarthy, black-haired young man of twenty named Thomas Mann Randolph, Jr. He had spent four years as a student in Edinburgh, and this may have been part of his fascination. Young Martha did not participate in her father's wish to go home, and on shipboard had remarked to a young man her own age that she hated the thought of exchanging the lively social life of Paris for the dull round of a Virginia plantation and the company of the unsophisticated farmers of Albemarle. Young Randolph, with the sheen of a European education still bright, obviously had a special appeal to her. In a matter of weeks, the young couple was discussing a wedding date with Jefferson.

The new Secretary of State was delighted with the match. He had spent his boyhood with the groom's father, Thomas Mann Randolph of Tuckahoe, and he was soon writing cheeefully to him: "The marriage of your son with my daughter cannot be more pleasing to you than to me. Besides the worth which I discover in him, I am happy that the knot of friendship between us, as old as ourselves, should be drawn closer and closer to the day of our death." Randolph replied in equally cordial terms and the two fathers immediately contracted for substantial wedding gifts to the young couple.

Jefferson felt he had good reason to rejoice. Instead of the blockhead he feared Martha might marry, the young man gave every evidence of being an ideal son-in-law, intensely interested in farming, the sciences and politics. Hoping to make him more son than son-in-law, Jefferson immediately began trying to entice

Randolph to settle near Monticello. But the elder Randolph had given his son a farm in a distant section of Virginia and the young couple, in a burst of independence, announced that they were going to set up housekeeping there and go it alone. This did not especially disturb Jefferson for the moment, because he himself was committed to spend the next months, perhaps years, away from Monticello. So he contented himself with the satisfaction of a son-in-law well captured.

As for Polly, he decided, no doubt with some powerful pleading on her part, to return her to the tender ministrations of Aunt Eppes at Eppington. He had taken Martha with him to Philadelphia when she was Polly's age, but Jefferson was shrewd enough to see that his second daughter was a totally different person, a more dependent, emotional girl who needed the constant companionship of loving friends and family to keep her well and happy.

With the two most important people in his life in good hands, Jefferson proceeded to obey the promise he had made in his letter of acceptance to George Washington "to postpone every matter of business however pressing" in order to get to New York as soon as possible to take up his duties as Secretary of State. Instead of spending months putting his farms in order and raising their productivity to the point where he could once more begin to pay off the debt he owed on the Wayles estate (which now, with interest, had almost doubled), Jefferson had to leave his lands in their still chaotic state and ask for a loan of $2,000 from the Dutch bankers, the Staphorsts, with whom he had dealt when he was ambassador to France. He pledged his land for the cash at 6 per cent interest. There is a certain wistfulness in his words: "I am only a farmer and have no resource but the productions of the farms." He planned to invest the money in these farms.

That done, Jefferson rode north, pausing only to mend a few political fences in Richmond, and accept an address of congratulation from the citizens of Alexandria, to which he replied with warm words in praise of France and freedom. In Philadelphia he stopped to visit with the bedridden Benjamin Franklin and fill him in on the fate of all his friends in France. They went down the long list, Jefferson later recalled, "with a rapidity and animation almost too much for his strength." In a month the sage would be dead.

On March 21, 1790, Jefferson stepped off a Hudson River ferry and made his way through the narrow, crooked streets of lower Manhattan to "the Broadway." Although it was Sunday, he presented himself to President George Washington as a citizen soldier of the Republic, ready for duty. He swiftly discovered that this duty was far more complex and more significant than his immediate responsibilities as Secretary of State. At forty-seven, Jefferson began a new career which was to renew in dramatic and unforeseen ways the commitment to freedom he had made in 1776.

BOOK
THREE

New World
of Politics

❧

T HE SECRETARY of State rented a small house in Maiden Lane
and went to work. A mountain of mail had accumulated on
his desk and his entire staff consisted of two chief clerks, two
assistant clerks, and a translator.

The new federal government, with its three branches, executive,
legislative and judicial, was already established and hard at work
restructuring the nation. Congress was no longer the old dawdling
one-chamber body Jefferson had known before he left for France.
There were dozens of Senators and Representatives to deal with,
and they had handed over to Jefferson a host of leftover items
which they had been unable to fit into the other three executive
departments. Indian affairs, weights and measures, lighthouses,
patents, internal improvements and other odd matters came under
Jefferson's purview. He spent much of his first months in office
toiling over a report on weights and measures which was considered
in its day a philosophical masterpiece, and would have placed the
United States on the metric system. Congress, alas, declined to
adopt it. More long hours were spent pondering a policy for the
Patent Office, which his inventive mind considered of prime
importance.

He did not neglect the international aspects of his job. Among
his first concerns was the re-establishment of communication with
his friends in France. To Lafayette, at the height of his power and
prestige, he wrote a significant letter.

Behold me, my dear friend, dubbed Secretary of State instead of
returning to the far more agreeable position which places me in the
daily participation of your friendship . . . I have been here ten days
harnessed in my new gear. Wherever I am, or ever shall be, I shall be
sincere in my friendship to you and to your nation. I think, with

others, that nations are to be governed according to their own interests: but I am convinced that it is their interest, in the long run, to be
grateful, faithful to their engagements even in the worst of circumstances, and honorable and generous always. If I had not known that
the head of our government was in these sentiments, and that his
national and private ethics were the same, I would never have been
where I am.

He added that Washington's health was "less firm" than it used
to be. But if the President could be "preserved a few years till
habits of authority and obedience can be established generally, we
have nothing to fear."

In the next few weeks, Jefferson slowly began to change this
sanguine opinion. As a national celebrity, he was deluged with
invitations, and being gregarious by nature, he was soon dining at
the best tables in New York. The conversation was, of course,
almost entirely devoted to politics. New York was America's first
capital and the town watched the proceedings of the new Congress
with almost hypnotic fascination. Although Madison had warned
him, Jefferson was amazed to hear opinions expressed at these
dinner tables that he might have expected to hear at the court of
George III. Democracy and "the people" were damned and
scorned with a virulence which left the Secretary of State blinking
with disbelief. "I had left France in the first year of her revolution,
in the fervor of natural rights and zeal for reformation. My con-
scientious devotion to these rights could not be heightened, but it
had been aroused and excited by daily exercise . . . An apostate I
could not be, nor yet a hypocrite; and I found myself for the most
part the only advocate on the republican side of the question."

Until recently, many historians have been inclined to discount
this statement of Jefferson, arguing that his French experience had
made him a flaming apostle of democracy, who saw a monarchist in
everyone who disagreed with him. But the editors of the Thomas
Jefferson papers have uncovered startling evidence that Jefferson's
opinion of New York society and the political temper of the new
government was by no means eccentric. The judgment is based on
the long-concealed papers of Major George Beckwith, a British
agent sent to New York by Lord Dorchester, the Governor of
Canada. Beckwith, who had been in charge of secret-service opera-

tions in New York during the last years of the Revolutionary War, had no difficulty whatsoever re-establishing relations with an astonishing range of pro-British Americans.

They included members of the United States Senate and the House of Representatives. Many seemed to have an almost instinctive dislike for Thomas Jefferson. William Samuel Johnson, the senator from Connecticut, told Beckwith, "Mr. Jefferson . . . is greatly too democratic for us at present, he left us in that way, but we are infinitely changed, and he must alter his principles . . ." William Paterson, senator from New Jersey, summed up Jefferson as "a man of some acquirements . . . but his opinions upon government are the result of fine spun theoretic systems . . . which can never be realized." These men were all part of a political party that was forming around the most important of agent Beckwith's contacts—the man he referred to in his secret reports as "Number Seven"—Alexander Hamilton, the Secretary of the Treasury.

By now Jefferson had often heard this name spoken with a kind of reverence by the so-called best people of New York. Men such as William Duer, "prince of speculators," who had made a fortune supplying the French and American armies during the war, and rode around New York with a ducal coat of arms emblazoned on his carriage, considered the thirty-five-year-old Hamilton a kind of hero. His report on public credit had projected with clarity and brilliance a plan to repay the almost defaulted $85,000,000 Revolutionary War debt which was ruining American credit in Europe. Overnight, at home and abroad, confidence in the United States among bankers and merchants, who had all but abandoned financial hope in them during the feckless years of the Articles of Confederation, magically revived.

Jefferson and Hamilton met at a dinner Washington gave for the Secretary of State not long after he arrived. The other two members of the cabinet, forty-year-old Henry Knox, the portly Secretary of War from Massachusetts, and thirty-seven-year-old Edmund Randolph, the handsome Virginian who was Attorney General, were also among the guests. Randolph, the young attorney to whom Jefferson had handed over his law practice, had acquired not a little experience and prestige. He had served a term as Governor of Virginia, and had been one of the leading figures at the Constitutional Convention. As Washington's personal lawyer, he was more intimate with the President than any other cabinet member. Knox, major general in command of Washington's artillery in the Revolution, had more than enough military prestige, to which he added the weight of some three hundred pounds. Yet Hamilton, the youngest man in the cabinet, who had held no political offices, and whose wartime rank of colonel had been achieved largely as a Washington aide, was clearly the dominant figure. His bold eyes and jutting jaw exuded command and determination. Washington showed him a deference which Jefferson must have found more than a little surprising.

Beside him, Jefferson himself at first glance seemed a poor second in personal power. His long lanky frame, his habit of sitting sideways, on one hip, one leg slung carelessly over his knee, his shyness in large gatherings, did not incline to an overwhelming first impression. One crusty Pennsylvania senator complained about Jefferson's "loose shackling air" and "laxity of manner" which was not "the firm collected deportment" the solon expected from a cabinet minister. Even in the matter of fashion, the Secretary of the Treasury seemed to outshine the Secretary of State. Born out of wedlock in the West Indies, Hamilton had been wretchedly poor as a boy. Now, married to the daughter of the immensely rich Philip Schuyler, he compensated for those early pangs of poverty with the finest, boldest-colored satins, the most expensive laces and ruffles of the day. Jefferson, on the other hand, felt peacock finery was out of place in a Republican government. He could preen himself in France, because American prestige was at stake. But now he was home, and he wore old clothes that seemed, according to the same critical senator, "too small for him."

New York's uncongenial atmosphere, with its ominous hints of the political conflicts Jefferson dreaded, brought on a two-month-long migraine attack which left him all but incapacitated during the spring of 1790. Another probable cause was the acute sense of separation from his daughters, after having enjoyed their company so much, during the last year in Paris, when they had moved from the convent to live with him. He was a compulsively paternal man and he wrote worried letters of advice to Martha, urging her to do everything in her power to please her husband and placate her rather difficult father-in-law, who was thinking of marrying again —a decision which undid the young couple's hopes for a large inheritance. When the newlyweds lingered in Richmond, he anxiously warned them that they were liable to grow bored living in town with nothing to do, and this might make them bored with each other. He urged them to set up housekeeping without delay.

Martha's reply revealed the enormous devotion she still felt for her father. She said that she considered all concerns in life as secondary to her love for her husband—"*except* my love for you." She also added news that Jefferson received with vast joy. Young Randolph had abandoned his idea of settling on the distant property given to them by his father and was now attempting to buy a part of his family's Edgehill plantation near Monticello. She did not mention what her husband told others: he had made the move "to gratify Patsy."

To Polly, or Maria, as he now began to call her, Jefferson's letters were more wistful. He urged her to study Spanish, practice her music and tell him whether she knew "how to make a pudding yet, to cut out a beefstake, to sow spinach? or to set a hem? . . . Love your aunt and uncle, and be dutiful and obliging to them for all their kindness to you. What would you do without them, and with such a vagrant for a father?"

II

In the political world, the main focus of attention was on the battle between Alexander Hamilton and another Virginian, with whom the Secretary of the Treasury had previously worked in harmony. James Madison and Hamilton had (with Chief Justice John Jay) co-authored *The Federalist* papers, a penetrating commentary on the Constitution which had done much to swing public opinion in its favor. Now, day after day, Madison was on his feet in the House of Representatives hammering away at Hamilton's plan to have the federal government absorb the war debts of the states.

This was the second stage in Hamilton's grand design to put the finances of the United States in order. Madison had backed Hamilton's first funding bill, which provided for repayment of the federal debt. But he had quarreled with Hamilton's insistence on paying the face value of the Continental dollars and bills of credit. By the year 1790, most of these pieces of paper had passed into the hands of a small group of wealthy speculators who had bought them up from needy ex-soldiers and small farmers at prices as low as one-eighth of their original value. Madison had argued that these speculators should be paid at the current market value of the paper, and the balance of the money handed on to the original owners who had risked their lives and property on behalf of the revolutionary cause. Hamilton and his circle had violently opposed this idea; for them a contract was a sacred thing, which could only be abrogated at the risk of anarchy. Madison's proposal had gone down to defeat.

The battle over assumption of state debts revived many of these inflammatory issues. Thanks to information supplied by William Duer, whom Hamilton had made assistant secretary of the treasury, speculators sent agents hustling up and down the nation buying up state bonds and other types of paper debts at rock-bottom prices, before the unsuspecting owners heard of Hamilton's plan. Since an assumption of state debts was an almost total surprise (in contrast to the assumption of the federal debt, which everyone had expected and approved), the speculators stood to reap truly juicy profits. Compounding this was the problem that some states, such as Virginia, had made great sacrifices to repay a large portion of their debts while others, such as Massachusetts, had done little or nothing. Virginians rose in wrath to ask their representatives in Congress if they now were going to be taxed to pay off the debts of the slackers, after having toiled through the lean postwar years to clear their obligations, as men of honor should.

This complication brought numerous congressmen to Madison's side of the argument, to the alarm of Hamilton and his friends, who had invested much of their cash on his assurance that the state assumption was a *fait accompli*. Soon Madison was five votes up on the Hamiltonians in Congress, and stage two of the Treasury's plan looked very dead.

A few days later, as Jefferson was entering the President's house on Broadway, he heard Hamilton calling to him. The Secretary of the Treasury had undergone a remarkable transformation. The vitality was gone from his commanding gaze, his leonine head drooped in near despair. Even his clothes, normally the essence of the New York mode, were sloppy and dirty. For a half hour Hamilton walked Jefferson up and down in front of the building, talking earnestly. The crisis in Congress was endangering the very existence of the infant union, he said. The creditor states, especially New England, were already talking about secession, if Madison and his largely southern cohorts insisted on blocking state assumption. Hamilton's own personal reputation was at stake, as well. If he could not persuade Congress to vote for the measure, he was a failure as the Secretary of the Treasury, and had no alternative but to resign. The majority against the assumption was so small, he was sure that an appeal from Jefferson to several of his southern friends would be enough to change the vote.

Jefferson protested that he was "a stranger to the whole subject." He had not had a chance to study the new financial system. But if Hamilton was right, and the question was threatening the Union, that was a disaster which was to be averted at all costs. Have dinner with me tomorrow, he told Hamilton. He would bring together "another friend or two." Jefferson was sure it was "impossible that reasonable men consulting together coolly could fail by some mutual sacrifices of opinion to form a compromise . . . to save the Union."

Jefferson kept his word, and arranged a dinner for Hamilton with Madison and two other members of the Virginia delegation. Madison, equally devoted to the Union, was as concerned as Jefferson by the bitterness assumption had aroused in Congress. When it was voted down, the House of Representatives had all but ceased to function, simply meeting each day and adjourning. The opposing groups were so inflamed, they were incapable of speaking civilly to each other. Madison agreed something should be done. But how could anyone make a compromise palatable to southern congressmen and their constituents?

Hamilton suggested a horse trade. Congress had wrangled almost as angrily over the eventual location of the national capital. New Yorkers intensely wanted it to remain where it was. Philadelphia was lobbying fiercely for it. Everyone sensed that whoever possessed the capital would have a major weapon for influencing the government. Southerners—including President Washington—were hoping to see it situated in a "Federal City" on the banks of the Potomac.

If Madison would persuade his cohorts to vote for assumption, Hamilton would swing his side to voting for the Potomac capital. This would sweeten the "peculiarly bitter" assumption pill that southern states would be asked to swallow. Madison agreed, but stipulated that he himself would not change his vote, because he had gone too far in opposition. The two southern congressmen, whose districts bordered on the Potomac, agreed to switch their votes. One did so, Jefferson noted, with an "almost convulsive" revulsion.

Later, Hamilton added a fillip to this arrangement, which handed Jefferson another wearying chore. When Robert Morris, the so-called financier of the Revolution and currently senator from Pennsylvania, threatened to subtract his state's votes from the Assumption Bill, Hamilton agreed to switch the capital to Philadelphia for the ten years it would take to erect the Federal City on the Potomac. Washington was unhappy about this transfer, because there was a good chance that in ten years the subtle Pennsylvanians might convince Congress that their city was the best compromise between New York and the more obviously southern Federal City.

In his anxiety, the President turned to Jefferson, and made him his unofficial assistant in pushing the business of laying out not-yet-named Washington, D.C. Selecting the architecture of the various public buildings, organizing the sale of lands in the ten-mile square district to individual investors was a complicated, frustrating job. Jefferson did more than anyone else, except President Washington himself, to bring the District of Columbia to the point where it was economically impossible for Congress to abandon it.

More important for the future of Washington, D.C., and American architecture, Jefferson gently pressured Major Pierre Charles L'Enfant, the French engineer who planned the city, toward the classic style, with its emphasis on space, order and dignity. Nothing illustrates the encyclopedic quality of Jefferson's advice better than his casual letter to L'Enfant: "I have examined my papers and found the plans of Frankfort on the Mayne, Carlsrhue, Amsterdam, Strasburg, Paris, Orleans, Bordeaux, Lyons, Montpelier, Marseilles, Turin and Milan, which I send in a roll by the post." Jefferson presided over the architectural competition for the national Capitol, which is considered by art historians "the birth of the profession of architecture" in America. He chose Dr. William Thornton's design for its "grandeur, simplicity and beauty."

For the White House, he submitted a design of his own, under a pseudonym. It was modeled on a Palladian villa, with a dome and porticos. President Washington preferred the simpler yet dignified plan of Irish architect James Hoban.

By and large, Jefferson welcomed this chance to exert his architectural influence—and at the same time to please the President. But he soon regretted the political results of the capital swap. He began complaining that he was "most ignorantly and innocently made to hold the candle" in the deal. Some historians have assailed Jefferson for this assertion, claiming that he knew perfectly well what was going on. Although he had only been in New York a few months, he had more than enough time to find out from his friend Madison exactly what was at stake in the assumption battle. But Jefferson was really voicing his regret at having helped install any part of the Secretary of the Treasury's financial engine.

At this point, Jefferson only perceived rather dimly Hamilton's overall intentions. He knew from his dinner-table conversations that Hamilton was a central figure in the New York–New England circle that looked with scorn on a government that encouraged democracy. It was the war crisis in the summer of 1790 that awoke Jefferson to the sweep and scope of Hamilton's ambitions and policies.

For centuries the European powers had tacitly admitted that the Pacific was a Spanish lake. But Great Britain, noting the accelerating decline of the Spanish Empire, had made bolder and bolder intrusions into this great uncharted sea. The Spanish retaliated by seizing a British expedition sent to occupy Vancouver Island. For several months war seemed imminent, and the problem became Jefferson's first challenge as Secretary of State. Both powers owned huge territories surrounding the United States. Should America go to war in support of one side or the other in the hope of acquiring some of this real estate? Or, if she should remain neutral, which way should her neutrality lean?

Jefferson outlined a policy that was neither pro-Spanish nor pro-

British. His idea was to send emissaries to both powers, with orders to bargain for major concessions. From the Spanish, Jefferson wanted free navigation of the Mississippi, and the right to sell the produce and products of the western states through the port of New Orleans, which Spain had acquired from France in 1763. From the English he hoped to wring the surrender of the western forts, which had been called for in the 1783 treaty of peace. Great Britain had stubbornly refused to yield these border bastions, arguing that various states had failed to fulfill their part of the bargain and pay loyalists for confiscated property and make good other debts owed to English citizens. Equally desirable was some sort of agreement with Great Britain, which would do something to redress the highly self-interested tactics being pursued by the mother country. Americans were still forbidden to trade with the West Indies, and there were innumerable other restrictions aimed at keeping a majority of the cargoes on the high seas in British hulls.

In cabinet meetings, Jefferson argued for this policy, and was, to his mounting exasperation, repeatedly opposed by Hamilton. With an eloquence that overwhelmed the more reticent Jefferson, Hamilton argued in favor of siding with Great Britain in the controversy. To add weight to his persuasion, Hamilton revealed his conversations with Major Beckwith. But only in this century have historians learned the real dimensions of Hamilton's boldness. Not only did he brazenly admit that he was in contact with an unauthorized British representative—in effect playing part-time Secretary of State—but he coolly misrepresented what Beckwith told him, holding out to Washington and Jefferson the possibility that Great Britain was willing to enter into an actual alliance with the United States. Then he went back to Beckwith, and misrepresented to him the tepid reception Washington and Jefferson had given this idea, telling the not-very-secret agent that the time was ripe to push for such an alliance, or at the very least for a solid commercial treaty.

Hamilton was convinced that America's salvation lay in an intimate partnership with the mother country. British cash was the essential ingredient in his vision of a dynamic American economy which would, incidentally, create an aristocracy of wealth that would dominate the country politically. Hamilton saw this domination as absolutely necessary, if any sort of genuine unity was to be brought out of the shaky American union. He had little faith in the current arrangement. In conversation he called the Constitution "a shilly-shally thing full of milk and water."

At the Constitutional Convention, Hamilton had proposed, in a masterful five-hour speech, a totally different kind of government, a compromise between monarchy and republicanism, obviously modeled on Great Britain. The President would be elected for life, and so would the Senate. The governors of the various states would be appointed for life. "All communities," he had insisted, "divide themselves into the few and the many. The first are the rich and well born; the other the mass of the people . . . Turbulent and changing, they seldom judge or determine right. Give therefore to the first class a distinct, permanent share in the government."

None of these ideas was palatable to Jefferson. He had just spent five years in a nation where the citizens were "ground to powder" by a government that had over the centuries absorbed all power into its grasping hands. As he listened to Hamilton, Jefferson began to suspect that he was face to face with more than a man. In this brilliant, forceful personality was concentrated a fundamental tendency of human nature that instinctively revolted Jefferson.

At first, true to his experience in the Virginia legislature, Jefferson tried to achieve some kind of understanding—at least a social friendship—with this strangely different man, twelve years his junior. He invited Hamilton to dinner with him and John Adams. Inevitably the conversation turned to politics, and to his considerable distress, Jefferson heard John Adams begin praising the British constitution. True, it had defects—the rotten boroughs, the corruption that flowed from the placemen of the court—but if these could be corrected it would be "the most perfect . . . ever devised by the wit of man."

Hamilton drank his wine and let the Vice President have his say. Then he airily disagreed with Adams' lamentations about British corruption. In his opinion it was the corruption itself that gave England "the most perfect government which ever existed." This was too much for Adams to swallow, and it gave Jefferson acute indigestion. A man who saw virtue in corruption was sitting at the head of the Republic's largest federal department in charge of policies that determined the flow and direction of the nation's wealth.

There was an even more alarming facet of Hamilton's character which Jefferson saw before the dinner was over. Looking around the room, the New Yorker noticed three portraits on the wall and asked Jefferson who they were. Jefferson quietly explained that the first was Francis Bacon, the second Isaac Newton and the third John Locke, "my trinity of the three greatest men the world has ever produced." Colonel Hamilton took another drink of his wine and coolly remarked, "The greatest man that ever lived, was Julius Caesar."

III

Hamilton frankly regarded himself as Washington's prime minister, with the responsibility for setting government policy in all departments. His political credo is summed up in a quote from Demosthenes, which he wrote in his artillery company account book during the Revolutionary War. "As a general marches at the head of his troops, so ought wise politicians, if I dare use the expression, march at the head of affairs." Without legislative experience, he had no concept of a loyal opposition and no interest in retaining the friendship of people who differed with him. Instead, his military frame of mind inclined him to think dark thoughts about treachery.

He was especially baffled by James Madison's opposition to his financial program. They had worked together brilliantly for the ratification of the Constitution. Hamilton saw his program as merely an extension of the same crusade for an ordered society. Did the arrival of Jefferson on the New York scene have something to do with Madison's defection? The Secretary of the Treasury became convinced that his fellow cabinet member was poisoning Madison's mind when the two Virginians teamed up to fight the heart of his financial program—the Bank of the United States.

Hamilton's model was the Bank of England. Its half-public, half-private nature was deliberately copied because Hamilton believed that such a bank solved the worst dangers of paper money in a democracy—the tendency of a government to print too much of it.

The Secretary of the Treasury capitalized the bank at $10,000,-000—a staggering figure for the United States at that time. The total capitalization of the three state banks then in existence was less than $2,000,000. With this proposition Hamilton submitted nothing less than a treatise on banking which deluged Congress with a blizzard of facts, figures and arguments. The bill sailed through the House of Representatives by a vote of 39 to 20.

Led by Madison, the southern states had voted against it, almost to a man. They saw it as one more gift bestowed by Hamilton on the largely northern men of wealth who surrounded and supported him. But Madison's cry, that the plan was a poor bargain for the public and unconstitutional besides, was buried in an avalanche of votes. "Congress may go home," fumed Senator William Maclay of Pennsylvania. "Mr. Hamilton is all-powerful and fails in nothing he attempts."

President Washington was very sensitive to anything James Madison said in the House of Representatives. He was also more than a little attuned to local rumblings in Virginia. Patrick Henry had persuaded the state legislature to vote a rip-snorting condemnation of Hamilton's funding and assumption bills as "dangerous to the rights and subversive of the interests of the people . . . and repugnant to the Constitution of the United States." The anxious President called for opinions on the constitutionality of the bank bill.

Madison based his main argument on his profound knowledge of the Constitutional Convention, pointing out that the framers had specifically voted down giving the government power to charter corporations. Jefferson, knowing little of the details of the convention, advanced a more far-reaching argument, which was wholly consistent with his philosophy of government. It has come to be called the "strict" construction of the Constitution, and it rested on the following proposition: whenever a clause of the Constitution was in dispute, it was to be interpreted in the light of the Tenth Amendment, which reserved to the states or the people all powers not delegated to the United States by the Constitution or prohibited to the states. "To take a single step beyond the boundaries thus specially drawn around the powers of Congress," he said, "is to take possession of a boundless field of power, no longer susceptible of any definition." In his mind's eye, Jefferson saw Hamilton's consolidated government turning the Constitution into a scrap of paper.

Attorney General Edmund Randolph concurred with his fellow Virginians that the bank bill was unconstitutional. Deeply perturbed, Washington now presented these three opinions to Hamilton. The Secretary of the Treasury realized that a profound crisis in his relations with Washington had been reached. He went home and spent a full week thinking out and writing a defense of his position that has since become a classic American state paper. Being in the rebuttal position in the argument, he had an immense advantage over Madison, Jefferson and Randolph, who had presented little more than skeleton versions of their views. Hamilton buried them with a massive document which argued with a brilliant combination of logic and persuasion that the Constitution could only become a living organism, growing with the republic, if the great charter was construed as containing "implied powers" which enabled the federal government to exercise the primary power granted to it.

Hamilton's powerful prose convinced Washington and he signed the bank bill into law. Victory did not make Hamilton look kindly on his opponents. For one thing, he saw that Jefferson's strict interpretation of the Constitution was a weapon that others could use to club his financial system to death. It was an ideal rallying cry for those who spoke for "the people"—a phrase synonymous with demagoguery to Hamilton. "Take mankind in general, they are vicious," he had said in the Constitutional Convention. For him, with his New York state background, the people were the thousands of restless small farmers, living as sharecroppers on the huge estates of the "patroons" such as his father-in-law Schuyler. The people were in favor of cheap money and against law, order and the Constitution.

To this ideological clash, Hamilton found it easy to add a personal note. Jefferson's opinion on the bank bill was, he said "marked by ill humor and asperity toward me." When Madison and his southern followers in Congress began calling for investigations of the Treasury Department, the Secretary of the Treasury thought he saw, again, Jefferson's hostile hand.

There is no doubt that Jefferson did encourage Madison—and through him other southern congressmen—to oppose Hamilton's program. In his view, they were speaking for the majority of Americans. It requires an effort of the historical imagination to appreciate Jefferson's position. Today our mighty business-industrial complex is often hailed as a tribute to Alexander Hamilton's vision. These admirers of Hamilton tend to see him as the all-wise realist, and Jefferson as the doctrinaire theoretician, undermining America's potential greatness with his quibbles.

But in 1791 there was no business-industrial complex. Well over 90 per cent of Americans were farmers. Jefferson's opposition to Hamilton's attempt to transfer huge powers to a comparatively tiny circle of wealthy and commercial-minded men flowed from his instinctive fear of radical change, especially when the change concentrated too much power in the hands of a clique. In 1791, Hamilton was the theorist, boldly staking out claims for an America which did not yet exist. Jefferson was the realist, who knew from experience that the average farmer had his hands full fighting his annual battle with nature, and could not cope with a "moneyed interest" who believed in high taxes, to keep capital flowing. Already, one of Hamilton's taxes, on whiskey, had caused severe unrest in western Pennsylvania, where converting grain into spirits was the only way a man could earn a little cash from his crops. Staggering under such imposts, farmers would, Jefferson feared, first mortgage, then lose their lands, ending up little better than rebellious serfs paying rack rents to Hamilton's financial barons.

Jefferson's intellectual hostility to Hamilton soon broadened into personal dislike on his side, too. He became more and more infuriated by Hamilton's interference in the affairs of the State Department. The Spanish-English war scare had evaporated, but not before the British, alarmed at Jefferson's balance-of-power diplomacy, hastily dispatched one of their best younger diplomats— plump, red-faced George Hammond, the personification of John Bull himself—to fill the post of ambassador, which they had contemptuously left vacant since the treaty of peace. Hamilton was soon as confidential with Hammond as he had been with his unaccredited predecessor, Beckwith.

In the extensive notes Jefferson had begun to keep on cabinet meetings, he bitterly observed, "Whenever, at any of our consultations, anything was proposed as to Great Britain, Hamilton had constantly ready something which Mr. Hammond had communicated to him, which suited the subject and proved the intimacy of their communication; insomuch, that I believe he communicated to Hammond all our views and knew from him in return the views of the British Court."

Historians probing the British state papers have amply confirmed Jefferson's suspicion. At the time he could do nothing about it, except battle Hamilton on every point. When fighting was face to face, across the cabinet table, Jefferson continued to be at a severe disadvantage. He lacked Hamilton's rapid-fire eloquence and ready logic, and he hated personal acrimony. He also lacked Hamilton's gift for intrigue. The Secretary of the Treasury soon made it clear that he was willing to tread along the precipice of treason to maintain his unofficial British alliance.

To pressure the British into complying with the treaty of 1783, and surrendering the western forts, Jefferson prepared one of his greatest state papers. It was a devastating destruction of the British arguments that their refusal to honor the treaty was in retaliation for prior American violations. He showed the paper to Madison and asked him for suggestions, then took it to Attorney General Randolph—and then to the Secretary of the Treasury. Caught off guard, Hamilton could only admit that most of Jefferson's arguments were unbeatable. He made a few minor suggestions, most of which Jefferson accepted. On one important point, the question of state debts, Hamilton favored a milder tone, while Jefferson was for emphatically vindicating the states' refusal to pay Great Britain until she fulfilled the treaty. Jefferson referred a decision on this matter to Washington, who sided completely with Jefferson and warmly approved the entire document.

Such a blast should have sent the British ambassador reeling to his desk to write panicky letters home for instructions. But instead, Hammond fled to his good friend Alexander Hamilton, and the Secretary of the Treasury proceeded to outdo all his previous double talk by assuring Hammond that he lamented the "intemperate violence" of the Secretary of State and then abandoned the truth completely by claiming that Washington had not read the paper and it did not represent the policy of the administration. With this kind of guarantee from the man they trusted most, the British simply ignored Jefferson's magnificent document. A full year after he had given it to Ambassador Hammond, the Secretary of State was asking, somewhat plaintively, why no reply had been made. Jefferson never knew how totally Hamilton had sabotaged this major effort, on which he had lavished weeks of concentrated work. But he suspected a Hamiltonian hand in the British ambassador's serene intransigence, and it made the Secretary of State do some very tough political thinking.

I V

At first glance, Hamilton and his "phalanx" looked irresistible. He completely controlled the country's most influential paper, *The Gazette of the United States.* Its editor, Massachusetts-born John Fenno, was fond of editorially declaring his contempt for democracy. "Take away thrones and crowns from among men and there will soon be an end of dominion and justice," he intoned. Hamilton did everything but set Fenno's type for him, urging his numerous wealthy friends to subscribe to the paper, even paying the editor's personal bills. The Secretary of the Treasury was rewarded by the kind of effusive praise with which court poets repaid their royal patrons. To Fenno, Hamilton was, among other glittering titles, "the highest jewel in Columbia's crown."

Jefferson groaned over Fenno's "pure toryism," and his "hymns and lauds" to Hamilton. But he was even more disturbed to see his old friend, Vice President John Adams, appear in Fenno's sheet. Adams had undertaken to educate the unilluminated with a series of essays called "Discourses on Davila," a discussion of political theory, based on the writings of an Italian historian of the French civil wars of the sixteenth century. Government by the people came out a very poor second and doom and disaster were predicted for the French Revolution unless it ended in a balanced government which satisfied the supposed essence of every man's motivations—"a passion for distinction." Adams, in Jefferson's view, was obviously leaning toward Hamilton's concept of a Senate elected for life, and a President with the same tenure.

In Congress, senators and representatives by the dozen were getting rich speculating in the wake of the funding and bank bills and their votes tended to reflect their profits. In the cabinet Henry Knox, the Secretary of War, was little more than a Hamiltonian echo. Attorney General Edmund Randolph seemed to waver toward Hamilton, whenever he thought that Washington leaned in that direction. Later, Jefferson became so infuriated at Randolph, he called him "the poorest chameleon I have ever seen."

This harsh judgment was unfair to the Attorney General. He was devoted on a deeply personal level to Washington, and the President was trying to govern the nation above party politics. Randolph was following his chief's idealistic leadership. Already, Jefferson saw that this was the height of unrealism for anyone without Washington's overwhelming prestige. Hamilton was in the process of forming a political party, and there was simply no alternative, short of defeat, but to play the same rough game.

Some people have accused Jefferson of stabbing Randolph in the back, especially since his "chameleon" remark stuck to the man, and was repeated by decades of historians. But Jefferson could hardly foresee this fate, which can be attributed as much to the difficulty of finding any sharp description for Randolph's bland, legalistic personality. Jefferson's angry condemnation is more significant as evidence of the intensely emotional response Hamilton's tactics aroused in him. He was no angelic intellect, detached from the body, this Jefferson, but a man who felt as deeply as he thought. Though he struggled to maintain a balance, there were times when his feelings spoke first.

Usually, however, Jefferson's cool, realistic intellect was in control of his politics. Analyzing the vote against the bank bill in the House of Representatives, Jefferson noted the sectional quality of the division. It did not take a higher mathematician to make it clear that the southern states alone could not hope to make any headway against a Hamiltonian phalanx that included both New England and the Middle States. So with studied innocence, Jefferson, the man who repeatedly and passionately pronounced every day he spent away from his family and his beloved Monticello worse than a sojourn in purgatory, departed on an extensive tour of New York state with James Madison. It was, they piously proclaimed, a combination sightseeing and scientific expedition. An insect known as the Hessian fly was raging in the state and the American Philosophical Society, of which Jefferson had recently been elected a vice president, had been studying the pest. There were the "botanical objects" of an unfamiliar section of the country and historic military sights and scenes, such as Saratoga, Crown Point, Ticonderoga.

The trip took one month and two days and covered 920 miles. The Virginians sailed up Lake George into Lake Champlain, and returned to New York City via Vermont and Connecticut. Jefferson did indeed note numerous trees and plants foreign to his beloved Virginia. He wrote long letters home to Polly and Martha praising the beauty of Lake George and other parts of the Empire State. But he and his diminutive companion also managed to spend more than a little time studying some of New York's human fauna.

Chief among these was George Clinton, who had served six terms as Governor of New York and was a dedicated foe of Alexander Hamilton. Equally well visited was the Livingston clan, owners of vast tracts of the Hudson River Valley and furious with Hamilton because he had arrogantly double-crossed them in their intricate political dealings with his father-in-law, Philip Schuyler. Finally there were some extended conversations with Colonel Aaron Burr, a thirty-four-year-old lawyer who had served for a time as Washington's aide during the Revolution, and was now discovering that a New York organization known as the Sons of St. Tammany had some unique virtues worth cultivating on election day. Jefferson left no immediate impression of this small, suave, cool gentleman whose superb manners and brilliant mind had already made him a legal wizard to New York's men and a Don Juan to their ladies.

Still another man with whom Madison and Jefferson conferred was slight, stoop-shouldered Philip Freneau, a gifted poet and staunch friend of Republican principles, who had been Madison's classmate at Princeton. The Secretary of State offered him a clerkship for foreign languages in his department, admitting that the annual salary, $250, was almost invisible, but assuring him that the work was likewise. The money would at least keep the poet alive in Philadelphia until he had launched a newspaper that would compete with the *Gazette of the United States*. After much dickering, Freneau agreed, with one major stipulation: "in the conduct and title of the paper it will be altogether [my] own."

Returning to the new temporary capital of Philadelphia, Jefferson was astonished to discover he was already playing a prominent, totally unexpected role in the newspapers. Before he had left on his tour of New York, he had read "The Rights of Man," a vigorous defense of the French Revolution by Tom Paine. Jefferson sent his copy on to a Philadelphia printer named Smith, who professed a wish to publish it. Impulsively, Jefferson had scribbled off a covering note. "I am extremely pleased to find it will be reprinted here and that something is at length to be publicly said against the political heresies which have sprung up among us.

"I have no doubt our citizens will rally a second time round the standard of common sense."

The printer decided Paine's propaganda needed some jacket copy to help it sell. Without bothering to ask Jefferson's permission, he printed his note on the frontispiece. Jefferson had learned about it in New York and realized that the person most likely to be offended was John Adams. The close connection between Jefferson's remark about "political heresies" and the "Discourses on Davila" was unmistakable to any alert reader.

Jefferson quickly wrote to Washington explaining that "the indiscretion of a printer" had probably entangled him with "my friend Mr. Adams, for whom as one of the most honest and disinterested men alive, I have a cordial esteem . . . Even since his apostasy to hereditary monarchy and nobility, though we differ, we differ as friends should do." Jefferson soon discovered that Adams had indeed taken the remark in precisely this fashion, and pugnacious as always, had struck back. A series of anonymous articles, signed by one Publicola, had begun defending Adams and raking Paine fore and aft. Jefferson assumed Adams was the writer; a little later Madison discovered that it was Jefferson's "adopted son" John Quincy, now twenty-four, who had taken up the public cudgels on his father's behalf. He had immediately been assailed in turn by numerous Jefferson-Paine supporters hiding behind pseudonyms such as Brutus, Agricola or Philodemus. Jefferson was deeply distressed. As he had told Washington, he was "mortified to be thus brought forward on the public stage." At the same time Jefferson did not flinch from associating himself unreservedly with this "popular and republican pamphlet" which "at a single stroke" would wipe out all the unconstitutional doctrines which "their bellwether Davila has been preaching for a twelve month."

The most impressive thing about the controversy was the haste and obvious sincerity with which Jefferson tried to heal the personal breach with John Adams. He wrote Adams a candid letter, telling him the whole story of how the printer came to use his words. He did not of course refer directly to Adams' "political heresies" as he did in letters to Washington, Madison and Monroe, among others, but he was frank enough. "That you and I differ in our ideas as to the best form of government is well known to us both," he said. "But we have differed as friends should do, respecting the purity of each other's motives, and confining our differences of opinion to private conversation." He disavowed all the anonymous pamphleteers who were answering Publicola and then, with just a hint of annoyance, suggested that a large part of the uproar was due, not to his inadvertently published remark, but to Publicola's lengthy rebuttal.

Adams replied warmly to the gesture of friendship, expressing his "great pleasure" at Jefferson's letter. But he pointed to a whole list of newspapers around the nation which had seized on Jefferson's charge to slander Adams as an enemy of free institutions. The printer's indiscretion, he wrote, "had sown the seeds of more evils than he can ever atone for." Adams insisted that he had no desire whatsoever to introduce a hereditary monarchy and aristocracy into America. He was arguing for a strong centralized government, especially a strong executive, which would embody the monarchial principle in an essentially democratic way. Adams ended his letter by declaring that "the friendship that has subsisted for fifteen years between us without the smallest interruption, and until this occasion without the slightest suspicion, ever has been and still is very dear to my heart."

In the midst of this controversy, Jefferson had an interesting encounter with Alexander Hamilton. The two antagonists were still on polite speaking terms, and Hamilton startled Jefferson by telling him how much he disliked the "Discourses on Davila." The essays were causing dissension, and this weakened the federal government, an evil in Hamilton's opinion. He admitted to Jefferson that he himself did not think, "though I do not publish it in Dan or Bersheba, that the present government is not that which will answer the ends of society, by giving stability and protection to its rights, and that it will probably be found expedient to go into the British form. However, since we have undertaken the experiment, I am for giving it a fair course, whatever my expectations may be." As Jefferson's eyes widened with disbelief, Hamilton went on to say that the government's success had been far greater than he had expected, and he was therefore encouraged, because he honestly felt that every conceivable effort should be made before giving up republicanism. "That mind must be really depraved, which would not prefer the equality of political rights, which is the foundation of pure republicanism," Hamilton said, "if it can be obtained consistently with order."

Jefferson thought this conversation was so extraordinary he wrote down every word of it immediately after Hamilton departed. If Hamilton intended it for a flag of truce, Jefferson declined to recognize it. On the contrary, he thought Hamilton was trying to throw him off his track by qualifying "some less guarded expressions" which he had made to Jefferson on other occasions.

Jefferson had good reason for suspecting Hamilton was trying to repair some damaged bridges in his rear. The Secretary of the Treasury's position was no longer quite so unassailable since the July 4, 1791, opening of the Bank of the United States in Philadelphia. Assured by Fenno in his *Gazette of the United States* "that no equal object of speculation is perhaps presented at any quarter of the globe" and inflamed by rumors that the bank could be expected to pay dividends of 12 per cent or more, a small army of get-rich-quick gamblers descended on the City of Brotherly Love and when the bank's doors opened "rushed in like a torrent," practically mobbing the clerks in their eagerness to exchange hard money for the bank's stock. "If a golden mountain had been kindled, emitting from its crater a lava of the purest gold," one observer said, "the crowd would not have been greater, or exhibited more intense eagerness to share in the plunder."

Hamilton himself expressed amazement at this frenzy. He had expected several months to elapse before the bank stock was completely sold, and he had also envisioned its achieving a wide distribution throughout all the states, thereby furthering his avowed desire to strengthen loyalty to the central government. But well over 90 per cent of the buyers had come from north of the Mason-Dixon line.

Watching the wild trading of the speculators, which each day sent the stock price soaring, Jefferson and his friends felt an instinctive revulsion. Their people, the farmer majority, were getting absolutely nothing out of this orgy, while the gambling few were getting richer and richer. Even Hamilton became so alarmed that he wrote an article in *The Gazette of the United States* under the signature, "A Real Friend to Public Credit," warning that all-out speculation might in the end "be ruinous to the fortunes of many individuals, and for a time hurtful to the public credit." William Duer, who had resigned from the Treasury under Congressional fire, paid no attention whatsoever and plunged deeply on the soaring stock, borrowing money from many people in and out of the government, including Secretary of War Henry Knox. Before the year was over, the stock took a stupendous nose dive and only emergency support from the Treasury Department rescued the nation from a serious financial crisis.

V

Jefferson soon learned that Hamilton's supporters were undaunted. If anything, the Secretary of the Treasury was more of a hero in Philadelphia than he was in New York. Few among the New York rich matched the conspicuous consumption and aristocratic pretensions of Philadelphia's high society. The dominant figure was Anne Bingham, Jefferson's old friend from his Paris days. She and her husband had returned from five years abroad to build a palatial residence called The Mansion House, in Third Street above Spruce. Three stories high, with a magnificent marble staircase, and three acres of grounds full of walks, statuary, shade trees and gardens, the house was a kind of shrine to Anne Bingham's beauty. Equally sumptuous was the Binghams' country house, Lansdowne, on the west bank of the Schuylkill, a mansion which had originally belonged to the Penns.

Washington was a frequent visitor at both Bingham houses. Mrs. Bingham's father, Thomas Willing, had been a partner of Robert Morris, the financier of the American Revolution. Her sister, Elizabeth Willing, was married to William Jackson, Washington's private secretary. Morris was, of course, an equally prestigious figure in this group, with a magnificent town house and an equally splendid country estate, The Hills. He was married to Mary White, daughter of Colonel Thomas White, who had been an outspoken Loyalist in the Revolutionary era. Willing and Morris had made their original fortune in the India trade. Inevitably the politics of Mrs. Bingham and her set were violently Hamiltonian, and pro-British.

British influence extended far beyond this elite circle. Each spring and fall when ships arrived from England, boxes and bales of English dry goods were piled high before the doors of importers along Front Street. Swarms of retailers crowded the warehouses to buy up the chintzes, muslins, calicos, all in the latest fashion. When a Mr. Whitesides opened a shop at 134 Market Street, he was proclaimed to be "in the true Bond Street style" and ladies were soon pouring in, to finger the fine mulmul and jaconet muslins. Visiting Europeans were amazed at "the profusion and luxury" in "the dresses of . . . wives and daughters."

What the aristocracy thought of themselves can be glimpsed in the remark of an English traveler. "Amongst the upper circles . . . pride, haughtiness and ostentation are conspicuous; and it seems that nothing could make them happier than that an order of nobility should be established, by which they might be exalted above their fellow citizens, as much as they are in their own conceit." Wealthy Hamiltonians, such as Harrison Gray Otis of Massachusetts, found nothing to criticize in this high-toned society. "The women, after presentations to the court of George III or Louis XVI," he wrote home, "transplanted into Philadelphia society the manners of the English aristocracy and the fashions of

Paris." Soon Otis was noting with satisfaction, "Democratic gentlemen and their families, no matter how high their social qualifications, were rigidly ostracized by the best society."

As a friend of Mrs. Bingham, and a member of the President's official family, Jefferson was not a target of this ostracism. He went to dinner at Robert Morris' mansion with Alexander Hamilton and President Washington. He made his bow at Mrs. Bingham's dinners and balls, but he was no happier here than he had been in New York. Again and again he found himself the only man at a well-set, glittering table upholding the republican point of view. He had no ideas in common with men such as Theodore Sedgwick, the tall, handsome and arrogant Federalist from Massachusetts, or Pierce Butler, the cool aristocrat from South Carolina, or his rotund fellow cabinet member Henry Knox and his equally fat wife, who was fond of sneering at the manners and speech of the lower classes.

More and more Jefferson found himself preferring the company of David Rittenhouse, America's foremost astronomer and president of the American Philosophical Society, and Dr. Benjamin Rush, a pioneer in the treatment of mental illness and an ardent Republican. Equally appealing was the company of Dr. George Logan, who lived on his handsome estate, Stenton, outside Philadelphia. Ex-Quaker Logan too was a friend of the French Revolution and of Republican freedom; he was also considered one of the best scientific farmers in the nation. He had a superb library, in which Jefferson, cut off from many of his own books, loved to browse.

But none of these men were intimate friends, and a hint of Jefferson's loneliness can be seen in his invitation to Madison to board with him. "Come and take a bed and plate with me," he wrote. "I have four rooms, of which any one is at your service . . . and can be in readiness to receive you in twenty-four hours. Let me entreat you, my dear sir, to do it, if it be not disagreeable to you. To me it will be a relief from a solitude of which I have too much . . ."

Madison, fearful of compromising his independence as a congressman by becoming too publicly linked with a member of the Executive Department, declined. James Monroe was also in town to fill an unexpired term as senator from Virginia. It was another important step in this ex-protégé's career as a parliamentary man. He had his wife along, which eliminated him as a boarder—but Jefferson probably would not have invited him, anyway. Fond as Jefferson was of Monroe, there was always something paternal in their relationship. Madison alone achieved with Jefferson that mixture of mutual respect and intuitive sympathy on which great friendships rest. To his brilliance Madison added the quality Jefferson prized above all, unfailing good humor. Madison's table talk, particularly his imitations—complete with accents and gestures—of their more quirky fellow politicians often made Jefferson laugh until tears ran down his cheeks.

The only boarder Jefferson was able to muster was Jack Eppes, son of Francis and Elizabeth Eppes of Eppington. He came to Philadelphia to study under Jefferson's supervision. It was a welcome opportunity to return with interest the loving care "Aunt Eppes" had given Maria over the years. Jefferson handed the young man a rugged schedule. "Jack . . . passes from two to four hours a day at the college, completing his courses of sciences and four hours at the law. Besides this he will write an hour or two to learn the style of business and acquire a habit of writing, and will read something in history and government . . . If we can keep him out of love, he will be able to go straight forward and to make good progress."

To ease his isolation Jefferson decided to bring Maria with him when he returned from a visit to Monticello in October, 1791. At thirteen, she was blossoming into a genuine beauty. She had lost none of the charm she effortlessly exerted on everyone she met. When Jefferson stopped at Mount Vernon to discuss the Federal City with the President, Miss Jefferson instantly became Martha Washington's favorite as well as a close friend of the First Lady's high-spirited, twelve-year-old granddaughter, Nellie Custis. Jefferson wrote good-humoredly to his son-in-law, Thomas Mann Randolph, "Mrs. Washington took possession of Maria at Mount Vernon, and only restored her to me here (Philadelphia)." Maria was, he said, "immersed in new acquaintances; but particularly happy with Nellie Custis, and particularly attended to by Mrs. Washington."

Maria was no scholar, but Jefferson decided a little more school-ing would not hurt her, and he enrolled her in an academy run by a Mrs. Pine. Jefferson was soon reporting she was "perfectly at home" there, "with young friends enough to keep herself in a bustle," plus the added pleasure of visits from her old friend of London days, Abigail Adams. When Maria visited her father on holidays, she soon renewed her old friendship with Jack Eppes. "Cousin Jacky" could not help noticing that his playmate of childhood years was on her way to becoming a strikingly beautiful woman. For the moment, Jack was determined to finish Jefferson's challenging course of studies. But he filed his thoughts about Maria for important future reference.

Jefferson still found Philadelphia trying, even with Maria for company. He wrote to Martha in a melancholy mood that his thoughts of her, and "the various scenes through which we have passed together in our wanderings over the world," were the only things that alleviated the "toils and inquietudes of my present situation." He yearned to exchange Philadelphia's "labor, envy and malice" for Monticello's "ease . . . domestic love and society; where I may once more be happy with you, with Mr. Randolph, and dear little Anne, with whom even Socrates might ride on a stick without being ridiculous."

"Dear little Anne" was his first grandchild, born earlier in 1791. To a jesting letter on the subject from Elizabeth Eppes, Jefferson replied, "I received with real pleasure your congratulations on my advancement to the venerable corps of grandfathers, and can assure you with truth that I expect from it more felicity than any other advancement ever gave me. I only wish for the hour when I may go and enjoy it entire."

For the time being, however, Jefferson took up what looked like a very permanent residence in Philadelphia. The furniture, the books, the works of art which he had purchased in France arrived not long after he had established himself in a spacious rented house in Market Street, west of 8th Street, three blocks away from Washington's Presidential mansion. No less than 80 packing cases were deposited on the docks, consigned to Mr. Jefferson, and it took 27 wagonloads to deliver them to his residence. Except for 15 crates of books, the bulk of this staggering cargo was furniture.

Some of it Jefferson sent on to Monticello, but most of it he used to equip his rented Philadelphia house. The exquisite Louis XVI chairs and tables, the French and Italian art on the walls made it clear that this friend of the common man could compete with Mrs. Bingham in the realm of taste, if he was so inclined. But Jefferson never let good taste twist into snobbery. Roughnecks like Congressman William Branch Giles of Virginia were as welcome to lounge on his satin cushions as swells like Pierce Butler.

Soon Jefferson discovered that no one could make this elaborate household run as smoothly as the redoubtable Petit, and he was pleading with him to emigrate. James Hemings could cook the food *à la français* well enough, but only Petit had the eye for buying the right ingredients. After negotiations worthy of a treaty of commerce, Petit finally agreed to come, and Jefferson was soon enjoying true French cuisine once more, and introducing it to his political followers. When Patrick Henry, back in Virginia, heard reports of what people were eating at Jefferson's table—lip smacking pot au feu, coq au vin, a strange but delicious new dessert called ice cream—the Tribune of the People decided to make a political issue out of it. Jefferson, he roared, had "abjured his native vittles."

Jefferson thought this was funny, and told the story for years. Nobody else paid much attention to Henry, whose political instincts failed him badly when he carped at Jefferson's menus. The Secretary of State's civilized approach to dining, art, and culture was a subtle part of his appeal as a political leader. He offered to the average citizen precious proof that the "good, the wise, and the rich," as Hamilton's friends liked to style themselves, did not have a monopoly on learning and taste. At a time when the Hamiltonians were attempting to make democracy synonymous with boorish ignorance, Jefferson provided the humble farmer and the unlettered workman with a stunning refutation.

VI

In spite of his momentary exposure in the newspaper clash with John Adams, Jefferson remained a largely invisible opposition leader. James Madison was still the man out front. The two friends had dinner together at least once a week and remained in close and concerned agreement on the state of the nation. When Hamilton submitted a "Report on Manufactures" to Congress, calling for the establishment of government-supported industries, Madison led a ferocious attack on the idea in Congress. The lawmakers tabled it, to Hamilton's considerable chagrin. Jefferson did not conceal his exultation.

Before the spring of 1792 was over, William Duer and his followers had borrowed themselves into another stock-market crash. The prince of speculators himself wound up in jail and there were other signs that the Hamiltonians, in Jefferson's hopeful words, were "tottering." Another reason for his optimism was Philip Freneau's *National Gazette*. For the first nine months of his paper's life, Freneau had played it rather cool, confining his criticism to indirect hints, and running articles by Madison and others that were more educational than political. But on April 2, 1792, he published a blast by Madison asking, *Who are the real friends of the Union?*. Naturally, Madison said they were *not* public officials who encouraged speculation and tried to pervert the Constitution. No, the Union's true friends were those who supported Republican policies and resolutely opposed "a spirit of usurpation and monarchy."

Throughout the spring of 1792, Freneau steadily escalated his criticism of Hamilton, until on July 4 he published a highly satiric set of rules for transforming the United States into a monarchy. They included:

Get rid of Constitutional shackles.
Persevere and indoctrinate the people with the notion of titles.
Interest legislators in speculation and speculators in legislation.
Establish a bank of enrichment of those who are to inherit the kingdom.
Arrogate all political power to the federal government under the slogan of "national welfare."
Secure a rich manufacturing class by making laws in its interest.

There was no possibility of mistaking Freneau's target, and Hamilton writhed with rage. Nothing was going well for him. His department was still under fire in Congress, with James Madison in command of the sharpshooters as usual. Reports from distant sections of the country made it clear that the fall elections were running heavily against his followers, who were already beginning to be called Federalists, for their devotion to a strong executive. It was easy enough to connect Freneau, Madison, and a certain tall, thin third party who remained in the background, his hostility masked by politeness. Brooding over his woes, Hamilton decided he sniffed a plot to destroy him and—he considered the two things synonymous—to undermine the government.

True to his military instincts, Hamilton decided that the best defense was a good offense. If his mouthpiece Fenno could not answer Freneau, except to splutter expletives such as "crash brain" and "grumbletonian," the Secretary of the Treasury would do the job himself and he would not stop with annihilating the Republican mouthpiece. He would simultaneously confound and put down the man who was "continually machinating against the public happiness"—Thomas Jefferson.

Early in August, 1792, Hamilton unlimbered his heavy rhetorical artillery in the *Gazette of the United States* under the signature "An American." He accused the Secretary of State of hiring Freneau to publish a paper aimed at subverting the government and wrecking the Constitution. These charges were the opening round in an all-out newspaper war. Freneau and other Republicans, including Attorney General Edmund Randolph, replied to Hamilton behind pseudonyms such as "Aristedes." Hamilton blasted back under the signatures of "Catullus" and "Scourge." Before the verbal smoke cleared, Jefferson had been called "the most intriguing man in the United States," "an intellectual voluptuary," "the inspiring turbulent competitor," "a man of profound ambition and violent passions," and a "revolutionary" wearing the mask of a modest, retiring philospher.

While this acrimony filled the air in Philadelphia, Jefferson vacationed at Monticello, playing hobbyhorse for his granddaughter Anne, and enjoying the company of his two daughters and his son-in-law. Without so much as lifting a finger on his own behalf, or writing a line, he was becoming the foremost leader of the anti-Federalist party. This was the paradoxical result of Hamilton's decision to single him out for special attack. That Jefferson was the intellectual leader of this unformed party, which for the moment was really more a floating consensus of feelings and ideas, was to some extent true. But other men—George Clinton in New York, James Madison in Congress—were in far more powerful positions to exert political leadership. By singling out Jefferson as the supposedly evil genius behind and above all the rest, pulling invisible strings and whispering subversive words into his cohorts' ears, Hamilton inadvertently added cubits to his antagonist's stature as a national figure.

VII

George Washington was acutely distressed by this newspaper war. He shot letters to both Jefferson and Hamilton, asking for explanations. From both men he got lengthy and vehement defenses of their respective positions. Jefferson's words made it clear that his distance from the verbal fusillades did not make Hamilton's accusations any easier to bear. He slashed back, wielding his pen like a rapier.

"I have never inquired what number of sons, relatives and friends of Senators, Representatives, printers or other useful partisans Colonel Hamilton has provided for among the hundreds of clerks of his department, the thousand excisemen [tax collectors] at his nod spread over the union . . ." That Hamilton would make an affair of state out of his appointing a poet as translating clerk at a salary of $250 a year was simply astonishing. John Fenno was the official printer of the U.S. Senate and of the Bank of the United States, government contracts worth $2,500 a year.

It was true, Jefferson admitted, that he had encouraged Freneau to publish a paper. But he could "safely declare" that his expectations from that paper looked only to "the chastizement of the aristocratical and monarchial writers and not to any criticisms on the proceedings of the government." He was ready to swear an oath before heaven "that I never did by myself or any other, directly or indirectly write, dictate or procure any one sentence or sentiment to be inserted in his or any other gazette to which my name was not affixed or that of my office."

Jefferson contrasted his policy with Hamilton's. There was no doubt of the identity of the gentleman who signed himself *An*

American. "Is not the dignity and even the decency of the government committed when one of its principle ministers enlists himself as an anonymous writer? . . ."

Summing up, Jefferson stated one of his deepest convictions. "No government ought to be without censure; and where the press is free, no one ever will. If virtuous, it need not fear the fair operation of attack and defense. Nature has given to man no other means of sifting out the truth." The government, he said, should neither "know nor notice" its supporters or its censors because it would be "undignified and criminal to pamper the former and persecute the latter."

As far as his personal reputation was concerned, Hamilton's abuse was intolerable. It was precisely the sort of thing he had dreaded when he accepted Washington's offer to become Secretary of State. It confirmed a decision he had already intimated to the President. He was retiring at the end of Washington's first term (which had only six months to run). He would make no attempt to reply to Hamilton's attacks in the meantime. "A regard for your quiet," he told the President, "will be a sufficient motive for my deferring it till I become merely a private citizen when the propriety or impropriety of what I may say or do may fall on myself alone."

This initial impulse to flee from a brawl reveals that the split in Jefferson's psyche between the scholar-recluse and the man of action was still unresolved. Once before, when flight seemed about to overwhelm the fight in his nature, James Madison had rescued him, in a spirit of friendship. This time the rescuer was George Washington, with an appeal that personified the man—duty.

VIII

On October 1, 1792, Jefferson, enroute to Philadelphia, stopped over at Mount Vernon. He was exultantly telling himself that it was almost the last time he would have to make the exhausting journey. In his mind, the letter he had written to Washington had become an official resignation.

The President sat with his Secretary of State on the broad veranda, facing the green lawn and the placid, peaceful Potomac.

In such a setting, it was almost inevitable that Washington spoke first about retirement. But it was not Jefferson's retirement. It was his own. He was "quite undecided" about accepting a second term. Only if there was strong evidence that his aid was necessary "to save the cause to which he had devoted his life" would he make the sacrifice. Unfortunately, friends whom he had asked to sound public opinion reported there was "a universal desire" for him to continue. Most of this news was from the North. What did Jefferson think of the South? Jefferson quietly told him that "there was but one voice there"—and that was for him to continue.

Jefferson did not have to add what he had already told Washington earlier that year. In a penetrating analysis of the political situation he had pointed out that the original opposition to the Constitution had come chiefly from the South. Since 1789, Congress had done nothing to soothe southern prejudices; creditors were largely in the North, debtors in the South. Only a small shift was needed to place the majority of southerners "on the other side"—against the Constitution. "This is the event at which I tremble," Jefferson had written, "and to prevent which I consider your continuing at the head of affairs as of the last importance. The confidence of the whole union is centered in you . . . north and south will hang together if they have you to hang on."

All right, said Washington, he would run again. But if he was prepared to make the sacrifice, didn't that mean that Jefferson should follow his example? The Secretary of State could not possibly pant for the peace of Monticello any more ardently than the President yearned for the tranquillity of Mount Vernon. Jefferson, learning the hard way why the British called Washington "the old fox," was all but hoisted on his own petard. He protested, rather feebly, that his role in the government could not be compared to the President's. As he had said in an earlier letter, it was "a thing of mere indifference to the public" whether he or someone else was Secretary of State.

Washington did not agree. He felt it was important to keep Jefferson in the administration because his opinions operated as "a check" which kept things "in their proper channel," and prevented them "from going too far." The "things" he was obviously referring to were the policies of Alexander Hamilton. As for the conflict between Jefferson and Hamilton, he had "never suspected it had gone so far in producing a personal difference." Could not he act as a mediator?

It was difficult to tell George Washington that not even he could negotiate a truce in this particular war. Jefferson could only sit there while the President tried to blunt some of the shafts he had flung at Hamilton. Washington did not think the Treasury's system had evil tendencies, nor did he think Congress had been corrupted by it. A certain amount of interested spirit was inevitable in any legislature, the President argued. As for the over-all results of Hamilton's system, only history could finally judge it. But as far as he was concerned, he had seen "our affairs desperate and our credit lost" and then seen the situation almost miraculously reversed by the measures of the Secretary of the Treasury. Jefferson was forced to drop the argument. It was all too clear that the President felt he was personally committed to Hamilton's policies.

Back in Philadelphia, Jefferson was dismayed to hear his closest political friends—Madison, Monroe, Giles—seconding Washington's summons to stay on the job. They told him that if he bowed out of the government while Hamilton was on the attack, his reputation as a public man would be lost forever. A retreat now would be interpreted by too many people as a confession of guilt at worst and a cowardly surrender at best. Mournfully Jefferson wrote to Martha, on January 26, 1793, that he had been "under an agitation of mind which I scarcely ever experienced before" because of this advice. He had "perfect reliance in the disinterested friendship" of those who had advised him and there was no doubt that they had shaken his determination—"a determination which I had thought the whole world could not have shaken." More and more it began to look like he would be "detained here into the summer."

When Jefferson made this reluctant decision, he had packed most of his furniture and books and shipped them to Monticello. Some local papers had already announced his resignation. Glumly, he rented a small house on the banks of the Schuylkill and informed Washington that he would stay as Secretary of State for another six months at least.

Two months later came news from Europe that made Jefferson's decision to stay on the job pivotal in the history of the infant nation. He must have sensed, instantly, as he read the dispatches from his ambassadors, and heard the tumult outside his windows in Philadelphia's streets, that his feud with Hamilton was about to be flung onto the world stage, embroiling them in issues that involved the very survival of the Republic. England and revolutionary France were at war.

IX

For the previous six months, the French Revolution had been a sputtering bomb beneath the surface of American life. Most Americans seemed to favor France when the revolutionary National Assembly declared war against Austria and Prussia in April, 1792. The crowned heads of those nations had made threatening gestures on behalf of beleaguered King Louis XVI. When Parisian mobs set up an insurrectionary commune and the assembly, under pressure from these extremists, abolished the monarchy and transformed itself into the National Convention which proclaimed the First Republic, again, most Americans seemed to applaud the change. When news of French victories against the invading Austrian and Prussian armies reached America there were public celebrations from Boston to Charleston. Church bells rang and barrels of rum were emptied to toast America's old ally, fighting, so it seemed, against a coalition of kings with the same spirit and principles that had animated America's revolution.

At the same time, the growing criticism of Hamilton's policies by Freneau and other newspapermen had awakened much of the nation to the possibility of a conflict between aristocracy and democracy in America. The Secretary of the Treasury and his friends were quick to get the message that local cheers for liberty, equality and fraternity were also aimed at the Federalists, the so-called party of privilege. Hamilton was soon inveighing against the "passion for a foreign mistress, as violent as it is irregular." A southern Federalist lamented the "almost idolatrous devotion of a great majority of the people for the French Republic."

Philip Freneau in his *National Gazette* was almost frenzied in his support of the Revolution. He publicly gloried in the name "Jacobin," the extremist party in the French National Assembly, wrote resounding poetry in praise of France and savagely attacked the heavily Federalist U.S. Senate for permitting portraits of Louis XVI and Marie-Antoinette to remain on the walls of its chamber. The headstrong poet even accused the Federalists of hoping for "the extirpation of liberty in France."

Then the French National Convention committed a blunder—at least as far as Americans were concerned. They found Louis XVI guilty of treason and cut off his head. When the news reached the United States it changed the minds of thousands of Americans about the Revolution. Church bells tolled, women wore black roses for the martyred King and the Republicans were astonished by the switch in national mood. One Republican spokesman wrote from Charleston that he was disgusted to see how "the death of one man" could "so affect the generality of the people" of his city. More than a few Philadelphians reacted with outrage when Freneau, growing more radical every day, republished in his paper a brutal poem which first appeared in the Pittsburgh *Gazette*, "Louis Capet Has Lost His Caput."

When the news that America's old enemy, England, had joined the coalition of kings, public emotion swung violently back to a pro-French extreme. The streets of Philadelphia were jammed with marchers shouting French slogans. Children mockingly sang the "Marseillaise" beneath the windows of Federalist merchants. In Charleston, South Carolina, a new French ambassador, Edmond Genet, was greeted with wild enthusiasm.

Now it was the Federalists' turn to lament the instability of the man in the street—something they had a predilection for doing anyway. Alexander Hamilton looked on the impulse for war against England as nothing less than destructive madness. The Hamiltonian system depended totally on the flow of cash and commerce from England and he immediately went to work to protect this vital lifeline. He wrote to fellow New Yorker, John Jay, Secretary of State under the old Articles of Confederation, to get his advice on a proclamation of neutrality. He wrote to Washington, away on a brief trip to Mt. Vernon, urging him to return to Philadelphia at once.

All this feverish activity on Hamilton's part preceded by several

days Jefferson's calm letter to the President, informing Washington of the grim news that war had broken out between America's
old ally and old enemy. Jefferson had also calmly stated his policy
recommendation. It would be necessary "to take every justifiable
measure for preserving our neutrality." But he wanted to renew his
favorite tactic of playing off the two combatants, to America's
maximum advantage. Even before the cabinet convened, Hamilton
was undermining this approach by playing his undercover game
with the British ambassador, assuring him that he and not the
Secretary of State had decisive influence on the foreign policy of
the United States. By the time Washington arrived in Philadelphia,
Hamilton had drawn up for him a list of "queries," thirteen in
number, for the President to submit to his cabinet. They covered
all aspects of the crisis confronting the nation, but, naturally, they
were heavily slanted in favor of the pro-British policies Hamilton
was recommending.

When Jefferson received his copy of the thirteen queries, he
immediately saw Hamilton's intrusive shadow, even though the
President had attempted to disguise the source by writing the
queries out in his own hand. "It was palpable from the style, their
ingenious tissue and suite, that they were not the President's,"
Jefferson noted in his diary. "They were raised upon a prepared
chain of argument. In short, that the language was Hamilton's and
the doubts his alone."

The doubts were all cast upon the validity of the Treaty of
Alliance and Commerce which America had signed with France in
1778, in return for the financial and military aid that had won the
Revolution. Under the terms of the treaty the United States was
supposed to support France in any defensive war. More immediately pressing was the question of whether Edmond Genet should
be received as Minister of the Republic of France.

The next morning, April 19, 1793, the cabinet met at 9 o'clock
in the President's office, with Jefferson in a fighting mood. The
first question on the list was: "Shall a proclamation be issued and
shall it embody a declaration of neutrality?" Hamilton seized the
floor and argued for an immediate, formal proclamation. Jefferson
bluntly contradicted him. He said it would be "better to hold back
the declaration of neutrality as a thing worth something to the

powers of war, that they would bid for it and we might reasonably ask a price." Great Britain still maintained those garrisons in forts along the western borders of the United States. Here, if ever, was a chance to use diplomatic leverage to pry loose these interlopers, who were continually arousing and often arming the Indians against the United States.

Hamilton, who had already assured the British minister of America's neutrality, insisted that silence was too dangerous. Great Britain might misconstrue it as a gesture of alliance with France and commit acts of war against American ships that would force the United States into the conflict. Attorney General Randolph and Secretary of War Knox sided with Hamilton. Jefferson fell back to his next line of defense and argued that if a "statement of public policy" must be issued it should omit the word neutrality. Hamilton yielded the point and neutrality, it was agreed, would not appear in the proclamation.

This was at best a minor victory; the main argument, the decision to issue the proclamation, had gone Hamilton's way. But Jefferson, eying the thirteen questions, was playing a shrewd game. As he explained it later in a letter to James Madison, it was "not expedient" to oppose the proclamation "altogether" because he did not want to "prejudice" his position on the next and far more crucial question—whether the new French ambassador, Edmond Genet, should be received, and whether such a reception should be "absolute" or "qualified." This, Jefferson told Madison, was "the boldest and greatest [question] that ever was hazarded," and it called for "extremities" if Hamilton prevailed.

To deny recognition of Genet would be nothing less than denying the legitimacy of the French Republic—an act which would place the American Republic on the side of the coalition of kings. The mere thought filled Jefferson with wrath. He had already written Gouverneur Morris, America's ambassador in Paris, sending official instructions to recognize the National Assembly as the duly constituted government of France. "We surely cannot deny to any nation," he had written Morris, "that right whereon our own government is founded, that everyone may govern itself according to whatever form it pleases, and change these forms at its own will." Hamilton gave ground before Jefferson's anger and agreed that they could not avoid receiving Genet. But should there be some "qualifications" in this reception?

Here, of course, was the meat of the matter, and Hamilton launched into a long speech aimed at convincing the President and the rest of the cabinet that France's change in government had made the treaty between the two nations void and this judgment should be made clear when Genet was received. Secretary of War Knox immediately agreed with Hamilton, "acknowledging," Jefferson noted in his diary, "like the fool he is that he knew nothing about it." Jefferson steadily maintained that the treaty remained valid. Randolph sided with him until Hamilton quoted an opinion from Vattel, an authority on international law, supporting his notion that a change in the nature of a government was grounds for voiding an alliance. Randolph declined to accept Vattel quoted out of context, and the President decided it might be best if written opinions on the question were submitted.

Hamilton sent in an immensely wordy disquisition. Jefferson's opinion was far briefer, but fighting on a field he knew well, he demolished Hamilton's arguments one by one, burying his expert, Vattel, with counterarguments from three other international lawyers. Jefferson even quoted Vattel himself against Hamilton, pointing out that the sage had written elsewhere: "He who does not preserve a treaty is assuredly perfidious since he violates his faith." Randolph came down on Jefferson's side of the argument in an independent opinion, and the President made the momentous—and to Hamilton galling—decision: the treaty was valid and Ambassador Genet would be received without any qualifications or quibbling.

"The President told me," Jefferson noted with some satisfaction in his cabinet diary, "he never had a doubt about the validity of the treaty; but that since a question had been suggested he thought it ought to be considered." Washington also advised Jefferson (and no doubt Hamilton) that "he thought it would be as well that nothing should be said of such a question having been under consideration."

Jefferson understood precisely what the President meant. In a letter to James Monroe, he had already noted the ominous domestic result of the British-French conflict. "The war has kindled and brought forward the two parties with an ardor which our own interests merely could never excite." He told Monroe how a French frigate had captured a British ship off the capes of the Delaware and escorted her into Philadelphia. "Upon her coming into sight thousands and thousands of the *yeomanry* of the city crowded and covered the wharves. Never before was such a crowd seen there; and when the British colors were seen *reversed* and the French flying above them, they burst into peals of exultation."

Here is graphic evidence that if Hamilton's views had prevailed, and the government had refused to receive Genet, there might easily have been an armed uprising in the United States. No government could have openly flouted the strong feelings of so many of its citizens, without a violent reaction. Hindsight also makes it clear that the French would have quickly aided this civil war with men and guns. They had already successfully revolutionized several European governments, and converted them into satellites in this same inside fashion.

Washington, struggling to stay out of party politics, regarded this violent Republican enthusiasm for France with distaste and alarm. Jefferson, committed even deeper than he yet realized to his struggle with Hamilton, could not—and did not—take such an aloof attitude. Even without Hamilton's opposition, Jefferson's years in France, his intense devotion to human freedom, would have made such an attitude impossible. He participated wholeheartedly in those Republican cheers for France.

At the same time, here, as he did throughout his life, Jefferson made a sharp distinction between his official words and actions, as a public servant, and his private feelings. He agreed completely with Washington that a war would demoralize and probably destroy America's fragile experiment in responsible government. With evident approval he wrote Ambassador Morris in France, "No country perhaps was ever so thoroughly against war as ours. These dispositions pervade every description of its citizens whether in or out of office." He added that the American people "cannot perhaps suppress their affections, nor their wishes. But they will suppress the effects of them so as to preserve a fair neutrality."

Jefferson continued to regret that he had not been allowed to bargain with the British minister for "the broadest neutral privileges." But he was far more incensed by Alexander Hamilton's efforts to reduce the American position to what Jefferson called "a mere English neutrality." In another letter to James Monroe, Jefferson told how "every inch of ground must be fought in our councils to desperation, in order to hold up the face of even a sneaking neutrality." Hamilton, he said, "is panic struck if we refuse our breech to every kick which Great Britain may choose to give it. He is for proclaiming at once the most abject principles such as would invite and merit habitual insults."

George Washington's enthusiasm for the French revolution diminished steadily after his favorite Frenchman, Lafayette, lost favor and had to flee from the fickle French mobs into the hands of his Austrian enemies. In France, many Americans who saw at firsthand the Revolution's brutal excesses began to change their minds even more drastically. Chief among these was Ambassador Gouverneur Morris, who had a New York grandee's predilection for aristocracy even before the French began to spill torrents of blue blood from their guillotines.

More disturbing to Jefferson was the defection of his ex-protégé, William Short, who had stayed behind in Paris as chargé d'affaires, and then, thanks to Jefferson, moved to The Hague as American minister to Holland. Short had fallen hopelessly in love with Rosalie, wife of the Duke de la Rochefoucauld, Jefferson's good friend. Both the duke and Rosalie's brother, also a Jefferson friend, were beaten to death by a French mob. Short was soon writing violently critical dispatches to Jefferson about the ominous tendencies of the Revolution.

These reports drew a stinging rebuke from Jefferson, which included the most emotional political statement he ever made. He admitted that some innocent persons had fallen "without the forms of trial," and that his "own affections have been deeply wounded by some of the martyrs to this cause." But rather than see it fail, "I would have seen half the earth desolated. Were there but an Adam & Eve left in every country & left free, it would be better than as it now is."

These words have been quoted by Jefferson critics for over a century, to indict him for bloodthirsty radicalism at worst and instability at best. They only tell us how personally involved

Jefferson was with the outcome of the French Revolution. By no stretch of fact or imagination would Jefferson have ever recommended such a program as a public man. Here once more the division between his personal feelings and public acts was even more sharply delineated. Those who refuse to accept this first principle of politics may call Jefferson a hypocrite. Jefferson, that most sophisticated of politicians, would have been amused by such a childish notion. Doing his thing, acting out his emotions was hardly the lodestar of his political life. On the contrary, he kept these emotions firmly subordinated to one political principle: the interests of America. A few years later, a shrewd Frenchman summed up Jefferson for his country's leaders. "Although a friend of liberty and science, although an admirer of the efforts which we have put forth to break our chains and dissipate the cloud of ignorance which oppresses the hope of humanity Jefferson . . . is an American, and by just so much, he cannot be sincerely our friend."

The new French ambassador, Edmond Genet, had to learn this lesson the hard way. His education would also give Jefferson some sleepless days and nights.

X

While Hamilton and Jefferson wrangled over his reception, Genet had been proving himself a very strange ambassador. From the moment he stepped off the frigate *Embuscade* in Charleston harbor, he acted more like an imperial legate to a conquered colony than an intermediary between free and equal republics. Handsome and headstrong, he spoke excellent English, and saw himself as a magnetic popular leader. The Francophiles in Charleston feted him with a round of dinners, which swelled his already overinflated ego to monstrous proportions.

At first Jefferson was deceived by Genet's apparent generosity. In an ebullient letter to James Madison, he wrote, "It is impossible for anything to be more affectionate, more magnanimous than the purport of his mission. . . . He offers everything and asks nothing." When he was presented to Washington, Genet suavely declared that he had no desire to invoke American aid in the war against Great Britain, as the 1778 Treaty of Alliance gave him the right to do. In the contrary, all he wanted was a "more liberal" treaty of commerce which would enable American goods, and especially American food, to flow into France's poorly stocked larder.

But it soon became apparent that Citizen Genet, as he styled himself, was prepared to ask for a great many things. On May 27, 1793, he coolly requested Jefferson to pay the entire residue of the American debt to France, some $2,500,000, although only one-fifth of this amount was payable in 1793. Washington passed this request on to Hamilton, who returned a predictably scathing negative. Meanwhile, Jefferson was being bombarded by complaints from the British minister about the depredations of American privateers commissioned by Genet at Charleston.

Simultaneously, Philip Freneau in his *National Gazette* plunged toward extremism. He condemned the Proclamation of Neutrality and boldly called for war on behalf of France. He ridiculed Washington and suggested that Hamilton and his party had extorted the proclamation by threatening to behead the President. This only multiplied Jefferson's difficulties with Washington.

Visiting the President to discuss the draft of a letter to the French government acknowledging Genet's arrival, Jefferson was amazed when Washington objected to the Secretary of State's description of the United States as "a republic." This was, apparently, an excuse to involve Jefferson in a discussion of the current political situation. In a moment Jefferson was listening to a Presidential lecture. If anybody wanted to change the government of the United States into a monarchy Washington was sure it was only a "few individuals" and that no man in the country would "set his face against it more than himself." But he was far more worried about danger from another quarter—anarchy. Waving a copy of the *National Gazette*, the President denounced "that rascal Freneau" in a voice that Jefferson described as "sore and warm."

Later, in his diary, Jefferson made it clear that he had gotten Washington's message—"that I should interpose in some way with Freneau, perhaps withdraw his appointment as translating clerk to my office. But I will not do it. His paper has saved our constitution, which was galloping fast into monarchy, and has been checked by no one means as so powerfully as by that paper." He admitted that "some bad things have passed through it to the public, yet the good have preponderated immensely."

Freneau's extremism did Jefferson no good in his daily struggles with Hamilton over the details of America's neutrality. Jefferson argued that the British ships seized by Genet's Charleston privateers belonged to the captors and the privateers themselves should be allowed to continue operating from American ports. Hamilton vociferously opposed both positions, Randolph wavered and Washington ruled against Jefferson, ordering restitution or compensation to the British, and the closing of American ports. As a slight concession to Jefferson, he agreed to permit the French to sell their captured prizes in American ports—a privilege that was denied the British.

Meanwhile Freneau grew wilder. In four "open letters to the President of the United States" appearing between the 1st and 12th of June, he abused Washington's foreign policy unmercifully. Had the President forgotten that his office was "temporary"? Did he feel himself "so buoyed up by official importance as to think it beneath his dignity to mix occasionally with the people?" Why had he allowed himself to be lulled by "an opiate of sycophancy?"

While Freneau ranted, Genet was swiftly proving himself an even more nightmarish liability. In impertinent tones, he rejected Jefferson's polite communication, informing him that America wanted no more privateers commissioned in her ports. He was, Genet informed the dismayed Secretary of State, willing to defer to the President's "political opinions" until Congress assembled and rejected them. With unbelievable effrontery Genet warned the government to respond to the call of the people whose "fraternal voice has resounded from every quarter around me!" Jefferson had to submit this and similar letters to the President and the cabinet. Hamilton, followed as always by Knox, found it almost ridiculously easy to convert them into anti-French ammunition.

These harassments were almost more than a sensitive man could bear. When James Madison urged him to reconsider his determination to resign, the scholar-recluse who was always hiding inside Jefferson the politician saw his opportunity and unleashed a cry of anguish to his friend.

The motion of my blood no longer keeps time with the tumult of the world. It leads me to seek for happiness in the lap and love of my family, in the society of my neighbors and my books, in the wholesome occupations of my farm and my affairs, in an interest or affection in every bud that opens, in every breath that blows around me, in an entire freedom of rest, of motion, of thought, owing account to myself alone of my hours and actions. What must be the principle of that calculation which should balance against these the circumstances of my present existence—worn down with labors from morning to night, and day to day; knowing them as fruitless to others as they are vexatious to myself, committed singly in desperate and eternal contest against a host who are systematically undermining the public liberty and prosperity, even the rare hours of relaxation sacrificed to the society of persons in the same intentions, of whose hatred I am conscious even in those moments of conviviality when the heart wishes most to open itself to the effusions of friendship and confidence, cut off from my family and friends, my affairs abandoned to chaos and derangement, in short giving everything I love in exchange for everything I hate, and all this without a single gratification in possession or prospect, in present enjoyment or future wish. Indeed, my dear friend, duty being out of the question, inclination cuts off all argument (. . .) let there be no more between you and me on this subject.

For the moment, escape was impossible. In vain Jefferson tried to correct Genet's absurd ideas about how the American government worked. There was no hope of Congress repudiating George Washington, and as for the French ambassador's idea of appealing to the people, this was even more fantastic. Genet replied by declaring his disgust with the American government and challenging the Secretary of State to throw aside "diplomatic subtleties" and explain matters "as a Republican." Jefferson did not even try to answer this absurdity, but merely informed the President of it at the cabinet meeting of June 22. At this same meeting came fresh evidence of Genet's arrogance. Only a few blocks from the President's house, the *Little Sarah*, a British brigantine captured by the French, was being transformed into a privateer with fourteen cannon already aboard. Genet was flinging defiance in the very face of the American government.

Jefferson requested Governor Thomas Mifflin of Pennsylvania to investigate the allegations about the *Little Sarah* in more detail.

Pennsylvania authorities soon confirmed that the ship was being outfitted for war. Alexander James Dallas, the Secretary of the Commonwealth of Pennsylvania and a devoted Republican, went to Genet's house at midnight on July 6 to warn him against ordering the ship to sea. Genet told him off in wildly extravagant language, reviving his threat of appealing over the heads of the authorities to the people. Dallas notified Jefferson, who rushed from his house on the Schuylkill for a personal confrontation with Genet. He too could barely get a word into the torrent of revolutionary rhetoric the ambassador flung in his face.

Genet declared he would convene Congress himself if Washington did not do it and scornfully denounced the American system of government, when Jefferson tried to explain it to him once more. Jefferson went home to write a mournful letter to Madison. "Never in my opinion," he said, "was so calamitous an appointment made as that of the present Minister of France here. Hotheaded, all imagination, no judgment, passionate, disrespectful and even indecent toward the P. in his written as well as verbal communications. . . . He renders my position immensely difficult."

Genet refused to guarantee that the *Little Sarah* would not sail. But in a memorandum to Washington, Jefferson said he felt the ambassador had "with look and gesture" given him his assurance as a gentleman that she would stay in the harbor. This did not satisfy Hamilton, and the next day Jefferson found himself locked in a furious cabinet battle with the Secretary of the Treasury. With the support of Secretary of War Knox, Hamilton wanted to erect a battery on Mud Island in the Delaware, with orders to fire on the *Little Sarah* if she put to sea. Washington was out of town, on a brief trip to Mount Vernon, and Attorney General Randolph was also absent, so Jefferson had to fight alone.

He rose to the challenge with a fierce combination of eloquence and logic. To risk an artillery duel with the *Little Sarah* was madness, he snapped. The vessel simply was not worth the possible consequences—war with France. Wasn't it inconsistent to "rise at a feather against friends and benefactors" when for ten years Americans had been putting up with the British habit of impressing American seamen for duty on their warships, and arrogantly seizing and searching American ships? Above all Jefferson said he "would not gratify the combination of kings with the spectacle of the two only republics on earth destroying each other for two cannon"—the number of guns on the *Little Sarah* which the Pennsylvania investigators had been able to certify were American made.

Jefferson won the argument, and no cannon were moved to Mud Island. The next day, Genet notified Jefferson that he was sending the *Little Sarah* to sea. The dismayed Secretary of State collapsed with an obviously psychosomatic fever. Genet had proved himself totally, finally, absolutely impossible.

Struggling out of his sickbed, on the following day Jefferson trudged to Washington's handsome brick mansion to confront a gloating Hamilton and a scowling President. Washington had already written the Secretary of State a very snappish letter about "the case of the *Little Sarah*." Jefferson sat quietly while Hamilton lamented and declaimed over Genet's plot to provoke a war between England and America.

Then Hamilton began recommending Genet's immediate recall, in "peremptory terms." Secretary of War Knox went even further, and proposed to revoke his diplomatic standing immediately. Jefferson came to life. Far better, he said, to forward the outrageous letters Genet had been sending the American government to Paris, with "friendly observations." If the French government had any brains at all, they would quietly recall Genet. Washington decided for the time being to do nothing.

Day after day, while the President sat, a silent, undecided judge, Jefferson fought Hamilton's demand for a hard line with the French government. Simultaneously he was keeping headstrong followers such as James Monroe in bounds by condemning Genet's conduct as "indefensible by the most furious Jacobin." He was also telling Madison to answer Hamilton's latest newspaper series, which brilliantly defended his pro-English neutrality under the pseudonym Pacificus. "Cut him to pieces in the face of the public," snarled Jefferson the politician.

Hamilton now urged Washington to lay all of Genet's correspondence before the Congress—which would mean instant publication in the newspapers. Jefferson blocked this move by threatening to resign. Back went the Secretary of the Treasury to demanding

Genet's recall in "peremptory terms." Again Jefferson disagreed, standing firm against his three fellow secretaries, and even the President, who was obviously leaning toward Hamilton.

The climax of this struggle came on August 2 when Hamilton opened the cabinet meeting with another three-quarter-hour harangue. Once more he demanded Genet's public embarrassment, and dwelt at length on the headstrong ambassador's latest *gaffe*— the founding of a "Democratic Society" alarmingly similar to the Jacobin clubs which had pushed the French Revolution into extremism.

Again Jefferson fought back with all the logic and rhetoric he could command. Hamilton wanted "to make the President assume a station of the head of a party, instead of the head of the nation," he declared. Genet's role in America was already exciting violent party conflict. It would be disastrous to let this division become a contest between the President and Genet. Once more he begged his fellow cabinet members and the President to remember that "friendly nations always negotiate little differences in private." On and on Jefferson talked, but he could see from the set of Washington's jaw that he was losing the argument. Secretary of War Knox, hoping to administer the *coup de grâce*, brought up one of the more atrocious newspaper assaults on Washington, which described the President's funeral, after he had been guillotined.

Washington exploded. "The President," Jefferson wrote in his diary ". . . got into one of those passions when he cannot command himself; ran on much on the personal abuse which had been bestowed on him; defied any man on earth to produce one single act of his since he had been in the government which was not done on the purest motives . . . that *by God* he had rather be in his grave than in his present situation; that he had rather be on his farm than to be made emperor of the world." On and on stormed the inflamed Chief Executive, turning at last on "that rascal Freneau" who sent him three copies of his paper every day as if he hoped to convert the President of the United States into his "distributor."

Washington's rage finally petered out, and he sat there in a semi-incoherent daze. Even Hamilton was appalled by a glimpse of the human volcano which smoldered beneath the President's iron self-control. The Secretary of the Treasury did not try to revive the argument. This meant Washington reverted to his usual policy, of permitting a department head to have his own way on matters within his domain. Thanks to Knox's heavy-handed overreaching, Jefferson won a victory by default. He immediately went to work on the delicate problem of writing the letter requesting Genet's recall.

While Jefferson toiled at his Schuylkill house, he received an unexpected visit from George Washington. On July 31, Jefferson had informed the President by letter that he wished to resign at the end of the month. A very distressed Chief Executive confronted him now with a plea to stay until the end of the year. He revealed to the surprised Secretary of State that three or four weeks ago Hamilton had written to him announcing his determination to retire. With surprising bitterness, Washington lamented that he had allowed Hamilton and Jefferson to talk him into another term, and now when he needed them most they were deserting him. But at least Hamilton was staying until the close of the next session of Congress. The President was obviously suggesting that Jefferson ought to do likewise.

Washington worried aloud about the "fermentation which seemed to be working on the mind of the public" and possible difficulties with a new Congress "perhaps of a different spirit." Indirectly, but not very subtly, Washington was telling Jefferson that he badly needed him in the government, because as long as he was there, he exercised a moderating influence on the extremists among his fellow Republicans. Fulminate though they might against Hamilton, and even against the President, they could not, with Jefferson in the cabinet, picture the government as entirely in the grip of a single party. As a symbol as well as a reality, Jefferson had become a vital stabilizing figure in Washington's attempt to govern turbulent young America.

A long discussion of Jefferson's possible successor followed, with no obvious candidate. The President's first choice was James Madison, but he knew he could never persuade him to take the office. A half dozen other men were ruled out for political and personal reasons. Then, having neatly boxed Jefferson in from every angle, Washington again asked him to stay till the end of the year. Eventually he knew he would have to release him but "like a man going to the gallows" he wanted to put it off as long as he could.

Once more, Jefferson really had no choice. His deep admiration for Washington, and his own very real appreciation of the political crisis, forced him to yield. He would make a flying visit to Monticello early in the autumn, and return to his labors until December 31. Within three days of this decision, the wisdom of Washington's persuasion was graphically apparent.

Hamilton and his followers recklessly escalated the Genet affair by revealing in a New York newspaper the Frenchman's threat to appeal to the people over Washington's head. The result, of course, was precisely what Hamilton had foreseen. In town after town and city after city, from Boston to Charleston, a chorus of indignation buried Genet and the few hapless Republicans who were foolish enough to attempt to defend him. "Is the President a consecrated character, that an appeal from his decisions must be considered criminal?" squawked Freneau, one of the diehards. The answer, when that President was George Washington, was obviously an overwhelming yes.

A more stubborn political leader might have tried to rally his followers in a desperate do-or-die stand behind Genet. But the day before the Hamiltonian revelation Jefferson had written a long confidential letter to Madison in Virginia, recommending that Republicans execute an immediate withdrawal from the disastrous ambassador. Genet was "absolutely incorrigible" and there was no choice but "quitting a wreck which could not but sink all that would cling to it." The party should "approve unequivocally of a state of neutrality . . . to abandon Genet entirely, with expressions of strong friendship & adherence to his nation & confidence that he has acted against their sense." To this shrewd practical advice Jefferson added one of his aphoristic gems, as true today as it was in 1793. "In this way we shall keep the people on our side by keeping ourselves in the right."

Madison swiftly conferred with James Monroe, and the two Republican chieftains organized a series of town meetings in Virginia which produced sets of resolutions along the lines Jefferson suggested, dumping Genet but attempting to retain popular feeling for France.

In Philadelphia, meanwhile, Jefferson had finished the letter requesting Genet's recall. The President and the cabinet went over it paragraph by paragraph. Although Jefferson felt in the end that "the expressions of affection" for the cause of France he had worked into it "were a good deal taken down," his reaction was similar to the pain he exhibited when Congress had manicured the Declaration of Independence. The document was essentially unchanged, and remains today one of the most skillful diplomatic papers in American history. Jefferson demolished Genet simply by quoting from the erratic ambassador's own letters. The Frenchman's contemptuous expressions about Washington and the American government were reported at length, but instead of denouncing them in the "peremptory" tones that Hamilton demanded, Jefferson smoothly added, "We draw a veil over the sensations which these expressions excite. No words can render them; but they will not escape the sensibility of a friendly and magnanimous nation, who will do us justice. We see in them neither the portrait of ourselves, nor the pencil of our friends; but an attempt to embroil both; to add still another nation to the enemies of his country, and to draw on both a reproach, which it is hoped will never stain the history of either."

On this victorious note, Jefferson closed his career as Secretary of State. On December 15, 1793, he was writing to Maria, who had preceded him to Monticello to escape an outbreak of yellow fever in Philadelphia: "I hope to be with you all about the 15th of January no more to leave you." On December 22 he told Martha that the President had made, the day before, "what I hope will be the last set at me to continue; but in this I am now immovable, by any considerations whatever." On the last day of 1793 he submitted his formal resignation to the President. "I carry into my retirement a lively sense of your goodness," he told Washington, "and shall continue gratefully to remember it." Washington in reply said, "The opinion which I had formed of your integrity and talents and which dictated your original nomination has been confirmed by the fullest experience."

Oddly, the publication of the letter recalling Genet (as part of a folio of diplomatic correspondence submitted to Congress) enabled Jefferson to depart with something approximating popularity among the Federalists. One of Hamilton's closest friends told the Secretary of the Treasury that the letter had "blotted all the sins of [Jefferson] out of the book of our remembrance; and with the sentiments and temper Jefferson appears at present to possess we would much regret that he should quit his post."

But not even regrets from this unexpected quarter could stop Jefferson now. By January 5, 1794, his bags were packed, his remaining furniture shipped. He said good-by to Madison and Monroe, both of whom were in the new Congress. In Madison's hands would now be the public defense of the Republican position. Jefferson honestly felt that his colleague was the better man for such a task. He was going home, he devoutly told himself, for good. Home to build Monticello into the mansion he had envisioned when his imagination was fired by his face-to-face contact with the architectural virtuosity of Europe. Home to domestic concord and love, "the best ingredient in human happiness." Home to pursue his studies of the flora and fauna of Virginia, to restore his neglected farms, to read books, and perhaps to write some.

Behind him he left a record of achievement as Secretary of State that ranks him with the greatest Americans to hold that crucial office. He had, against strenuous and often vicious opposition, charted a foreign policy that was neither servile nor arrogant. More important for Jefferson personally, he had met Alexander Hamilton, the most formidable of opponents, in bruising, almost daily combat. The scholar and theorist had, momentarily, triumphed, and Jefferson was retreating. But the realist, the practicing politician had been immensely toughened by the experience. Moreover, Jefferson had had a priceless opportunity to study the inner workings of the new Republic at the summit. Though he would have vehemently denied it as he rode south to Monticello, it was an experience too precious for a realistic man to waste. As James Madison, that perennial student of his complex friend, might have put it in his oblique but penetrating style—there was more than a little chance that Mr. Jefferson was not permanently retiring from politics.

BOOK FOUR

Birth of

a Candidate

A T MONTICELLO, politics vanished totally from Jefferson's immediate horizon. For more than three months he did not write a single letter on the subject. He was busy planning the rehabilitation of his farms and enjoying the company of his first two grandchildren, Anne Cary Randolph, now three years old, and Thomas Jefferson Randolph, two. Like many a grandparent before and since, he found himself playing baby-sitter, while the young mother and father visited at another Randolph plantation. At one point he wrote somewhat plaintively that the children "will forget you if you do not return soon." But on the whole he enjoyed the toddlers immensely, as can be seen from a letter he wrote to Martha during one of her absences in the following year. The two youngsters, he assured her, "have never had even a finger-ache since you left us. Jefferson is very robust. His hands are constantly like lumps of ice, yet he will not warm them. He has not worn his shoes an hour this winter. If put on him, he takes them off immediately and uses one to carry his nuts, etc. in. Within these two days we have put both him and Anne into mockaseens, which being made of soft leather, fitting well and lacing up, they have never been able to take them off . . ."

To Horatio Gates he wrote, "The length of my tether is now fixed for life between Monticello and Richmond." He urged his old teacher George Wythe to visit and enjoy his library, which he somewhat immodestly declared was "now certainly the best in America." For three years Jefferson lived this comfortable, charming country life with his two daughters, his grandchildren and the usual stream of visiting relatives.

Back in Philadelphia the political caldron continued to bubble, and not a little of its contents were Jefferson's ideas. Before he departed from the capital, he had submitted to Congress a report on America's commercial relations with England, France and other foreign nations. It clarified with a wealth of devastating statistics England's continuing attempts to keep the United States in a colonial position, by imposing all sorts of humiliating restrictions on American shipping. Madison made the report the basis for a series of resolutions calling for retaliation against England and the controversy fanned to furious proportions anti-British feeling among the mass of Americans.

With incredible stupidity, England's ministers added fuel to this conflagration by committing more outrageous depredations against American ships on the high seas. The Republican Party rode this emotion to new heights of popularity. These developments were thoroughly satisfying to Jefferson and strengthened his conviction that the nation was doing very well without him. He plunged ever deeper into the management of Monticello. To a friend whom he had last seen in France, Jefferson wrote that his days were spent "in my farmer's coat, immersed soul and body in the culture of my fields, and alive to nothing abroad except successes of the French Revolution, and the welfare of my friends." He had plenty of work to do. Of the 10,647 acres he carefully listed in his farm book for the year 1794, little more than 2,000 were under cultivation. In an era when new lands were constantly opening up in the west, it was difficult if not impossible to get good men to spend their days as employees on another man's farm. Thus Jefferson, Washington, and Madison were perpetually struggling with inept or indifferent overseers who failed to plant or harvest on time, ignored intelligent crop rotation and often stole or wasted shocking proportions of what they harvested. With no other source of income, and the perpetually mounting interest of the Wayles debt as well as other notes to pay, it was a life-or-death matter for Jefferson to organize his lands profitably.

By now, Jefferson was no longer a young man. Long hours on horseback in all weather brought on a debilitating attack of inflammatory rheumatism. For three months he was unable to leave the house and without his immediate supervision, the overseers once more lapsed into their usual pattern. In his farm book for

1795 he gloomily noted that "the fall of 1794 had been fine, yet little plowing was done . . ." In desperation, Jefferson sent for his French *maître*, Petit, whom he had left behind in Philadelphia, and persuaded this faithful foreigner to take on the unlikely task of superintending Monticello.

Petit got things moving on the farm side, and Jefferson turned his ever restless mind to another potential source of income. He started a nailery at Monticello, training a dozen young slave boys, under his personal supervision, until they were producing a ton and a half of nails a month. Jefferson used persuasion, praise, and cash bonuses to boost his monthly production to such a startling level so quickly. Here, as elsewhere at Monticello, he never permitted an overseer to whip a man. In fact he soon made one of the best workers, a rugged commanding Negro named Isaac, the nailery boss.

Once a nailery worker stole several hundred pounds of nails and hid them in a wooden box, hoping to sell them at an opportune moment. He was caught and brought before Jefferson for punishment. Weeping, he begged for forgiveness. Jefferson turned to the overseer and said: "Ah, sir, we can't punish him. He has suffered enough already."

Sadly, Jefferson told the fellow how disappointed he was in him, but hoped that he had learned his lesson. Then he sent him back to the shop. There the chastened thief said to Isaac, "Well, I'se been aseeking religion a long time but I never heard anything before that sounded so or made me feel so as I did when Master said, 'Go and don't do so anymore'; and now I'se determined to seek religion till I find it." A few days later he asked to be baptized.

Jefferson was not benevolent to the point of sainthood, however. He could display his frontiersman's temper when the occasion called for it. One day he told one of his younger servants to go to the Charlottesville post office for his letters and papers. The boy came back and informed the master of Monticello that there was not a horse available except the blood pair, used for Jefferson's carriage. Though it was against his own inclinations, Jefferson told the boy to ask Jupiter, his coachman, to let him have one of those horses for the brief errand. The boy came back a few moments later to report that "Old Jube" had kicked him out of the stable, declaring that nobody could run his horses on errands. Jefferson smiled, and told the boy to explain to Jupiter that the matter was urgent and he was under orders from Jefferson himself. Again the boy returned, eyes wide, to report that Jupiter had declared that "neither of his horses should go for anybody."

"Tell Jupiter to come here," said Jefferson. Rarely had anyone at Monticello seen such a look on Jefferson's face. Jupiter, when he appeared, took one glance and began backing water desperately, pleading that he could not keep his precious horses the way Jefferson wanted them, if they were to be "ridden round by boys." Fortunately, by now Jefferson had regained control of his temper, and he let his favorite off with a warning not to be quite so blunt the next time about "telling his mind."

Jefferson sold his nails direct to retailers and fellow farmers throughout Virginia, and sometimes used them for barter with merchants. But most of the time he was his own best customer, because he was devoting a major portion of his and his workmen's energies to rebuilding Monticello. Jefferson undertook nothing less than a complete restructuring of the house which enlarged it to almost three times its original size. His library, which occupied much of the second floor, was to be brought down to the first floor and housed in a new south wing. The entire roof was to be ripped off and a dome of Jefferson's own design was to rise above a reorganized second floor, which would be used exclusively for bedrooms. At the same time, his artistic instincts inclined him to make this commodious Virginia mansion look like a one-story house. He wanted the building to fit snugly on its hilltop and resemble the elegant one-story town houses he had visited in Europe. He specially liked the way these houses eliminated "great staircases . . . which are expensive & occupy a space which would make a good room in every story." Monticello's staircases, he decided, would be small and hidden from the visitor's eye. He was equally interested in Monticello's landscaping, and during his first year home set 2,400 cuttings of weeping willow to border the lower paths of the mountain, and sketched plans for "terrases" of fig and other fruit trees, strawberry beds and a vineyard.

Busy as his isolation was, it nevertheless produced an unexpected effect on Jefferson. In the language of modern psychology, he simply could not adjust to the change from turbulent sophisticated Philadelphia to the simpler world of Monticello. Several years later he admitted in a confidential letter to his daughter Maria that the experience had completely reversed his long cherished vision of idyllic privacy on his mountain. He spoke of being "severely punished" by a "state of mind" that made him "anti-social and misanthropic." It left him "unfit for society" and "uneasy" when he met outsiders. That inner war between the scholar-recluse and the realistic politician was obviously not ending the way Jefferson had anticipated. After a decade of steady growth, the man of action was not going to be displaced by a mere change of scene. He was serving notice on Jefferson that he was here to stay.

II

The world of politics was equally persistent in pursuing the would-be retired grandfather. James Madison sent as many as three letters a week from Philadelphia, and Monroe and other Republican leaders wrote frequently. Thus Jefferson continued to get an insider's view of what was happening in the nation's capital.

He watched with indignation and alarm the Hamiltonian reaction to the so-called Whisky Rebellion. The citizens of western Pennsylvania had never looked with favor upon the Secretary of the Treasury's tax on whisky. They regarded the brew as more than a source of idle pleasure; for them it was their economic staff of life. They had challenged the tax first by nonpayment, then by assaulting federal collectors, and finally by an armed uprising that sent federal officials fleeing for their lives and threatened the town of Pittsburgh with riotous destruction. There was bold talk of joining the western counties of Virginia in a new independent nation.

When a Presidential proclamation failed to restore peace, Washington reluctantly yielded to Hamilton's urgings, and assembled a militia army of 15,000 men. The sight of this armed host turned the extremist leaders' backbones to jelly, and most fled to Spanish territory. Elsewhere in the area, moderate Republicans led by Albert Gallatin, a Swiss immigrant who had already risen high in the councils of the party, persuaded many of the would-be rebels to submit without violence. To Jefferson the entire episode reeked of Hamiltonian power grabbing, especially when the Secretary of the Treasury took it upon himself to accompany the troops.

Jefferson was even more incensed when Washington, in his message to Congress later that year, associated the rebellion with certain "self-created societies"—the Democratic Societies which had been founded throughout the country during Genet's emotional reign. These were, of course, all stanchly Republican, and Washington's denunciation hit them like a blast of fire. Nothing, neither individuals nor groups nor even a whole party, could withstand Washington's immense popularity, Madison sadly informed Jefferson, and the Democratic Societies withered away in the glare of the President's disapproval.

In a reply to Madison, Jefferson called the denunciation of the Democratic Societies an "extraordinary act of boldness" on the part of the "monocrats." He did his utmost to exonerate Washington. "It was wonderful indeed that the President should have permitted himself to be the organ of such an attack on the freedom of discussion, the freedom of writing, printing and publishing . . ." But the denunciation made it clear to Jefferson and everyone else that Washington had moved much closer to Hamilton's position. Edmund Randolph, who had succeeded Jefferson as Secretary of State, would soon be driven out of the cabinet by a Federalist smear that he was in the pay of the French minister, thus removing the last vestige of Republican influence on the President. Randolph found that not even Washington's friendship could protect a man without a party, in the escalating political ferocity of the day.

There was vast alarm at Monticello when Madison, newly married to vivacious Dolley Payne Todd, began to wonder if retirement might give him more happiness than battling Washington's prestige.

"Hold on then, my dear friend," Jefferson begged him, "that we may not ship wreck." With shrewd insight into the new Mrs. Madison's social inclinations, he urged her to keep her husband on the job "for her own satisfaction and the public good." At the same time Jefferson struggled to keep the more headstrong Republicans in a reasonably moderate frame of mind. He assured the splenetic William Giles that "the tide against our Constitution is unquestionably strong, but it will turn. . . . Hold on then like a good & faithful seaman till our brother-sailors can rouse from their intoxication & right the vessel." Nor was it just of his party that Jefferson was thinking. The threat of the dismemberment of the fragile republic was always before his eyes. "Make friends with the Transalleghenians," he urged Giles. "They are gone if you do not. Do not let false pride make a Tea Act of your excise law."

Scarcely was the whisky crisis over when a new political hurricane struck the new nation. In a desperate attempt to avert war with England, Washington had sent John Jay, Chief Justice of the Supreme Court, as a special envoy to resolve the mounting tension between the two nations, and settle all the outstanding differences. Jay returned with a treaty that was woefully deficient in British concessions, except for the evacuation of the western forts and some minor relaxation of British barriers against American ships in the West Indies trade. To Jefferson and Madison, this was the final sellout, the denouement of Hamilton's policy of appeasing Great Britain.

Madison blasted it in Congress, and Jefferson sent scorching opinions of it hurtling from his mountaintop, like flaming arrows. To a fellow Virginian, he reverted to his favorite metaphor of the ship and described his neighbors "in considerable fermentation" because . . . "while all hands were belowdecks mending sails, splicing ropes and everyone at his own business, & the captain in his cabin attending to his log book & chart, a rogue of a pilot has run them into an enemy's port." When Hamilton took to the newspapers to defend the treaty as the only alternative to war, Jefferson once more urged poor Madison to do battle with him. "Hamilton is really a colossus to the anti-Republican party," Jefferson admitted. "Without numbers, he is an host within himself . . . in truth when he comes forward, there is nobody but yourself can meet him."

Though Madison manfully obeyed Jefferson's summons, and Republicans in the Senate and the House declaimed against the treaty and their newspapers denounced it and George Washington in the most violent terms, Jay's treaty was ratified by the Senate on June 24, 1795. The Republicans continued to fulminate against it, and as late as March, 1796, Madison led Republican congressmen in an attempt to torpedo the agreement by denying the appropriation for enforcing its provisions. This proved to be a mistake. Washington made it a personal as well as a constitutional test, by bluntly refusing to submit papers relating to the treaty to the House. The Federalists shouted that the Republicans were trying to shove the country into war with Great Britain, on behalf of their patron France. Sadly Jefferson wrote to Madison, "The people have everywhere been made to believe that the object of the House of Representatives in resisting the treaty was war, and have thence listened to the summons 'to follow where Washington leads.' "

III

The battle over Jay's treaty made it grimly clear to Jefferson that the success of the Republican cause was by no means guaranteed. Madison, in the thick of the fight, had known this all along, and he welcomed a hint that Jefferson dropped on the subject late in 1794. Under no circumstances should Madison retire, Jefferson said, "Unless to a more splendid and more efficacious post. There I should rejoice to see you . . ." Madison immediately replied that his mind was shut "against the admission of any idea such as you seem to glance at." He declined to say more in a letter, preferring to wait for "the latitude of a free conversation." But he told Jefferson, "You ought to be preparing yourself . . . to hear truths which no inflexibility will be able to withstand." This was a diplomatic prelude to telling Jefferson that he was the only man who could lead the Republican Party to victory in the Presidential election of 1796.

Both men knew that Washington would not run again. The President made this clear to the nation at large when he published his Farewell Address on September 19, 1796, in the Philadelphia *Daily American Advertiser*. Jefferson continued to insist wistfully that Madison was still his choice, but he had to admit the political facts of life. Madison's battles with Hamilton in Congress and in the press had made him too much of a partisan figure. Moreover, it was becoming more and more apparent that the Federalists would put forward Vice President John Adams as their candidate and the Republicans could not hope to withstand him without Jefferson, who shared the golden glories of 1776. So Jefferson reluctantly allowed himself to become a candidate.

But we should not accept this reluctance too literally. Washington had made nonambition for office the prevailing Presidential style. In 1796, and for many years thereafter, no man who hoped to become President campaigned for the job. This smacked of egotism and ominous lust for power. The decision to run required no exertion on the part of Jefferson, or any other candidate, only silence. The one act permitted a potential candidate was public withdrawal, and this Jefferson conspicuously failed to do. His silence was in itself a confession that the man of action had triumphed over the scholar-recluse, and Jefferson was more than ready to abandon Monticello's isolation for the great world once more.

Throughout the campaign, neither Jefferson nor Adams made a single speech propounding their policies, nor even a single comment on each other's respective merits. But their partisans in the newspapers were not so gentle. Republican editors industriously pictured Adams as "The Duke of Braintree," a monocrat in love with the British Constitution, while Federalists viewed Jefferson as an atheistic Francophile who yearned to introduce the guillotine into American politics. Some struck even lower blows, blaming Jefferson for Virginia's helplessness during Cornwallis' invasion, and sneering that he showed a lack of "fortitude" when he fled Monticello before Tarleton's cavalry. Others said that Jefferson showed a "weak, wavering, indecisive character" that might fit him to be a professor in a college, president of a philosophical society or even a Secretary of State, but not the Chief Executive of the nation. The Republicans matched these absurdities by ominously pointing out that John Adams had sons who might try to succeed him to the Presidential "throne" while Jefferson had only daughters.

These attacks could only affect the moron vote. Jefferson and his party were far more seriously damaged by a new French ambassador, Pierre Adet, who boldly tried to influence the election by publishing a series of letters in the newspapers, strongly hinting that Jay's treaty had made it obligatory for France to declare war on the United States, unless Jefferson was elected. This gave the Federalists a marvelous new club to belabor the Republicans once more as the war party, and the enemies of Washington and peace. "Adet's note," groaned Madison to Jefferson, "is working all the evil with which it is pregnant."

Behind the Federalist scene, Alexander Hamilton was playing a game of his own. Forced to acquiesce in John Adams' candidacy, he secretly hoped to throw the election to the Federalist Vice Presidential candidate, Thomas Pinckney of South Carolina. Under the idealistic system laid down by the framers of the Constitution, each state elector had two votes. The rise of political parties had not been envisioned; it was simply assumed that the electors would choose the two best men available and the man who received the most electoral votes would be President, the runner-up Vice President. Hamilton connived with Federalists in South Carolina to vote for Pinckney, but to throw away their second vote which should have gone to Adams. Assuming that other Federalists would vote down the line for the party's two candidates, Pinckney would come out eight votes ahead of Adams and be the legally elected President—and, incidentally, Alexander Hamilton's puppet.

Unfortunately for Hamilton, news of the plot leaked out, thanks largely to the political shrewdness of Jefferson's Vice Presidential candidate, Aaron Burr. The suave New Yorker had recently distinguished himself as a U.S. senator and as a politician who combined practicality with a very large ambition. He had boldly put himself forward as a Vice Presidential candidate in 1792, before John Adams had decided to run again, and had proved himself a potent vote getter in New York, thanks to his organization of the less well born under the banner of the Sons of St. Tammany. The Republicans had rewarded him with the nomination for Vice President. But Burr liked to dabble with both parties. He warned New England electors of Hamilton's scheme and they made sure they threw away enough second votes to guarantee that their favorite son, John Adams, would run well ahead of Pinckney.

The race between Adams and Jefferson was a seesaw affair with Jefferson sweeping the South, and Adams New England, dividing the middle states and finally coming down to Pennsylvania, the last state to vote (there was no single Election Day) with Adams ahead. If Jefferson carried the Quaker State, he could, on a strict party vote, hope to tie Adams in the Electoral College.

Jefferson won Pennsylvania by one half of one per cent, thanks largely to the "whisky boys" of the western counties. But to everyone's amazement, one Republican elector, sentimentally remembering Adams' revolutionary services, threw one of his two votes to him. The same thing happened in Virginia, and in North Carolina, states the Republicans also carried. The final vote was Adams 71, Jefferson 68. Pinckney got 59 votes, and Burr, a relative stranger to southerners, won little support below the Mason-Dixon Line and finished a poor fourth with 30. John Adams was President by 3 votes in what Alexander Hamilton grumpily called "a sort of miracle."

Madison, on the job in Philadelphia, foresaw the result before the final returns trickled in. He sent a warning to Jefferson, "You *must* reconcile yourself to the secondary as well as the primary station if that should be your lot."

Jefferson's reply is the best possible proof of his ever-present concern for the stability of his country. The talk of electors north and south throwing away second votes had already made him wonder if he and John Adams might finish in a tie and the final choice of a President depend on the House of Representatives. There, he noted, "it seems also possible that the Representatives may be divided. This is a difficulty from which the Constitution has provided no issue. It is both my duty and inclination, therefore, to relieve the embarrassment should it happen; and in that case, I pray you and authorize you fully to solicit on my behalf that Mr. Adams may be preferred. He has always been my senior, from the commencement of our public life and the expression of the public will being equal this circumstance ought to give him the preference."

When the Adams miracle was confirmed, Jefferson reiterated his satisfaction with the final decision. "I have no ambition to govern men," he told Edward Rutledge of South Carolina. "No passion which would lead me to delight to ride in a storm."

IV

Thinking of John Adams as President of the United States, Jefferson's generous spirit overflowed, and he sat down and wrote the warmest letter a defeated Presidential candidate has ever written to his successful opponent.

Dear Sir—The public & the papers have been much occupied lately in placing us in a point of opposition to each other. I trust with confidence that less of it has been felt by ourselves personally. . . . Our latest intelligence from Philadelphia at present is of the 16th inst. but tho' at that date your election to the first magistracy seems not to have been known as a fact, yet with me it has never been doubted. . . . I never one single moment expected a different issue; and tho' I know I shall not be believed, yet it is not the less true that I have never wished it. . . . It is impossible that you may be cheated of your succession by a trick worthy of the subtlety of your arch-friend of New York who has been able to make of your real friends tools to defeat their and your just wishes. Most probably he will be disappointed as to you; and my inclinations place me out of his reach. . . . No one then will congratulate you with purer disinterestedness than myself. . . .

Jefferson closed with the hope that Adams would be able to "shun for us this war by which our agriculture, commerce & credit will be destroyed." If he succeeded, "the glory will be all your own." He hoped Adams' administration would be "filled with glory, and happiness to yourself and advantage to us." After Jefferson finished this letter, he had an attack of second thoughts. Was it too effusive? Would Adams believe it or try to see a trick hidden in this rush of genuine emotion? He decided to send it to Madison for a first reading with instructions to forward it if he approved.

Madison read, pondered, and advised against sending it. He told Jefferson that Adams was already aware of his kind feelings. There was also the problem of Adams' "ticklish" temper. But most important, in Madison's opinion, was the possibility that Adams might be a far from satisfactory President to the Republicans. Giving him such a testimonial now might prove in the future "distinctly embarrassing."

Both Jefferson and Madison hoped they could work closely with Adams and drive a wedge between the President and his followers, and the rest of the Federalist Party, who tended to gravitate toward Hamilton. But Jefferson made it clear to Madison that he would under no circumstances participate in the "executive cabinet." Both duty and inclination "shut that door." With a flash of old bitterness, he told Madison, "I cannot have a wish to see the scenes of '93 revived as to myself & to descend daily into the arena like a gladiator, to suffer martyrdom in every conflict." As to duty, the Constitution made it clear that the Vice President was simply the presiding officer of the Senate, and that was all Jefferson intended to be. Whatever work they might do with Adams would be in the area of party politics.

Jefferson almost declined to appear for his inauguration as Vice President. The journey in the month of February, he told Madison, would be "a tremendous undertaking." He toyed with the idea of taking the oath at Monticello, "or wherever else I could meet with a Senator." Finally "respect to the public" forced him to decide to brave the icy rivers and muddy roads of winter. But he added, "I hope I shall be made a part of no ceremony whatever. I shall escape into the city as covertly as possible." This is precisely what he did. He drove his phaeton and pair to Alexandria and took the public mail coach the rest of the way to Philadelphia, arriving on the 2nd of March.

An interesting contrast between Jefferson and the Federalists can be glimpsed in the comment that Jefferson made to the French philosopher Constantin Volney, explaining why he preferred to take public stage coaches. It gave him "an opportunity of plunging into the mixed characters of my country, the most useful school we can enter into, and one which nothing else can supply the want of." Around the same time Joseph Cotton Smith, Federalist lawmaker from Sharon, Connecticut, told how he and four fellow Federalists hired a private carriage in New York so they could "enjoy each other's company without democratick annoyance." In the public stage coach, he explained, they would "have to endure the presence of social inferiors"—the passengers often included "squalling children and Republicans smoking cigars."

The Vice Presidency was not the only office Jefferson was coming to Philadelphia to accept. The president of the American Philosophical Society, David Rittenhouse, had died and the members of this small but potent intellectual powerhouse agreed that there was only one possible successor, Thomas Jefferson. He was sworn in the day after he arrived. But he waited a week, until the political inaugurations were over, before submitting to the society one more proof of his stature as a scientist. He had carried with him from Monticello the bones of a huge animal, recently found in a cave in Virginia's Greenbrier County. Jefferson named it Megalonyx or "Great Claw," and wrote a paper on it in which he compared it to a more complete skeleton recently discovered in Paraguay which had been identified as an early ancestor of the sloth. He was excited by the discovery because the size of the bones confirmed for him his old argument with Buffon about the relative size of European and American animals. Here was a sloth the size of the mammoth! Though he did not realize it at the time, Jefferson was founding another American science—paleontology.

For the moment, politics was more important. Madison had reserved a room for him at his boardinghouse, and after depositing his bags, Jefferson called on the President-elect. The next day, John Adams returned the call and made a startling gesture of conciliation and co-operation.

As a result of the Jay treaty, American relations with France had sunk to an unparalleled low. Washington, in the closing days of his administration, had recalled Ambassador James Monroe, and sent Charles Cotesworth Pinckney of South Carolina, a Federalist, as a replacement. The French Directory, the latest inheritors of the revolution, refused to receive Pinckney, and ordered him out of the country. This was only a tiny step short of war, and John Adams now had the power to take this step. But he made it clear to Jefferson that he abhorred the possibility almost as much as the most pro-French Republican. Would Jefferson be willing to undertake a special mission to France, to heal the breach?

The two old friends debated whether the Constitution permitted the Vice President to undertake such a role, and decided it probably did not. Jefferson said he had no desire ever to go abroad again, thinking no doubt of what a sea voyage would do to his rheumatism. Adams then suggested sending James Madison and Elbridge Gerry, a Massachusetts Independent, and asked Jefferson to intercede with Madison. Jefferson warned him that he was unlikely to succeed, but promised to try.

A few days later, the two men met again at dinner with ex-

President Washington. As they walked back to their lodgings, Jefferson told Adams that he had attempted to persuade his fellow Virginian, but Madison's dread of long sea voyages was as inveterate as ever. With scarcely concealed embarrassment, Adams told Jefferson that it was just as well. "Some objection" to Madison's nomination had been raised which he had not foreseen. They parted at the corner of 5th and Market Streets and Jefferson noted wryly in his diary, "he never after that said one word to me on the subject, or ever consulted me as to any measures of the government." Jefferson decided that "Mr. Adams in the first moments of the enthusiasm of the occasion . . . forgot party sentiments. . . . That Monday, the 6th of March, being the first time he had met his cabinet, on expressing ideas of this kind, he had been at once diverted from them and returned to his former party views."

The truth was not far from this shrewd guess, although Jefferson was being a little unkind to his old friend from Massachusetts. That morning the President had indeed met with his cabinet. Hatchet-faced Timothy Pickering, Secretary of State, was a dedicated detester of France; so was suave Oliver Wolcott, Alexander Hamilton's ex-assistant, and now his successor as Secretary of the Treasury. The Secretary of War, mild-mannered James McHenry, devoutly believed that Alexander Hamilton was the greatest man in the universe; the Attorney General, Charles Lee, was an archconservative whose sole qualification was his Virginia birth. All of these gentlemen regularly consulted with Alexander Hamilton before venturing so much as an opinion to the President. In some respects, they were far more intransigent than the party leader himself. While Hamilton in New York was recommending Madison as a member of a mission to France, Pickering, Wolcott and company threatened to resign en masse the moment John Adams suggested appointing him. Adams backed off and dropped the idea. It was a fateful turning point in the history of John Adams' administration. If he had accepted resignations on the spot, he would have been a far different President.

Instead, surrounded by such counselors, Adams drifted inevitably into the Federalist orbit around Alexander Hamilton. He never made another attempt to work with Jefferson, and the excesses of party politicians on both sides soon drove the two old friends farther and farther apart. One of the first explosions came in May, 1797, when Jefferson returned to Philadelphia for a special session of Congress. A year before, he had written a letter to his ex-neighbor Philip Mazzei, who had retreated to his native Tuscany. Incensed over the Jay treaty and the general drift of the American government toward war with France, Jefferson had let his emotions guide his pen.

The aspect of our politics has wonderfully changed since you left us. In place of that noble love of liberty, & republican government which carried us triumphantly thro' the war, an Anglican monarchical, & aristocratical party has sprung up, whose avowed object is to draw over us the substance, as they have already done the forms of the British government. The main body of our citizens, however, remain true to their republican principles; the whole landed interest is republican and so is a great mass of talents. Against us are the Executive, the Judiciary, two out of three branches of the legislature, all the officers of the government, all who want to be officers, all timid men who prefer the calm of despotism to the boisterous sea of liberty, British merchants & Americans trading on British capitals, speculators & holders in the banks & public funds, a contrivance invented for the purposes of corruption, and for assimilating us in all things to the rotten as well as the sound parts of the British model. It would give you a fever were I to name to you the apostates who have gone over to these heresies, men who were Samsons in the field & Solomons in the council, but who have had their heads shorn by the harlot England. In short, we are likely to preserve the liberty we have obtained only by unremitting labors & perils.

Mazzei had unwisely translated this personal communication into Italian, and published it in a local paper. An alert reader had forwarded it to Paris, where it had been translated into French. From there it bounded across the Atlantic, was retranslated into English, and published in arch-Federalist Noah Webster's *Minerva* in New York. In the course of these complicated travels, the word "forms" had been mistranslated into "form"—which gave the distinct impression that Jefferson considered the Constitution itself a tool of the British interests. Many years later Jefferson explained that by *forms* he meant "the birthdays, levees, inauguration pomposities, etc. on which the Federalists doted."

Webster denounced the letter as treasonable, and he and other Federalist editors took up the cry that Jefferson, in his reference to Samsons in the field, had slandered Washington. Again, this was partisan politics at its worst. Although Jefferson had in his private letters become increasingly critical of Washington about the time of the Jay treaty, believing him to be almost totally the captive of the Hamiltonians, he never altered his admiration for Washington's fundamental integrity. The Samsons to whom he referred were the numerous ex-soldiers, from General Knox through Hamilton to McHenry, who were in the Federalist camp.

The letter raised a tremendous political storm. Jefferson's first impulse was to answer it, pointing out the important mistranslations, and an extra sentence which the French editor had added making him sound blatantly pro-French as well as anti-English. Monroe, writing from New York, urged Jefferson to follow this course, but Jefferson himself hesitated, and finally decided to say nothing. Really to defend the points he made in the letter would have taken a full-length book, and would have forced him to uncover the confidential cabinet meetings of Washington's administration. The best course was silence. A conversation with Madison confirmed this difficult choice, and for the next months Jefferson grimly continued to say nothing, while Federalist papers called upon him either to avow or disavow the "abominable letter."

Meanwhile, President Adams' speech at the special session of Congress dilated at length upon the French refusal to receive Charles Cotesworth Pinckney and denounced the Directory's farewell statement to outgoing Ambassador Monroe, in which they had pointedly praised Monroe and by implication his Republican friends, and arrogantly rebuked the American government. The President also called on Congress to strengthen the Navy and reorganize the militia. Jefferson considered this performance much too provocative, in the delicate state of Franco-American relations. But he approved Adams' decision, a few weeks later, to send three special envoys to France, in a last effort to resolve the crisis.

Separated from Adams by his Hamiltonian cabinet, Jefferson nevertheless urged Elbridge Gerry to accept the President's appointment to the special French mission. He reiterated his wish "that we could take our stand on a ground perfectly neutral and independent towards all nations." The problem, as he saw it, was that England was not "content with equality. . . . They have wished a monopoly of commerce with us." He wisely pointed out "the insults and injuries committed on us by both the belligerent parties from the beginning of 1793 to this day and still continuing cannot now be wiped off by engaging in war with one of them."

Repeatedly Jefferson recommended a policy of international independence and neutrality. "Our countrymen have divided themselves by such strong affections to the French and the English," he said, "that nothing will secure us internally but a divorce from both nations; and this must be the object of every real American." With these views, it was inevitable, given the position of the President, that Jefferson should slowly abandon all hopes of cooperation, and move gradually into the role of opposition leader.

Another large reason for this development was the retirement of James Madison from Congress. Worn out by his battles over the Jay treaty, and longing to enjoy the company of his delightful Dolley in the relative privacy of his plantation, Madison had refused to stand for re-election, and turned down an offer to make him the unanimous choice for Governor of Virginia. In the House of Representatives this left swarthy Albert Gallatin as the Republican leader. No one could touch him on matters of finance, but his Swiss birth and heavy French accent made him a dubious spokesman on the far more crucial international situation. As for Madison, Jefferson did not let him really retire, any more than Madison had allowed him to escape the political wars during the previous three years at Monticello. Reversing positions, Jefferson now became the political correspondent, sending a stream of brilliant commentaries to Madison at his Orange County estate, Montpelier.

V

Jefferson's leadership was also desperately needed by his party. In the House of Representatives the difference between Federalists and Republicans was balanced on a hair, with three or four moderate Federalists and the same number of moderate Republicans liable to vote either way. Moreover the Federalists were on the offensive. Adams went out of his way in his speech to Congress to call James Monroe a "disgraced minister" and Federalist papers were full of slanderous stories about Monroe speculating with American state funds while in France. Monroe struck back with a slashing pamphlet, bitterly criticizing American policies toward France, sparing not even Washington from abuse.

In the Senate, dominated by the Federalists, Jefferson had to sit mute while senators rose to denounce the author of the Mazzei letter and accuse him and other Republicans of treason. No wonder Jefferson was soon writing home to his daughter Martha, "I become more and more disgusted with the jealousies, the hatred, the rancorous and malignant passions of this scene, and lament my having ever again been drawn into public view."

His weary spirit was gladdened, however, by the best possible news from Monticello. Nineteen-year-old Maria was in love. Her choice was Jack Eppes, Jefferson's ex-student with whom Maria had spent so many happy childhood years at Eppington. Wealthy, charming and intelligent, he seemed to Jefferson the perfect son-in-law and he joyously turned from the embitterments of politics to write a sunny letter to his daughter.

I learn, my dear Maria, with inexpressible pleasure that an union of sentiment is likely to bring on an union of destiny between yourself and a person for whom I have the highest esteem. A long acquaintance with him has made his virtues familiar to me and convinced me that he possesses every quality necessary to make you happy and to make us all happy. This event in compleating the circle of our family has composed for us such a group of good sense, good humor, liberality and prudent care of our affairs, and that without a single member of a contrary character as families are rarely blessed with. It promises us long years of domestic concord and love . . .

As with Martha, he immediately proposed to settle the young couple near Monticello, at the Pantops Plantation. To Martha he wrote in equally exultant terms. "After your happy establishment which has given me an inestimable friend, to whom I can leave the care of everything I love, the only anxiety I had remaining was to see Maria also so associated as to assure her happiness. She could not have been more so to my wishes if I had had the whole earth free to have chosen a partner for her."

Five months later, on October 13, 1797, Maria was married to

John Wayles Eppes at Monticello. Although Jefferson repeated his urgent wish for them to live at Pantops and even began building a house for them there, the young couple chose to spend the first months of their marriage at Eppington, where Maria had so many happy memories. Jefferson, dreading and lamenting his fate, returned to the political wars in Philadelphia.

VI

In the capital, the news from France continued to be bad. The Directory had ordered French men-of-war to seize all ships having merchandise aboard them which was produced in England or her colonies. This made American ships returning from Britain or the West Indies fair game. Extreme Federalists demanded that American merchantmen arm for self-defense. President Adams sent a belligerent message to Congress denouncing France and the French in such extreme terms that Jefferson in a private letter to Madison called it "insane."

"To do nothing & to gain time is everything with us," Jefferson told Madison, and he advised the Republicans in Congress to try to adjourn the session "in order to go home & consult their constituents on the great crisis of American affairs now existing." Unfortunately, the congressmen declined to take his advice, and instead boldly opened a debate on whether the government was contemplating war with France. A fierce exchange erupted, and soon the Republicans were clamoring for the correspondence between the special envoys and the French Directory. They confidently proclaimed that the President was withholding these papers because they proved France's peaceful intentions. Solemnly President Adams forwarded the papers to Congress, and sat back like a man who had just given his worst enemy an exploding cigar.

The papers revealed a shocking tale of French arrogance and duplicity. Charles Maurice Talleyrand, the French Minister of Foreign Affairs, had vaingloriously informed the envoys that his government considered President Adams' speech of the previous May an insult which could only be erased by an immense American loan—$12,800,000 was the figure suggested—plus a personal bribe of $250,000 which Talleyrand and the Directors were presumably to share. Charles Cotesworth Pinckney stood firm when Talleyrand's agents (discreetly designated by President Adams as X, Y and Z) suggested the bribe. "No, not a sixpence," he snapped.

The X Y Z papers struck Jefferson and his fellow Republicans with hurricane force. "Trimmers dropt off from the Party like windfalls from an apple tree in September," gloated Federalist leader Fisher Ames. Jefferson ruefully admitted to Madison that the X Y Z revelations and their "artful misrepresentations" had "produced such a shock on the Republican mind as has never been seen since our independence."

Spurred by gleeful Federalist editors, the nation plunged into a frenzy of anti-French emotion. Patriotic testimonials poured into the capital from individuals and towns. Young men sporting black cockades—a Federalist symbol—paraded in military formations on Philadelphia's streets, and assaulted any and all Republicans they could find. President Adams addressed them, with a matching black cockade in his hat, and a sword on his hip. Fifers and drummers played the "Rogue's March" under Jefferson's windows, and smeared the statue of Benjamin Franklin with mud, because his grandson, Benjamin Franklin Bache, was the editor of the violently Republican newspaper *The Aurora*.

Jefferson grimly refused to lose his head; he made no attempt to counter the first wild rush of emotion. But he insisted in his letters to Madison that there was still no real cause for war. France's conduct was admittedly outrageous, but thus far there was no proof that the government itself was involved in Talleyrand's dirty dealing. Madison agreed, commenting that he was more appalled by Talleyrand's stupidity than by his corruption, which was well known. But when Jefferson asked him to write "a well digested analysis" of the X Y Z papers for the press, claiming that it could "now decide the future turn of things," Madison declined. He knew an impossible task when he saw one.

What added acutely to Jefferson's distress was the man who seemed to be gaining the most public acclaim for defying X Y Z— John Marshall of Virginia. He was a cousin—they both had Randolph blood in their veins—but this was the only iota of similarity Jefferson found in this lanky, surprisingly indolent but charming young lawyer. Through a sister's marriage he was linked with Robert Morris, and with that financier's money was involved in huge land speculations in Virginia. This naturally made him an avowed Federalist, and he had swiftly become the leading spokesman of the party in Virginia. On his side, Marshall's political antagonism to Jefferson was bolstered by a strange coincidence. He had married the daughter of Rebecca Burwell Ambler, that unattainable Belinda whom young Jefferson had pursued in colonial Williamsburg. Perhaps it was his half-hearted pursuit, perhaps his bumbling shyness in the crunch, but the Ambler family always had a marked antipathy for Thomas Jefferson.

Marshall wrote the report on the X Y Z confrontation, a bristling indictment of the French and France. When he returned to Philadelphia, he was greeted as a conquering hero. Three corps of cavalry met him outside the city, church bells rang, cannon thundered, and congressmen flocked to his rooms to congratulate him. At a dinner in his honor, the often quoted toast was offered: "Millions for defense, not one cent for tribute." For his eleven months in France, and his highly political dispatches, the Secretary of State, Timothy Pickering paid Marshall $19,963.97. His financial backer, Robert Morris, had gone bankrupt, and Marshall was desperate for cash. Jefferson wryly noted in his diary the report that Marshall had called the money a "God-send." It was three times more than he ever made from his law practice.

Jefferson and the Republicans could only watch helplessly while Congress rammed through some twenty acts, abrogating the French treaty, raising an army, equipping a navy, and putting the nation on a war footing. George Washington was summoned from retirement to head the army, and to Jefferson's dismay and John Adams' considerable mortification, the aging general insisted on having Alexander Hamilton as his second in command and chief of staff. Since Washington made it clear that if war came he had no intention of leading in the field, Hamilton was the army's real commander in chief. Jefferson, knowing his old antagonist's fondness for Julius Caesar, found this appointment extremely alarming.

Meanwhile, in Congress the Federalists did not stop with defensive measures. Riding a hitherto unknown popularity, they decided to take advantage of it to crush Jefferson and his Republicans for good. Jefferson saw the storm brewing as early as April

26, 1798, within a month of the X Y Z revelations. "One of the War Party," he told Madison, "in a fit of unguarded passion, declared some time ago they would pass a Citizen Bill, an Alien Bill, and a Sedition Bill." The chances of stopping them were slight. Some Republican congressmen had gone over to the war hawks and others, such as the once aggressive Giles, decided to go home, cowed by the Federalist policy of keeping the country in a panic.

William Cobbet, the chief Federalist editor, who wrote under the name Peter Porcupine, ranted daily about the imminence of a French invasion. A newspaper exchange with an obscure Republican inspired Alexander Hamilton to announce he was threatened with assassination. The Chief Justice of the Supreme Court, Oliver Ellsworth, turned a grand-jury charge into a vicious assault on Jefferson and his party. When Dr. George Logan, the Pennsylvanian whom Jefferson admired as a scientific farmer and an ardent Republican, sailed to France as an unofficial seeker after peace, Federalist editors screamed that he had been sent by Jefferson and company to summon a French army of invasion.

For Jefferson, with his detestation of personal acrimony, these were painful times. He complained to one correspondent, "At this moment all the passions are boiling over, and one who keeps himself cool and clear of the contagion is so far below the point of ordinary conversation, that he finds himself insulated in every society." When dining out he had to sit in silence most of the time, a disagreeable practice for a man who delighted in social banter. Another reason for his silence was his growing conviction that the Federalists were spying on him constantly, hoping to get evidence that could convict him under the forthcoming Sedition Act. On April 15, 1798, he wrote to James Monroe that he would "hereafter seal my letters with wax, & the same seal. Pay attention if you please to the state of the impression." His suspicions were well founded. The Federalists were scrutinizing all the mail they could lay their hands on. Oliver Wolcott, the Secretary of the Treasury, forced a traveler from France to surrender a personal letter to Jefferson from the American consul in Paris. It was found in Wolcott's private papers fifty years later.

In their final form the Alien and Sedition Acts extended the waiting period for citizenship from five to fourteen years and gave the President the power to deport at his discretion any alien he considered dangerous. The sedition act made it a crime to conspire "with intent to oppose the government, to incite riots or insurrections against the laws of Congress"—a declaration sufficiently vague to make every man who attended a Republican political meeting suspect—and Federalist legislators virtually omnipotent. This was bad enough. The law also declared it a crime "to publish false, scandalous or malicious writings against the government, either house of Congress or the President, with intent to bring them into contempt, stir up sedition, or to aid or abet a foreign nation in hostile designs against the United States." The bills, Jefferson said, were "so palpably in the teeth of the Constitution as to show they mean to pay no respect for it." They were also palpably aimed at crippling the Republican Party. Numbers of French and Irish refugees had flocked to America to escape their troubled countries and had gravitated naturally to the Republicans. They could now be banished at a stroke of the President's pen. The sedition bill was even more serious. It gave the Federalists the power to muzzle the Republican press.

Still Jefferson continued to keep calm. Instead of denouncing the Federalists, he did his utmost to restrain seekers after extreme solutions in his own party. When John Taylor, one of Virginia's leading thinkers, wrote to Jefferson strongly intimating that it was time for Virginia to secede from the Union (adding that North Carolina was willing to join her), Jefferson answered him with a philosophical and psychological analysis of the nature of political man that still has profound meaning.

True, he admitted, Massachusetts and Connecticut, the heartland of Federalist strength, were riding the South hard. But "in every free and deliberating society, there must from the nature of man, be opposite parties, and violent dissensions and discords; and one of these, for the most part must prevail over the other for a longer or shorter time . . . but if to rid ourselves of the present rule of Massachusetts and Connecticut we break the union, will the evil stop there?"

No, Jefferson said. Even North Carolina and Virginia alone would fall to quarreling and when they split up, Virginians would soon have party quarrels among themselves.

"Seeing therefore, that an association of men who will not quarrel with one another is a thing which never yet existed, from the greatest confederacy of nations down to a town meeting or a vestry; seeing that we must have somebody to quarrel with, I had rather keep our New England associates for that purpose, than to see our bickerings transferred to others."

"A little patience," he assured Taylor, "and we shall see the reign of witches pass over, their spells dissolved and the people recovering their true sight."

But as always, Jefferson geared his optimism to action. He did not think that the Alien and Sedition Acts could be defeated simply by enduring them. The people had to be rallied, and early in July, when the passage of the bills became a certainty, he abandoned his thankless role as president of the Senate and headed for Virginia. En route, he stopped overnight at Montpelier and had one of his most important conversations with James Madison. He then jogged on to Monticello and a happy reunion with his grandchildren, who now numbered three. Martha had given birth to another girl, Ellen, destined to be his favorite, in 1796.

Back in Philadelphia, the hard-riding Federalists began wielding their Sedition Act sword. Matthew Lyon, a brawling, indecorous Republican congressman from Vermont, was arrested for publishing in his newspaper a scalding attack on President Adams. He was found guilty, fined a thousand dollars, and thrown into a filthy jail in a small Vermont town. Next came an indictment against Benjamin Franklin Bache, followed by prosecutions against some twenty other Republican editors. There were signs that the Federalists did not intend to confine their witch hunting to editors. "Long John" Allen, a fanatically anti-Republican representative from Connecticut, ominously reported that Jefferson had been "closeted" with the indicted Bache.

Obviously, once an editor was convicted of sedition, it was only a step to prove his friends guilty by association. Jefferson himself spoke darkly of "Maratists" who might make a personal attempt to seize him, and he told one correspondent that he was "prepared to meet them" in a manner that would do justice to his personal honor. His fear of Federalist espionage also deepened. "I know not which mortifies me most," he told John Taylor, "that I should fear to write what I think, or my country bear such a state of things."

In this atmosphere, it is hardly surprising that Jefferson made his next political move with a stealth worthy of a secret agent. To Monticello came Wilson Cary Nicholas, long a Jeffersonian leader in the Virginia Assembly. A solid, balding, rather colorless man, he had inherited from his austere father, Robert Carter Nicholas, a reputation for absolute integrity. In Jefferson's spacious library, with the works of the greatest thinkers on politics and history around them, the two men discussed the grim political situation. There was no hope of repealing the Sedition Acts in Congress, or of seeking protection from them in the solidly Federalist courts. The Republicans had to fall back to their last line of defense—the states.

Angrily, Jefferson spelled out for Nicholas what he had in mind. Madison was going to write a set of resolutions to be introduced into the Virginia Assembly, protesting the hateful acts. He, Jefferson, was writing another set, which he wanted Nicholas to deliver to a certain Republican in the North Carolina assembly, for introduction there. It had to be done in total secrecy. Jefferson was Vice President of the United States. For him to be caught publicly attacking the government, in the present political atmosphere, could easily put him on trial for treason.

Nicholas agreed to play courier, and Jefferson went to work on the resolutions. He wrote them in a violent mood, at a headlong pace. They are the sloppiest public document ever to come from his pen, repetitious, and more than a little shrill. They are the words of a man fighting for his political life, and risking his actual life to do so.

The resolutions denounced the Sedition Acts in blazing terms, and declared that in forming the union the states never intended to permit themselves to be subjected to "undelegated and consequently unlimited powers." On the contrary, when the federal government exceeded its delegated powers, the states had the right to "nullify of their own authority" the excessive laws. This was political dynamite. Jefferson made this even clearer when he closed the resolutions by warning that "these and successive acts of the same character, unless arrested at the threshold [will] necessarily drive these states into revolution and blood."

Nicholas was, privately, staggered by the intensity of the resolutions. He decided they were far too dangerous to entrust to the unnamed Republican in North Carolina, who could have easily been connected with their author. Like a true Virginian, he decided blood alone could be trusted with such explosive material. Nicholas' older brother George was a political power in Kentucky. Oddly, he was the same George Nicholas who had caused Jefferson so much mental anguish by calling for an investigation of his governorship. They had long since composed that difference, and George was a devoted Jeffersonian. By happy coincidence, one of George's closest friends, John Breckinridge, was visiting Wilson Nicholas at his Albermarle plantation, Warren. He too was an Albermarle man who had emigrated to Kentucky.

First swearing him to secrecy, Nicholas gave him the resolutions to introduce in the Kentucky legislature. Breckinridge too was shaken by their intensity, and asked if he could go to Monticello to discuss possible changes in them. Nicholas vetoed the idea. It was too risky to link him with Jefferson, even through a casual visit.

Madison meanwhile was completing his resolutions for the Virginia legislature. Neither Madison's life nor his career was on the line. This fact, plus his cooler, more logical mind, produced a much more moderate statement. But it was bold enough to join Jefferson's Kentucky bellow of defiance.

The two sets of resolutions were issued at the height of the Sedition Act frenzy. Coming from the giant Virginia and her smaller but symbolically potent western satellite, Kentucky, they spoke to the Federalists, and the whole nation, rallying disarrayed Republicans and warning their arrogant opponents that there was a limit to their power.

Madison later persuaded a calmer Jefferson to abandon his nullification idea. It was clear to the architect of the Constitution that in the wrong hands, it could destroy the union—which it almost did, in 1832, and in 1861. Jefferson's resort to this extreme position is one more proof that he was no angelic intellect, above the political battle; he was human, he made mistakes, as every man does when he is fighting for his life, and for ideas that he has cherished from youth. It is also proof of his devotion to freedom, and his genuine fear that this supreme value was about to be destroyed by the reckless Federalists. The union, the nation itself, was not more valuable to Jefferson than freedom.

At the same time, he remained the consummate realist. He made it clear that he saw no cause for playing Samson in the temple of government. Only "repeated and enormous violations" would justify revolution or secession. For the present he refused to do anything "which would commit us further." Peaceful protest, he assured his friends, would win the day. "Firmness on our part, but a passive firmness," he told Madison, "is the true course." Anything rash or threatening might check "the favorable dispositions" which he saw rising among the people on his return to Philadelphia.

Jefferson foresaw the factors that had begun eroding the popularity which the Federalists had seized during the X Y Z furor. Congress had passed a direct tax on houses and land to pay for the enlarged army and navy. Every time a voter paid this tax, he stopped to ask himself what, exactly, he was getting for it. The longer the French invading army failed to appear, the more he wondered. Then he saw the army put to the sort of use that the Republicans had long been predicting. In Bucks County, Pennsylvania, an auctioneer named Fries organized a group of seven hundred farmers to resist the tax, and they chased the federal collectors out of the neighborhood. The government responded with massive force; squadrons of cavalry thundered up and down the countryside, pursuing a nonexistent revolutionary army, finally hauling Fries off to a federal court, where he was condemned to death. President Adams pardoned him, practically admitting that the whole affair was close to an absurdity.

Meanwhile, the popular reaction against Sedition Act prosecutions was creating a host of Republican martyrs. Samuel Adams, the man who had begun the American Revolution, strode into a Boston jail and publicly announced his sympathy through the bars to imprisoned Republican editor Thomas Adams (no relation). When the newsman died three weeks after his release from prison, the Republicans bitterly claimed it was the result of his sufferings in the dank, damp cell. Matthew Lyon had his thousand-dollar fine paid by popular subscription, and was re-elected to Congress while behind bars. His journey to Philadelphia was nothing less than a triumphant progress, with thousands of Republicans turning out to greet him in towns and cities along the way. At one point his partisans vowed the crowd following him was twelve miles long.

Jefferson was also heartened by the way conservative statesmen, such as Edmund Pendleton, his old antagonist in the Virginia legislature, and John Dickinson, once his angry foe in the Continental Congress, rallied to his cause. He urged Madison, Pendleton, every politican who could wield a pen to write for the papers, to reach the people. "The press is the engine," he told Madison. "Every man must lay his purse and his pen under contribution."

VII

While Jefferson was holding the line with resolutions, exhortations and advice, behind closed doors the Federalist Party was quietly destroying itself. John Adams was truer to that profound patriotism Jefferson admired in him back in 1776 than his old friend believed. Adams still did not want a war with France, and he slowly came to realize that the wild rumors of a French invasion were nonsense. "At present there is no more prospect of seeing a French army here, than there is in heaven," he growled to Secretary of State Timothy Pickering, in October, 1798. The experience of creating an army and a navy had been very enlightening to the President. The way his cabinet supported Washington's preference for Hamilton, and the almost abject deference of McHenry, his Secretary of War, to Hamilton's opinions, made the President finally realize that the New York colossus was running the government, not only in Congress, but in Adams' own cabinet.

Early in 1799 he heard through several channels (one of them the much abused George Logan) that the French were anxious to compose the differences which had their sailors fighting an undeclared war off the American coasts. To give Adams and the Federalists their due, the U.S. Navy's show of strength undoubtedly had something to do with bringing the French around to a more reasonable attitude. But Hamilton and his followers presumed that these naval duels were only the opening shots in an all-out conflict.

Once war was declared, Hamilton planned to use the American

army to crush all opposition at home, and then march south, to liberate the Floridas and Louisiana. With these vast territories secured, the army, with the co-operation of the English fleet, would embark on the liberation of the Spanish colonies of South America. With an empire in his pocket, the American Caesar would then have coolly divided the civilized world with his British colleagues.

The hinge on which this entire scheme swung was a declaration of war by France. If it came from the French, it would demolish the last shred of support for Jefferson and his party. Hamilton would have no difficulty rallying the army against the external enemy and their internal friends. But John Adams, finally declaring his own independence, proceeded to unbolt this hinge by appointing a new peace-seeking mission to France. The Federalists, Hamilton above all, were appalled and did everything in their power to delay the mission. But as usual, they overreached themselves. Secretary of State Pickering sent a public letter to Boston denouncing the mission and, indirectly, the President for sending it. That was enough for honest John Adams. He bounced Pickering out of the cabinet, and replaced him with Virginia's John Marshall. He had already retired Hamilton's chief toady, Secretary of War McHenry, and he now proceeded to dismantle the skeleton army on which Hamilton's dreams depended.

This finished Adams as far as Hamilton was concerned. But who could replace him as a candidate? The harried Federalist chief decided that his only hope was George Washington. But a cautious letter, exploring the possibility of a third term, had brought from the sixty-seven-year-old general a very sharp reply, asking when the Federalists would be strong enough to stand on their own feet. Still Hamilton had not given up hope, and in December he had persuaded another stanch Federalist and friend of Washington, Gouverneur Morris, to write a second, even more pleading letter. It arrived the day after Washington succumbed to a throat infection he had contracted supervising Mount Vernon's far-flung farms in winter weather. In his dismay at the news, Hamilton blurted out his real feeling for the Father of the Country. "Perhaps no man in this community has equal cause with myself to deplore the loss. . . . He was an aegis very essential to me."

Jefferson, fearing that the Federalists would turn the departed hero into a political weapon, did not leave Monticello early enough to join Congress on the day of formal mourning, set for December 26. He arrived in Philadelphia two days later, and immediately met a barrage of criticism from the Federalist press for his absence. Though he mourned Washington as a friend, the great man had drifted so far into the Federalist camp that politics made it impossible for Jefferson to comment on his death. Even a note to Mrs. Washington might have been twisted and misinterpreted by the Federalists into new accusations of hypocrisy or a confession of past mistakes.

Washington was not the only great name to pass in this final year of the old century. Patrick Henry had succumbed in June, after running one last time for the Virginia Assembly on a violently anti-Jefferson, pro-Sedition Laws platform.

As far as personal grief was concerned, Jefferson expressed a keener sense of loss about another death—his faithful servant and traveling companion, Jupiter. The black man had insisted on accompanying Jefferson from Monticello to Fredericksburg, where he caught the public stage for Philadelphia, although Jefferson could see that he was not well. "Toward the end of the second day's journey, I saw how much he was worsted," he said later, "and pressed him to wait at Hyde's, a very excellent house, till the horses should return, & I got the promise of a servant from there. But he would not hear of it. At Fredericksburg again I engaged the tavernkeeper to take care of him until he should be quite well enough to proceed." But Jupiter returned to Monticello and unwisely made another journey to the home of a Jefferson relative, where he collapsed and died.

Still another death distressed Jefferson deeply early in the year 1800. Maria was pregnant, and perhaps because of her close resemblance to his wife Jefferson fretted and fussed over her condition. He had her doctor writing him reports of her health and his letters were constant repetitions of statements such as, "I become daily more anxious to hear from you, and to know that you continue well." On the last day of the old year, Maria gave birth to a daughter. It was a tiny baby, probably premature, and lived only a few weeks. Early in February, Jefferson wrote mournfully to her:

"How deeply I feel it in all of its bearings, I shall not say, nor attempt consolation where I know that time and silence are the only medicines." Maria herself was very ill after the birth, and this news made Jefferson almost frantic. "I feel inexpressibly whatever affects either your health or happiness," he wrote her. "My attachments to the world and whatever it can offer are daily wearing off, but you are one of the links which hold to my existence, and can only break off with that."

Fortunately, the mounting tempo of politics did not permit Jefferson much time for personal grief. The nation was roaring into the election of 1800—a conflict that even then was recognized as a crucial turning point in the history of America—and the world.

VIII

On the Federalist side, Hamilton, still disgusted with John Adams, began playing his by now familiar game. There was no hope of dumping Adams, Federalist congressmen made that clear. The President had built up a strong popular following as a result of his defiant stand on the X Y Z affair. So Hamilton began scheming for a repetition of the same plan he had failed to put across in 1796—the nomination of a South Carolinian as Vice President on the Federalist ticket, followed by enough juggling in the electoral college to make this man the legal President. For his candidate he chose the brother of the man who had failed to do the trick for him last time—Charles Cotesworth Pinckney.

Jefferson was the inevitable candidate of the Republicans—who by now were beginning in some places to call themselves the Democrat-Republicans. He made no attempt to avoid the responsibility. On the contrary he saw it as the climactic battle of his life. At stake, in his view, was the future of freedom in America. Those words he had written twenty-three years ago in the Declaration of Independence were demanding the ultimate commitment—and Jefferson was ready. To underscore his seriousness, he wrote to numerous friends, telling them not to expect much correspondence from him for at least a year. He was determined not to repeat his old mistake of letting personal letters get into the mails, with violent political consequences.

The west front of Monticello. The pond was used to stock fresh fish. One of Jefferson's favorite pleasures, after he retired from the Presidency, was romping with his grandchildren on this lawn. *Culver Pictures, Inc.*

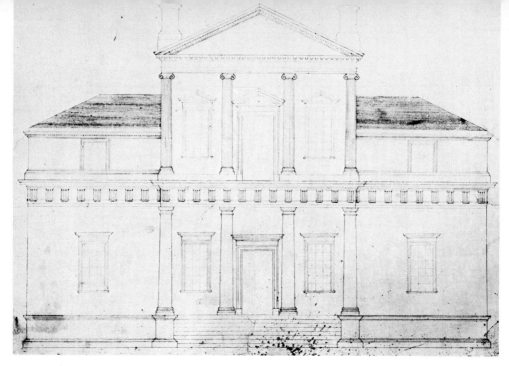

Jefferson's original plan for Monticello did not include the dome. He built all of this house except the upper portico and, when he returned from France, tore much of it down to create Monticello as it appears today. *The Bettmann Archive.*

"The honeymoon cottage"—the small, one-room building in which Jefferson and his bride spent their first days at Monticello, while the mansion was being completed. It was also Jefferson's residence during the last of his bachelor days, when he lived alone on his mountain waxing cynical over women. *Culver Pictures, Inc.*

The entrance hall of Monticello, which Jefferson called "the museum." In his day it contained some eighteen paintings and pieces of statuary, as well as a cabinet of mammal bones, Indian antiquities and curiosities brought back by Lewis and Clark from their expedition to the Northwest. The seven-day clock on the wall, run by Revolutionary War cannonball weights, was designed by Jefferson. The bust to the far right is of Alexander Hamilton, testimony to Jefferson's willingness to concede his greatness and to forgive and forget their historic animosity. *The Bettmann Archive.*

Jefferson's dumbwaiter, probably the first in America. It brought wine up from his cellar. "Good wine is a necessity of life for me," he said. Whiskey, on the other hand, "was destroying one-third of our population." *The Bettmann Archive.*

Another example of Jefferson's ingenuity. Food was placed on the shelves in the hall. The door was turned and the food was in the dining room. It enabled him to do without servants in the dining room when he was having confidential conversations about affairs of state. *The Bettmann Archive.*

Jefferson designed this chaise longue (which revolved) and table so that he could simultaneously relax and write. In his 77th year, he wrote a staggering 1,667 letters. *The Bettmann Archive.*

The Polygraph, the device which enabled Jefferson to write letters and simultaneously make copies. He considered it one of the most important inventions of the age. *The Bettmann Archive.*

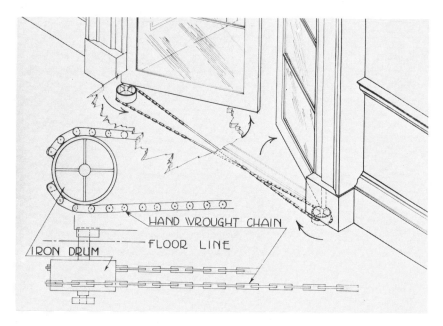

Yet another Jefferson invention. The doors from the entrance hall to the parlor of Monticello open simultaneously thanks to the figure-eight chain and drums concealed in the floor. The mechanism still works perfectly. *Culver Pictures, Inc.*

The parlor at Monticello, looking west to the Blue Ridge. The parquet floor was one of the first in America. Even the draperies were made to Jefferson's own design. Family weddings, christenings, musicales were all held in this room.

Photo by Frank Moscati.
Copyright © Reader's Digest Association 1968.

Poplar Forest, the Jefferson-designed-and-built home in Bedford County, where he went to escape the crowds at Monticello in the summer months. The house is an exact octagon, the first of its kind in the United States. Here the neighbors called the ex-President "the Squire" and let him relax with one or two of his favorite grandchildren. "He interested himself," one later recalled, "in all we did, thought or read." *Culver Pictures, Inc.*

The inner court of the University of Virginia, including Jefferson's "last and best dome," modeled on the Pantheon. Original as always, Jefferson rejected the barn-like college architecture of his area and created this "academical village." *Photo by Ed Roseberry, courtesy University of Virginia.*

In Philadelphia, he boldly played the part of party chieftain. Night after night, he huddled with his followers at the Indian Queen Tavern, plotting the next day's strategy in Congress. Party leaders from other states wrote or visited to discuss local tactics and problems. Aaron Burr came from New York for several long conferences on Republican chances in that key state. Burr, still assiduously building up the Sons of St. Tammany, told Jefferson that the prospects were good. But he made it clear that this time, if he received the Republican nomination for Vice President, he wanted guarantees that southerners would not throw away their votes and dump him as they had in 1796. Jefferson was quick to assure the dapper New Yorker that the honor of the gentlemen of the South, pledged through him, would be inviolable. This promise was reinforced by the pledge of the Republican caucus in Congress, when Jefferson and Burr were nominated.

Burr proceeded to perform handsomely in New York. That state's elections for the legislature—from which the electors would be named—were held early in 1800. Hamilton, anxious to have men he could control to further his dump-Adams schemes, put up a slate of mediocrities. Burr persuaded two Revolutionary War heroes, ex-Governor George Clinton and Major General Horatio Gates, to come out of retirement and head his Republican slate. He set up what may have been the first finance committee in American politics, and, combining tireless industry, personal charm and ample funds, he led the Sons of St. Tammany to a startling upset victory over the complacent Hamiltonians.

Fighting back, the desperate Federalists rammed through a new election law in Pennsylvania which divided that state's Presidential electors on a proportionate basis, abolishing the unit system that gave the entire electoral vote to the winning party. This carved at least seven votes out of the total Jefferson had won in 1796, though it still left him well ahead of Adams, for whom the loss of New York was a devastating blow. But the Federalists still thought they had a chance to win if they could carry South Carolina. John Marshall told Charles Cotesworth Pinckney that the Pennsylvania decision would "exclude Mr. Jefferson provided he gets no vote in South Carolina but it is now reduced to an absolute certainty that any success in your state elects him."

As for Hamilton, his detestation of Adams was now so complete he began saying that if the country was going to shipwreck, he would rather see it run aground with Jefferson at the helm, so they could at least blame the disaster on the Republicans. Jefferson, sensing the advantage, urged his followers to redouble their efforts. Since his "botanizing" expedition to New York in 1791, Jefferson had slowly constructed the first genuine political party in the United States. Hamilton never approached the thoroughness with which Jefferson organized his followers, state by state. The Federalists relied on the influence of "the good, the wise and the rich" to percolate from the top, downward into the electorate. Jefferson worked from the opposite direction. Each state had a party chief and he in turn labored to organize subchiefs and committees for each town, city, county. In New York it was Burr, in Pennsylvania it was Governor Thomas McKean, in South Carolina it was Peter Freneau, hulking Rabelaisian brother of Philip, editing a paper in the best scathing family tradition, and Charles Pinckney, ex-Governor, an aristocrat with democratic enthusiasms. Everywhere, in response to Jefferson's urgings, papers were set up, often two, to replace the ones struck down by the Sedition Act prosecutions. (Matthew Lyon established four.) To all his followers Jefferson laid out a party platform—attack the Land Tax, the swollen army and navy with nothing to fight, the tyranny of the Sedition Acts. Always, as he told Edmund Pendleton, the writing must be "short, simple, and level to every capacity." He urged Madison to "set aside a portion of every post day to write what may be proper for the public." When X Y Z negotiator Elbridge Gerry returned from France with further proof that peace was possible, Jefferson called for a "capitulation . . . so concise, as, omitting nothing material, may yet be printed in handbills, of which we could print and disperse ten or twelve thousand copies under letter covers, through all the United States by the members of Congress when they return home."

Gone were Jefferson's lamentations about the petty bickerings and acrimonies of politics. These had obviously been produced by the frustrations of the years when the Federalists rode high. Now, with the smell of victory in his nostrils, Jefferson was the consummate party leader, infinitely superior to Hamilton because he led with ideas and never attempted to control the minutiae of his followers' words and acts. The best possible proof of this is Jefferson's calm retirement from Philadelphia in the midsummer of 1800. With the platform created, the newspapers publishing and the local state leaders carrying the fight to every farm and hamlet, he retreated to Monticello, and spent the rest of the campaign there, tending his farms and enjoying his children and grandchildren.

IX

Perhaps it was just as well that Jeffeerson was not in the center of the conflict. The campaign of 1800 was the dirtiest in the history of the nation. Everything that had ever been said against Jefferson by Hamilton and others was repeated, embellished and multiplied. But it was against his religion, his supposed fondness for the atheistic worship of reason, that the Federalists chose to hurl their strongest thunderbolts. Part of this was defensive. The enthusiasm for the French Revolution among young people, especially, had brought an alarming decline in orthodoxy. There had been, for instance, only one professed Christian in a recent Yale class. Ministers of the gospel, seeking for a scapegoat, found Jefferson an ideal target. His reputation as a scientist and political philosopher made him a kind of magnet for thinking men who came to America, often as refugees from reactionary governments in Europe. Unfortunately for Jefferson, at this point in history, most of these men were sloughing off the wordy theology of traditional Christianity, in search of a simpler view of God. Typical of these men were Joseph Priestley, the great pioneer chemist, and his friend Thomas Cooper, who were driven out of England in 1794 because of their sympathy for the French Revolution. Jefferson also welcomed and entertained the freethinking philosopher, Comte de Volney, and the equally independent French economist Pierre Samuel du Pont de Nemours.

While Jefferson scrupulously avoided public statements on religion, these friends felt no such compunction. Volney and Priestley in particular were outspoken foes of traditional Christianity and the Federalists, using the old canard of guilt by association, held Jefferson responsible for their hard-hitting books.

The preachers conjured up before their congregations a picture of the nation collapsing into total moral and social anarchy if Jefferson was elected. The Reverend John M. Mason declared the issue in the election was "national regard or disregard to the religion of Jesus Christ." The churchman found in Jefferson's *Notes on Virginia* "ten thousand impieties and mischiefs, including disbelief in the deluge, in the story of Adam and Eve and the idea of the Jews as God's chosen people." The Reverend Mason vowed that by voting for Jefferson "you will do more to destroy a regard for the gospel of Jesus, than the whole fraternity of infidels with all their . . . industry and their intrigues."

The New England *Palladium*, an all-out Federalist sheet, thundered, "Should the infidel Jefferson be elected to the Presidency, the seal of death is that moment set on our holy religion, our churches will be prostrated, and some infamous prostitute, under the title of the goddess of reason, will preside in the sanctuaries now devoted to the worship of the Most High." The Reverend Cotton Mather Smith charged him with obtaining his personal fortune by defrauding a widow and her children as the executor of their estate. Another divine conjured up the totally mythical story of the day Jefferson and Mazzei were out riding and the Italian commented on the dilapidated state of a local church. Jefferson supposedly replied, "It's good enough for Him who was born in a manger."

Some Republicans panicked at the ferocity of these religious attacks. One wrote Jefferson asking him bluntly, "Do you believe there was a deluge and do you believe that mankind originally sprang from one pair?" Jefferson stubbornly refused to make any statement about his religious beliefs, though his followers strenuously defended him in newspapers and pamphlets. The attacks did move him to write a private letter to his close friend, Dr. Benjamin Rush. Earlier he had told Rush in conversation that he "believed in the divine mission of the Savior of the world, but he did not believe that he was the son of God in the way in which many Christians believed it. . . ." He believed likewise in "the resurrection, and a future state of rewards and punishments." Rush, like many others, urged him to make a public statement. After giving the matter much thought, Jefferson replied at the height of the campaign, that he had decided to remain silent. He said that his religious opinions "ought to displease neither the rational Christian or Deist" but he had no hopes of satisfying the organized clergy, particularly the Episcopalians of Virginia, and the Congregationalists of New England. These two groups still hoped to see the "establishment of a particular form of Christianity thro' the U.S." But Jefferson noted wryly, "The returning good sense of our country threatens abortion to their hopes, & they believe that any portion of power confided to me will be exerted in opposition to their scheme. And they believe truly, for I have sworn upon the altar of God eternal hostility against every form of tyranny over the mind of man."

Thus his religious critics inspired Jefferson to write one of his most immortal lines, the one which is inscribed on the Jefferson Memorial in Washington, D.C.

Religion was not the only stick the Federalists seized to beat Jefferson. He was called an "intellectual voluptuary," a secret drunkard (on his French wines), a physical coward for his retreat over Carter's Mountain before Tarleton's dragoons, a moral coward for slandering George Washington in the Mazzei letter. His scientific experiments supposedly included the awful crime of vivisection, and Monticello was renamed "Dog's Misery." Other editors pilloried him as a "Negro Driver" who debauched and abused his slaves. He was pictured as a coarse vulgarian, his conversation a constant stream of blasphemies and curses, and a bloodthirsty Jacobin who could not wait to set up a guillotine on every street corner.

The real Jefferson was the best possible antidote to these slanders. Perhaps the best example of how a meeting with the man could dispel Federalist myths is the story of his visit to a young Washington housewife, Margaret Bayard Smith. Her husband, Samuel Harrison Smith, was a Philadelphia newspaperman whom Jefferson, with his usual eye for talent, had spotted as a comer. Industrious, well-educated, Smith was intellectually superior to most newsmen of the time; he proved it by winning a prize for an essay on liberal education from the American Philosophical Society when he was only twenty-five. Jefferson had encouraged Smith to move with the times, and transfer his newspapering to the new national capital, Washington, D.C. He had done so, beginning the publication of the *National Intelligencer* in October, 1800. A few weeks later his young bride was busy setting up house on New Jersey Avenue, when, as she described it, "the servant opened the door and showed in a gentleman who wished to see my husband."

Outgoing and pretty, Mrs. Smith was used to men fussing over her, and she was "somewhat checked by the dignified and reserved air" of the visitor. But the chilled feeling was only momentary. "In a free and easy manner" he took the chair she offered him and "carelessly throwing his arm on the table near which he sat, he turned towards me a countenance beaming with an expression of benevolence and with a manner and voice almost femininely soft and gentle entered into a conversation on the commonplace topics of the day."

Before she was conscious of it, Margaret Smith was drawn into "observations of a more personal and interesting nature. I know not how it was," she said, "but there was something in his manner, his countenance and voice that at once unlocked my heart, and in answer to his casual inquiries concerning our situation in our new home, *as he called it*, I found myself frankly telling him what I liked or disliked." The interest with which he listened to her "artless details" finally convinced her that he was some intimate acquaintance or friend of Mr. Smith's and she was soon so "perfectly at my ease" that she forgot that he was not a friend of her own.

A moment later her husband arrived and introduced the stranger as "Mr. Jefferson."

Margaret felt her cheeks burn and her heart throb. Her father, James Bayard, was a stanch Federalist, as was her adopted brother, the congressman from Delaware. Though her husband Samuel was an enthusiastic Jeffersonian, Margaret had heard reams of Federalist slander from her blood relatives. She entertained "kindly dispositions" toward Jefferson because of his political and personal friendship with her husband, yet she still believed that "he was an ambitious and violent demagogue, coarse and vulgar in his manners, awkward and rude in his appearance, for such had the public journals and private conversations of the Federalist Party represented him to be." Now she could only ask herself in bewilderment, "Was this the bold atheist and profligate man I have so often heard denounced by the Federalists? Can this man so meek and mild yet dignified in his manners, with a voice so soft and low, with a countenance so benignant and intelligent, can he be that daring leader of a faction, that disturber of the peace, that enemy of all rank and order? I felt that I had been the victim of prejudice, that I had been unjust. The revolution of feeling was complete and from that moment my heart warmed to him with the most affectionate interest."

X

In the Presidential campaign, John Adams was going his own highly unpredictable way. He indignantly rejected the charge of irreligion against Jefferson, irascibly asking what a man's religion had to do with his qualifications for public office, and insisting that Jefferson was "a good patriot citizen and father." These kindly comments filled high Federalists with alarm, especially when Abigail joined heartily in her husband's sentiments. "The Good Lady," Fisher Ames said of Abigail, "is as complete a politician as any lady in the old French court." Did this mean that Adams and Jefferson were forming a coalition behind the scenes? Even more alarming was the report, forwarded to Hamilton by Vice Presidential candidate Pinckney, that Adams was describing Jefferson as "the man in the United States fittest for President." These stories were bad enough, but what totally unstrung Alexander Hamilton were hard-hitting attacks by Adams on what he called "the British faction" in American politics. Everyone knew this was a shaft aimed straight at the New York colossus, and Hamilton now decided, once and for all, that Adams had to go.

A tour of New England found high Federalist leaders disposed to play the dump-Adams, push-Pinckney game, but the lowest ranks of the Party were still loyal to old "John Yankee," as Adams liked to call himself. To separate them from this emotional allegiance, Hamilton wrote a letter "Concerning the Public Conduct and Character of John Adams," which was intended for private circulation among Federalist leaders. Aaron Burr, by now a past master of political intrigue, got his hands on a copy and published the juiciest passages in two Republican papers. Hamilton then released the entire letter to the press, on October 22, 1800. It gave Jefferson and the country the almost unbelievable spectacle of the leader of the Federalist Party flaying alive his official candidate for President. Hamilton even admitted he had tried to steer Thomas Pinckney into the Presidency in 1796 because of the "disgusting egotism, the distempered jealousy, and the ungovernable indiscretion of Mr. Adams' temper." He descanted upon Adams' "paroxysms of rage, which deprived him of self-command." The Federalists reeled in disbelief. Noah Webster told Hamilton, "Your ambition, pride and overbearing temper have destined you to be the evil genius of the country."

There was no need for Jefferson to tell his Republican editors what to do about this unbelievable good fortune. "Alexander Hamilton and the New York Feds have split upon the Adamantine rock," the *Philadelphia Aurora* chortled. "If the Federalists are all as bad as they paint each other," crowed the Portsmouth *Ledger*, "can anyone hesitate to say that Mr. Jefferson is the most suitable . . . for President?"

So the election steamed into the home stretch, with charges and countercharges sulphuring the atmosphere. As state after state went to the polls, it was evident from Congressional and local elections that a Republican swing was in the making. But the Presidential race remained extremely close. In New Jersey, the Federalists discovered a legal loophole which permitted women to vote, and they marched enough wives and daughters to the polls to swing the state to Adams. Maryland, where both sides had hoped for victory, dropped its unit election ban and each party came away with five electoral votes. Delaware, where Jefferson's old friend of 1776, Caesar Rodney, was Republican leader, went Federalist by three hundred votes.

Meanwhile, Aaron Burr was sending a stream of letters and personal representatives to Jefferson and his lieutenants, to make sure that the southern gentlemen kept their promise not to "lurch" him. One who called on Jefferson personally was young Joseph Alston of South Carolina, who was engaged to marry Burr's beautiful and brilliant daughter, Theodosia. Neither Jefferson nor Madison, whom Alston also visited en route, knew of this imminent connection with the Burr family, so Alston was able to pose as an honest and disinterested southerner, carrying Burr's plea for "the integrity of the southern states."

Early in November, Madison had another visitor, George W. Irving of Boston. He had been rushed to Montpelier by James Monroe, now Governor of Virginia, with some very alarming rumors that Burr was contriving to hold southern votes in line, while intriguing to throw away northern votes for Jefferson, which would make Burr the President of the United States. The forthright Monroe had never trusted Burr because he tended to seesaw between the two parties. But Madison's confidence in the New Yorker was restored by a letter from David Gelston, Burr's right-hand man. Gelston said he had heard that Virginia planned to throw away one or two votes from Colonel Burr to make sure the election did not end in a tie. Gelston called upon "the honor of the gentlemen of Virginia" and then added a blatant lie. "We are well aware from good information that three states, two at least, will give Mr. J three or more votes more than Mr. B will have, but I trust that it never will be said that either Virginia or New York could be guilty of such a subterfuge."

Thus, with the complete approval of Madison and Jefferson, Virginia's electors cast 21 votes for Jefferson and 21 for Aaron Burr. In New York a far different scene took place. One Republican elector, Anthony Lispinard, abruptly refused to give a pledge to vote for Jefferson. Only a last-minute resolution requiring all 12 electors to show their ballots to one another held him in line. Thus Aaron Burr's first attempt to seize the Presidency by deception was blocked by Republicans loyal to Jefferson.

Meanwhile, government officials and congressmen were slowly filtering into the new federal city of Washington, which was now the national capital. Ten years of sporadic building had made little impression on what seemed at first glance a near wilderness. Only one part of the Capitol was finished, and the White House, better known as the President's "Palace," still dripped of wet plaster. Congressmen had to jam into two boardinghouses on opposite sides of New Jersey Avenue. Streets were seas of mud and not even President Adams could get anyone to chop enough wood to keep him and Abigail warm. Luxury-loving Gouverneur Morris, senator from New York, said with fine irony, "This is the best city in the world to live in—in the future."

Jefferson had arrived in the city he had labored so hard to create

on November 27, in his usual unobtrusive fashion. He took rooms
with the Republicans at Conrad and McMunn's boardinghouse.
The twenty to thirty lodgers ate each day at a common table and
Jefferson absolutely declined to sit at the head of it, close to the
fire, even though as Vice President he was the ranking politician in
the house. Instead he took a chair wherever chance landed him,
usually well below the salt, near the drafty door. But seating
arrangements were hardly a major topic of conversation. The still
undecided Presidential election absorbed every politician's waking
thoughts. The vote, as things now stood, was:

Jefferson	65
Burr	65
Adams	65
Pinckney	64

8 votes from South Carolina—undecided

For the first time it dawned on the Republicans that Jefferson
and Burr might finish in a tie. The Republicans had a small
majority in the South Carolina legislature, which would choose the
Presidential electors. Jefferson, therefore, stood a good chance of
winning, but Burr was equally determined to stay in the race. His
future son-in-law, Joseph Alston, was working mightily for him in
the legislature, and the candidate himself sent a New York lawyer,
Timothy Green, as a special agent to persuade South Carolinians to
support him. They succeeded handily, and South Carolina voted
down the line for both candidates.

The final choice for President would be made by the House of
Representatives.

Federalist politicians instantly saw a marvelous opportunity to
rescue their fading cause from the political disaster that had engulfed it. Gouverneur Morris wrote in his diary shortly after the
news arrived: "Burr must be preferred to Jefferson."

XI

The revival of Federalist confidence rested on another political
oddity—Presidential terms began in those days on March 4, and a
lame-duck Congress and President were in charge until the chang-

ing of the guard. This meant that the Federalists still had a strong cadre in the House of Representatives. Moreover, the vote would be taken by states, and the winner would need two-thirds—nine—to become President.

Jefferson, scanning the state delegations with the astute eye of a party leader, immediately predicted that he could be sure of only eight states; the Federalists had six. Two other state delegations were tied, which in effect gave them no vote. Thus a deadlock appeared all too possible, in which the country would have no President.

This did not disturb many Federalists. They talked of having the Senate elect a President pro tempore, perhaps John Marshall, the Secretary of State, who was next in line after the President and Vice President. It was, they declared, only a mild "stretch" of the Constitution.

In New York, Colonel Burr was proving himself very evasive when it came to an honest statement of his intentions. He wrote smooth, plausible letters to Jefferson, vowing his complete support of him. But when Samuel Smith, a Baltimore Republican congressman, published a letter Burr had sent him before the final tally stating that Burr would utterly disclaim all competition with Jefferson, Burr became extremely angry, and made it clear that General Smith had been authorized only to "declare" his sentiments but not to print them in the newspapers. Smith, highly alarmed, asked Burr to meet him in Philadelphia and Burr agreed. Smith wanted the slippery little colonel to say plainly that he would *not* accept the Presidency, under any circumstances. The Marylander brought along with him Benjamin Hichborn, a Republican from Massachusetts. The three men talked for hours, but at no point would Burr make the concession Smith and Hichborn wanted to hear. Instead he told them, "We must have a President and a Constitutional one in some way."

"How is it to be done?" Hichborn asked. "Mr. Jefferson's friends will not quit him, and his enemies are not strong enough to carry another."

"Why," said Burr, "our friends must join the Federalists and give them the President."

The following morning at breakfast Burr reiterated his carefully phrased availability. "We cannot be without a President, our friends must join the Federal vote."

"But," Hichborn said, "we shall then be without a Vice President; who is to be our Vice President?"

"Mr. Jefferson," answered Colonel Burr.

At this point Jefferson was still convinced that Burr was trustworthy. The very day that Smith, Hichborn and Burr were meeting in Philadelphia, Jefferson was writing his daughter Maria, "The Federalists were confident at first they could debauch Colo. B. from his good faith by offering him their vote to be President, and have seriously proposed it to him. His conduct has been honorable and decisive, and greatly embarrasses them."

Acting very much like a President-elect, Jefferson had the day before crossed the Potomac and paid a visit to George Washington's widow, who greeted him cordially and asked eagerly after Maria, whom she remembered from Presidential days in Philadelphia. Jefferson even began planning White House visits for Maria. "This new destination"—Washington, D.C.—made the distance "so moderate" that he hoped a journey to the White House "would be scarcely more inconvenient than one to Monticello."

Twelve days later, after he had heard Hichborn's report of the Philadelphia conference with Burr, he was writing to his older daughter in a far different frame of mind. "If I am fixed here, it will be but three easy days' journey from you; so that I should hope you and the family could pay an annual visit here at least. . . . On this subject, however, we may hereafter converse, lest we should be counting chickens before they are hatched."

Jefferson was also wrestling with another problem—how to deal with his old friend John Adams, still in the White House, in possession of the Presidential power for another two months. Jefferson may have already seen that Adams could block the Federalist scheme of a temporary president with a stroke of his pen—vetoing the bill that created the monster. Aside from this possibility the winning candidate also felt he owed the loser the courtesy of a visit, and he sensed that the timing was all important. If he came too soon, he might look as if he were exulting over Adams' downfall; if he waited too long, Adams' hypersensitivity might construe the delay as a slight.

Aiming at what he hoped was a middle date, Jefferson paid his call. He instantly saw that he had come too soon. Adams charged him like a querulous bulldog, shrilling: "You have turned me out, you have turned me out!"

"*I* have not turned you out," Jefferson said gently. Mustering all his charm, he told Adams that it had never been a personal contest. They were both simply symbols of "the political division" in the country. If both of them died tomorrow, two other men would step forward, to play the identical roles. In fact, Jefferson added, without Adams' personal popularity, the Federalists would have been beaten far more badly. This mollified John Yankee and the two men sat down as friends. Mournfully, Adams revealed another reason for his black mood, beyond politics. The very day he had heard the bad news from South Carolina, he had learned that his son Charles, a handsome young man who had "once been the delight of my eyes and the darling of my heart," had died of alcoholism in New York.

Even though it was obvious that Adams was unlikely to help solve the Presidential deadlock, Jefferson remained optimistic. As he wrote Governor Thomas McKean of Pennsylvania, "six individuals, of moderate character any one of whom coming over to the Republican side" would give him the needed state. Among these were Delaware's lone representative, thirty-three-year-old James A. Bayard, and Maryland's two Federalists George Bear and William Craik, who had both opposed war with France. The other two Maryland Federalist congressmen were also considered moderates. Then there was Federalist Lewis Morris of Vermont, nephew of Gouverneur Morris. A switch on his part would bring the Green Mountain State into Jefferson's column.

But Burr, counting votes from his side of the aisle, obviously thought his chances were almost as good—and he was right. New Jersey was divided 3 to 2 for Jefferson, but this was Burr's native state. His father had been president of Princeton and one of the three Republican congressmen, Dr. James Linn, was a standing joke in Congress for his wavering between the parties. In equally divided Maryland the Burrites were depending on George Dent, who had taken to voting with the Republicans but had been elected as a Federalist. In the New York delegation, divided 6 to 4 for Jefferson, Burr had two intimate personal friends, Congressmen Edward Livingston and Theodorus Bailey. Then there was Tennessee, whose lone vote, held by William C. Claiborne, might lean toward Burr because in his Senate days he had lent them powerful support in their fight for statehood.

By mid-January, Edward Livingston was telling his friends that he would cast his first ballot for Jefferson, and switch to Burr. Twice during this month of suspended animation, New Yorkers claiming to speak for Burr appeared in Washington and did their utmost to persuade New Jersey and New York congressmen to swing to their man. Each time, when worried Jeffersonians, including the Presidential candidate himself, wrote the colonel, asking him by what authority these men spoke, he blandly disowned them. But it was becoming more and more apparent to Jefferson and everyone else that Burr was in the game for the Presidency.

All he had to do, if he wanted to dynamite the Federal scheme, was make a quick trip to Washington and state publicly that he was not a candidate for the first place as Jefferson had done for John Adams in 1796. Instead, Burr retreated to Albany and pretended to be absorbed in legislative affairs and preparations for his daughter's wedding. When Samuel Smith wrote, trying one more time to get a positive statement out of him, Burr replied coyly that he stood by his original letter in which he disclaimed all competition with Jefferson. Beyond that, "to enter into details would take reams of paper and years of time." As one historian has since noted acerbicly, "It would have taken little of either to get out of the race."

In his letter to Martha on January 16, Jefferson added a footnote which announced the strangest of the many twists and turns in this Presidential drama. "Hamilton is using his uttermost influence to procure my election rather than Colo. Burr's." It was the truth. When Hamilton heard the first hints of the Federalists' scheme, he thought it might be shrewd politics to "throw out a lure" for Burr "to tempt him to start for the plate," and thus lay the foundation of "dissension between him and Jefferson." But when he discovered his fellow Federalists were in earnest, Hamilton declared that he felt "in the awkward situation of a man who continues sober after the company are drunk." He sent a stream of letters

pouring into Washington, begging his followers to regain their
senses. Burr, he said, was "the most unfitted, dangerous man in the
community." He compared him to Catiline, the dissolute intriguer
who almost destroyed the Roman Republic. "Like Catiline he is
indefatigable in courting young men and profligates," Hamilton
told James McHenry. "He knows well the weak sides of human
nature . . . by natural disposition the haughtiest of men, he is at
the same time the most creeping to answer his purposes. . . . He
will court and employ able and daring young scoundrels of every
party and . . . attempt an usurpation."

"No mortal can tell what his political principles are," Hamilton
insisted. "He has talked all around the compass. . . . If he has any
theory, 'tis that of simple despotism."

Compared to Burr, Hamilton insisted, Jefferson was almost a
blessing. He at least had pretensions to character, though he conceded Jefferson was "a contemptible hypocrite."

But Hamilton's influence with his party was gone. He had destroyed it with his reckless attack on Adams and his schemes to
frustrate the electoral process by making presidents out of Pinck-
neys. The Federalists in Congress were only taking a leaf from
their ex-leader's book in the game they were playing with Burr.
Their letters to him are dismaying evidence of how totally they
had become captives of their own invective against Jefferson. John
Marshall piously rejected Hamilton, declaring: "The morals of the
author of the letter to Mazzei cannot be pure." House leader
Theodore Sedgwick admitted that everything Hamilton said about
Burr was true. "There is no disagreement as to his character. He is
ambitious—selfish—profligate. His ambition is of the worst kind; it
is a mere love of power, regardless of fame; his selfishness excludes
all social affections; and his profligacy unrestrained by any moral
sentiments and defying all decency."

Nevertheless Sedgwick maintained that Burr's "manners are
plausible" and he was "a mere matter of fact man" holding "no
previous theories." Therefore, this distinguished leader of his party
was able to blandly ask Hamilton "to what evil shall we expose
ourselves by the choice of Burr, which we should escape by the
election of Jefferson?"

Hamilton was indeed dealing with men so drunk with party

bitterness they no longer made sense. But he did Jefferson one service which may have been crucial. He persuaded the head of the powerful Livingston clan, Chancellor Robert Livingston, to write a "very peremptory letter" to his brother Edward warning him not to switch his vote to Burr.

Meanwhile, the Republicans were engaged in some fierce politicking of their own. A caucus of the New Jersey and New York Congressional delegation was held on January 31. The pro-Jefferson majority forced everyone to take a pledge to stay with their man under any and all circumstances. Three of the four Maryland Republicans had a similar meeting, and joined in a similar pledge. But when they invited their fourth member, Joseph Nicholson, to join them, they were alarmed to discover he had taken to his bed with a high fever, and might not be able to vote. This would throw Maryland to Burr, 4 to 3.

On February 10, 1801, the Federalist majority in the House set the rules for the Presidential vote. One of them, passed over strong Republican objections, stipulated that the House could not adjourn until a choice was made. Learning of Nicholson's illness, the Federalists hoped to capture the vote of his state when he collapsed.

The next day, the electors' votes were duly counted and Jefferson as president of the Senate calmly announced the well-known result. The electors had failed to choose a President, he declared. The solemn task now passed to the House of Representatives.

XII

During the night, a snowstorm had blanketed the "federal village." The unfinished chamber of the House of Representatives was unheated and filled with chilling drafts. Yet Congressman Nicholson of Maryland braved the slush outside and the temperature inside to take up his post on a cot in a committee room, his wife beside him, a bottle of medicine in her hand. The voting began, and on the first ballot, the predicted split occurred—8 states for Jefferson, 6 for Burr. It was not the first, but the second ballot which the 104 members awaited with mounting excitement. They crowded around the New York ballot box, waiting to see if

Livingston and Bailey had switched. But they remained true to their caucus pledge, and New York as well as the other 7 Republican states remained firmly in the Jefferson column. Nicholson, so feeble that his wife had to guide his hand, again managed to scrawl the single word Jefferson on his all-important ballot.

Grimly the balloting resumed. All through the day and into the night the bitterly divided congressmen voted. Some stumbled off to committee rooms to snatch a few moments of rest and reeled back into the chamber to vote with old-fashioned nightcaps sprouting on their heads. On the twenty-eighth ballot, at 8 A.M. on February 12, the line still held firm on both sides. Federalist energy wavered, and they agreed to adjourn until 11 A.M. As the representatives staggered out, a Federalist senator noted, "They looked banged badly."

At noon, and another ballot, not a vote had changed. The Federalists wearily agreed to another adjournment, until 11 o'clock the next day, Friday. Now the real politicking began. Jefferson, huddling with his fellow Republicans at Conrad and McMunn's, heard what was going on behind the scenes. Federalists were making wild offers on Burr's behalf. Bayard of Delaware had guaranteed Samuel Smith of Maryland the secretaryship of the navy. The same Federalist had told Edward Livingston that he was insane not to switch to his friend Burr, he had "everything to expect if he would come over." Before wavering, Linn of New Jersey was dangled the governorship of his home state. Bayard said he was "authorized" to make these offers. Another Federalist congressman went to Matthew Lyon of Vermont and asked, "What is it you want, Colonel Lyon? Is it office, is it money? Only say what you want, and you shall have it."

Simultaneously, the Republicans were applying their own kind of pressure. Petitions poured in from the Maryland district of Federalist John Chew Thomas telling him that two-thirds of his constituents wanted him to switch to Jefferson, but he remained immovable.

All day Friday the congressmen balloted and still the deadlock persisted. After three more ballots on Saturday, there was another adjournment and Jefferson through a third party got a significant feeler from Senator Gouverneur Morris. "How comes it that Burr who is four hundred miles off, has agents here at Washington with great activity, while Mr. Jefferson, who is on the spot, does nothing?" Jefferson instantly saw that the senator was ready to trade his nephew's vote for a price. A little later, when the Vice President was coming down the steps of the Capitol, the peg-legged New York aristocrat hailed him and struck up a conversation on the crisis. He told Jefferson that his opponents were chiefly concerned about three things. One, that he would turn all the Federalists out of office. Two, that he would abolish the navy (which Republicans had criticized and opposed) and, three, repudiate the public debt. All he had to do, Morris assured Jefferson, was declare that he would not "take these steps" and he would be "instantly" elected.

Jefferson calmly told him he would "leave the world to judge of the course I meant to pursue by that which I had pursued hitherto."

For the present he would "certainly make no terms." Never would he go into the office of President "by capitulation, nor with my hands tied."

Jefferson's friends in Virginia and Pennsylvania were taking a more impatient view of the situation. Governor James Monroe made it clear through Virginia congressmen that he was ready to summon the state's militia to march on Washington. Rumblings from Pennsylvania announced that Governor Thomas McKean was ready to take the same route the moment the Federalists attempted to install a temporary president. The leaders of these large states also said that they intended to call a convention to write a new Constitution in which the small states would have their present privileges drastically reduced. The *Gazette of the United States* warned that any such moves by Virginia and Pennsylvania meant civil war.

Jefferson, always anxious to avoid even a show of force, returned to the half-finished White House and asked John Adams to declare that he would veto any bill to install a temporary president. Adams testily declined. He saw no threat of civil war, and thought a temporary president was "justifiable." Adams told Jefferson he could become President in five minutes if he would give the Federalists the assurances they had recently demanded, through Morris. Wearily, Jefferson reiterated his refusal to capitulate to his enemies, and insisted he should be judged on his past record as a responsible public servant.

The rumors of civil war and a new federal convention did much to weaken a key Federalist, James Bayard of Delaware. His little state could easily be swallowed up by his powerful Republican neighbors, Pennsylvania and Virginia. The present Constitution was his only protection. He went to a Virginia congressman and asked him if he could get guarantees from Jefferson on the points Morris had outlined. The congressman assured him he had nothing to worry about, but Bayard insisted on "an engagement." Bayard next turned to Samuel Smith of Maryland, who had been toiling so assiduously on Jefferson's behalf. Like all politicians, Bayard got down to specific cases. He wanted to be sure one of his oldest friends, Allen McLane, was retained as collector of the port of Wilmington.

Living in the same boardinghouse as Jefferson, it was easy for Smith to bring up the subject. Whether he specifically said that he was bringing a request from Bayard, or whether he "fished" the answer out of Jefferson by throwing out McLane's name as an example in a general conversation, remains something of a mystery. But Jefferson told Smith that he considered McLane, who had been a distinguished soldier in the Revolution, "a meritorious officer" and that he "would not be displaced, or ought not to be displaced."

This was as close as Jefferson came to making any deals. On Sunday, February 15, he wrote proudly to Monroe, "Many attempts have been made to obtain terms and promises from me. I have declared to them unequivocally that I would not receive the government on capitulation, that I would not go into it with my hands tied." Obviously, he was referring to the larger issues on which Gouverneur Morris had quizzed him. The fate of collector McLane was hardly a major policy decision.

On Monday, February 16, when the congressmen met again, the mood of the city was growing ugly. A mob swarmed around the Capitol "like a thunder cloud . . . their indignation ready to burst." Republicans, who thought that Bayard would come over on the first ballot, were angrily disappointed when, instead, he called for a Federalist caucus. In this private party meeting he demanded to know if anyone had heard a word from Aaron Burr.

Without some statement from him, what was the point of bringing down the government? Were they going to elect a man who owed nothing to either party? That would make him "the most dangerous man in the community." Hamilton was right, Bayard declared, the country was safer with Jefferson.

New England fanatics leaped to their feet shouting, "Deserter! Deserter." But Bayard was immovable. He was going to vote for Jefferson.

The next morning, the Federalists fell apart completely. Lewis Morris of Vermont withdrew, giving that state to Jefferson, the four Maryland Federalists handed in blank ballots, giving Jefferson ten states, one more than he needed. Looking like a man who had just swallowed a porcupine, Speaker Theodore Sedgwick had to announce that Thomas Jefferson was officially elected the third President of the United States. Outside, the news reached the crowd and there were volleys of cheers. Cannon boomed in Virginia and that night at Conrad's boardinghouse there was a sumptuous celebration. Candles blazed in the windows of dozens of homes. It was in fact a night for rejoicing. The infant republic had passed through the worst crisis since its founding.

Inevitably, people's minds now turned to another, more difficult question. Could Jefferson resolve the deeper crisis—the appalling divisions between parties and sections that the Presidential campaign and its aftermath had made so painfully evident? Two of the most prominent men in the nation, John Adams and Alexander Hamilton, did not think so. They were convinced the ship of state was headed for the rocks. Jefferson, pondering the problem in his modest room at Conrad's boardinghouse, sat down to write the most important paper he had undertaken since the Declaration of Independence—his inaugural address.

BOOK

FIVE

*Rebirth
of a Nation*

O N THE MORNING of Jefferson's inauguration, he strolled casually into the dining room of Conrad's boardinghouse and headed for his usual seat at the bottom of the table. The wife of the senator from Kentucky offered him her seat at the head of the table but the President-elect declined it with a smile and took his usual place below the salt. The lady later said she felt indignant, and for a moment almost hated the leveling spirit of democracy.

The incident struck the note which Jefferson insisted on maintaining throughout his Presidency. "Republican simplicity" was a phrase he loved, and he was determined to show the people that the pomp and ceremony, the "forms" of monarchy which he had criticized in his letter to Mazzei, were no longer part of the federal government. At noon, dressed "like a plain citizen without any distinctive badge of office," Jefferson left Conrad's boardinghouse and, flanked by several members of Congress, ambled the two blocks to the Capitol. He could, of course, do nothing about the huge crowd that streamed in his wake. Thousands of plain citizens had swarmed in from the Virginia and Maryland countryside to celebrate the great day. Nor could he stop federal artillerymen from firing a magnificent salute as he mounted the steps of the Capitol.

An estimated one thousand people jammed into the small Senate chamber. The Senate sat on one side, while the Representatives gallantly surrendered their seats to the ladies. "Every inch of ground was occupied," Margaret Bayard Smith said.

On the dais, Aaron Burr, already sworn as Vice President, vacated the presiding officer's chair. Jefferson took the familiar seat, between Burr and Chief Justice John Marshall, recently

[273]

appointed by outgoing President Adams. Old "John Yankee" himself was conspicuously absent. As a last gesture of New England irreconcilability, Adams had jounced out of the darkened capital at 4 A.M. in the morning, heading back to Quincy, Massachusetts. Not far behind him in another private carriage was Speaker of the House Theodore Sedgwick. Thus the gaping national wounds which challenged Jefferson were visible to the expectant audience.

Jefferson waited a few moments for the crowd to subside. Then he rose and delivered his inaugural address. His voice was low and tense; he knew he was no speaker and he made no attempt to overcome his deficiency. He had given an advance copy of his speech to the *National Intelligencer*, which would have papers on the street by noon. It is a relatively forgotten inaugural speech today, overshadowed by the more polished oratory of Lincoln, Roosevelt and Kennedy. But Lincoln's great appeal for reconciliation failed. Jefferson's succeeded. For that reason alone, Americans might well ponder the heart of Jefferson's message.

During the contest of opinion, through which we have passed, the animation of discussion and of exertions has sometimes worn an aspect which might impose on strangers unused to think freely and to speak and to write what they think.

But this being now decided by the voice of the nation, announced according to the rules of the Constitution, all will, of course, arrange themselves under the will of the law, and unite in common efforts for the common good. All, too, will bear in mind this sacred principle, that though the will of the majority is in all cases to prevail, that will, to be rightful, must be reasonable; that the minority possess their equal rights, which equal laws must protect, and to violate which would be oppression.

Let us then, fellow citizens, unite with one heart and one mind. Let us restore the social intercourse, that harmony and affection without which liberty and even life itself are dreary things. And let us reflect that having banished from our land that religious intolerance under which mankind so long bled and suffered, we have yet gained little if we countenance a political intolerance as despotic, as wicked, and capable of as bitter and bloody persecutions.

During the throes and convulsions of the ancient world, during the agonizing spasms of infuriated man, seeking through blood and slaughter his long lost liberty, it was not wonderful that the agitation of the billows should reach even this distant and peaceful shore; that this should be more felt and feared by some, and less by others; that this should divide opinions as to measures of safety.

But every difference of opinion is not a difference of principle. We have called by different names brethren of the same principle. We are all Republicans—we are all Federalists.

If there be any among us who would wish to dissolve this union or to change its republican form, let them stand undisturbed as monuments of the safety with which error of opinion may be tolerated where reason is left free to combat it.

I know, indeed, that some honest men fear that a republican government cannot be strong; that this government is not strong enough. But would the honest patriot, in the full tide of successful experiment, abandon a government which has so far kept us free and firm, on the theoretic and visionary fear that this government, the world's best hope, may by possibility want energy to preserve itself?

I trust not. I believe this, on the contrary, the strongest government on earth.

I believe it the only one where every man, at the call of the laws, would fly to the standard of the law and would meet invasions of the public order, as his own personal concern.

Sometimes it is said that man cannot be trusted with the government of himself. Can he then be trusted with the government of others? Or have we found angels in the forms of kings to govern him? Let history answer this question.

About to enter, fellow citizens, on the exercise of duties, which comprehend everything dear & valuable to you, it is proper that you should understand what I deem the essential principle of this government, and consequently those which ought to shape its administration. I will compress them in the narrowest compass they will bear, stating the general principle, but not all its limitations.

Equal and exact justice to all men, of whatever state or persuasion, religious or political.

Peace, commerce, and an honest friendship, with all nations—entangling alliances with none.

The support of the state governments in all their rights, as the most competent administration for our domestic concerns and the surest bulwarks against anti-republican tendencies.

The preservation of the General Government in its whole Constitutional vigor, as the sheet anchor of our peace at home and safety abroad.

A jealous care of the right of election by the people—a mild and safe corrective of abuses which are lopped by the sword of revolution where peaceable remedies are unprovided.

Absolute acquiescence in the decisions of the majority—the vital principle of republics, from which there is no appeal but to force, the vital principle and immediate parent of despotism.

The supremacy of the civil over the military authority.

Economy in the public expense, that labor may be lightly burdened.

The honest payment of our debts and sacred preservation of the public faith.

Encouragement of agriculture, and of commerce as its handmaid.

The diffusion of information and the arraignment of all abuses at the bar of public reason.

Freedom of religion; freedom of the press; freedom of person under the protection of the habeas corpus; and trial by juries impartially selected.

These principles form the bright constellation which has gone before us, and guided our steps through an age of revolution and reformation: the wisdom of our sages, & blood of our heroes, have been devoted to their attainment: they should be the creed of our political faith, the text of civic instruction, the touchstone by which to try the services of those we trust: and should we wander from them, in moments of error or alarm, let us hasten to retrace our steps and to regain the road which alone leads to peace, liberty and safety.

I repair then, fellow citizens, to the post which you have assigned me.

With experience enough in subordinate offices to have seen the difficulties of this, the greatest of all, I have learned to expect that it will rarely fall to the lot of imperfect man to retire from this station with the reputation and the favor which bring him into it.

Without pretension to that high confidence reposed in our first and great revolutionary character, whose pre-eminent services had entitled him to the first place in his country's love, and destined for him the fairest page in the volume of faithful history, I ask so much confidence only as may give firmness and effect to the legal administration of your affairs.

I shall often go wrong through defect of judgment. When right, I shall often be thought wrong by those whose positions will not command a whole view of the ground.

I ask your indulgence for my own errors, which will never be intentional; and your support against the errors of others, who may condemn what they would not if seen in all its parts. . . .

And may that infinite power which rules the destinies of the universe

lead our councils to what is best, and give them a favorable issue for
your peace & prosperity.

Thus Jefferson commenced what he afterward called "the second American revolution." Thanks almost entirely to him, it was a
peaceful revolution, without a bayonet drawn or bullet fired. A
new sense of hope pervaded the mass of the nation. "This day a
new era commences," wrote Samuel Harrison Smith in the *National Intelligencer*. Governor Thomas McKean of Pennsylvania
had used the same phrase in a letter, congratulating Jefferson before
the inauguration.

As always, Jefferson did not rely solely on glittering generalities.
He knew that the nation was not going to be reunited by mere
words. The new President was planning to use that most realistic
of tools, which he had done so much to invent—the political party.

When he said, "We are all Republicans—we are all Federalists,"
his purpose was not only healing wounds, but bringing over to the
Republican Party a majority of the Federalists. Jefferson's political
realism was never more evident than in the letter he wrote to James
Monroe on March 7, 1801, two days after his inauguration. "The
leading objects" of his inaugural address, he said, were "conciliation and adherence to sound principle." He knew it was "impracti-
cable" to conciliate the Federalist leaders "whom I abandon as
incurables . . . but with the main body of the Federalists, I believe it very practicable."

The threat of anarchy the Federalist leaders had created by their
reckless support of Burr had caused thousands of their followers
"to desire anxiously the very event they had just before opposed
with all their energies, and to receive the election which was made,
as . . . a child of their own. These people . . . look with a certain
degree of affection and confidence to the administration, ready to
become attached to it, if it avoids in the outset acts which might
revolt and throw them off. To give time for a perfect consolidation
seems prudent."

History has confirmed the brilliance of Jefferson's political insight. By firmly following the policy he laid down here, he united
the nation behind the Republican Party so totally that he created
what James Madison proudly called in later years "the Republican
ascendancy." Jeffersonians were to hold the White House for

twenty-eight years, one of the longest consecutive rules by a single party in the history of the nation.

Jefferson did not accomplish this near-miracle without a fight with extremists within his own party. "Sweeping Republicans" such as Congressman William Giles of Virginia and William Duane, the editor of the Philadelphia *Aurora*, thought there should be a wholesale purge of Federalists from government jobs. Monroe, more headstrong than Jefferson, also leaned in this direction, but Jefferson calmly pointed out to him the political folly of such a policy. "Deprivations of office, if made on the ground of political principles alone, would revolt our new converts." He was realistic enough to admit that some changes must be made but he insisted "they must be as few as possible, done gradually and bottomed on some . . . disqualification."

A major problem intimately connected with the question of jobs had been dumped in Jefferson's lap by his old friend John Adams. In the last days of his term, Adams had appointed scores of Federalists to offices in the various government departments. Most galling of these "midnight appointments"—he signed some of the commissions between 9 P.M. and 12 P.M. on his final day in office—were twenty-three additional federal judges voted by the lame-duck Congress, supposedly to ease the burden on the Supreme Court. With John Marshall, his most inveterate enemy in Virginia, already seated as Chief Justice, Jefferson complained angrily that the Federalists, driven from control of two branches of the government, were hoping to destroy the Republican program by entrenching their stalwarts in the judiciary. (Marshall grabbed two of these judgeships, plus a U.S. attorney's job, for three of his relatives.) There was little Jefferson could do but complain, since the Constitution stipulated that federal judges were appointed for life.

Before he could attack this or any other problem, Jefferson had to organize his cabinet. James Madison's appointment as Secretary of State was almost a foregone conclusion. Jefferson was urging him to come to Washington well before the inauguration. For the equally vital Treasury post, Jefferson turned to Albert Gallatin, who had shown himself, as the Republican leader in the House, the equal of Hamilton in the labyrinthine intricacies of public finance.

For his Attorney General, Jefferson chose a Massachusetts man, Harvard-educated Levi Lincoln. The Secretary of War was Henry Dearborn of Maine, a solid Revolutionary War soldier. Robert Smith, brother of Maryland's Republican stalwart Samuel Smith, became the Secretary of the Navy.

Madison naturally brought his charming Dolley with him to Washington and while they were searching for a house in the sparsely populated Federal City, Jefferson invited them to stay at the White House. In a matter of weeks, the dismayed President discovered that the malice toward him among the leading Federalists had by no means diminished. These embittered politicians were soon whispering all around Washington that Jefferson and Dolley were conducting an amour under poor Jemmy Madison's nose. "I thought my age & ordinary demeanor would have prevented any suggestions in that form, from the improbability of their obtaining belief," wrote the President, sadly.

This was the beginning of a campaign of slander against Jefferson that stooped lower than the assaults made on him when he was running for President. Much of the smut emanated from one man, James Callender, a dissolute Scottish newspaperman who had written virulent assaults on Presidents Washington and Adams. Hunted down under the Sedition Act, Callender had been tried in Richmond by Judge Samuel Chase of the Supreme Court, with a vindictiveness that shocked the entire state. Callender had been fined $200 and sentenced to nine months in jail. Jefferson sympathized with Callender, as he did with all the victims of the Sedition Act. Unfortunately, proximity inspired Callender to single out Jefferson as his benefactor, and he bombarded him with long, begging letters and copies of the book he was writing, *The Prospect Before Us*.

With only the slightest personal acquaintance, Jefferson had no idea that Callender was spiraling steadily downward morally and psychologically. Sympathy, and Callender's constant wheedling, persuaded Jefferson to send him $200 over the course of some dozen months. Even more unwisely, Jefferson had commented on the proof sheets of the first section of *The Prospect Before Us*. "Such papers cannot fail to produce the best effect." The later parts of the book degenerated into a scurrilous attack on Washington and Adams which impugned their patriotism, honesty and honor.

One of Jefferson's first acts as President was to pardon all the victims of the Sedition Act, who were still in jail, including Callender. He also ordered his $200 fine refunded, but the federalist U.S. marshal in Richmond refused to accept the opinion of the Attorney General that it was legal to do so. Callender, in desperate need of money, turned up in Governor Monroe's office, shouting bitter denunciations of Jefferson, weeping hysterically, and demanding money for a trip to Washington. Next he appeared in Madison's office at the State Department, where another violent scene took place. By now he was snarling blatant threats about a "piece of small history that Jefferson's enemies would love to possess." The price of his silence, he insisted, was the postmastership of Richmond.

Jefferson refused to consider such a deal, but he made the mistake of trying to refund Callender's fine through subscriptions from himself and his friends. He donated $50, listing it in his account book as "charity." Callender, by now completely "fermented," to use Madison's description, arrogantly told Jefferson's secretary, Meriwether Lewis, that he received the money "not as charity, but a due, in fact as hush money." When no more money was forthcoming, Callender went back to Virginia, wangled the editorship of a paper called the *Recorder*, and began attacking Jefferson savagely. He started with the purely political libel that Jefferson had literally employed him and furnished material for his low road attacks on Washington and Adams. From there Callender proceeded to scour Virginia, collecting every dirty rumor ever whispered about Jefferson. Some he printed himself, others he secretly circulated to the Federalists.

Perhaps the vilest was the story that Jefferson had fathered numerous children with Sally Hemings, the pretty Negro slave who had accompanied little Maria to Paris. In the Federalist magazine, *The Portfolio*, supposedly dedicated to literature, the following song appeared on October 2, 1802, subtitled, "Supposed to have been written by the Sage of Monticello."

> Of all the damsels on the green
> On mountain, or in valley,

A lass so luscious ne'er was seen
As Monticellian Sally.

Yankee Doodle, who's the noodle?
What wife were half so handy?
To breed a flock of slaves for stock,
A black amour's the dandy. . . .

When press'd by load of state affairs,
I seek to sport and dally,
The sweetest solace of my cares
Is in the lap of Sally.

Yankee Doodle, etc.

What though she by the glands secretes;
Must I stand shill-I-shall-I?
Tuck'd up between a pair of sheets
There's no perfume like Sally.

Yankee Doodle, etc.

The Federalists expanded the saga of Sally until Jefferson was pictured setting her up as queen of Monticello, ordering his daughters to call her "Mother."

The kernel of fact in this unpleasant story was the origin of Sally Hemings. She and her brothers James and John and her mulatto mother, Betty, had come to Monticello after the death of John Wayles, as part of Martha Jefferson's inheritance. Betty was the daughter of an English ship captain and a Wayles slave girl. It is probable, though by no means certain, that Sally and her brothers were the children of John Wayles. Jefferson seems to have been aware of their special status, and treated them accordingly. Sally and her mother were among Monticello's chief house servants. John became an expert carpenter and James a French chef under Jefferson's tutelage.

Further grist for the slander mill is the undoubted fact, recorded in Jefferson's Farm Book, that Sally Hemings gave birth to four children at Monticello, between 1798 and 1808. The father, according to Edmund Bacon, Jefferson's overseer at the time, was one of Jefferson's Carr nephews. Jefferson himself was only an occasional visitor at Monticello during these years. Whether he knew the parentage of Sally's children is uncertain. Neither of his daughters was living at Monticello. The secret might easily have been concealed from him. What he could have done about it, even if he did know, is equally uncertain. Such sexual license between young whites and slave girls was not unusual at the time. It was one of the "boisterous passions" Jefferson alluded to when he condemned slavery in his book, *Notes on Virginia*.

That Jefferson himself would have committed such an indiscretion—and then recorded the results in his Farm Book in his own hand—at the very time when he was a committed candidate for the Presidency, and continued the relationship throughout his two terms, when he was under the most relentless personal attack by the Federalists, is almost a refutation in itself. But no special set of facts disproves the possibility of a liaison between Jefferson and Sally. The fundamental pattern of Jefferson's whole life is the best answer. That such an idealistic man could, at the age of fifty-five, have openly maintained this illicit relationship and retained the respect and affection of his daughters and the numerous other relatives who visited Monticello is simply incredible.

Jefferson never made the slightest attempt to refute the story in his lifetime. He obviously considered it beneath contempt. Gritting his teeth, he continued to believe in the freedom of the press. He reiterated his confidence that by encouraging responsible newspapers such as Samuel Harrison Smith's *National Intelligencer*, good reporting would eventually drive out the bad.

One day Jefferson received a visit from Baron Alexander von Humboldt, the distinguished German scientist who had come to America to see its "great men." As he waited for the President in his study, the baron picked up a Federalist newspaper that was filled with the usual slanders against Jefferson. When he came in, the agitated German asked him: "Why is not this libelous journal suppressed, or its editor at least fined and imprisoned?"

Jefferson smiled. "Put that paper in your pocket, Baron, and should you hear the reality of our liberty, the freedom of the press, questioned, show this paper, and tell where you found it."

As usual the best antidote to these lies was a personal meeting with Jefferson. Sometimes these encounters took rather strange forms. Every afternoon between twelve and three, Jefferson was fond of mounting his horse and riding about the outskirts of

Washington. He always rode alone and his plain clothes made him completely incognito.

One day the President's magnificent steed, Wildair, caught the eye of a Connecticut Yankee who stopped and asked him if he was interested in a horse trade. The conversation soon drifted to politics, and the man from the State of Steady Habits pompously declared that he had no use for Jefferson.

The President murmured that he thought there was at least a point or two in his favor.

"Come, come, mister," said the Yankee, "I guess you don't see the moral sin of niggery; but it ain't only that. This Thomas Jefferson—did you ever see him?"

Jefferson nodded.

"Well, that's more luck than I've had; but that doesn't matter. Now I hear that this Jefferson is a very wasteful chap with our hard-earned money. . . . They tell me he never goes out but he's got clothes on his back that would sell for a plantation. . . . He's a couple of watches or more. . . . Rings on all his fingers; and a frill to his shirt."

Jefferson could not help it—he burst out laughing. He assured the man from New England that the President usually went out dressed no better than himself. During this exchange, they had been cantering along toward the White House. In a moment they reached it, and Jefferson suggested his new friend meet the man he was denouncing. In the entrance hall, a servant addressed Jefferson as "Mr. President." The Yankee froze, his eyes bulged, and before Jefferson could say a word, he ran for his life.

Another day, on his daily ride, Jefferson met a Kentuckian who was also no friend of the administration. When he began repeating some of the slanderous stories Callender had been circulating, Jefferson dared him to come to the White House and meet the President personally, so he could judge for himself whether the stories were true. The next day, the man appeared at the appointed time. But he was no fool. He had realized in the interim who the stranger on horseback was, and he appealed for mercy. "I have called, Mr. Jefferson, to apologize for having said to a stranger—"

"Hard things of an imaginary personage, who is no relation of mine," Jefferson said with a laugh. Quickly he turned the conversation to other matters, and before the man realized it, a servant was announcing dinner, and he was sitting at the Presidential table enjoying the finest wine and the best food he had ever tasted. It hardly needs to be added that he and all his clan became fiery Jeffersonians for life.

William Paterson, the violently Federalist senator from New Jersey who later became a U.S. Supreme Court Justice, admitted somewhat ruefully to Margaret Bayard Smith, "No man can know Mr. Jefferson and be his personal enemy." One congressman, a Jefferson admirer, told his wife: "I have known one of his political adversaries . . . enter into his presence with a sentiment formed from the Opposition gazettes, as if he was going to see a fury or a monster, and return from the interview undeceived and disappointed, praising him as a well-bred, well-informed gentleman."

But the Federalists remained poised to twist and distort Jefferson's acts and opinions. He gave them an ideal opportunity when he extended a friendly hand to Thomas Paine.

Like his friend Lafayette, Paine failed to stay aboard the tiger that the French Revolution became, and he had spent some time in Parisian jails in imminent danger of being shortened by a head. Bitter because President George Washington did not make a stronger effort to protect him, Paine wrote an insulting public letter to the man he had once revered. It was printed widely in Republican newspapers toward the end of Washington's second term. Later, Paine published a book, *The Age of Reason*, which was an attack on traditional Christianity in his usual scathing style.

By 1800, Paine was on the brink of starvation in Paris and he wrote Jefferson asking permission to return to the United States. But he expressed great trepidation about traveling aboard an ordinary merchant ship. He was considered an outlaw and a traitor by the British government and he trembled at what might happen to him if his merchant ship was searched by a British cruiser. Would it be possible, he wondered, to get a berth aboard an American frigate if one touched at a French port? Jefferson immediately offered Paine passage on the American warship *Maryland*, which was preparing to sail home from France.

Word of Jefferson's generous gesture somehow leaked out and the Federalists shouted from pulpits and in newspapers that the

President had sent an American warship to France solely to pick up Tom Paine, the atheistic slanderer of Washington. Rather than embarrass Jefferson, Paine declined the President's offer and took the risk of crossing in a merchant ship. He landed in the fall of 1802 at Baltimore and Jefferson promptly offered him the hospitality of the White House. The Federalists set up another fantastic hue and cry. One declared that the President and his "blasphemous crony" should be hanged on the same gallows. Federalist Senator William Plumer of New Hampshire was scandalized when he called at the White House and Paine treated him with the familiarity of "an equal." At sixty-five Paine was more pathetic than dangerous. He had contracted agonizing rheumatism in prison, and the pain gave him an excuse to drink dangerous amounts of brandy which in turn gave the Federalists an excuse to call him a sot. Jefferson's own daughters, both stanch members of the Episcopal Church, objected strongly when he invited the supposed atheist to Monticello. But Jefferson calmly insisted on asserting his prerogative, and Paine, on his best behavior, succeeded in charming Martha and Maria with his vivid stories of Revolutionary days in America and France.

II

In the day-to-day life of the White House, Jefferson steadily pursued his goal of Republican simplicity. He abolished the formal levees John Adams and George Washington had held twice a week, and announced that the White House would be open to visitors—all visitors—every morning. This news inspired a brief revolution among the capital ladies who cherished levees as a marvelous opportunity to see and be seen in the latest fashions. A group of Congressional wives, largely Federalists, gowned and bejeweled themselves and marched on the White House one traditional levee day, determined to embarrass Jefferson into changing his mind. The servants showed them graciously into the public rooms, then suavely informed them that the President was out. Where? On his usual horseback ride around Georgetown and the outskirts of the city. The ladies said they would wait.

When Jefferson returned, he instantly understood what was

happening. Instead of being cowed, and rushing to change into his best satins and ruffles, he greeted the ladies in his dust-covered riding clothes—but exuding all his formidable Virginia charm. He dazzled them with anecdotes of Paris days, reminiscences of 1776, passing from one group to another, greeting every lady with the same cordiality. Whenever anyone left, he begged her to stay a little longer, urging her to sample the wines and cakes the servants laid out on the buffet table. Finally, totally baffled, the ladies withdrew and never tried to force a levee on Jefferson again.

To the astonishment of more than one Federalist, Jefferson dressed as simply as he lived. Senator Plumer rushed back to his boardinghouse to tell his diary what he had seen on his first White House visit. "A tall, high-boned man came into the room; he was drest, or rather undrest, with an old brown coat, red waistcoat, old corduroy small clothes, much soild—woolen hose—slippers without heels. I thought this man was a servant. . . . It was the President."

If this informality startled the starchy New Englander, it left the new British ambassador, Anthony Merry, quivering with rage. This gentleman appeared in his full royal regalia, accompanied by Secretary of State James Madison in his usual sober black. The sight of Jefferson in his heelless slippers shocked this formalist so much that he completely ignored the fact that the President greeted him cordially, led him to a chair and conversed with him in a very friendly, open manner. Merry complained hotly to Madison that the President's outfit was an insult. Madison told him he had received the Danish minister in exactly the same costume. That did not mollify Mr. Merry. The Dane, he huffed, was a diplomat of the third rank.

Madison apparently hesitated to tell His Majesty's ambassador, for the moment, that President Jefferson had abolished all such distinctions. The memory of the absurd protocol of the French court, when he had (at first) been the lowest ranking ambassador in Paris and had been treated accordingly, still irked him. Thus he announced, to the consternation of the Washington diplomatic corps, that the President would consider every minister "as the representative of his nation and equal to every other, without distinction of grade."

Ambassador Merry soon experienced still another Jefferson innovation. The President had announced that at any public ceremony to which the government invited foreign ministers and their families, "no precedence or privilege will be given them, other than the provision of a convenient seat with any other strangers invited." Moreover, "at dinners in public or private, and on all occasions of social intercourse, a perfect equality exists between the persons composing the company whether foreign or domestic, titled or untitled, in or out of office." Either Mr. Merry declined to read these democratic rules, or he was afraid to mention them to Mrs. Merry, who was a very large, commanding lady. Margaret Bayard Smith noted that when they appeared together in public, Mrs. Merry did all the talking, and her smaller unassuming husband was practically invisible.

When the Merrys came to their first White House dinner, they discovered the Madisons, the Gallatins, several Congressional couples, the Spanish ambassador, the Marquis de Casa Yrujo, a handsome dandy, and his American wife, Sally, as well as Louis André Pichon, the young, agreeable French chargé d'affaires, and his vivacious wife. The company chatted in the drawing room until dinner was announced. Jefferson, who happened to be talking with Dolley Madison at the moment, offered her his arm and strolled to the table. Madison escorted Mrs. Merry, but appalled both husband and wife by seating her below the Spanish minister. Jefferson placed Dolley on his right, and Madame Yrujo on his left. Mr. Merry reached for the chair next to Madame Yrujo, but was elbowed aside by a hard-charging congressman. The distraught ambassador finally found himself seated eyeball to eyeball with M. Pichon, from a nation with whom England was at war.

A few days later, Madison invited the Merrys to a dinner at his house. This time, in the parade to the dining room, Madison gave his hand to Mrs. Gallatin. Merry, waiting for someone to escort his formidable spouse, found himself left alone with her and as M. Pichon gleefully described it, "astonished, had to give her his hand." Merry bombarded Madison with official objections and complained wildly to his home office of a plot "to degrade the character of a foreign minister" by placing him "on a level with the lowest American citizen." The haughty Yrujo joined the Merrys in what amounted to a strike. They refused to accept invitations to White House dinners.

This tactic inflicted pain on no one but themselves. Not even the most hardened Federalist could resist an invitation to a White House dinner, prepared by Chef Julien, under the all-seeing French eye of steward Etienne Lemaire, successor to Maître Petit. One Federalist noted in his diary: "Dined at the President's. Rice soup, round of beef, turkey, mutton, ham, loin of veal, cutlets of mutton, fried eggs, fried beef, a pie called macaroni which appeared to be a rich brown crust . . . an Italian dish. Ice cream, very good, crust wholly dried crumbled into thin flakes; a dish somewhat like a pudding—inside white as cream or curd, very porous and light, covered with cream sauce . . . very fine. Many other jimcracks, a great variety of fruit, plenty of wines and good." This amazing variety was seldom served to more than fourteen guests. The table was round "to encourage general conversation."

The Federalists, who prided themselves on being the party of intelligence and culture, presented a hilarious picture as they gasped to keep up with Jefferson's wide-ranging mind. John Quincy Adams, who arrived as a Federalist senator from Massachusetts in 1803, recorded in his diary one dinner at which Jefferson entertained the New York physician and Republican congressman, Dr. Samuel Latham Mitchill, whom contemporaries described as "a living encyclopedia." The talk began with a dissertation on wines from Jefferson, which left the Federalists reeling. Then the President veered to philosophy and suggested that the Epicurean system was much misunderstood and misrepresented. He talked enthusiastically about a contemporary Italian commentary on it and remarked that someone should translate it. Mitchill brought up Fulton's steamboat as an invention of epochal importance. Jefferson coolly replied that he thought Fulton's torpedo was equally valuable. The talk shifted to chemistry, geography, zoology, paleontology, with Jefferson drawing Mitchill out on "oils, gasses, beasts, birds, petrifactions." Finally Jefferson switched to agriculture, about which he professed to know "nothing." But he managed to talk about it for the rest of the evening.

Others talked too. Jefferson never permitted conversation to degenerate into a monologue by himself or anyone else. "He took the lead and gave the tone," said Margaret Bayard Smith, who was a frequent White House visitor, "with a tact so true and discriminating that he seldom missed his aim which was to draw forth the talents and information of each and all of his guests and to place everyone in an advantageous light, and by being pleased with themselves, being able to please others."

He never allowed any individual to sit through dinner unnoticed. The moment he saw anyone lapsing into such a condition, he would single him out for his personal attention and skillfully draw him into the general conversation. One day he found himself confronted by a special challenge of this sort. A young man, just returned from Europe, found himself seated in company so distinguished and so talkative that he could not find a word to say. His long residence abroad had left him a stranger in his own country; unknown, he was totally ignored. Jefferson turned the conversation toward rice farming, then nodded to the young man and declared, "To you we are indebted to this benefit, no one more deserves the gratitude of this country." Although the young man was as astonished as everyone else, he instantly became the center of attention. "Yes, sir," the President continued, "the upland rice which you sent from Algiers, and which thus far succeeds, will, when generally adopted by the planters, prove an inestimable blessing to our southern states." Fortunately, no one else at the table knew enough about rice planting to ask difficult questions and the conversation swiftly turned to other matters. But the young man had been transformed from a cipher to a person of importance and he was no longer ignored by the other distinguished guests.

Jefferson liked to tell tall stories, in which he slyly pulled the legs of pompous visitors. Serious, precise John Quincy Adams, who should have known Jefferson well enough to be on the inside of these jokes, was often gulled by them. Jefferson airily informed one dinner party that he had learned Spanish on his voyage to Europe with nothing but *Don Quixote* for a textbook. Another time he made eyes bulge by gravely declaring that during one six-week period in Paris, the temperature stood immovably at 20 below zero, Fahrenheit. He topped even that one by solemnly claiming that when he went to Paris he had left in Virginia some ripe pears,

sewed up in tow bags, and six years later, found them not only perfectly preserved—but self-candied! "You can never be an hour in
this man's company without something of the marvelous, like these
stories," wrote the younger Adams, in his usual querulous tone.

Jefferson was not above kidding a Republican with this kind of
humor, especially one as solemn as the learned Dr. Mitchill. One
day Mitchill asked him just where he had stood to view the
Potomac, for his famous description of Harpers Ferry in *Notes on
Virginia*. Jefferson put on his most mournful face, and sighed that
the spot no longer existed. During President Adams' administration, the Federalists had ordered troops to blast the rock with
gunpowder, so that future travelers, attempting to duplicate the
view, would think Jefferson was a liar. Mitchill swallowed the
story whole and denounced this "vandalic revenge" in his next
letter home.

Doctors were another favorite subject for Jefferson jokes. He
used to say that he never saw two medical men on the road without
looking up to see if there was a circling buzzard overhead. He was
particularly sarcastic at the expense of "Philadelphia doctors" who
followed his friend, Benjamin Rush, in his theory of "heroic
measures" to defeat disease. Jefferson often told, with mordant
humor, the story of the time he stopped at a tavern and found the
landlady in tears. She was just returning from the funeral of a very
fine young man, carried off unexpectedly by one of the unknown
diseases of the era. After bemoaning his loss at length, the woman
finally wiped her eyes and said: "At least we have the consolation
that the doctors did everything possible for him—he was bled six
and twenty times."

He had heard enough risqué stories in his Paris years to tell a few
of his own without blushing. A favorite concerned Benjamin
Franklin and a certain American lady who was seated next to him
at dinner and who made it a point to correct the sage's awful
French. Unfortunately, her own was equally atrocious. In the
middle of the dinner, Temple Franklin, the great man's exotic
grandson, proceeded to go around the room, kissing every woman
at the table. The last of these was Mrs. John Jay, who blushed
deeply. Franklin, trying to make light of his grandson's bizarre
ways, asked her why she was blushing. The intrusive American

lady immediately butted in: *"Parce qu'il a lui baisé le derrière"*—instead of *"la dernière."*

The Federalists, baffled by Jefferson the host, could only growl their frustrations to their diaries. Epicure Gouverneur Morris, forced to admit his dinner was superb, descended to mere carping. "His constrained manner of reception showed his enmity," he wrote, "and his assiduous attentions demonstrate his fear." Another complained mightily because no blessing was asked, "although two clergymen were present." Still another grumped, "I wish his French politics were as good as his French wines."

Nothing, not even stupidity, could mar Jefferson's good humor at his dinners. Once a very lightheaded lady, trying to make conversation, asked him if he lived near Carter's Mountain. This was, of course, where he had sought refuge from Tarleton's raiders, and the Federalists had labored endlessly to make the name synonymous with Jefferson's cowardice.

The woman's husband was turning red, but Jefferson remained unruffled. He blithely told the lady he lived very close to Carter's Mountain. "It is the adjoining mountain to Monticello."

"I suppose it is a very convenient place?" the lady asked.

By now the husband was strangling. But Jefferson, although he could not suppress a smile, refused to embarrass his guest.

"Why, yes," he said. "I certainly found it so in wartime."

This was typical of the gallantry which women found irresistible in Jefferson. One day a lady congratulated herself that she never felt cold in winter.

"Go where I will," she said, "I can always fancy it's summer."

"And when you are under my roof," declared Jefferson with a bow that any courtier of Louis XVI would have envied, "I partake your impression!"

"There is a degree of ease in Mr. Jefferson's company that everyone seems to feel and to enjoy," said Benjamin H. Latrobe, the architect of the Capitol and a frequent White House visitor. He told of one dinner he attended, where Martha Jefferson Randolph was a guest. Martha drank a toast to a fellow Virginian on the other side of the table. Jefferson gently told her that she was breaking his law against drinking healths at the table. A health (or toast) always brought a reply: "To *your* health, madame."

This in turn could produce a counter reply and so forth until everyone was reeling. Martha replied that the law must have been passed in her absence. The President could hardly fault this impudence. He let it pass with a smile, and reiterated the three laws of his table—"no healths, no politics and no restraint."

III

Early in Jefferson's first term, a delegation of Washingtonians called on him to find out his birthday, so they could celebrate it. He instantly squashed the idea. The only birthday he ever celebrated, he informed them, was his country's birthday. Jefferson had never approved of the celebration of Washington's birthday, feeling it smacked too much of hero worship. But after Washington retired, he had encouraged Republicans to attend the celebrations (which mortified President John Adams, because no one ever suggested celebrating *his* birthday). Jefferson wanted to drive home to the public the idea that the nation should venerate the hero of the Revolution, not the President.

President Jefferson made sure the 4th of July was a gala day. The Marine Corps band turned out, and soldiers, sailors and marines paraded on the wide lawn in front of the White House. Temporary tents and booths were scattered about, with vendors selling food and drink to the crowd that came from both city and country. Jefferson, in a simple black suit, and "Republican" shoes (without buckles), stood on the White House steps with his cabinet and the foreign ministers while the military passed in review. Then everyone was invited into the White House where sideboards and tables were filled with cakes, wine, punch, lemonade. Jefferson stood in the center of what is now the Blue Room, shaking the hand of each visitor as he entered and exchanging a genial sentence or two. The marine band played in the hall, and for three hours the White House was public property. Cabinet officers and their wives chatted with clerks, and snobs such as the Merrys were appalled to find themselves greeted by their grocers.

On New Year's Day, another reception took place indoors; it was more formal and socially glittering. There was the same profusion of cakes, wines and punch, but the ladies wore their gorgeous best, and most of the visitors were congressmen, government employees, diplomats and their wives. Sometimes Jefferson displayed items sent to him to show off American manufacturing and farming prowess. Once he invited a group of Federalists to admire a mammoth 1,236-pound cheese shipped from Vermont. It was made, the President told the Federalists solemnly, from milk drawn exclusively from Republican cows.

In spite of his dinner parties and receptions, Jefferson found life in the White House rather lonely. He complained to his daughter Martha that he and his secretary, Meriwether Lewis, were rattling around the huge rooms like "two mice in a church." He did his utmost to persuade his daughters to visit him; his original plan was to have Maria as his hostess in the spring and Martha in the fall. But this rotation never was achieved; illness, childbirth and husbands busy with farms of their own intervened. Only once, in the fall of 1802, did the two girls spend a month at the White House together.

As always, the auburn-haired Maria's beauty dazzled everyone. But she was "timidity personified when in company" and her more outgoing, confident older sister enjoyed the experience far more. Margaret Bayard Smith described Martha as "rather homely, a delicate likeness of her father . . . more interesting than Mrs. Eppes." Her manners were, she said, "so frank and affectionate that you know her at once, and feel perfectly at ease with her." The young editor's wife was almost as fascinated by little Ellen Randolph, who she thought was "one of the finest, most intelligent children I ever met with." Ellen was already in love with poetry and when Mrs. Smith recited a few lines for her, she flung her arms around the older woman's waist and begged her for more. They were soon such good friends they were spending whole days together.

Martha handled with consummate tact a brush with the aggressive Mrs. Merry. The haughty virago, as Jefferson called her, sent in a note, asking Martha if she were visiting the White House as the President's daughter or the wife of a Virginia gentleman. If the first, Mrs. Merry would deign to call; if the second, Mrs. Merry expected Mrs. Randolph to call on her. Martha coolly answered that she was visiting as the wife of a Virginia gentleman. But she expected Mrs. Merry to call on her because she was a stranger in the capital, and her father, the President, had stated clearly in his new democratic rules of etiquette that all residents of the capital should call first on visiting strangers. Mrs. Merry was reduced to sulky silence.

Jefferson's loneliness in the White House was relieved later in 1802 by the arrival of his two sons-in-law as congressmen from Virginia. There is no evidence that he encouraged either of them to enter politics, nor did he give them any assistance. In fact, he tried to dissuade Thomas Mann Randolph from running in Albemarle against another Republican, Samuel Jordan Cabell, who protested heatedly that during the hectic days of February, 1801, he had "spent two nights on a blanket" to make Jefferson President. Randolph scraped through with a mere thirteen-vote majority. John Wayles Eppes won handily.

Jefferson invited both young men to live with him in the White House. They were totally different types. Jack Eppes was a Jeffersonian in temperament as well as politics, a charming, gracious young man, and a natural leader. Thomas Mann Randolph had inherited more than his share of the moody, hypersensitive temperament of his family. At thirty-four he was also beginning to experience an acute sense of inferiority. In October, 1802, before he impulsively ran for Congress, he had written Jefferson a very disturbing letter in which he had lashed himself as unworthy to be included "within the narrow circle" around the President. He was, he said, "so essentially and widely different from all within it, as to look like something extraneous . . . the proverbial 'silly bird' who could not feel at . . . ease among the swans." Part of the problem was obviously his overwhelming awe of Jefferson. "The sentiment of my mind when it contemplates yourself alone, is one of the most lofty elevation and most unmixed delight." His heart overflowed with "gratitude and affection . . . when I attempt to estimate the value to the whole human race . . . of the incredibly inconceivably excellent political system which you created, developed & at last I think, permanently established."

There is more than a hint here that the person who made Randolph feel like a "silly bird" was his wife. (The emphasis on "yourself alone.") Although he had retained a lively interest in botany, Randolph had in other respects become little more than a typical Virginia farmer, with only vestiges of the sophisticated European scholar whom Martha had married. Moreover their poverty, which Randolph proudly concealed from Jefferson, was acute. In later years his son Thomas Jefferson Randolph told of shivering at night under a single blanket in a room little bigger than a closet, and walking miles along icy roads to school, with no shoes.

Jefferson hastily tried to rescue his son-in-law from self-abasement. "The shade into which you throw yourself," he replied to Randolph's letter, "neither your happiness nor mine will admit that you remain in. . . . I hold the virtues of your heart and the powers of your understanding in a far more exalted view than you place them in." In the White House the President did his utmost to treat his two sons-in-law with scrupulous equality. He also let them make their own way in the House of Representatives, independently of him.

This was not easy. The prickly Virginia Republican John Randolph of Roanoke, already eager to announce his independence of Jefferson, took exception to a resolution John Eppes had offered and declared to the House that he would form his "opinion of every resolution that shall come before this House, without reference to the quarter from which it shall proceed." Jefferson hastily tried to reassure the querulous Virginian. "No men on earth are more independent in their sentiments than they are," he said of his sons-in-law. "We rarely speak of politics, or of the proceedings of the House, but merely historically. . . ."

John Eppes did not let Randolph's acid tongue bother him in the least and soon marked himself as one of the Jeffersonian leaders, entering freely into the often violent debates of those days. Thomas Mann Randolph, on the other hand, sat in almost total silence throughout his first term in Congress. He was equally invisible throughout his second term until he rose to reply to some remarks by John Randolph, which he thought reflected on a few words he had spoken in a recent debate. He accused his cousin of using language "behind the shield of the dignity of the House, which he would not venture to make use of elsewhere." After adding that Randolph was "bankrupt forever as a popular states-man," because of his frequent opposition to Jefferson, the Presi-dent's son-in-law strolled out of the House chamber.

In the Virginia of the early 1800's, these were shooting words, and John Randolph was a famous duelist. Jefferson had to use all his power, both persuasive and political, to resolve this crisis. He had scarcely managed this thorny task, when Randolph abruptly bolted out of the White House, accusing Jefferson of showing "preference" for Eppes. He moved to a Washington boarding-house largely patronized by Federalists, and lived like a hermit, eating all his meals in his room. Jefferson begged him to return, telling him that his accusation had "given me a pang under which I am overwhelmed." He admitted he had for some days noticed in Randolph "a gloom which gave me uneasiness. I knew there was a difference between Mr. Eppes & yourself, but had no idea it was as deep-seated as your letter shows it to be." He vowed that his affections for them both "were warm, as well for your respective merits, as for the sake of the dear objects"—Martha and Maria—"which link them. What acts of mine can have induced you to suppose that I felt or manifested a preference of him, I cannot conceive."

But Martha's moody husband ignored these warm words, and continued his isolationist policy. Even when he became seriously ill with one of the district's prevalent fevers, he refused to let Jeffer-son bring him back to the Executive Mansion. Instead he crept home to Albemarle, and announced he was through with politics. John Eppes, on the other hand, continued his lively political career and his close, if not intimate, relationship with Jefferson for an-other ten years, becoming one of his party's chief spokesmen in Congress.

I V

On the political front, Jefferson made the Federalists squirm by repealing the Judiciary Act, which had enabled John Adams to appoint his midnight judges. This shot the jobs out from under the judges, and put the Supreme Court back on circuit again. Jefferson also successfully impeached one lower-court judge who was certifiably insane, and tried to impeach Associate Justice Samuel Chase of the Supreme Court, who was fond of making arrogant Federalist speeches from the bench. The U.S. Senate acquitted Chase, largely because of his earlier reputation as a Revolutionary patriot and signer of the Declaration of Independence. But the two trials served notice on the Federalists that Jefferson and his party were not going to let the judicial side of the government checkmate the other two branches, without some vigorous counterassaults to maintain a genuine balance.

Elsewhere, Jefferson confronted the ambiguities of power, the agonizing decisions a President must make where the case is neither black nor white. A prime example was the Yazoo fraud. In 1795 thousands of people, from all walks of life, including a considerable number of New Englanders, had invested millions in three land companies which bought from the state of Georgia the greater part of the territory now making up Alabama and Mississippi. The legislature that made the grant was bribed to a man, and the following year a new legislature rescinded the act. It also became clear that Georgia had only shadowy claims to the land in the first place.

The claimants sought relief from the federal government, and President Jefferson asked Madison and Gallatin to arbitrate the dispute. They settled on a formula which should have satisfied any reasonable man—repayment of the original investment, plus some modest interest—to the innocent stock buyers, and the purchase of the disputed lands by the United States, to be formed into the Mississippi territory. But John Randolph decided he was purer than the President. He called the Yazoo settlement a fraud, and strutted about Washington, D.C., in his flapping black cloak and jockey's cap, swearing that Madison was in on the deal.

There must have been times when Jefferson wished he had never heard the word Randolph. Their "high-toned" explosive temper and overall emotional instability, sometimes bordering, as in John Randolph's case, on insanity, disrupted his life again and again.

In still another area of moral ambiguity, political jobs, Jefferson hewed to his gradualist policy. In May, 1803, he drew up a list of Federalists he had removed. They totaled a modest 113, and only 23 of these were for "misconduct or delinquency." Secretary of

State Madison did not fire Jacob Wagner, his department's chief clerk, although the man was a bitter and outspoken Federalist. As one of his "midnight appointments" John Adams had named his son-in-law, William Smith, Surveyor of Customs for New York. No doubt remembering their cheerful breakfasts with "old Hump" in Paris, Jefferson let Smith keep the job, although he insisted all of Adams' appointments after he had been defeated were "null" and could be abrogated by the new President. A few years later, when Smith was indicted for his role in an adventurous scheme to revolutionize Venezuela, Jefferson tried to defend him as "a man of honor and integrity" who had been deceived into believing the expedition had the approval of the American government. But the puritanical Gallatin insisted on Smith's resignation, and Jefferson reluctantly yielded.

Like all presidents, Jefferson was bombarded with requests for jobs. James Madison saved this one, no doubt because it gave him and the Chief Executive a private laugh.

I should be very glad to get some publick office of moderate emoluments, and the duty of which not very intricate, so as I could discharge the duty of, with Credit and ease. You will I presume Say that one Foible I possess, aught to be done away, before it would be prudent to trust any publick post or office to me. I am perfectly Sensible from experience that the long habit in drinking to excess rendered me less Capable of doing my duty, as I aught to have done, which on reflection, hurt my feelings as it hurt my Consequence. . . .

Jefferson did his best to follow Washington's rule of firmly barring appointments to friends and, above all, to relatives. Only with his old friend John Page did Jefferson waver. Page was in severe financial difficulties, and Jefferson made sure he had a series of obscure but reasonably rewarding federal jobs in Virginia. But he declined to appoint his ex-protégé, William Short, to an ambassadorship, because it would have violated a rule he had set up, that no diplomat abroad more than six years should be reappointed without being brought home to get reacquainted with the country.

"The transaction of the great interests of our country," Jefferson told one correspondent," costs us little trouble or difficulty. There the line is plain to men of some experience. But the task of appointment is a heavy one indeed. He on whom it falls may envy the lot of a Sisyphus or Ixion. Their agonies were of the body: this of the mind. Yet like the office of hangman it must be executed by someone."

The time and attention Jefferson gave to this Sisyphean task can be seen in this memorandum to Albert Gallatin.

Candidates for the office of Surveyor of Smithfield (Va):

Doctor Purdie—His father I know. He is a good man. But they are tories.

Wilson Davies—He was a collector of the direct tax which is sufficient evidence he is a tory. He is recommended too by John Parker appointed by our predecessors, ergo a tory.

Dr. Southall—His father was an excellent man and whig. His brother is said to be a very bad man. Of himself I know nothing. Col. Davies's favor makes his politics suspicious.

Cunningham—Recommended by T. Newton junr but not on his own knolege. A republican of 75. He does not live at the place and would be to remove.

John Easson—Strongly recommended by Col. Newton the father, from an intimate knolege of him, as a very honest man, republican, and living on the spot. He was not long since a member of the Senate of Virginia . . . a good testimony of respectability and a shield for us in his appointment.

Easson got the job.

On other fronts, Jefferson let the detested Alien and Sedition Acts expire, and gradually repealed the hated whisky tax and the other internal taxes that had caused the government so many collection troubles. He firmly backed the severe economy in government policy of his Secretary of the Treasury, Gallatin, which was soon reducing the national debt by almost $3,000,000 a year. Internationally, the world was at peace. England and the new ruler of France, Napoleon Bonaparte, were regrouping for another death battle, but the interregnum gave Jefferson an opportunity to economize on army and navy appropriations.

The modest naval force that remained—some fourteen ships—Jefferson soon found an opportunity to use, in a way that fulfilled one of his oldest ambitions. The United States, like the European nations whose ships used the Mediterranean, had been paying tribute—some $10,000,000 during the Washington and Adams administrations—to the bandit states of Morocco, Algiers, Tunis and Tripoli. This galled Jefferson even more than it had in his ambassadorial days, when he had tried to organize a coalition against these seagoing shakedown artists. Now the Bashaw of Tripoli announced that the most recent U.S. payment did not purchase peace, but only his willingness to negotiate a peace. Jefferson promptly sent most of his tiny navy to the Mediterranean to teach these "pirates" a lesson. With the marines attacking overland and the navy bombarding from the sea, the bashaw finally saw the error of his ways and negotiated a genuine treaty of peace.

This was little more than a minor interlude as far as Jefferson was concerned. The main focus of his diplomacy was England and France, the two great powers, and Spain, weaker but still a potent force in world affairs. Now, at last, he had an opportunity to pursue the policy of playing one off against the other, to the ultimate profit of the United States. Not even he realized, in the first months of his administration, the stupendous diplomatic triumph this policy would produce.

V

The specter of Napoleon's growing arrogance and steadily more naked imperialism was a daily nightmare. The policy of the Republican Party had always been friendship with France. But could anyone risk friendship with this reckless militarist, who swallowed up countries and overturned rulers and constitutions with a scratch of his pen and an order to his apparently irresistible armies? Although France and England were at peace, the question was by no means a speculation for future reference. From the very beginning of the administration, Jefferson and Madison heard rumors that made them think they might soon have Napoleon for a next-door neighbor.

The vast territory known as Louisiana, stretching from New Orleans to the Canadian border and encompassing the heartland of the continent, between the Mississippi and the Rockies, had been ceded to Spain in 1763, to repay her for the losses she had suffered as France's ally in the Seven Years' War. Thanks to diplomatic initiatives which Jefferson had opened when he was Secretary of State, the Americans had negotiated a very advantageous treaty with the Spanish, guaranteeing them free navigation of the Mississippi and the use of the port of New Orleans. Now rumors and messages from various unexpected quarters—one came from an American soldier of fortune serving in the French Expeditionary Force to repress the Negro revolt in Santo Domingo—suggested that Spain, completely under the domination of Napoleon, had secretly ceded this vast domain back to France.

Jefferson instantly proved how wrong his enemies were when they accused him of being a French puppet. In a secret letter to Robert Livingston, the American ambassador, he bluntly stated his wholly American reaction to this news. "There is on the globe one single spot, the possessor of which is our natural habitual enemy. It is New Orleans, through which the produce of three-eighths of our territory must pass to market." He went on to predict that these western territories would soon yield half of the total American farm production and contain more than half of the nation's population. "The day that France takes possession of New Orleans," he said, "we must marry ourselves to the British fleet and nation."

Jefferson, the supposed theorist and dreamer, showed his consummate realism. Much as he detested England and her arrogance, he was ready to enter into a temporary alliance with her to block a far more obvious threat to America. Jefferson called on Livingston "to return again and again to the charge" and persuade France as soon as possible that she did not need Louisiana. Convince Bonaparte, Jefferson urged, that the best way to reconcile the two nations would be to cede to the United States the "island" of New Orleans and the Floridas. (West Florida included much of what is now southern Louisiana. East Florida was, roughly, the present state.) "Every eye in the U.S. is now fixed on this affair," the President told his minister. "Perhaps nothing since the Revolutionary War has produced more uneasy sensations through the body of the nation."

The reason for this agitation was a move by Spain. The Intendant at New Orleans had suddenly closed the port to all American goods. Petitions poured in from the western territories demanding war, and the Federalists, eager to make trouble for Jefferson, joined the cry. Jefferson skillfully blunted this passion by dispatching James Monroe as an envoy extraordinary to France with orders to settle the Mississippi question once and for all. If the French failed to co-operate, he was to "enter into conferences with the British government through their ambassador at Paris to fix principles of alliance."

At home, meanwhile, Jefferson and Madison played a superb game of alternately soothing and terrifying France's representative in Washington, André Pichon. On January 12, 1803, Jefferson told the Frenchman that there was no danger of war. The administration was determined to "try peaceful means to the last moment," and they hoped that France would be disposed to concur. Then Madison called Pichon to his office and blandly told him that if France "should" obtain Louisiana and the Floridas (as yet Napoleon had not publicly admitted his ownership) they must either cede all territory east of the Mississippi to the United States for perhaps two or three million dollars or "force" the United States to expand beyond the Mississippi—in short, seize all of Louisiana. These conversations were, of course, duly reported to France by Pichon.

Then Jefferson, using his dinner table as a stage for the carefully arranged drama, turned the next screw and began to direct more and more of his conversation to the members of the British diplomatic mission. Soon the agitated Pichon was writing home, "Necessity is forcing Mr. Jefferson to give up his pretensions and scruples against an English alliance. I have observed at table that he redoubles his kindness and attention to the British chargé d'affaires." Pichon's reports passed through the hands of Talleyrand, to be read by Napoleon himself. The First Consul needed money to finance the renewed war he was planning with England. Since the secret of Louisiana's return to France was out, the English with their superiority on the seas would certainly seize it the moment war was declared. With the strained relations between the United States and France, the Americans might even grab it first. In either case, Napoleon told himself he did not care. Once he settled John Bull's hash, he could bring to bear the immense power of his consolidated empire on the New World.

For weeks, Talleyrand had been parrying all Robert Livingston's attempts to negotiate until the desperate diplomat had been reduced to pleading for the mere restoration of American rights at New Orleans. Now Napoleon's Foreign Minister suddenly asked: "Would the United States wish to have the whole of Louisiana?"

Incredibly, Livingston at first said no, all America wanted was New Orleans and the Floridas. Somewhat impatiently, Talleyrand pointed out that without New Orleans, the rest of Louisiana was practically valueless to France. "What would you give for the whole?"

The reeling Livingston suggested four million.

"Too low," said Talleyrand. "Reflect and see me tomorrow."

Talleyrand did everything in his power to stall the negotiations, largely because the British had offered him a hundred thousand pounds to keep Napoleon at peace. But the First Consul handed the negotiations over to his Finance Minister, François Barbé-Marbois, the man whose queries had inspired Jefferson to write his *Notes on Virginia*. James Monroe arrived in Paris to give the jittery Livingston invaluable support, and after a week of bargaining over money the real-estate deal of the century was clinched. America doubled its size for $12,000,000, picking up a million square miles of the continent for about 2¢ an acre.

The envoys rushed the treaty to Washington by the fastest available ship, with apologies for exceeding their instructions. Jefferson did not waste a moment to seize the bargain. At the President's order, Secretary of State Madison told the negotiators not to worry about their instructions. Buying all of Louisiana was "not deemed . . . within the frame of probability." It was, Madison wrote in a later letter, "a truly noble acquisition." Jefferson was equally jubilant. To numerous correspondents he expressed his pride at winning such an enormous territory without firing a shot. The Louisiana Purchase does in fact remain one of the largest peaceful acquisitions of territory in the history of nations.

Throughout the United States the news evoked wild celebrations, bonfires, parades, and banquets hailing Jefferson. Only the Federalists held aloof. Although they had been urging Jefferson to go to war only a few months before to conquer the territory, now they screamed that Jefferson had turned the Constitution into a blank scrap of paper and destroyed the federal union. Fisher Ames declared, "Acquiring territory with money is mean and despicable." Senator Plumer of New Hampshire announced that it was now "optional with the old states to say whether they would longer remain in the present confederacy." The Federalists saw instantly that if this new territory was carved into states, their already waning power and influence would dwindle to a cipher. With Jefferson as their father, the new arrivals would inevitably be Republican. But not all the Federalists were so petty. The statesmen among them—Alexander Hamilton, Gouverneur Morris and John Quincy Adams—approved, and young Adams, voting in the Senate to ratify the treaty, made himself anathema to his Massachusetts constituents.

Jefferson himself, with his strict construction of the Constitution, felt that an amendment was needed to make the purchase completely legal. "In the meantime," he told his old opponent in the Continental Congress, John Dickinson, "we must ratify & pay our money . . . and rely on the nation to sanction an act done for its great good, without its previous authority." Then came news from France that the mercurial Napoleon was regretting the deal, and looking for ways to abrogate it. To admit the deed was done outside the Constitution would give him an irresistible opening. So, although he would have preferred the constitutional route, Jefferson, for the good of the nation, proceeded to take advantage of his party majority in Congress, and win approval for the treaty of purchase and the money to pay for it. Federalists were quick to point out in the course of the debates that Republican congressmen sounded very much like Alexander Hamilton in their discussion of the implied powers of the Constitution.

Jefferson himself, justifying his decision in later life, took a different and a higher ground. A strict observance of the written laws, he argued, is one of the high duties of a good citizen but it is not the highest. "The laws of necessity, of self-preservation, as saving our country when in danger, are of higher obligation. To lose our country by a scrupulous adherence to written law, would be to lose the law itself with life, liberty, property and all those who are enjoying them with us; thus absurdly sacrificing the end to the means." Abraham Lincoln was to use this same argument to justify his suspension of habeas corpus and other portions of the Bill of Rights during the early days of the Civil War.

Jefferson did not think this principle gave every citizen the right to ignore the laws. "It is incumbent on those only who accept of great charges, to risk themselves on great occasions, when the safety of the nation, or some of its very high interests are at stake. Then the good officer will make his decision at his own peril, and throw himself on the justice of his country and the rectitude of his motives."

The more Jefferson thought of the immense new territory, the more optimistic about it, and America, he became. In the fall of 1803 he began to talk about "an empire for liberty," expanding his new conviction that the larger America became, the healthier her democracy. "By enlarging the empire for liberty," he told another correspondent, "we multiply its auxiliaries & provide new sources of renovation, should its principles, at any time, degenerate, in those portions of our country which gave them birth." A few years later he wrote to Madison, "I am persuaded no constitution was ever before so well calculated as ours for extensive empire and self-government."

The mass of the American people obviously agreed with him, especially when he announced in his message to Congress that thanks to continued economies, there would be no need for new taxes to pay the bill for Louisiana. Jefferson's popularity soared to hitherto unbelievable heights, and the Federalists all but collapsed into despair.

VI

The glory and the satisfaction of this political triumph was soon dimmed for Jefferson by personal tragedy. His beloved Maria began to slip away from him. It began with a strange reluctance to visit Washington, even after her husband was elected to Congress. She stayed home, and seldom answered Jefferson's troubled letters urging her to visit. Part of it was psychological; she obviously had no taste for the backbiting, gossipy world of capital society. But much of it was also physical. Some evidence suggests that she had inherited the disease that killed her mother, and childbirth was a medical and physical crisis for her. Early in 1804, she gave birth to a baby girl and never recovered from the ordeal.

Jefferson had her carried to Monticello on a litter and each day he personally brought her out on the lawn in a kind of rolling chaise which he would let no one except himself move from place to place to catch the sun. In spite of the agonizing memories that must have welled up, he was her nurse and companion, even more than Maria's sorrowing husband. But neither love nor the mediocre medical skills of the day could save her, and early in April, 1804, while Monticello was wrapped in a soft dreamy haze of early spring, and the trees were budding and the flowers blooming, Maria closed her eyes.

Jefferson was prostrated. His daughter Martha left him alone for hours. When she returned she found him with the Bible in his hands searching mournfully for words of consolation. To his old friend John Page, now (thanks to Jefferson) Governor of Virginia, he poured out his heart. "Others may lose of their abundance, but I, of my want, have lost even the half of all I had." Many other friends wrote him letters of sympathy, but the one Jefferson treasured most came from Massachusetts. Abigail Adams remembered the little auburn-haired girl who had clung to her in London. The woman in her proud puritan soul welled up. Secretly, without saying a word to her still embittered husband, she wrote a deeply personal letter to Jefferson. "Had you been no other but the private inhabitant of Monticello, I should e'er this time have addresst you, with that sympathy, which a recent event has awakend in my bosom. But reasons of various kinds withheld my pen until the powerful feelings of my heart have burst through the restraint, and called upon me to shed the tear of sorrow over the departed remains of your beloved and deserving daughter." She signed it "Who once took pleasure in subscribing herself your friend."

Jefferson answered her with more than his customary warmth, telling her that Maria had never forgotten Abigail's kindness in London. "To the last," he wrote, "on our meetings after long separations, whether I had heard lately of you, and how you did, were among the earliest of her inquiries." He went on to say how much he regretted that "circumstances should have arisen, which have seemed to draw a line of separation between us." He vowed that his friendship remained unbroken with both her and the ex-President. "I can say with truth, that one act of Mr. Adams' life, and one only, ever gave me a moment's personal displeasure. I did consider his last appointments to office as personally unkind." Eventually, Jefferson said, "after brooding over it for some little time, and not always resisting the expression of it, I forgave it cordially. . . ."

The words are a touching testimony of how deeply Jefferson treasured not only friendship, but the feeling of it in his own large heart. He almost admitted to Abigail that he had said too much, but "without knowing how it will be received, I feel relief."

Abigail Adams did not receive it very well. She replied with a waspish defense of her husband, and with an accusation that Jefferson could expect no better treatment, when he hired human refuse like Callender to attack President Adams. Jefferson tried in vain to defend himself and explain Callender, but Abigail abruptly "closed the correspondence." Poor Jefferson was left where he started.

Meanwhile, he was having troubles of another, meaner, variety. James Callender had published in his Richmond *Recorder,* with vast exaggerations, the stories of Jefferson's assault on Betsey Walker's virtue, in his bachelor days. Betsey's husband had become a Federalist, and had whispered the story to several Virginia Federalists who in turn told it to Callender. Some thirty years after the fact Walker was prodded by his political friends to "demand satisfaction" from Jefferson—apparently a written statement that Betsey had repulsed him. Federalist editors seized on the story with obscene glee and soon it was being printed around the nation, expanding steadily until Betsey was repulsing Jefferson every night for the better part of a year before she finally got around to telling her husband about it. Inevitably this was connected to Jefferson's supposed immorality with Sally Hemings. Among his friends, Jefferson made no attempt to disguise the truth. He told Levi Lincoln, his Attorney General, "I plead guilty to one of their charges, that when young and single I offered love to a handsome lady. I acknowledge its incorrectness. It is the only one founded in truth among all their allegations against me."

Federalist editors persisted in smearing this mud on Jefferson to the point where his belief in absolute freedom of the press wavered. He wrote to Governor McKean of Pennsylvania remarking that "a few wholesome prosecutions" on the local level might restore these madmen to their senses. Republicans in Pennsylvania and New York instantly went to work and indicted the editors of two papers. Alexander Hamilton emerged from near retirement to undertake the defense of Harry Croswell, editor of the Hudson *Wasp*, in the New York State Supreme Court. Croswell was tried under the old-fashioned law of seditious libel, which made the truth or falsity of the charges irrelevant. This was the law of New York State, and most other states, at the time. The Federalists quickly made the Republicans look rather foolish by shouting that the moribund law gave those in power the right to muzzle the press on the pretext that they were stirring up dissatisfaction with the government, hardly in line with the Republicans' protestations on behalf of freedom.

Hamilton made one of his most impassioned and brilliant speeches on Croswell's behalf. Though it failed to move the Republican majority on the court it persuaded the New York legislature to pass an entirely new libel law, in which truth was the deciding factor. Other states followed suit, and thus the two great antagonists, by indirection, created the principles which control newspaper excesses today.

At the height of the Croswell trial the Federalists threatened to call Callender as a witness, and even Jefferson himself. But Callender conveniently drowned himself in three feet of James River water; he apparently fell into it and was too drunk to get out. Some say he committed suicide. No one argued with the writer who said he found his grave in "congenial mud."

VII

Their dependence on Callender only proved the Federalists' desperation, and the Presidential election of 1804 fulfilled their worst forebodings. Jefferson swept every state except Connecticut and Delaware and these he lost only by handfuls of votes. Even mighty Massachusetts, once the bastion of Federalism, fell before

Jefferson's calm, steady appeal for reconciliation, bolstered by the triumph of the Louisiana Purchase. His majority in the Electoral College was an astonishing 162 to 14.

The victory was deeply satisfying to Jefferson. It justified his faith in the good sense of the common man. He devoted a major portion of his second inaugural address to discussing the failure of the Federalist slander campaign.

During this course of administration, and in order to disturb it, the artillery of the press has been leveled against us, charged with whatever its licentiousness could devise or dare. These abuses of an institution so important to freedom and science, are deeply to be regretted, inasmuch as they tend to lessen its usefulness, and to sap its safety. . . .

Nor was it uninteresting to the world, that an experiment should be fairly and fully made, where the freedom of discussion, unaided by power, is not sufficient for the propagation and protection of truth—whether a government, conducting itself in the true spirit of its constitution, with zeal and purity, and doing no act which it would be unwilling the whole world should witness, can be written down by falsehood and defamation. The experiment has been tried; you have witnessed the scene; our fellow citizens have looked on, cool and collected; they saw the latent source from which these outrages proceeded; they gathered around their public functionaries, and when the Constitution called them to the decision by suffrage, they pronounced their verdict, honorable to those who had served them, and consolatory to the friend of man, who believes he may be entrusted with his own affairs.

In a letter about a month later, he told James Sullivan, Republican Governor of Massachusetts, another reason why newspaper excesses worried him. "The circle of characters equal to the first stations is not too large, & will be lessened by the voluntary retreat of those whose sensibilities are stronger than their confidence in the justice of public opinion. I certainly have known, & still know, characters eminently qualified for the most exalted trusts, who could not bear up against the brutal hackings & hewings of these heroes of Billingsgate." He added an interesting observation on George Washington. "I may say, from intimate knowledge, that we should have lost the services of the greatest character of our country, had he been assailed with the degree of abandoned licentiousness now practiced. The torture he felt under rare & slight attacks, proved that under those of which the Federal bands have shown themselves capable, he would have thrown up the helm in a burst of indignation."

Jefferson began his second administration with high hopes for an era of domestic tranquillity and international peace. With England, he wrote one friend, "we are in cordial friendship: with France in the most perfect understanding; with Spain we shall always be bickering, but never at war." But his hopes were to be dashed by two familiar international troublemakers—England and France—and an equally familiar domestic one, Aaron Burr.

Jefferson, with the full support of his party, had kept the dapper Vice President at arms' length throughout his first term. After appointing a few of his followers to jobs, it became clear that Burr did not control very much of the Republican Party in New York. Powerful George Clinton and his ambitious nephew, De Witt Clinton, were far stronger, as well as more acceptable, and Jefferson soon shifted most federal patronage to their followers. Burr, meanwhile, flirted outrageously with the Federalists. He attended a Washington's Birthday dinner and before the largely Federalist audience offered a toast "to the union of all honest men."

Everyone, including Burr, knew that after that he had no hope of being renominated as Vice President. His one chance of staying alive politically was to regain control of New York, and he decided to run for governor in 1804. Although he styled himself an independent, he actually was running with Federalist support, hoping his name would still split off enough Republican votes to carve out a victory. But it soon became evident to this astute politician that his chances of wooing Republicans were nil, without Jefferson's blessing. So, on January 26, he paid a visit to the White House, for the first of several fateful conversations on which Jefferson made extensive notes.

Burr told the President that he had only accepted the Vice Presidential nomination "to promote Jefferson towards fame and advancement, and from a desire to be with [him] whose company and conversation had always been fascinating to him." He avowed that his feeling for Jefferson had been "sincere, and was still unchanged" and coolly declared that he was ready to "retire" from the Vice Presidency lest "a disadvantageous schism" take place in the party. But he wanted "some mark of favor" from Jefferson which would "declare to the world" that he retired with the President's confidence.

Perhaps Burr believed the Federalist caricature of Jefferson as a timid theorist; more likely this was one more illustration of his totally amoral gambler's approach to politics. Either way, he lost. Jefferson had no intention whatsoever of letting Burr ride to victory on his name. Imperturbably, he replied that he never electioneered for anybody, including himself. As for Burr's offer to retire to avoid a party schism, Jefferson, if he had wanted to be unkind, could have laughed in his face. When the Republican Congressional caucus nominated Jefferson unanimously for a second term, there were seven contestants for the Vice Presidency. George Clinton of New York won it on the first ballot and Burr, in the words of an observer, "had not one single vote, and not a word was lisped in his favor at the meeting." But Jefferson was too shrewd to give this arrogant little man cause for resentment. Instead he smoothly turned the conversation "to indifferent subjects" and the Vice President soon departed. Jefferson noted in his diary that Burr "must have thought that I could swallow strong things in my own favor" with his remarks about the fascination of Jefferson's company and conversation.

Burr went back to New York, where he began running not merely for the governorship, but for the possible Presidency of a new nation. He was deep in the intrigues of extreme New England Federalists, who, despairing of defeating Jefferson, were planning to dismember the United States. They needed New York to add strength and prestige to this dubious venture. Burr as usual made no commitments to anyone, suavely courting Republicans and Federalists out of opposite sides of his mouth. But Alexander Hamilton, invited to join the cabal, responded with a scathing rejection. When the Federalist malcontents turned to Burr, Hamilton came flailing out of retirement to spur the remnant of his followers into violent opposition. During these same months he became involved in the uproar over the prosecution of the editor, Harry Croswell, and while he was getting in a few licks against Jefferson, Hamilton did not forget the more immediate menace of

Burr. At dinner with a group of Albany Federalists, Hamilton spoke of Burr as "a dangerous man" and, according to a friend who wrote the letter reporting the dinner conversation, threw in "a still more despicable opinion."

Clinton and his followers beat Burr badly in the election, finishing him in New York. In his bitterness, Burr looked for a scapegoat, and found one in Hamilton. He charged the former Secretary of the Treasury with "base slanders," and asked for satisfaction. Some historians speculate that Hamilton, whose son had been killed in a duel two years before, might have refused, but for the public excitement he had generated in his defense of Croswell, which was really an attack on Jefferson. This return to the spotlight had revived his dreams of political and military glory, and he accepted Burr's challenge on the theory that he could never hope to become America's Bonaparte if people considered him a coward. So the famous duel was fought on the cliffs of Weehawken, N.J., on the morning of July 11, 1804. Burr cut Hamilton down with a single shot, and Jefferson's great antagonist died at 2 o'clock on the following afternoon. Indicted for murder in both New York and New Jersey, Burr fled south pursued by Federalist vituperation for killing their party's hero.

Really finished as a politician now, Burr turned to treason. A few months later the British minister, Anthony Merry, was writing home.

I have just received an offer from Mr. Burr, the actual Vice President of the United States (which situation he is about to resign) to lend his assistance to His Majesty's government in any manner in which they may think fit to employ him, particularly in endeavoring to effect a separation of the western part of the United States from that which lies between the Atlantic and the mountains, in its whole extent.

Around the same time, Burr began conferences with General James Wilkinson, corpulent commander in chief of the American army which Jefferson had sent to occupy New Orleans and the rest of Louisiana. One of the most corrupt characters in American history, Wilkinson was on the payroll of the Spanish government, to report any and all American secrets to them; he also secretly detested Jefferson and his party for reducing the army, and had a grandiose vision of himself, if not as a Bonaparte, at least a marshal to one. Burr had no trouble in convincing him he was the man to play the Napoleonic role.

Burr's ability to fascinate and often to dominate men was truly remarkable. On his last day as Vice President, he made a farewell speech to the Senate. It was an apostrophe to the virtue of duty. *The Washington Federalist*, which had been extremely abusive of Burr, reported the speech was "the most dignified, sublime and impressive that was ever uttered." Senator Plumer of New Hampshire told his wife, "we were all deeply affected, and many shed tears." The Senate responded by voting Burr a franking privilege for life—an honor heretofore given only to ex-presidents.

While the senators dried their eyes, Burr returned to plotting treason. Totally bankrupt now—his fine home in New York had been sold for debts—Burr began traveling extensively in the West, supposedly to lay claim to huge tracts of land in which he had speculated. Actually, he began exercising his sinister charm on everyone he met, from Andrew Jackson through United States Senator John Adair of Kentucky to the Roman Catholic Bishop of New Orleans. Burr pretended to have the secret backing of the Jefferson administration, and told all but a few of the chief conspirators that his goal was to liberate Mexico and the Floridas from the feeble hand of Spain. In the East, meanwhile, he managed to win the ardent support of a number of Federalists, such as Senator Jonathan Dayton of New Jersey. Burr's son-in-law, Joseph Alston, on his way to the governorship of South Carolina, was his chief agent in the Deep South.

But a scheme so grandiose required too many conspirators. Burr was forced to reveal his real plan too often, and various versions of the truth were soon floating throughout the West and even in Washington. Joseph Hamilton Daveiss, Federal District Attorney of Kentucky, picked up the scent of treason, and sent Jefferson a warning. Unfortunately, Daveiss was John Marshall's brother-in-law and a strong Federalist. His list of Burr's suspected supporters was a western Republican Who's Who. Jefferson, suspecting a plot to discredit his party, asked for more information. Meanwhile, the *Gazette of the United States* was asking, "How long will it be before we shall hear of Colonel Burr being at the head of a revolutionary party on the Western Waters?"

Then came a White House visit by William Eaton, one of the

heroes of the fight against Tripoli. He told Jefferson that Burr had first invited him to join an expedition to Mexico. Then he "laid open his project of revolutionizing the territory west of the Allegheny; establishing an independent empire there; New Orleans to be the capital and he himself to be the chief; organizing a military force on the waters of the Mississippi and carrying conquest to Mexico." Eaton's solution was to offer Burr an ambassadorship to Paris, London or Madrid. Jefferson scotched the idea with a tart remark that he preferred to place his confidence in the loyalty of the West.

Burr made other mistakes. He at first depended on what seemed to be a sure thing—a war with Spain. The Spanish government resented mightily the French sale of Louisiana to the United States in direct violation of a promise Napoleon had made to them. They resisted American attempts to argue that the Floridas were included in the bargain, and declined to negotiate other aspects of Louisiana's boundaries. The American government made a number of belligerent statements, but President Jefferson was playing the old diplomatic game of using threats of war to negotiate a peaceful settlement and Burr was soon lamenting, "We are to have no Spanish War, except in ink and words." Moreover, he was having trouble wooing westerners away from their personal loyalty to Jefferson. His chief lieutenant, Wilkinson, had tried to entice several of his officers and some prominent political friends into the scheme, and gave up in disgust. "The West is bigoted to Jefferson and democracy," he told Burr. So the colonel made one more visit to the White House.

Burr began rather belligerently by telling Jefferson that he never asked for a job. "He asked aid of nobody but could walk on his own legs and take care of himself." Then he complained that Jefferson had always "used him with politeness, but nothing more," a rather accurate description of the way the President had handled this treacherous gentleman. Burr protested that he had aided "in bringing on the present order of things" and he added significantly that he could "do Jefferson much harm." But he smoothed over this threat by assuring the President that he wished to be "on different ground." He would be in town several days and ready to listen to anything Jefferson might "propose to him."

Jefferson made it plain that he had no intention of proposing anything. He told Burr he admired his "talents" but the public had "withdrawn their confidence" from him and in a democratic administration, it was essential to employ men "who had a character with the public, of their own."

Truculently, Burr growled that if we "believed a few newspapers, it might be supposed he had lost the public confidence."

Wryly, Jefferson replied that he meant the Presidential election, when "not a single voice" was raised to keep him in the Vice Presidency.

As for harming him, Jefferson told Burr he was trying to frighten the wrong man. He feared "no injury which any man could do to me"; and added that he had "never done a single act, or been concerned in any transaction, which I feared to have fully laid open, or which could do me any hurt, if truly stated."

Those who are inclined to look with compassion on Burr think this interview was his last try at respectability. If Jefferson had given him a decent post, as Eaton had suggested, he might have remained loyal. More likely, Burr was making one more try to gull Jefferson into aiding his schemes. If the President had given him any federal appointment Burr would have used it as proof that the government was really behind the secret army he was already building in the West.

By now Burr was also in the pay of the Spanish government. They advanced him $2,500 to aid his recruiting, convinced that his main plot was a western revolution which would split America in half. Burr went back to Kentucky, and Jefferson, by now thoroughly alarmed by reports reaching him from all directions, ordered the secretary of the New Orleans territory to get on Burr's trail with discretionary powers to arrest him. Gunboats were ordered to New Orleans and officials throughout the territory were warned of the plot, and the possibility that General Wilkinson might be implicated. But Burr, knowing he was watched, did as little as possible himself and Jefferson was soon hearing "not one word . . . of any movements by Colonel Burr." Still dreading a party and administration scandal (Wilkinson, after all, was his appointment), Jefferson canceled the orders to the gunboats, and resumed his policy of watchful waiting. Then came a thunderbolt from New Orleans.

General Wilkinson, getting word from Burr that he was about

to start his descent of the Mississippi with a well-armed advance guard, suddenly developed an acute case of cold feet. He fired off a letter to Jefferson denouncing "a deep, dark, wicked and wide-spread conspiracy" and enclosed a letter Burr had sent him from which he had eliminated all incriminating references to himself. Jefferson immediately issued a proclamation vigorously denouncing Burr's expedition and calling on the governors of all the western states and territories to prevent the gathering of the 1,300-man army Burr had already recruited. While this Presidential blast was traveling west, Burr was displaying the kind of duplicity he might have used on a far larger scale if Jefferson had succumbed to his threats, and given him some governmental post. When Tennesseeans, led by Andrew Jackson (not yet the hero of New Orleans), became suspicious of Burr and began asking him some hard questions, the wily little colonel pulled from his pocket a blank commission with Jefferson's name forged to it. "Gentlemen," he said, "I suppose this will satisfy you."

The Presidential proclamation, and the publication of Burr's cipher letter to Wilkinson in which he revealed his secessionist plans, exploded Burr's scheme. Andrew Jackson's reaction was typical and it also explained why Burr was able to tempt so many prominent men to join him. "I would delight to see Mexico reduced," Jackson growled, "but I will die in the last ditch before I . . . see the Union disunited." Burr's ungathered army dissolved and Wilkinson arrested Burr's New Orleans lieutenants and shipped them to Washington. Burr himself was captured, with one still faithful aide, by a troop of soldiers as he fled in disguise through the Mississippi territory.

The more Jefferson learned of the breadth and depth of Burr's conspiracy, the angrier he became. The ex-Vice President had plotted to destroy by treachery the empire of liberty—the Louisiana Purchase—which Jefferson considered the triumph of his Presidency. John Randolph, eager to make trouble for Jefferson, introduced a resolution in the House of Representatives, calling for a Presidential report on the conspiracy. Jefferson was obviously reluctant to say anything. He was still not sure that Burr's disunion intrigues had been completely stamped out. But once he started writing, his anger controlled his pen. Like a good lawyer, he first said that "neither safety nor justice" would permit him to expose the names of all the conspirators. If he had stopped there, he would have been the philosopher-statesman legend has painted him. But the flesh-and-blood Jefferson, boiling with rage at Burr, added a fateful phrase—"*except that of the principal actor whose guilt is placed beyond question.*"

This was a blunder, and it soon rebounded on the President. Federalists rushed to Burr's defense screaming that he was a victim of government persecution. John Adams, who had lost his temper more often than any other President in history, piously declared that "the first magistrate" should not have publicly prejudged Burr's guilt. Federalist fervor for the fallen hero was in part motivated by the fact that two of their senators were implicated in the plot. But most of their enthusiasm came from sheer hatred of Jefferson. This was especially true in Richmond, where the small clique of Federalist lawyers, led by Chief Justice John Marshall, nursed an intense antipathy for the President.

Jefferson's old cabinet colleague, Edmund Randolph, consented to become Burr's senior defense attorney. When the colonel arrived in Richmond for trial, the ladies of the capital immediately adopted him as their pet. Harmon Blennerhassett, an Irish-born accomplice of Burr's, noted in his journal that Mrs. David Randolph, sister to Jefferson's son-in-law, "ridiculed the experiment of a republic in this country . . . and as for treason, she cordially hoped whenever Burr, or anyone else, again attempted to do anything, the Atlantic states would be comprised in the plan." Finally Chief Justice John Marshall announced that he would personally sit at the trial.

Jefferson's alarm and anger exceeded all previous bounds. "The Federalists make Burr's cause their own," he fumed. The combination of treason and Federalism rampant in its judicial stronghold aroused Jefferson to use every iota of power he possessed to convict Burr. Signed Presidential pardons were offered to Burr's fellow conspirators, if they agreed to turn state's evidence. The President bombarded George Hay, the chief prosecuting attorney, with dozens of letters advising him on every move down to the minutiae of what precedents to plead. Federal district attorneys throughout the country rounded up over a hundred witnesses.

But all this energy was in vain. Chief Justice Marshall was equally determined to see Burr acquitted. In an unprecedented display of judicial partisanship, Marshall had dinner with Burr and his chief attorney before the trial began and he managed to wangle Edward Carrington, his brother-in-law, onto the jury as foreman. Carrington's wife was simultaneously sending jellies and soups to the prisoners. During the grand-jury hearing, Marshall allowed Burr and his lawyers to handle government witnesses so roughly that one spectator wrote Albert Gallatin it was questionable whether "the court is trying Burr or Burr the President." Marshall permitted Burr to issue an insulting subpoena to Jefferson personally, which the President rejected as "preposterous," and at one point the Chief Justice openly declared in the courtroom that the government wanted to convict Burr without evidence.

Marshall never let most of the government's witnesses get to the stand, siding with the defense argument that an "overt act" of treason had to be proven before witnesses could testify to a conspiracy. Since Burr consistently acted through intermediaries, who were not likely to turn state's evidence against him, Marshall's rulings left the government hamstrung.

Finally, in one of the longest opinions he ever wrote—it took him over three hours to read it and it cited more decisions, treatises and histories than all the rest of his major Constitutional opinions combined—Marshall declared it was not treason merely to "advise or procure" treason, and insisted that the intention to go to war (against the United States) had to be proved by "open deeds." This completely reversed a previous decision by the Chief Justice himself that it was only necessary to prove that an assembled armed force intended to commit treason.

The jury at least had the gumption to tell Marshall what they thought of his opinion by conferring for only twenty-five minutes, and then announcing, "Aaron Burr is not proved to be guilty under this indictment by any evidence submitted to us." Defense lawyers angrily demanded to know if the jury was censuring the court. Foreman Carrington intimated that he would be willing to alter the peculiar language of the verdict, but Jeffersonians on the jury said they would sit till doomsday before they agreed to change it. Marshall, satisfied that Burr was free and the President frustrated, ordered the verdict to be filed as given.

The jury thus offered Jefferson an opportunity to prosecute Burr for treason in other parts of the nation, outside of Marshall's jurisdiction, and for a while he was inclined to do so. He did order him prosecuted for misdemeanor—levying war against Spain—and tried to get the trial shifted to another jurisdiction. But Marshall declined to co-operate, and he saw to it that this effort too ended in acquittal. Discussions with his cabinet finally made Jefferson realize he was in danger of turning Burr into a martyr, and instead he sent the proceedings of the treason trial, including the depositions of the numerous witnesses Marshall had not permitted to testify, to Congress for publication. He remained convinced that Marshall's ruling on treason was "equivalent to a proclamation of impunity to every traitorous combination which may be formed to destroy the union."

General Wilkinson did almost as much damage to the government's case as Chief Justice Marshall. Rumors of his Spanish pension, and the considerable evidence that he was deeply involved with Burr, made it easy for Jefferson haters to conjure up a government plot to destroy the New Yorker. But Jefferson refused to disavow his portly, red-faced general, in part because he had appointed him, but also because there was no real evidence to support the Spanish-pension story. Jefferson was hardly inclined to pay attention to charges in Federalist newspapers, after the years of lying abuse they had heaped on him.

Wilkinson demanded a court-martial to refute "the foul slander of his pension." The Spanish Governor of West Florida acquitted him with a testimonial that there was no document whatever in his archives that supported the story. The Governor was able to tell this white lie because he had sent the incriminating material to the archives in Havana. Decades later, when historians finally penetrated these archives, many, in a kind of rebound effect, began picturing Burr to be as innocent as the Federalists piously proclaimed him. Actually, proof of Burr's willingness to play the traitor is overwhelming. But his scheme was flexible enough to permit him to drop the secessionist section of it, when the West's loyalty to Jefferson proved too strong for his serpentine wiles. He then shifted his sights to the second stage of his Bonapartean dream, the revolutionizing of Mexico.

Perhaps the best proof of this is Burr's later conduct. Totally discredited by Jefferson's publication of the government's evidence, and hounded by creditors, he fled to Europe, where he made a proposition to the French to carve a satellite nation out of Louisiana, Florida and Mexico—the identical plan he had dangled before Wilkinson. When Napoleon turned him down, Burr dropped the American portion of the plan, and urged the simple seizure of Mexico—again identical with his original maneuvers. Napoleon never answered these lengthy memoranda, still on file in the French archives. The colonel drifted aimlessly around Europe, trying to sell his schemes and services to Great Britain, Russia, Denmark, and carefully listing his almost nightly visits to prostitutes in his letters home to his adoring daughter. He finally crept back to the United States in 1812, and spent the rest of his life obscurely practicing law in New York. Jefferson wrote his epitaph, when Burr was on his way to Richmond for trial. "No man's history proves better the value of honesty. With that, what might he not have been!"

VIII

Before the drama with Burr ended, Jefferson got some better news from the West. Soon after he became President, he had suggested an expedition to explore the unknown part of the continent. He had obtained permission from Spain, France and England to send a small body of soldiers to the headwaters of the Missouri, in the hope of finding a water route to the Pacific. Jefferson personally selected the expedition's two leaders, Meriwether Lewis, his private secretary, and William Clark, younger brother of Jefferson's old friend, General George Rogers Clark, and an experienced soldier and frontiersman. The purchase of Louisiana made the expedition all the more urgent, and in the spring of 1804 the two young Virginians, 26 soldiers, 2 interpreters, and a Negro servant, York, and an Indian squaw, Sacajawea, started up the Missouri.

Jefferson has often been hailed for sponsoring the expedition, but as with so much of his life, the intimate details are far more revealing of the man. He browbeat a parsimonious Congress into providing the funds—$2,500. Lewis was not just selected because he was Jefferson's secretary. He was extremely well educated in science, languages and mathematics. He spent a full year, before he departed, studying a Jefferson-outlined brush-up course in astronomy, botany, mineralogy, cartography, zoology and Indian history. Jefferson devoted weeks to what we would call "briefing" the two leaders on the purpose of the expedition, which was nothing less than a scientific exploration of the unknown half of the continent.

Two and a half years later, on October 20, 1806, Jefferson heard "with unspeakable joy" that the expedition had returned safely to St. Louis, after exploring the Missouri, the Yellowstone, the Snake and the Columbia Rivers, reaching the Pacific near present-day Astoria, Oregon. Proudly, in his message to Congress several weeks later, Jefferson told how his hand-picked young lieutenants had "learned the character of the country, of its commerce and inhabitants." They had also brought back reams of information on the soil, plants, animals and Indians of the West. Their surveys, he declared, now made it possible for the first time to begin an accurate map of the Mississippi and its western waters. Thus Jefferson, who had already done so much to bring order and national unity to America's westward expansion, created a new and vaster frontier.

In this same message to Congress, Jefferson also congratulated his fellow citizens on a bill successfully maneuvered through Congress earlier that year—the suspension of the African slave trade, as of 1808. The citizens of the United States, Jefferson said proudly, were now withdrawn "from all further participation in those violations of human rights which have been so long continued on the unoffending inhabitants of Africa, and which the morality, the reputation, and the best interests of our country, have long been eager to proscribe." The bill had been passed over violent southern objections, and had split the Virginia delegation wide open, driving into outraged opposition their leading spokesman, reedy, voluble John Randolph, who now became Jefferson's most dangerous Congressional foe.

Jefferson would have preferred a bill to abolish slavery entirely, but he was too realistic to try for the impossible. A year before, when Dr. George Logan, the Pennsylvania idealist, asked him to subscribe to the publication of a long antislavery poem called "Avenia," Jefferson candidly explained his policy toward slavery. It was, he said, "highly painful" to him to hesitate to say yes on a matter "which appears so small," but he had "most carefully avoided every public act or manifestation on that subject." Why? Because he knew "that little irritating measures," such as the subscribing to books, would accomplish nothing and would only lose the good will of moderates by inflaming proslavery men to intemperate attacks. What Jefferson was waiting for was "an occasion . . . in which I can interpose with decisive effect." Then he said he would "certainly know & do my duty with promptitude & zeal."

But Jefferson was gradually abandoning his hope that this opportunity would come in his lifetime. Early in 1805 he wrote to his secretary, William A. Burwell: "I have long since given up the expectation of any early provision for the extinguishment of slavery among us. There are many virtuous men who would make any sacrifice to effect it, many equally virtuous men who persuade themselves either that the thing is not wrong, or that it cannot be remedied. And very many with whom interest is morality. The older we grow, the larger we are disposed to believe the last party to be. . . ." The only hope, Jefferson saw, was the decline in the value of slaves in the southern economy, which might bring "interest . . . over to the side of morality." This movement would be "goaded from time to time by the insurrectionary spirit of the slaves."

He had also changed his mind about confining slavery to the original states. He told John Dickinson in 1807 that by "dividing the evil" and letting men take slaves into the new territories, there was more hope of eventual emancipation. The fewer the slave owners in a state, the more likely a vote for emancipation, was his reasoning. Jefferson was also convinced that in the long run slavery could not compete with free labor. A mixed economy in the territories and the states they eventually formed could be slavery's downfall.

In the meantime, Jefferson had to face all the grim realities of owning slaves. On July 31, 1806, he sent the following letter from Monticello to Joseph Dougherty, the White House handyman.

In the first place say not a word on the subject of this letter but to Mr. Perry, the person who delivers it to you. He comes in pursuit of a young mulatto man, called Joe, 26 years of age, who ran away from here the night of the 29th inst. without the least word of difference with any body, & indeed having never in his life received a blow from any one. He has been about 12 years working at the blacksmith's trade. We know he has taken the road towards Washington, & . . . he may possibly trump up some story to be taken care of at the President's house till he can make up his mind which way to go, or perhaps he may make himself known to Edy [a female slave working at the White House] only, as he was formerly connected with her. I must beg of you to use all possible diligence in searching for him in Washington & Georgetown, and if you can find him, have aid with you to take him as he is strong & resolute. . . .

A few days later Dougherty replied that he had met Joe "going from the President's House and being informed of his marks & clothing by Mr. Perry I knew it must be him. I took him immediately and brot him to Mr. Perry & has him now in jail. Mr. Perry will start with him tomorrow for Monticello."

This must be balanced against a letter the President wrote the following year to an Albemarle neighbor.

. . . Nobody feels more strongly than I do the desire to make all practicable sacrifices to keep man & wife together who have imprudently married out of their respective families, & I had accordingly told Moses that if it should be your pleasure to sell his wife personally, I would buy her when I could with convenience: for I assure you that nobody is less able to make purchases than myself, or more pressed for money. . . .

IX

Throughout his second term Jefferson continued his hospitable White House ways. Superb wines and gourmet cooking disappeared so rapidly into the interiors of visiting congressmen and diplomats that his expenses invariably outran his $25,000 annual salary. When a friend wrote him for a thousand-dollar loan, the President was mortified to confess that he simply did not have the money.

He also continued to ride more or less incognito about the District of Columbia, striking up conversations with unsuspecting travelers. Often he converted this daily relaxation into a scientific expedition. One Washingtonian of the era said it was a common sight to see the President get off his horse and "climb rocks or wade through swamps to obtain any plant he discovered or desired. . . . Not a plant from the lowliest weed to the loftiest tree escaped his notice."

Although Jefferson repeatedly emphasized that he was not a professional scientist but an "amateur"—a man who loved it—his reputation made him a symbol of scientific learning. As president · of the American Philosophical Society, he was in constant contact with leading scientists throughout the nation and abroad. Dr. Benjamin Waterhouse of Harvard Medical School sent him samples of a new smallpox vaccine, made from cowpox, and discussed his results in lengthy letters. Jefferson immediately asked him for more of the vaccine which he used to inoculate dozens of his own people at Monticello. He then persuaded doctors to try it on a mass scale throughout Virginia. It was the first public health campaign in the nation's history.

People sent Jefferson an endless stream of scientific requests. One man wanted him to correspond on optics. A second asked for some seeds of the senega root. A third wanted his help in identifying some unusual grapevine leaves. Humboldt sent him his latest work on astronomy. Dr. Benjamin Rush corresponded with him on medicine. William Short, in business in Philadelphia, sent him a micrometer and telescope which he knew Jefferson would be interested in seeing. The skin of a Rocky Mountain sheep, dead Hessian flies, stuffed birds, coins of Rome and Denmark, shells, specimens of horn, streamed into the White House.

Jefferson used some of this diversified material to set up a kind of scientific museum in the East Room. The main attraction was a huge collection of fossil bones dug out of Big Bone Lick, in Kentucky. He also displayed the model of a new plow which he had invented and used at Monticello for five years, before bringing it to the White House. Called the "moldboard plow," it was one of the first attempts to standardize this key farming implement, and at the same time enable it to dig a much deeper furrow than the usual eighteenth-century plow. It could, Jefferson proudly declared, be made by "the most bungling carpenter" without varying "a hair's breadth in its form but by gross negligence."

He continued to improve this technological breakthrough, for which he received a gold medal from the Agricultural Society of Paris, borrowing a dynamometer from Robert Fulton to test the amount of force required to operate it, and shortening it some six or eight inches in response to suggestions from farmers who used it. Typically, Jefferson never bothered to take out a patent. To a fellow inventor he wrote, "You will be at perfect liberty to use the form of the mold-board, as all the world is, having never thought of monopolizing by patent any useful idea which happens to offer itself to me. . . ."

Also on display in the White House was a dry dock the President had designed. It seemed to him the perfect answer to combining economy with a strong navy. In the days of wooden ships, men-of-war were constantly rotting away. Jefferson envisioned the possibility of running vessels into his dry docks, pumping the water out of them, and thus keeping them preserved "through the long intervals of peace which I hope are to be the lot of our country." His friend, Dr. Samuel L. Mitchill of New York, liked the idea, but his favorable committee report was killed by Congress.

As a public man, Jefferson lacked the time to be an inventor on a large scale. But he managed to find spare moments enough to design a startling variety of gadgets which were all over the White House. One visitor noted "an odd but useful contrivance for hanging up jackets and breeches on a machine like a turnstile." Another man was intrigued by a set of circular shelves set up on the dining-room door so that they turned into the room loaded with dishes "on touching a spring." In the "cabinet," as he called his study, Jefferson showed Margaret Bayard Smith a small piece of furniture he had designed. He touched a spring and little doors flew open, disclosing a goblet of water, a decanter of wine, a plate of light cakes, and a night candle. When he sat up late reading, Jefferson used this emergency kitchen rather than bother a servant.

With this love of small, practical things, Jefferson continued to combine his passion for architecture. He conferred and corresponded at length with Benjamin Latrobe on the design for the

Capitol, and on additions to the White House. How thoroughly professional he could be is evident in this note: "Though the spheroidical dome presents difficulties to the executor, yet they are not beyond his art . . . would it not be best to make the internal columns of well burnt brick, moulded in portions of circles . . . ?" Jefferson also continued to toss off strikingly beautiful house plans for his friends. Perhaps the best of these is Bremo, still standing in Fluvanna County, Virginia. It is a lovely variation on Monticello, with terraces containing the service quarters running out to porticoed pavilions. Robert Mills, who later claimed, with some justification, to be the first native-born professional architect, worked for two years under President Jefferson as a draftsman.

One might wonder how Jefferson accomplished all these things and still ran the country. The only answer is his fantastic industry. He rose before the sun, and was usually at his desk from dawn until 1 or 2 P.M. Letter after letter flowed from his tireless pen. Memoranda, reports, messages to Congress, all were written by the President, personally, in the same clear firm hand. Washington and Adams had often relied on numerous talented ghosts—Adams used John Marshall—but President Jefferson did all his own writing. Only when he wanted advice on the tone or political prudence of a speech or message did he turn to Madison or Gallatin for help.

The gadget President Jefferson loved most was one he did not design—the polygraph. This was a writing desk with from two to five pens attached to it, suspended from wires in a way that enabled the other pens to duplicate the work of the number-one pen. Jefferson, staggering under his enormous correspondence, hailed it as "the finest invention of the present age . . . a most precious possession." It freed him and his secretary from the drudgery of making copies of letters—and it could not reveal state and personal secrets. Jefferson suggested several improvements in the device, which were incorporated in later models. It never won the popularity in the United States he thought it deserved, largely because few people had so many letters to write, or were concerned about the importance of making copies.

In the windows of his study, Jefferson grew roses and geraniums. Above these was suspended the cage of the favorite White House pet, Dick the mockingbird. When Jefferson was alone, he would let Dick fly about the room and eventually he became so tame he would perch on Jefferson's shoulder, and take food from his lips. Often he flew upstairs after him to his bedroom, and would perch on the headboard of the bed, chirping away. "How he loved this bird! How he loved his flowers! He could not live without something to love," said Margaret Bayard Smith. "And in the absence of his darling grandchildren, his bird and his flowers became the objects of tender care."

X

In 1806, Jefferson finally persuaded his daughter Martha to pay him a visit with her children. Margaret Bayard Smith dropped in one evening to find the President literally up to his ears in young Randolphs, "one standing on the sofa with its arms around his neck, the other two youngest on his knees, playing with him." (By now Martha had six children, five of them girls.) Baron von Humboldt called on another evening, and found Jefferson on the floor all but buried by a half dozen shouting, wrestling youngsters. The Baron stood in the doorway for several minutes before Jefferson noticed him. When he finally escaped from his playmates and shook hands with his distinguished visitor, the President was cheerfully unembarrassed. "You have found me playing the fool, Baron," he said, "but I am sure to you I need make no apology."

Martha gave birth to her second son during this White House visit. As with earlier children, the Randolphs let Jefferson select the new arrival's name. He decided James Madison Randolph had the right ring for the first child born in the Presidential mansion. The next boy, born (in Virginia) in 1808, became Benjamin Franklin Randolph. Two later boys were called Meriwether Lewis, after the explorer of the continent, and George Wythe, for Jefferson's old law professor and collaborator on revising the laws of Virginia. It was another sign of the almost too abject reverence with which Thomas Mann Randolph regarded Jefferson that he insisted on his father-in-law naming his children. Jefferson did not ask for the privilege. Once, when he delayed, obviously hoping Randolph would do the job, Martha wrote a plaintive letter, asking for a name, so the baby could be baptized.

Whether they were at Monticello or at the White House, Martha's children were Jefferson's favorite escape from "the Feds," as he called the Federalists, and similar headaches of state. He carried on a delightful correspondence with all his grandchildren, solemnly debating with Anne the momentous question of whether she should change her name to "Anastasia," and getting letters from Ellen, when she was in the midst of a romantic poetry phase, signed "Eleanora." Anne was his favorite gardener, and he shipped her everything from flowering peas sent from Arkansas by Meriwether Lewis to rare Algerian chickens to superintend at Monticello. Ellen was more intellectual. Whenever she had a question such as "What is the seventh art?" she would fire it off to the White House. Jefferson dodged that one, saying the number had never been fixed by general consent and inclining himself to include poetry, oratory and gardening.

The President always kept track of whether there was "a balance" of letters in his or the child's favor. When Ellen fell behind, he warned her that her balance was badly out of line "and unless it be soon paid off I shall send the sheriff after you."

With Ellen he played another game. Whenever he was about to pay Monticello a visit, he would warn Ellen that he expected "to catch her in bed." Ten-year-old Ellen loved it and wrote tartly to him. "I do not intend to let you catch me in bed that day [of his arrival] as I will get up with the sun that you may not. For I should be very sorry if you found me as averse to getting up early as I was when you left us." A few weeks later Ellen submitted her reading list to him. It included Grecian history, "in which I am very much interested," Plutarch in French and Lord Chesterfield's letters.

The freedom with which all his granddaughters wrote to Jefferson obviously delighted him. In 1807, when Burr and other political matters pressed him for time, he wrote mournfully to Ellen, "I am afraid I shall be bankrupt in my epistolary account with Anne and yourself." Ellen promptly replied: "Your fear of being bankrupt is not badly founded." Tongue in cheek, Jefferson defended himself: "Whether this proceeds from your having more industry or less to do than myself I will not say." Ellen gravely replied: "I suspect that it would be more reasonable to think that your owing me three letters proceeds from my having more time than industry, although [she proudly added] a very little part of this winter has been spent by me in idleness. Still, however, I think that you must have a great deal more to do than I have."

The younger children even sent Jefferson their babyish scrawls. He told Ellen to thank four-year-old Mary for her letter, "but tell her it is written in a cypher of which I have not the key. She must, therefore, tell it all to me when I come home." Ellen replied cheerfully: "Mary says she would tell you what was in her letter gladly if she knew herself."

Little Cornelia Jefferson Randolph was cleverer, and got Ellen to write the letter for her. "Every day I get a piece of poetry by heart and write a copy," she told him proudly. "I have not yet begun arithmetic yet but I hope I soon shall." In a companion letter, Ellen grandly reported: "Cornelia goes on very well with her writing."

Anne's letters reveal an impressive growth in gardening skill under Jefferson's guidance. In November, 1807, she wrote him matter of factly:

The tuberoses and amaryllises are taken up. We shall have aplenty of them the next year. The tulips and Hyacinths I had planted before I left Monticello. They had increased so much as to fill the beds quite full. The Anemonies and Ranunculuses are also doing well. Fourteen of Governor Lewis's Pea ripened which I have saved. The Pinks, Carnations, Sweet Williams, Yellow Horned Poppy, Ixia Jeffersonia, everlasting Pea Lavetera, Columbian Lily, Lobelia Lychinis, double blossomed Poppy and Physalis failed . . . Ellen and myself have a fine parcel of little Orange trees for the greenhouse against your return.

But it was Ellen who was best at giving Jefferson the "small news" he loved.

In compliance with my promise I take up my pen to write to my dear grandpapa. . . . I am in a fair way to raise some bantams as the hen is now setting. She has taken up her residence in the cellar. Has laid 13 eggs and I hope will hatch some chickens. Mr. Ogilvie has broken up keeping school and Jefferson [her older brother] is going to the Green Springs to a Mr. Maury who they say is a very good teacher. . . . I heard yesterday from Aunt Virginia. There has been a terrible riot at Williamsburg [the College of William and Mary]. Fifteen boys were expelled and five thrown in jail and fined $20 a piece. . . . Mamma is a little unwell today. . . . How is Mrs. H. Smith? Tell me when you answer this. Are all the birds and flowers well? I soon will have a garden of my own in which I shall plant the seeds you gave me. The orange trees look very well but one of the finest is dead. We had a visit yesterday from Colonel Munroe. . . . Virginia reads a little and Mary can spell words of three letters. She imagines that she is far before Cornelia although she often expresses apprehensions lest Cornelia should catch her and learn to read before she does. James is a sweet little fellow, speaks quite well and has really grown handsome. He thinks of nothing but guns, horses and dogs. Mamma and sister Anne send their love to you. Give mine to Mrs. S.H.S. [Samuel Harrison Smith]. . . . Cornelia says will you soon answer her letter. She hopes the next you get from her will be in her own hand writing. . . . We have not had such a thing as a ball for a long time in Milton and my dancing school is over so that I have not been to a dance for a long time. . . . My dear grandpa will excuse this long catalogue but I have no news to tell him and rather than not write I will relate to him what passes among us which though rather dull and uninteresting to another will serve to show him that rather than not write at all I will this. . . .

Jefferson replied: "Your letter of the 11th is received and is the best letter you have ever written me because it is the longest and fullest of that small news which I have most pleasure in receiving. With great news I am more than surfeited from other quarters. . . ."

With his oldest grandson, Thomas Jefferson Randolph, the President tended to be more serious. When this husky—he grew to be 6'4"—young man went to school in Philadelphia at fifteen to continue his education, Jefferson wrote him a letter, rich in wisdom and in personal revelation.

Thrown on a wide world, among entire strangers, without a friend or guardian to advise, so young too and with so little experience of mankind, your dangers are great, & still your safety must rest on yourself. . . . When I recollect that at 14 years of age the whole care & direction of myself was thrown on myself entirely, without a relation or friend qualified to advise or guide me, and recollect the various sorts of bad company with which I associated from time to time, I am astonished I did not turn off with some of them, & become as worthless to society as they were. I had the good fortune to become acquainted very early with some characters of very high standing, and to feel the incessant wish that I could ever become what they were . . . many a time have I asked myself, in the enthusiastic moment of the death of a fox, the victory of a favorite horse, the issue of a question eloquently argued at the bar, or in the great council of the nation, well, which of these kinds of reputation should I prefer? That of a horse jockey? A fox hunter? An orator? Or the honest advocate of my country's rights? Be assured, my dear Jefferson, that these little returns into ourselves, this self-catechizing habit, is not trifling nor useless but leads to the prudent selection & steady pursuit of what is right.

Above all things Jefferson urged his grandson to cultivate good humor. He called it "among the most effectual . . . preservatives of our peace & tranquility." Its effect, he said, "is so well imitated and aided, artificially, by politeness, that this also becomes an acquisition of first-rate value."

Jefferson advised the young man never to argue with anyone. "I never saw an instance of one of two disputants convincing the other by argument. I have seen many, on their getting warm, becoming rude, & shooting one another. Conviction is the effect of our own dispassionate reasoning, either in solitude, or weighing within ourselves, dispassionately, what we hear from others, standing uncommitted in argument ourselves. It was one of the rules which, above all others, made Dr. Franklin the most amiable of men in society, never to contradict anybody." If he was urged to announce an opinion, he did it rather by asking questions, as if for information, or by suggesting doubts. "When I hear another express an opinion which is not mine, I say to myself, he has a right to his opinion, as I to mine; why should I question it? His error does me no injury, and shall I become a Don Quixote, to bring all men by force of argument to one opinion?"

There are, Jefferson said, two classes of "disputants" that are especially common. The first is . . . young students . . . the other consists of the ill-tempered & rude men in society, who have taken up a passion for politics. From both, Jefferson urged, "keep aloof, as you would from the infected subjects of yellow fever or pestilence. Consider yourself, when with them, as among the patients of Bedlam, needing medical more than moral counsel."

XI

Even as he wrote this long letter, Jefferson was being challenged to cope with a political bedlam worse than any he had yet faced.

On June 22, 1807, the 36-gun frigate U.S.S. *Chesapeake* stood out from Baltimore for the Mediterranean. She was overhauled by the 50-gun frigate *Leopard*, part of a British squadron patrolling off the American coast. The British captain of the *Leopard* sent an officer aboard the *Chesapeake* with a letter informing him that he was under orders to search the American warship for deserters from British ships. The American captain refused this insulting demand, but only then noticed that the *Leopard*'s decks were cleared for action. Before the *Chesapeake* could load a gun, the *Leopard* poured broadside after broadside into her, bringing down her masts, ripping 22 holes in the hull, and killing 3 and wounding 18 sailors. Forced to strike their colors, the Americans had to submit to the humiliation of British officers mustering the crew. In spite of desperate denials, four men were seized as deserters and returned to His Majesty's fleet, where one of them was hanged.

The nation exploded. Mobs surged through the seacoast towns attacking British sailors and property. If ever there was a time when a President might have confidently declared war on behalf of a united nation, it was now. The *Chesapeake* was the last and worst in a long series of British assaults on American ships. Jefferson had done his utmost to bring the British to their senses, sending Monroe and William Pinckney to London to negotiate a new treaty, and repeatedly warning British diplomats in Washington that America's patience was not inexhaustible. But the treaty Monroe and Pinckney brought back was so poor, in terms of British concessions, Jefferson did not even submit it to the Senate.

Never was a more martial Fourth of July celebrated in Washington. Navy Yard cannon boomed, militia paraded before the White House and Federalists struggled to be first in line at the reception in the East Room. At a banquet that night, there was frenzied cheering when one Republican proposed a toast, "The President of the United States—the hand that drafted the Declaration of Independence—will maintain inviolate the principles that it recognizes."

But Jefferson was to prove once more that "peace was his passion." He issued a proclamation, denouncing "this enormity" in scathing terms, and barring all British armed vessels from the harbors and waters of the United States—a harsh blow in an era when men-of-war depended on friendly ports to replenish their supplies of fresh water and food regularly. But he also stated that he hoped the blundering arrogance of the British naval commander would "strengthen the motives to an honorable reparation." As he explained it a few days later to a correspondent, "Both reason and the usage of nations required we should give Gr. Britain an opportunity of disavowing & repairing the insult of their officers."

To his son-in-law, Congressman Jack Eppes, a few days later, Jefferson wrote candidly that if Britain had "the good sense to do us ample justice, it will be a war saved. But I do not expect it, and every preparation therefore is going on & will continue, which is in our power." That Jefferson meant what he said is evident from the record of his cabinet meetings. He sent an account of the *Chesapeake* incident to Tsar Alexander of Russia, with whom he had been conducting a friendly correspondence, in the hope of turning that mighty monarch against Great Britain. A call went out to the state governors for 100,000 militia with orders to prepare for a winter expedition against Canada. At the same time Jefferson resisted all pleas for a special session of Congress, because in the country's present mood, the lawmakers would have almost certainly voted for war.

In previous crises with Great Britain, and with France, Jefferson had always advocated playing off one antagonist against the other, thus forcing them to make some concessions to American trade, or pay a little more respect to neutral rights. But now the situation was acutely complicated by a new development. The two giants were in their climactic death grapple and Napoleon, in a series of pronunciamentos known as The Berlin and Milan Decrees, declared the British Isles in a state of blockade, forbidding all commerce and communication with them and authorizing the seizure and confiscation of vessels and cargo. This was the French Emperor's imperial reply to the British blockade of France and her allies. Scores of American ships were seized, and the Federalists had ranted that Jefferson was in the pay of Bonaparte because he did not go to war with France immediately.

Napoleon's decrees were still very much in force. Thus France was abusing America's neutral rights almost as much as Great Britain and it left Jefferson little or no room to maneuver. If war was to be declared on the basis of outrages committed, the infant republic should logically attack both France and England. This was so absurd that Jefferson decided there was only one truly neutral course left: an embargo.

Thus began the greatest experiment in search of an alternative to war in the history of the world. The law, passed on December 22, 1807, declared that all ships of the United States were herewith forbidden to sail to any foreign port. No measure of Jefferson's long career drew more violent criticism, both from contemporaries and from historians of later generations. Jefferson haters, a high proportion of them New Englanders, have used it as the quintessential proof that he was an impractical theorist. Others used it to accuse him of seeking a "Chinese isolation" of the United States.

Jefferson's own words are the best answer to these charges. The embargo was never intended to be permanent. As early as March, 1808, Jefferson said in a letter to Madison, "War will become preferable to a continuation of the embargo after a certain time. Should we not therefore avail ourselves of the intervening period to procure a retraction of the obnoxious decrees peaceably if possible?" Several times Jefferson admitted to Albert Gallatin and other members of the cabinet that the embargo was an "experiment." But it was worth making because of its "immense value for the future as well as on this occasion." There was also an extremely realistic side to the measure. As Jefferson told another correspondent, it gave American "time to call home 80 millions of property, 20, or 30,000 seamen, & 2,000 vessels." The seamen and the ships were especially vital, if the nation was to have any hope of fighting Great Britain, "the whale of the ocean," as Jefferson called her. Above all, the decision was based on Jefferson's intimate knowledge of European conditions. Napoleon's counterblockade had shut Great Britain out of all her continental markets. Even in peacetime, America imported one-third of all England's manufactures. If the American people stood solidly behind him, Jefferson was sure he could bring the English economy to a dead stop in a matter of months.

The embargo hurt. Farm prices dropped and stocks faltered. Small businessmen with limited capital reserves were driven to the wall. Inevitably, these hardships caused some discontent, especially in New England, where seafaring was a major industry. Still, the majority of the nation supported the President. But the Federalist leaders could not resist one last try at destroying Jefferson. They exploited the minority's discontent in their most vituperative style, and did their utmost to create more of it.

The leader was John Adams' ex-Secretary of State, Senator Timothy Pickering of Massachusetts. Few figures in American history are easier to dislike than this long, lean, sour fanatic. When George Rose came from England as a special ambassador to settle the *Chesapeake* affair, Pickering had immediately entered into a secret correspondence with him. Jefferson and Madison rejected Rose's arrogant satire on negotiation, and Pickering openly sided with the British minister. Now the Senator wrote an open letter to the Governor of Massachusetts, published as a pamphlet, calling on him to summon a New England convention to nullify the embargo law. From there he proceeded to a pious defense of the British Orders in Council, which permitted their navy to seize American ships and impress American seamen almost at will. The real reason for our difficulties with England, the Senator declared, was "the mysterious conduct of our affairs after the attack on the *Chesapeake*." The real purpose of the embargo was to starve England into submission. It was all part of a secret deal Jefferson had made with Napoleon. As for standing behind the President, the whole trouble with the nation, Pickering shrilled, was its blind confidence in Thomas Jefferson.

Pickering sent his letter to ex-Ambassador Rose in London, where it was reprinted in the midst of a campaign by Englishmen friendly to America for the repeal of the Orders in Council. Their chief argument was, of course, the determination and unity with which Americans backed the embargo. The letter made these men look like fools. "Your modesty would suffer," Rose wrote to Pickering, "if you were aware of the sensation produced in this country by the publication." The mortified American ambassador, William Pinckney, called for a rebuttal. "Have you prohibited the exportation of all pamphlets which uphold our rights and our honor?" he asked Secretary of State Madison. Naturally, the King's ministers, eager to justify their aggressive policies, seized on Senator Pickering's ranting as proof that Americans lacked the willpower and self-sacrifice to see the embargo through. This vastly stiffened their resistance to it.

Along the Canadian border, and in some New England ports,

violations of the embargo became organized and almost treasonous. Private armies guarded rafts loaded with flour and corn moving up Lake Champlain to Montreal. Coastal traders, permitted under the law, repeatedly sneaked to Bermuda or the British West Indies, blandly claiming they were "blown off course." When the good, the wise and the rich urge men to resist their government, and that resistance, by happy coincidence, involves a chance to make stupendous profits, was it surprising that many could not resist the temptation?

Pickering's letter had one good effect. It drove John Quincy Adams completely into the Republican Party. The son of John Yankee wrote a ferocious pamphlet, castigating this "Senator of the United States, specially charged with the maintenance of the nation's rights against foreign powers, and at a moment extremely critical of pending negotiations," for his "formal abandonment of the American cause, this summons to unconditional surrender to the pretensions of our antagonists." But his answer, appealing to men's minds, lacked the impact of Pickering's appeal to their pockets.

Secretary of the Treasury Gallatin, who bore the major burden of enforcing the law, was soon lamenting to Madison, "The people have been taught to view the embargo less as a shield protecting them against the decrees and orders of foreign powers than as the true if not primary cause of the stagnation of commerce and depreciation of produce. . . . I had rather to encounter war itself than to display our impotence to enforce our laws." Jefferson himself admitted mournfully, "I did not expect a crop of so sudden and rank growth of fraud and open opposition by force should have grown up in the United States."

Privately, Jefferson admitted to Gallatin: "This embargo law is certainly the most embarrassing one we have ever had to execute." But he did not let this emotion interfere with his determination. Instead, he got tough. Collectors of customs who failed to do their jobs were fired. The navy was ordered to patrol the New England coasts, and first local militia, and next the regular army was sent to smash the smuggling rings along the Canadian border. As violators squirmed around clauses that permitted coastal shipping, and the importation of foodstuffs in cases of genuine want, Jefferson replied with tighter federal regulations. Pickering and company inevitably shrilled that he was seizing more arbitrary power than John Adams ever dreamed of wielding at the height of the Sedition Act frenzy. But Jefferson was not exercising his power for the sole purpose of crushing his political opponents. He was obeying his sworn oath to enforce the laws of the United States. Enforce them he did, with a firmness and decision that made it clear to everyone that there was no weakling in the White House.

Ironically, Jefferson's policy was also attacked by the extreme idealists of his own party. John Randolph, of course, was in opposition as usual. But the President's old friend, George Logan of Pennsylvania, who had risked his life and reputation to help avert war with France in 1798, now accused Jefferson of attempting to win a victory by starving "the wretched inhabitants—men, women and children" of the manufacturing towns of New England. Logan swore he could not conceive of a policy "more barbarous or more dishonorable to our nation."

The embargo gave Jefferson personal as well as political headaches. One of his ex-secretaries, William A. Burwell, wrote him a worried letter from Richmond, telling him that the numerous Federalists in that city were accusing Jefferson of selling his tobacco at a good price, after personally leaking a rumor that the embargo would be suspended. Wouldn't it be a good idea, Burwell asked, to refund the price to the buyer? Calmly and at length Jefferson explained the entire transaction to the worried young disciple. Ten months ago, he had told his factor in Richmond to sell his tobacco whenever he could get $7 a hogshead. He had nothing whatsoever to do with the rumor that the embargo would be suspended. As for relinquishing the contract, "Your suggestion," Jefferson said, "has not I think been well weighed. The consequence would inevitably be that instead of giving me credit for a liberal act, the Federalists would consider it as a plea of guilty, and give to the story a new form of ten-fold malignity & difficulty to refute. 'Conscious of having cheated the purchasers, he has slunk out of a transaction which he knew could not be supported, & claims merit for his meanness as if it were a liberality' As sure as we live this turn, or a worse one, if they could find a worse, would be given it. And the inference of guilt would be rendered more plausible. . . ."

But the most acute of Jefferson's embargo headaches was its

timing within the American political framework. It ran straight into an election year. Early in 1808, Jefferson made it clear that he would not run again. It was also clear to every realistic political observer that if he had wanted a third term, all he had to do was remain silent. The legislatures of New York, Pennsylvania, Maryland, New Jersey, North Carolina, Rhode Island, Vermont and even Massachusetts sent resolutions to the White House urging him to serve again. Jefferson replied that he thought it was better for the country if a "proper period" was set, either by the Constitution or "by practice" to the Presidential office. He also believed that "representative government, responsible at short periods of election, is that which produces the greatest sum of happiness to mankind," and he was determined to perform "no act which shall essentially impair that principle." Finally, he was getting old, and he feared the "mental effect" of advancing years. He might have added that the strain of the job was obviously telling on him. Throughout his second term, he had been dogged by a recurrence of his old "head-ach" which left him incapacitated and in agony for days.

For the first time the Democrat-Republicans were confronted with the problem of choosing a candidate. In their first three Presidential runs, Jefferson had been a foregone conclusion. While the President scrupulously refrained from making a public statement, he made it clear that as far as he was concerned, there was only one possible successor: James Madison. The Secretary of State had been the alter ego of his administration, the man who had helped him shape all the crucial foreign-policy decisions. His years as a Congressional leader made him equally expert in domestic affairs.

But the embargo and conflicts, personal and political, within Jefferson's own party made Madison, for a while at least, an uncertain candidate. John Randolph of Roanoke had carried with him into opposition a small band of Republicans known as the "Tertium Quids," or "Third Somethings." More to embarrass Jefferson than anything else, they decided to back James Monroe. This earnest, volatile man was feeling more than a little disgruntled with Madison, blaming him for the decision not to submit his English treaty to the Senate for ratification. At the same time, aging Vice President George Clinton began to preen himself as another alternative. He was easy enough to handle, but the prospect of a contest between Madison and Monroe distressed Jefferson deeply. There is no better example of Jefferson's personal power than the letter he wrote to Monroe on February 18, 1808, in which he masterfully reaffirmed his friendship—and edged him out of the race.

I see with infinite grief a contest arising between yourself and another, who have been very dear to each other, and equally so to me. I sincerely pray that these dispositions may not be affected between you; with me I confidently trust they will not. For independently of the dictates of public duty, which prescribe neutrality to me, my sincere friendship for you both will ensure its sacred observance. I suffer no one to converse with me on the subject. . . . The object of the contest is a fair & honorable one, equally open to you all; and I have no doubt the personal conduct of all will be so chaste, as to offer no ground of dissatisfaction with each other. But your friends will not be as delicate. I know too well from experience the progress of political controversy, and the exacerbation of spirit into which it degenerates, not to fear for the continuance of your mutual esteem. . . . My wish for retirement itself is not stronger than that of carrying into it the affections of all my friends. I have ever viewed Mr. Madison and yourself as two principal pillars of my happiness. Were either to be withdrawn, I should consider it as among the greatest calamities which could assail my future peace of mind.

Monroe was soon writing Jefferson that he intended to remain "an inactive spectator" during the approaching election. He did not raise a hand or speak a word to take advantage of the extremist support offered to him by the strangest of bedfellows, Randolph of Virginia and Pickering of Massachusetts. Both, of course, dreamed of humiliating Jefferson by alienating one of his chief lieutenants. But they misjudged the depths of Monroe's loyalty to the President. In a frank correspondence which does credit to both men, Monroe admitted how badly his feelings had been hurt by the rejection of his treaty with England. But he had never forgotten "the proofs of kindness and friendship" he had received from Jefferson when he was a footloose and alienated young ex-soldier. Monroe was soon telling his supporters that he absolutely refused to become an anti-administration candidate, proof that he meant it when he told Jefferson that the national interest and Jefferson's advancement and fame "were so intimately connected as to constitute essentially the same cause."

Without Jefferson, the Monroe-Madison feud would have shattered the Democrat-Republican Party. Instead, the quarrel merely smoldered and neither man supplied material for either smoke or flame. The combustible stuff all came from outsiders. In spite of the embargo and the usual Federalist campaign of slander, the Clintonian disaffection in New York, and the caterwauling of Randolph and his Virginia dissidents, Madison cruised to a Presidential victory in November that was not far behind the massive majority of Jefferson's re-election. He rolled up 169 electoral votes, to 47 for the Federalists.

Yet more than one historian has claimed that Jefferson's second term ended in a rout. They have discussed his "humiliation" and the "loss of his popularity." There is no sane way to read the vote but as an overwhelming endorsement for Jefferson. No rational observer could claim that the mild, diminutive Madison, with his totally unprepossessing public manner, was the man who rescued Jefferson's popularity. It was Jefferson's towering figure that carried Madison into the White House. The President's popularity did, it was true, dip in New England, but that cantankerous province was not the whole country, difficult as it has always been for them to accept that plain truth. The vote made it clear that four out of every five Americans were still behind Thomas Jefferson.

As for the embargo, nothing could be more honest than Jefferson's discussion of it in his eighth and last message to Congress. "This candid and liberal experiment" had, he said, "failed to force either of the belligerents into revoking their obnoxious decrees." He also admitted that the "losses and sacrifices of our citizens, are subjects of just concern." But he made it clear that the only possible alternative to the embargo was war, not the craven submission to the British Orders in Council which Pickering and his Federalists were recommending. This, Jefferson said, "sacrificed a vital principle of our national independence." The decision, he said, rested with "the wisdom of Congress . . . bringing with them as they do from every part of the union, the sentiments of our constituents."

Then with obvious pride, Jefferson pointed to the fundamentally healthy state of the union. In spite of the embargo, revenues remained high, and the government was able to maintain its steady reduction of the national debt. In six and a half years, $33,580,000 of the debt had been repaid. There was a surplus of $14,000,000 in the Treasury, and the interest savings from the lower debt would add an additional $2,000,000 annually to this comfortable bulge. Jefferson urged an amendment to the Constitution, to permit the federal government to begin the construction of "roads, canals, rivers, education and other great foundations of prosperity and union."

There was a Hamiltonian ring to this last suggestion, as there was earlier in the message, when Jefferson referred with pride to the growth of American factories, thanks to the embargo. He was no longer so fearful of Presidential power, when it was in Republican hands, and he now saw more than a little value in his great antagonist's desire to build up American industry, to make us genuinely independent of Europe. But his continuing distrust of unlimited federal power is also evident, in the call for a Constitutional amendment.

After considerable debate, Congress decided to repeal the embargo in June, 1809, and to declare war on both France and England at the same time. But Federalist ranting, and Republican losses in the local and Congressional elections of New England and New York, shook party leaders from those states and Congress wavered badly. Instinctively they looked to Jefferson for leadership but he was silent. There were only days left in his administration and he did not want to inflict a policy on the friend who was to succeed him. Both he and Madison were especially sensitive on this point because throughout the Presidential campaign, Pickering and his friends had ranted that "from the top of Monticello" Jefferson would "direct all the movements of the little man at the Palace."

So Congress was given its head, and instantly lost it. Stampeded by the New England and New York Republicans, they repealed the embargo, salving the national honor by forbidding all commercial relations between France and between England. This was no solution and the members knew it; the British and French decrees would still enable them to seize American ships wholesale. Jefferson predicted that the policy would lead to war, which it did three years later. But he signed the bill repealing the great experiment on his last day in office.

The peculiar timing of this Congressional shift has enabled more than one historian to picture it as a repudiation of Jefferson's entire administration. To some extent, the atmosphere of defeat was Jefferson's own fault. Once he admitted the embargo was a failure, he should have suspended it immediately. This would have required a special session of Congress, and it would have necessitated, as Jefferson made clear, a simultaneous declaration of war. This last fateful decision, Jefferson could not bring himself to make. It would have probably meant a third term for him. It was almost impossible then, as now, to hand on a war to a presidential successor. It would have meant all the government policies Jefferson detested—high taxes, a swollen debt. Compared to these personal and public evils, the embargo was easy to view as a comparative blessing. So Jefferson clung to it, month by month, hoping the British would crack. But events in Europe combined with Federalist sabotage to frustrate him. A revolution in Spain kicked out the French and opened that country and its numerous colonies to British goods. This guaranteed the embargo's failure. But from the perspective of a century of total war, it has gained the stature of a noble failure.

There is no evidence in any of the descriptions of the final days in the White House, or Madison's inauguration, to give the smallest hint that Jefferson was a man writhing in the fires of humiliation and defeat. The notion is ridiculous. His party had scored an overwhelming victory in the Presidential elections. His best friend was succeeding him as President, so there was not the smallest doubt that the government would be administered on identical principles for the next four years. No wonder the eyewitness accounts of Jefferson at the inauguration picture a man almost radiantly happy.

He rode to the inauguration accompanied only by his burly grandson, Thomas Jefferson Randolph. He was upset to hear that a detachment of cavalry and infantry was preparing to escort him to the Capitol and left early to avoid them. They met on Pennsylvania Avenue and Jefferson merely touched his hat to the bewildered troops and galloped past them. President-elect Madison had invited him to ride with him and Dolley in his carriage, but Jefferson refused, explaining to those who wondered, "I wished not to divide with him the honors of the day, it pleased me better to see them all bestowed on him." The ex-President hitched his horse to a picket fence near the Capitol, just as hundreds of other ordinary citizens were doing, and inside took a seat below the dais—again over the protests of the committee on arrangement. But Jefferson had insisted, saying, "This day I return to the people and my proper seat is among them."

When he discovered, after the inauguration, that there was a plan afoot among many of the capital women to pay their respects to the new President, Mr. Madison, and then go on to the White House to pay a farewell visit to him, Jefferson once more protested, "This day should be exclusively my friend's." He kept on insisting, at Madison's reception, "I am too happy in being here to remain at home."

But the ladies also insisted, and he finally made a bow of acquiescence and slipped out of the crowd to return to the White House in time to greet them. There Samuel Harrison Smith and his wife found him full of jokes. Editor Smith teased him about his sex appeal. The ladies insisted on following him, he said. Jefferson chuckled and said that was just as well, "since I am too old to follow them."

"I remember in France when his friends were taking leave of Dr. Franklin," he said, "the ladies smothered him with embraces, and on his introducing me to them as his successor, I told him I wished he would transfer these privileges to me, but he answered, 'You are too young a man.'"

That night, Dolley Madison began a great Washington, D.C., tradition, with the first inaugural ball. Jefferson came, and cheerfully told everyone that he needed advice on how to behave; it was forty years since he had been on a dance floor. Margaret Bayard Smith said Jefferson's face "beamed with benevolent joy. I do believe father never loved son more than he loves Mr. Madison, and I believe too that every demonstration of respect to Mr. M. gave Mr. J. more pleasure than if paid to himself."

The day after the inauguration, Jefferson began packing. Resolutions of good will and testimonials from towns and state legislatures poured in. One of the most touching came from a group of Washihgtonians who declared that the world knew him as a philosopher, a scientist, a statesman, in all of which he had achieved greatness. But they knew him as *a man*, a friend and neighbor, and it was to this Jefferson that they paid tribute.

That touched Jefferson deeply. On another level he was stirred by the tribute of the Virginia legislature.

In the principles on which you have administered the government, we see only the continuation and maturity of the same virtues and ability which drew upon you in your youth the resentment of Dunmore. From the first brilliant and happy moment of your resistance to foreign tyranny until the present day, we mark with pleasure and with gratitude the same uniform and consistent character—the same warm and devoted attachment to liberty and the republic, the same Roman love of your country, her rights, her peace, her honor, her prosperity.

Perhaps the most revealing words Jefferson himself wrote in these last days were in a letter to his good friend, Pierre DuPont. "Never did a prisoner released from his chains," he said, "feel such relief as I shall on shaking off the shackles of power. Nature intended me for the tranquil pursuits of science, by rendering them my supreme delight. But the enormities of the times in which I have lived, have forced me to take a part in resisting them, and to commit myself on the boisterous ocean of political passions. I thank God for the opportunity of retiring from them without censure, and carrying with me the most consoling proofs of public approbation."

Here, finally, Jefferson was speaking with an undivided mind. The man of action had fulfilled himself. He had achieved the summit of reasonable ambition, and seen the ideas for which he had pledged his life triumphant in the nation. He could, as a bonus, look forward to watching his friends who had battled beside him in the years of defeat and uncertainty go forward under the banner of his name. There was not much more a realistic man could ask. So, on March 11, 1809, Thomas Jefferson, the politician, rode out of Washington, D.C., never to return.

BOOK
SIX

The Country

Gentleman

〰〜

Before Jefferson left the Presidency, his daughter Martha asked him how he planned to live in retirement. The Randolphs were planning to move to Monticello from nearby Edgehill. With nine children, Martha was understandably a little anxious about the possibility that she would find herself running a Virginia version of the White House. Jefferson's reply was reassuring. "I shall live," he said, "like a plain country gentleman." It was a tribute to his optimism, as well as his constant underestimation of his own fame.

It was also a grim testimony to the harsh financial realities which greeted Jefferson when he tried to balance his books, before he left Washington. In an era when greed among the rulers of men was taken for granted, and the Bonapartes were looting Europe, Jefferson departed from eight years of power much poorer than he had gone in. He had to borrow $8,000 from a friend in the capital to clear his Washington, D.C., debts alone.

At home he found himself still dogged by part of the old Wayles debt and other notes he had taken out on his farms during the long years of absence. Worse, he found his lands in the inevitable state of disarray and neglect which his absence always created, and at sixty-six the task of putting them straight was neither easy nor pleasant. He lamented in one letter that he had forgotten what little he ever knew about farming, a startling change in mood and tone from the delight in growing things which he evinced in earlier years. Even his flower garden seemed too much for him. His favorite gardener, Anne Randolph, had married at seventeen, as her mother had before her, and he wrote her mournfully that he scarcely knew one bulb from another, or how to tend them.

But a few months at Monticello, surrounded by his grandchildren, restored Jefferson's spirits and energy. He was soon boasting of being in the saddle from dawn until dusk, "reading the newspapers but little and that little but as the romance of the day."

Jefferson's disengagement from politics was by no means as complete as he pretended. Less than a month after he reached home, he was hard at work trying to repair the political rupture between Monroe and Madison. He paid Monroe a visit, and was soon writing to President Madison describing his "hour or two's frank conversation." Monroe had been so badly beaten by Madison in his halfhearted contest for the Presidency, he was unsure of his standing in the party. Jefferson told him his "wish to see his talents and integrity engaged in the service of his country again, and that his going into any post would be a signal of reconciliation, on which the body of Republicans, who lamented his absence from the public service, would again rally to him." Jefferson assured Madison that Monroe "has quite separated himself from the junto which had gotten possession of him & is sensible that they had used him for purposes not respecting himself always. He & JR [John Randolph] now avoid seeing one another, mutually dissatisfied. . . . On the whole I have no doubt that his strong & candid mind will bring him to a cordial return to his old friends." Thus Jefferson took the lead in the delicate reconciliation, which eventually led Madison to offer Monroe the post of Secretary of State in his cabinet, thereby designating him the Presidential heir apparent.

Jefferson also played a vital role in persuading the restless Gallatin to remain in Madison's cabinet. When the Swiss financier told Jefferson he was inclined to submit his resignation, Jefferson told him it would be "a great public calamity." Gallatin was under fire from dissident Republicans in Pennsylvania. Jefferson soothed his wounds by assuring him that the public paid no attention to these potshots. "None of us ever occupied stronger ground in the esteem of Congress than yourself," he declared. "I hope, then, you will . . . consider the eight years to come as essential to your political career. I should certainly consider any earlier day of your retirement, as the most inauspicious day our new government has ever seen." This was hardly the voice of the disinterested political spectator.

Jefferson corresponded steadily with Madison throughout the eight years of his friend's administration. He never hesitated to give Madison advice and commentary, and backed him firmly in his numerous crises. But there was never a hint that he expected Madison to take his advice, nor did Jefferson ever descend to the minutiae of government. True to his principles of independence, Jefferson wanted his great little friend to make his own way, and he rejoiced in his triumphs and suffered in his misfortunes. In the last days of his life, Jefferson almost inadvertently made a comment that summed up Madison's chief problem as President. After discussing Madison's wisdom, his learning, his great abilities, Jefferson said, with a sigh, "But, ah! he could never in his life stand up against strenuous opposition."

For John Randolph, often the fountainhead of this strenuous opposition Madison encountered, Jefferson dipped his pen in wormwood. He called him "the most invenomed enemy to a democratical republican government which it has ever seen." When his son-in-law John Eppes spoke of retiring from Congress, Jefferson exhorted him to run against Randolph and defeat his "adder tongue." Eppes ran and won, to Jefferson's huge delight.

Jefferson groaned when the war with England he had foreseen and tried to avoid finally exploded in 1812. The first years of the conflict went badly, and the British climaxed Madison's misfortunes by burning Washington, D.C. Jefferson manfully defended his unhappy friend. "Nobody who knows the President can doubt but that he has honestly done everything he could to the best of his judgment. And there is no sounder judgment than his," he told John Eppes. To Lafayette, he explained: "Our thirty years of peace had taken off or superannuated, all our revolutionary officers of experience and grade; and our first draught in the lottery of untried characters [was] most unfortunate. . . ."

He was soon rejoicing that a naval victory on Lake Champlain "has been happily timed to dispel the gloom" of the disaster at Washington. To Lafayette he proudly described the series of smashing American victories in the third and final year of the war. He even began to declare the burning of the capital a blessing in disguise. It had aroused the nation and made the British odious around the world.

Aside from the trouble the sack of the capital caused Madison, what disturbed Jefferson most was the destruction of the Library of Congress. He immediately wrote to Samuel Harrison Smith, and offered his own great collection of books, to serve as the foundation of a new library. "I have been fifty years making it," he told Smith, "and have spared no pains, opportunity or expense to make it what it is." He had already placed in his will a provision that Congress would have an opportunity to buy it at "their own price," but now the loss of the national library "makes the present the proper moment . . . without regard to the small remnant of time and the barren use of my enjoying it." After some legislative dillydallying, Congress accepted, and Jefferson's books became the foundation for the present world-famous collection still called the Library of Congress.

II

Affairs of state were by no means Jefferson's only preoccupation. He told one correspondent, "I have (. . .) been rubbing off the rust of my mathematics contracted during fifty years engrossed by other pursuits, and have found in it a delight and a success beyond my expectations." He remained President of the American Philosophical Society until 1815 and continued to correspond with scientists around the world.

What Jefferson hoped to make the great intellectual work of his retirement was destroyed by a scoundrel. In a trunk shipped from the White House to Monticello were notes and observations he had accumulated over fifty years, on Indian languages and dialects. He planned to write a definitive book on the Indian language, which would help trace their origins, by comparing their basic linguistic patterns to those of other cultures. With his knowledge of Anglo-Saxon, Greek and a half dozen other languages, Jefferson was superbly qualified for the task. But a thief broke into the ship while it was en route to Monticello, and stole this irreplaceable trunk. Finding nothing salable in it, he threw it into the James River. Friends managed to fish out a few of the manuscripts that drifted to shore and sent them to Jefferson, mud-smeared and illegible. But all hope of doing a comprehensive work was gone.

Aside from the hours spent supervising his farms, Jefferson devoted most of his time, in the early years of his retirement, to completing Monticello. Throughout the last years of his Presidency, he had pushed work on the main building. The triumphant white dome, constructed from thousands of individual pieces of wood, rose above the red brick walls. On the east or front entrance, Jefferson blended his own and his mentor Palladio's architectural genius, to achieve the appearance of a comfortable one-story house, by lowering his second-story windows to the floor, so that from the outside they seemed extensions of the tall first-floor windows. Behind this deceptive façade was a three-story, thirty-five-room mansion.

Inside, the house abounded with still more details of Jefferson's taste and ingenuity. On the wall above the front door was a huge gold-faced seven-day clock which ran on a series of pulleys attached to Revolutionary War cannonballs which in turn rose and fell on the two side walls, marking the days of the week in the process. Past the entrance hall, which Jefferson called "the museum," double glass doors opened into the drawing room. The doors opened simultaneously on both sides, at the touch of a hand. The secret was a figure-eight chain attached to two drums inserted into the floor beneath them. In Monticello today they still operate with noiseless perfection, 164 years after their installation.

Both in the drawing room (or parlor) and in the entrance hall, Jefferson accepted the prevailing taste of his time, and literally covered the walls with paintings and drawings. With typical independence, however, he mixed art and artifacts, and placed his paintings, a surprising number of them on religious themes, such as the Crucifixion, beside old Indian maps and sketches. Young George Ticknor of Boston, destined to be one of Harvard's greatest professors, visited Jefferson in 1815, and noted "in odd union with a fine painting of the Repentance of Saint Peter, is an Indian map on leather, of the southern waters of the Missouri, and an Indian representation of a bloody battle . . ."

Ticknor's traveling companion, Francis Calley Gray, noted that the Louis XVI furniture Jefferson had brought with him from France was showing signs of age. "The bottoms were completely worn through and the hair sticking out in all directions." But

Ticknor admired the "large and rather elegant" drawing room with its parquet floor "formed of alternate diamonds of cherry and beech, and kept polished as highly as if it were of fine mahogany."

Off the drawing room, to the north, was the dining room. The walls were a delicate blue, matching Wedgwood medallions set in the mantel, as well as the blue-bordered dishes. In the fireplace Jefferson had installed dumb-waiters that brought his beloved wine up from the cellar by the most direct route. On the door to the kitchen he had placed the same wide shelves he had used in the White House to revolve the food into the dining room, thus dispensing with a parade of servants.

Just off the dining room was a small octagonal tea room in which Jefferson mounted busts of men he admired most. Among them were Washington, Lafayette, Franklin, and, in later years, Alexander Hamilton. As the memory of their personal antagonism dimmed, Jefferson was able to concede Hamilton's greatness as a public financier.

South of the entrance hall Jefferson constructed three rooms for himself, a bedroom, a study, and a library. He began replenishing his shelves immediately after he sold his major library to Congress, and before long had rebuilt his collection to several thousand volumes. "I cannot live without books," he often said. Just off his study, opening onto the terrace, was a small greenhouse which enabled him to grow in all weather the flowers he liked most. Jefferson called this part of the house his *sanctum sanctorum* and no one—grandchildren, visitors, not even Martha—entered it without an invitation.

When Margaret Bayard Smith and her husband visited Jefferson in 1809, she found Monticello largely completed (though Jefferson's greenhouse was as yet empty) and Jefferson was now turning his attention to landscaping his mountain. "My long absence from this place has left a wilderness around me," he told the Smiths. But he was already hard at work, creating new "roundabouts" through the woods on the mountain slopes. He took Mrs. Smith and his granddaughter Ellen in a small carriage to explore those he had already completed.

Mrs. Smith's description of the ride refutes for all time the Federalist canard that Jefferson was physically timid and shrank from danger. "The first circuit," she said, "the road was good, and I enjoyed the views it afforded and the familiar and easy conversation. . . . But when we descended to the second and third circuit, fear took from me the power of listening to him, or observing the scene. . . . We went along a rough road which had only been laid out . . . driving over fallen trees and great rocks which threatened an overset . . . and a roll down the mountains to us."

Jefferson apparently saw the terror in Mrs. Smith's eyes and tried to reassure her. "My dear Madame," he said, "you are not to be afraid, or if you are you are not to show it; trust yourself implicitly to me, and I will answer for your safety; I came every foot of this road yesterday on purpose to see if a carriage could come safely; I know every step I take, so banish all fear." Mrs. Smith tried, but when they came to a point in the road where one wheel of the carriage was in midair above the almost perpendicular slope, she disobeyed orders and jumped out. "The servant who attended on horseback rode forward and held up the carriage as Mr. J. passed." Poor Ellen, she noted, "did not dare to get out."

Mrs. Smith gave a vivid description of Monticello's routine, during the first dozen years of Jefferson's retirement. "At breakfast the family all assembled, all Mrs. R.'s children eat at the family table, but are in such excellent order, that you would not know, if you did not see them, that a child was present. After breakfast, I soon learned that it was the habit of the family each separately to pursue their occupations. Mr. J. went to his apartments, the door of which is never opened but by himself. . . . Mr. Randolph rides over to his farm and seldom returns until night; Mr. Bankhead [Anne's husband], who is reading law, to his study; a small building at the end of the east terrace. [This was the honeymoon cottage. Opposite to it, on the west terrace, Jefferson built a matching one-room red brick cottage, which his son-in-law Thomas Randolph used for an office.] These buildings are called pavilions," Mrs. Smith noted. Thomas Jefferson Randolph "went to survey a tract of woodland, afterwards made his report to his grandfather. Mrs. Randolph withdrew to her nursery, and excepting the hours housekeeping requires, she devotes the rest to her children, whom she instructs. As for them, they seem never to leave her for an instant, but are always beside her or on her lap."

At 3:30 the dinner bell rang, and the family began to reassemble. Between 4 and 5 o'clock, dinner was served in the dining room, in Jefferson's usual sumptuous style. After dinner it was the fashion to take walks, converse, and, for the children, to play games with Grandfather Jefferson on the lawn. Races were among the favorite sports. Jefferson always organized the contestants carefully, placing them according to size. Then, Mrs. Smith said, "he gave the word for starting and away they flew; the course round this back lawn was a quarter of a mile, the little girls were much tired by the time they returned to the spot from which they started and came panting and out of breath to throw themselves into their grandfather's arms, which were open to receive them. . . . He was sitting on the grass and they sat down by him, until they were rested. . . . They now called on him to run with them. . . ." In spite of his sixty-seven years, Jefferson joined them in a sprint.

III

Mrs. Smith was by no means the only visitor to Monticello. In fact, it soon became evident that Jefferson's dream of living as a plain country gentleman was one of his few purely visionary ideas. His granddaughter, Ellen Randolph, in later years described the deluge of guests. "They came of all nations, at all times and paid longer or shorter visits. I have known a New England judge bring a letter of introduction to my grandfather and stay three weeks. . . . We had persons from abroad, from all the states of the union, from every part of the state [Virginia]—men, women, and children. In short, almost every day for at least eight months of the year, brought its contingent of guests. People of wealth, fashion, men in office, professional men, military and civil, lawyers, doctors, Protestant clergymen, Catholic priests, members of Congress, foreign ministers, missionaries, Indian agents, tourists, travelers, artists, strangers, friends. Some came from affection and respect, some from curiosity, some to give or receive advice or instruction, some from idleness, some because others set the example. . . ."

Deeply imbued with Virginia's tradition of hospitality, Jefferson rarely turned anyone away. Added to this crowd of comparative strangers were the dozens of relatives and close friends who came to Monticello as a matter of course. One brought with him his family of six, and remained ten months. The Carrs and all their kin and children, Martha's children and their children, all of these people were equally welcome. Hospitality on such a vast scale put a terrible strain on Jefferson's already straitened finances. It took no less than thirty-seven house servants to keep Monticello running. Visitors' horses consumed staggering amounts of costly feed. One of Jefferson's first biographers asked a surviving house servant if Monticello's three carriage houses were often filled.

"Every night in summer," answered the old Negro, "and we commonly had two or three carriages under that tree."

"It took all hands to take care of your visitors?"

"Yes, sir, and the whole farm to feed them."

Martha Jefferson Randolph was once asked what was the greatest number of guests she remembered in the house at one time.

"Fifty," she replied.

Not all of these people were invited guests. Total strangers frequently wandered up the mountain and into the house, as if it were a public museum. One woman punched out a windowpane with her parasol, to get a look at Jefferson in his study. People lingered in the passage between his study and his dining room, and bunches of them stood at a cautious distance to stare at the ex-President and his family when they were sitting on the porticos in the dusk. Once a young man with an introduction from a friend came to see Jefferson, and met a stranger in the hall. Jefferson greeted them both, and invited them to dinner. The conversation was general, as usual, and after dinner the stranger shook hands with Jefferson and departed. Apologetically, Jefferson remarked to the young man with the introduction that he had not caught "his friend's" name. The young man said he had no idea who he was. Jefferson sighed and said, "I thought he came with you."

To escape the flood of visitors during the summer months, Jefferson built a small house on his Bedford County plantation, Poplar Forest. A granddaughter described it as "very pretty and pleasant. It was of brick, one story in front, and owing to the falling of the ground, two in the rear. It was an exact octagon [the first such house in America], with a center hall twenty feet square, lighted from above. . . . Round it were grouped a bright drawing room looking south, my grandfather's own chamber, three other bedrooms and a pantry. . . . There was a portico in front connected by a vestibule with the center room, and in the rear a veranda."

Jefferson usually took his granddaughter Ellen and one of her younger sisters with him to this retreat. Years later they still remembered these trips as marvelous adventures. "His cheerful conversation, so agreeable and instructive, his singing as we journeyed along, made the time pass pleasantly. . . . Our cold dinner was always put up by his own hand; a pleasant spot by the roadside chosen to eat it, and he was the carver and helped us to our cold fowl and ham, and mixed the wine and water to drink with it."

"We always stopped at the same simple country inns," recalled another granddaughter, "where the country people were as much pleased to see the 'Squire,' as they called Mr. Jefferson, as they could have been to meet their own best friends."

At one of these inns Jefferson struck up a conversation with a traveling clergyman. The man happened to mention some new machines which he had recently witnessed. Jefferson's inquiries and remarks soon convinced the traveler that he was conversing with some eminent engineer. The conversation turned to farming, and Jefferson's discussion of this subject convinced the minister that he was dealing with one of the foremost planters of Virginia. Finally they turned to religion and here, after several minutes, the man of the cloth began to wonder if his fellow traveler was not another clergyman. His only problem, as he told it later, was trying to decide to what particular sect this fascinating stranger belonged. When Jefferson retired for the night the clergyman asked the landlord who he was.

"You mean the Squire?" asked the landlord. "Why, that's old Tom Jefferson."

The granddaughters loved Poplar Forest because it gave them a chance to see more of Jefferson. "He interested himself in all we did, thought, or read," one recalled. "He would talk to us about his own youth and early friends, and tell us stories of former days. He seemed really to take as much pleasure in these conversations with us, as if we had been older and wiser people. . . . I not only listened with intense interest to all he said, but answered with perfect freedom, told my own opinions and impressions, gave him my own views of things, asked questions, made remarks and, in short, felt as free and as happy as if I'd been with companions of my own age."

One thing Jefferson could never resist, no matter how bad his finances became, was expensive gifts for his granddaughters. Ellen Randolph recalled:

From him seemed to flow all the pleasures of my life. To him I owed all the small blessings and joyful surprises of my childish and girlish years. His nature was so eminently sympathetic, that with those he loved, he could enter into their feelings, anticipate their wishes, gratify their tastes and surround them with an atmosphere of affection. I was fond of riding, and was rising above that childish simplicity when, provided I was mounted on a horse, I cared nothing for my equipments, and when an old saddle or broken bridle were matters of no moment. I was beginning to be fastidious, but I had never told my wishes. I was standing one bright day in the portico, when a man rode up to the door with a beautiful lady's saddle and bridle before him. My heart bounded. These coveted articles were deposited at my feet. My grandfather came out of his room to tell me they were mine.

When about 15 years old I began to think of a watch, but knew the state of my father's finances promised no such indulgence. One afternoon the letter bag was brought in. Among the letters was a small packet addressed to my grandfather. It had the Philadelphia mark upon it. I looked at it with indifferent, incurious eye. Three hours later an elegant lady's watch with chain and seals was in my hand, which trembled for very joy. My Bible came from him, my Shakespeare, my first writing table, my first handsome writing desk, my first leghorn hat, my first silk dress.

One day Jefferson heard ten-year-old Cornelia talking to herself, while going up Monticello's narrow stairs. "I never had a silk dress in my life," she said, undoubtedly with a sob in her throat. The next day a silk dress arrived from Charlottesville, and to make sure there were no more tears, a pair of pretty dresses for Cornelia's two younger sisters. One of these granddaughters recalled how Jefferson was standing nearby one day when she caught one of her good dresses on a broken pane of glass, and "tore it sadly." A few days later Jefferson strolled into Martha's sitting room and handed the young lady a bundle. "I have been mending your dress for you," he said, handing her a beautiful replacement, which he had selected himself.

Another time, this same young lady heard that one of their neighbors was moving to the West and wanted to sell a valuable guitar. But the price was so high that "I never in my dreams aspired to its possession." One morning, she came down to breakfast and there was the guitar on her chair. Jefferson said it was hers, if she solemnly promised to learn to play it.

Maria Jefferson had left behind her a son, Francis. Jefferson insisted on sharing the expenses of his education with his protesting father, claiming that if he did not, he feared the young man might feel, when he grew older, that he had been slighted in favor of the Randolphs. When his father was away in Congress, or on any other pretext Jefferson could invent, the boy became one more boarder at Monticello. As Francis grew older, Jefferson wrote him long letters full of the sort of sound advice that he had earlier given Jefferson Randolph. Good humor was emphasized, once more, as one of life's sovereign goods. No matter what happened, Jefferson never lost his faith in looking for the bright side of people.

This faith was severely tested, in these years, by the sad decline of his son-in-law, Thomas Mann Randolph. The ex-congressman continued to sink into a mournful spiral of debt. He had some bad luck, losing thousands of dollars on the speculative manufacture of flour during the War of 1812. But his chief problem was an inability to reconcile himself to limited circumstances. He was, literally, generous to a fault. He loaned money repeatedly to deadbeats and signed bank notes for men who were certain to fail him. Above all, he seemed to plunge into inexplicable depressions at crucial moments. He was considered one of the best farmers in the state, and would spend months toiling to bring in the crop, and either leave it in his barns, or let overseers haul it to Richmond too late to catch the top of the market. It was a common saying among Jefferson's neighbors that "no man made better crops than Colonel Randolph, and no man sold his crops for worse prices."

His own economic situation depressed Jefferson badly in the first years of his retirement. In 1810 he wrote to Thaddeus Kosciusko, the Polish volunteer who had fought in the American Revolution.

"Instead of the unalloyed happiness of retiring unembarrassed and independent, to the enjoyment of my estate, which is ample for my limited views, I have to pass such a length of time in thraldom of mind never before known to me. Except for this, my happiness would have been perfect." Most of the $23,950 Congress finally paid for Jefferson's great collection of books went immediately to his more demanding creditors.

But Jefferson's financial situation was not totally desperate. Occasionally, farm prices leaped and he was able to show a profit. He had plenty of land, and he told himself that if real-estate values rose, he could sell off two or three thousand acres and swim clear of red ink for good. Being in debt was nothing new in Virginia. A shortage of hard cash was traditional in a farming economy. "I steer my bark," he told one friend, "with hope ahead and fear astern."

IV

Along with his visitors, his farms, his books and his building, he found time to renew old friendships and heal old wounds. The chief triumph of this kind was Jefferson's reunion with John Adams.

It was a reunion via the U.S. mails; both men were too old to endure the rugged traveling of the era. But it was as real as a handclasp to both of them. The mediating angel was their mutual friend, Dr. Benjamin Rush. This signer of the Declaration of Independence never ceased regretting the separation of his two friends. He chastised both of them for it and testified, from their joint correspondence, that they were now in complete agreement on all points of the political compass. Both ex-Presidents cautiously admitted they would like to renew the friendship. Then came a verbal report from two of Jefferson's neighbors who had visited Adams on a trip to Boston late in 1811. They reported to Monticello that Adams had said, "I always loved Jefferson and still love him."

"This was enough for me," Jefferson wrote immediately to Rush. "I only needed this knowledge to revive towards him all the affections of the most cordial moments of our lives. . . ." All he

wanted now, Jefferson said, was "an apposite occasion" to show
Adams his "unchanged affections for him." But in the same letter
he made it clear that he did not want to correspond with Abigail
Adams. The disaster of their attempted reconciliation after Maria's
death was still too vivid in Jefferson's memory.

Rush discreetly omitted this proviso and sent the warm parts of
Jefferson's letter to Adams. On New Year's Day, 1812, Old John
Yankee took up his pen and wrote a letter to Monticello, beginning
the greatest correspondence in American history. From cautious
discussions of politics in which they did indeed discover their views
were now astonishingly similar, the letters broadened over the
years into philosophy, religion, history and the psychology of men
and nations. They even discussed the Sedition Act without too
much acrimony. Usually it was Jefferson who turned away Adams'
wrathful outbursts with a disquisition on the Greek language or
some other scholarly topic.

In their speculations on politics both men spun off jewels of
insight still worth pondering. Jefferson suggested, "The same
political parties which now agitate the United States have existed
through all time. Whether the power of the people or that of the
[aristoi] should prevail were questions which kept the states of
Greece and Rome in eternal convulsions, as they now schismatize
every people whose minds and mouths are not shut up by the gag
of a despot. . . . The terms of Whig & Tory belong to natural
history, as well as civil. They denote the temper and constitution
of mind of different individuals."

Both agreed there was a natural aristocracy among men. But
Jefferson worried about the problem of distinguishing between the
natural one based on virtue and talents and the artificial one based
on wealth and birth. "That form of government is the best, which
provides the most effectually for the pure selection of these natural
aristoi into the offices of government. . . ." He disagreed sharply
with Adams' idea of placing the rich or "pseudo-aristoi" in a
separate senate of the legislature in order to protect wealth against
the assaults of the have-nots. The wealthy can take care of themselves, Jefferson insisted. There was no need to worry about a
demagogue persuading the people to vote an equalization of property. The people, he said, reiterating his deepest faith, will, with
only an occasional error, "elect the really wise and good."

In 1813, Jefferson sent as a postscript his regards to Abigail Adams. In a P.S. to a following letter, her husband replied that she responded in kind. Jefferson answered with a letter to Abigail, and this friendship too was soon restored to much of its former warmth. But Jefferson never ventured onto the prickly terrain of politics with this formidable lady. They stuck to neutral themes such as grandchildren and rheumatism.

A favorite Adams-Jefferson topic was religion. Adams told Jefferson that in religion as well as government "checks and balances . . . however you and your party may have ridiculed them, are our only security, for the progress of mind, as well as the security of body. . . . Every species of these Christians would persecute deists, as soon as either sect would persecute another, if it had unchecked and unbalanced power. Nay, the deists would persecute Christians and atheists would persecute deists, with as unrelenting cruelty, as any Christians would persecute them or one another. Know thyself, human nature!"

Jefferson replied: "I very much suspect that if thinking men would have the courage to think for themselves, and to speak what they think, it would be found that they do not differ in religious opinions as much as is supposed. . . . We should all then, like the Quakers, live without an order of priests, moralize for ourselves, follow the oracle of conscience. . . ."

As he grew older, Jefferson became more and more devoted to the doctrines and the person of Jesus. Perhaps it was a reaction against the numerous slanders flung at him in the political wars, portraying him as a wild-eyed amoral atheist. "The greatest of all the reformers of the depraved religion of His own country," he told one correspondent, "was Jesus of Nazareth. Abstracting what is really His from the rubbish in which it is buried, easily distinguished by its lustre from the dross of his biographers, and as separable from that as the diamond from the dunghill, we have the outlines of a system of the most sublime morality which has ever fallen from the lips of man."

In 1819, Jefferson wrote to Ezra Stiles, the president of Yale College, what many consider the summation and crystallization of his religious views. "You say you are a Calvinist. I am not. I am of a sect by myself, as far as I know. I am not a Jew, and therefore do not adopt their Theology, which supposes the God of infinite justice to punish the sins of the fathers upon their children unto the third and fourth generation; and the benevolent and sublime Reformer of that Religion has told us only that God is good and perfect, but has not defined Him. I am, therefore, of His theology, believing that we have neither words nor ideas adequate to that definition. And if we could all, after this example, leave the subject as undefinable, we should all be of one sect, doers of good and eschewers of evil. . . ."

From his White House years Jefferson had brought back to Monticello with him a small book which he called "The Philosophy of Jesus." He put it together in two or three nights "by cutting the texts out of the book [the Bible] and arranging them on the pages of a blank book, in a certain order of time or subject. A more beautiful, or precious morsel of ethics I have never seen; it is a document in proof that I am a *real Christian*, that is to say a disciple of the doctrines of Jesus. . . ." Some time during his retirement years Jefferson added to the English text "Greek, Latin and French texts in columns side by side." He had the final compilation bound in red leather with gold tooling. Often, in the last decade of his life, this was the book he took to bed with him for "an hour or a half's . . . reading of something moral whereon to ruminate in the intervals of sleep."

This Jefferson Bible, as it has come to be called, was purchased from his descendants and placed in the United States National Museum in Washington, D.C., in 1895. It was published by the Government Printing Office in 1904, and has since been reissued many times by the government and by private publishers.

V

When James Madison returned home to Montpelier in 1817, leaving President James Monroe to carry on the Jeffersonian tradition, he was greeted by a letter from Monticello. "I sincerely congratulate you on your release from incessant labors, corroding anxieties, active enemies & interested friends, &, on your return to your books & farm, to tranquility & independence. A day of these is worth ages of the former. But all this you know."

To John Adams, Jefferson confidently asserted he had no worries "for the happiness of our brother Madison in a state of retirement. Such a mind as his . . . can never know ennui. Besides, there will always be work enough cut out for him to continue his active usefulness to his country."

Those last words spelled trouble for the White House-weary Madison. Jefferson at seventy-four was embarked on the great project of his old age, the founding of the University of Virginia, and he swiftly made Madison his right-hand man. For nine years the two old pros exerted all their formidable prestige and political know-how on the penny-pinching legislators of Virginia, squeezing out of them by slow degrees the necessary cash. The school was, of course, Jefferson's dream; he had proposed it in his "Bill for the More General Diffusion of Knowledge," presented to the Virginia Assembly in 1779. During his Presidency the Virginia Assembly had made some vague noises about establishing such a college, and he had rushed reams of advice to them. But nothing had come of it. Now the hapless locals found themselves confronted by an extremely determined old man, and no matter how they twisted and turned, he was ready for them.

Jefferson first helped establish a private school, which he shrewdly named Central College, in Charlottesville. After much backing and filling, the legislature voted a piddling $15,000 for the benefit of a state university and appointed twenty-four commissioners to decide on its site. Jefferson was one of the commissioners, and he came to the meeting equipped with a personally drawn map which proved, with blizzards of statistics, that Charlottesville was the "central" point in the state. Also in his portfolio was a complete set of plans for buildings, a course of instruction, a system of rules for the students. To make the victory total, the overwhelmed commissioners let Jefferson write the report. He did his usual superb job, and his friends in Richmond reprinted it as a pamphlet, and distributed it to the legislature. One of his old lieutenants from the political wars, Wilson Cary Nicholas, was in the Governor's chair, and he naturally lent all his influence and persuasive skills to the cause. The legislature voted overwhelmingly to make Central College the new state university.

The victory was another tribute to Jefferson's ability to combine the practical and the ideal. When his freethinking friend Dr.

Thomas Cooper scolded him for incorporating a professorship of theology in the new school, Jefferson replied with one of his philosophic gems. "We cannot always do what is absolutely best. Those with whom we act, entertaining different views, have the power and the right of carrying them into practice. Truth advances and error recedes step by step only; and to do to our fellow men the most good in our power, we must lead where we can, follow where we cannot, and still go with them, watching always the favorable moment for helping them to another step." Jefferson did his utmost to hire Cooper as a professor of medicine and chemistry but the English refugee was too unorthodox and outspoken in his religious opinions, and Jefferson had to beat a strategic retreat before clerical criticism. Nevertheless, in spite of a meager budget from the penny-pinching legislators, Jefferson managed to recruit a first-rate faculty, largely from Europe. At the same time, he put all his remaining strength and energy into the planning and building of the school.

His approach, as usual, was original. He despised the traditional college architecture of the day, which housed the students in huge, ugly dormitories. Instead he conceived "an academical village"— rectangular one-story cottages with rooms for 109 students interspersed by "pavilions" modeled on various Greek and Roman temples, ten of which were faculty houses, six "hotels for dieting the students." At the head of his village, Jefferson placed his last and best dome, the "Rotunda." Modeled on the Pantheon, it would house the university library, while the inside of the dome would double as a planetarium. The pavilions echoed such classical buildings as the Theater of Marcellus and the Temple of Trajan. All these were connected and united by a colonnade whose graceful white arches and pillars made architectural poetry against the sturdy red brick of the buildings.

The energy Jefferson poured into this project, at the age of seventy-six, was incredible. First came endless hours at the drawing board, planning the buildings. He consulted the best architects in the nation. He pored through the works of his old master Palladio. He plowed through winter mud to confer with Madison at Montpelier. Rheumatism tormented him, a fall from his horse broke his wrist again, still he kept on working.

He personally surveyed the ground and supervised the construction of the first buildings. When a shortage of skilled labor developed, he gave on-the-job training to bricklayers and carpenters. One visitor recalled with amazement following Jefferson from Monticello to the site of the university, and watching him show an Italian sculptor, imported through his efforts, how to turn a volute on a pillar. Then he mounted his blood horse "with the agility of a boy." By now he was seventy-nine.

When younger men, such as his chief supporter in the legislature, Joseph Cabell, grew weary, he exhorted them back into line. "What object of our lives can we propose so important? What interest of our own which ought not to be postponed to this? Health, time, labor, on what in the single life which nature has given us can these be better bestowed than on this immortal boon to our country?" As for himself, he was prepared to "die in the last ditch."

Jefferson's educational village also had a shrewd political value. He was able to begin work on the school, even though the legislature had yet to vote him even a tenth of the money he needed. Session after session, he extracted more grants from the protesting legislature, appealing simultaneously to their patriotism and parsimony. When someone asked him why he demanded small appropriations, he gave them the look of a fox who had just outwitted the hunters and bagged a pheasant in the bargain. No one, he said, liked to have more than one "hot potato" at a time crammed down his throat. The legislators fumed at the crack, but they kept on doling out the money. Before Jefferson was through with them, they had anteed up $300,000—about four times as much as they had ever dreamed of spending. Once Jefferson had them on the run, he never wavered in his insistence on achieving the total plan. Again there was hardheaded practicality in his idealism. "The world will never bear to see the doors of such an establishment locked up," he confidently told Madison. Once more he reiterated his deep faith, which in him was synonymous with determination "to pursue what is best, and the public will come right and approve us in the end."

Finally, in March, 1825, the university opened. Jefferson, naturally, was the first rector. Two or three times a week, he invited the young students up to Monticello to dine with him, and he poured out for their benefit anecdotes and recollections of Revolutionary days that he told no one else. One of them once asked how he felt after he had signed the Declaration of Independence. Fire suddenly flashed from Jefferson's old eyes, and another generation glimpsed for a moment the defiant emotions of 1776. "Pretty much," he said, "as you may imagine anyone with a halter around his neck."

"Old books and young society," George Ticknor said, were the two things Jefferson loved most. "After an introduction and being in his company but a short time," one student recalled, "I felt almost as much at home with him as with my own grandfather." Another said there was only one word that summed up the feelings the students had for him, "love—or something more akin to it than I have words otherwise to express." Jefferson astonished them by how much he knew about their families. He told one boy things about his dead father that he had never heard before. They gave him, the young man said, "such a view of his character as made his home and memory still dear to my heart."

Another attraction of Monticello was Jefferson's numerous granddaughters and their visiting female cousins. There was, according to one young man, great "kick up dancing" in the south pavilion of Monticello, to the tunes of the fiddle and the harpsichord. Family tradition tells how Jefferson used to tiptoe close enough to watch the young bloods and belles in action, tapping his foot to the music and perhaps remembering his youthful dancing days at the Raleigh in Williamsburg. If the youngsters caught sight of him, he always retired immediately, saying that an old codger like himself would only spoil their fun.

VI

Throughout these years of labor on the university, Jefferson maintained his prodigious correspondence. At the end of the year 1820, he stopped to count, and found he had written 1,667 letters in the previous twelve months. The discovery caused him to exclaim: "Is this life? At best it is but the life of a millhorse." But he persisted in personally answering almost every letter he received.

Each was added to the enormous, carefully catalogued files of letters which Jefferson had written throughout his long life. He sometimes referred to these as his autobiography. A man's letters, he maintained, written in the pulse and passion of the moment, were far more authentic than a carefully contrived memoir. His heirs would find a staggering 36,000 letters in these files.

He continued to exchange ideas vigorously with numerous old friends. As he grew older, he mellowed on some topics which had once aroused him to warfare. He declared himself solidly in favor of encouraging American manufacturing. As for the Constitution, it was no idol, to be worshiped. It could and should be changed by amendment, to meet the needs of future generations. He never abandoned his hostility to federal judiciary and their steady accumulation of power. In his eighties, he was still inveighing against these "sappers and miners" of freedom. But no political question agitated Jefferson as deeply as the Missouri Compromise.

Missouri, carved from the Louisiana territory, petitioned Congress for entrance to the Union as a state. Largely settled by southerners, her Constitution permitted slavery. A New York congressman introduced an amendment providing that all children born of slaves in Missouri after its admission would become free at the age of twenty-five. A fierce debate erupted in which one of the leading voices was the Federalist senator from New York, Rufus King, who boldly asserted that Congress had the power to forbid slavery in Missouri. The confrontation that was to imperil the nation in 1860 began, as southern congressmen rallied furiously to the cause of state's rights against federal power. Finally, with the help of Kentuckian Henry Clay, a compromise was worked out. Maine, which had separated from Massachusetts, was admitted as a free state, Missouri as a slave state, and slavery was prohibited forever in the Louisiana territory, north of latitude 36° 30'.

To Jefferson, the debate and the solution were equally ominous. "In the gloomiest moment of the Revolutionary War I never had any apprehensions equal to what I feel from this source. . . . Like a fire bell in the night [it] awakened and filled me with terror." It was, he said, "the knell of the union. For the moment it is hushed . . . but this is a reprieve only, not a final sentence." He predicted that "a geographical line, coinciding with a marked principle, moral and political, once conceded and held up to the angry passions of men, will never be obliterated; and every new irritation will mark it deeper and deeper." Bitterly he added, "I can say, with conscious truth, that there is not a man on earth who would sacrifice more than I would to relieve us [the South] from this heavy reproach, in any *practicable way*. The cession of that kind of property, for so it is misnamed, is a bagatelle which would not cost me a second thought, if, in that way, a general emancipation and expatriation could be affected; and gradually, and with due sacrifices, I think it might be."

In another letter a few weeks later, he condemned the Missouri question as "a mere party trick." The leaders of Federalism, he said, "defeated in their schemes of obtaining power . . . have changed their tack, and thrown out another barrel to the whale. They are taking advantage of the virtuous feelings of the people to effect a division of parties by a geographical line; they expect that this will insure them, on local principles, the majority they could never obtain on principles of Federalism. . . . They are wasting jeremiads on the miseries of slavery, as if we were advocates for it. Sincerity in their declamation should direct their efforts to the true point of difficulty, and unite their councils with ours in devising some reasonable and practicable plan of getting rid of it."

Throughout his retirement, Jefferson discussed with many correspondents a variety of such plans. But the vast, and constantly growing, Negro population confounded him and everyone else. He was most hopeful about a scheme to persuade the Virginia legislature to emancipate every newborn Negro child, raise them under the care of the state, and at an appropriate age, ship them to the black Republic of Santo Domingo, or to a colony set up in Africa, at American expense. When the legislature chose Thomas Mann Randolph as Governor of Virginia in 1820, he called on the lawmakers to work out a system of gradual emancipation. But they failed to respond. They were still dominated by the slave-owning eastern section of the state and Randolph, working under the same constitution that had hamstrung Jefferson during his governorship, disgustedly declared that he was "no more than a . . . signing clerk." Yet Jefferson refused to be discouraged. He wrote proudly to a friend, "Mr. Randolph . . . has had the courage to propose to our legislature a plan of general emancipation & deportation of our slaves. Although this is not ripe to be immediately acted on, it will, with the Missouri question, force a serious attention to this object by our citizens."

But the grim forces of economics and human inertia were working steadily against Jefferson's dream of gradual emancipation. A Connecticut Yankee named Eli Whitney had guaranteed the triumph of interest over morality when he invented the cotton gin. The machine, combined with slave labor, was already turning the hot bottom lands of the Mississippi territory to gold, and cotton was swiftly replacing tobacco as the South's number-one crop. The politicians from these new Gulf states became slavery's most vociferous defenders. Their blindness eventually fulfilled Jefferson's dark prophecy about the passions of men.

One might ask, now, why Jefferson did not take the lead, and boldly emancipate his slaves. Several correspondents hinted at this solution to him and always he patiently explained that abrupt emancipation would do more harm than good, especially when done by scattered individuals. Under Virginia law, emancipated slaves had to leave the state. To support themselves in a free economy, they needed training. To one Virginian who took this course, and himself left the state, Jefferson wrote, "Are you right in abandoning this property, and your country with it? I think not. My opinion has ever been that, until more can be done for them, we should endeavor, with those whom fortune has thrown on our hands, to feed and clothe them well, protect them from all ill-usage, require such reasonable labor only as is performed voluntarily by free men, & be led by no repugnancies to abdicate them, and our duties to them."

He constantly sought for evidence to refute his earlier impression that the Negro was inferior to the white man. To one correspondent he wrote, "No person living wishes more sincerely than I do to see a complete refutation of the doubts I have myself entertained and expressed on the grade of understanding allotted to them [Negroes] by nature, and to find that in this respect they are on a par by themselves." In 1815, he invited to Monticello Julius Melbourn, a mulatto who had been born a slave. He greeted him with enthusiasm, and Melbourn later described the long and learned conversation in which Jefferson spoke frequently of "our colored brethren." They discussed political philosophy, English history and other weighty topics.

One man who urged Jefferson to lead a crusade against slavery received a mournful reply. "This, my dear sir, is like bidding old Priam to buckle the armor of Hector. . . . No, I have overlived the generation with which mutual labors & perils begat mutual confidence and influence. This enterprise is for the young; for those who can follow it up, and bear it through to its consummation. It shall have all my prayers, and these are the only weapons of an old man."

VII

If Jefferson could no longer lead a great social movement—which emancipation finally became—he remained a counselor to whom presidents instinctively turned. One subject which he discussed in detail over the years with both Madison and Monroe was South America. He watched with sympathy and intense interest the stirrings of independence in America's southern neighbors. Yet he had no illusions about their immediate future. They were not, he told Lafayette in 1813, "capable of maintaining a free government. Their people are immersed in the darkest ignorance, and brutalized by bigotry & superstition. Their priests make of them what they please, and tho' they may have some capable leaders, yet nothing but intelligence in the people themselves can keep these faithful to their charge. Their efforts, I fear, therefore, will end in establishing military despotisms. . . ."

At the same time he projected an astounding vision of a future in which there would be "a cordial fraternization among all the American nations and . . . their coalescing in an American system of policy, totally independent of and unconcerned with that of Europe. . . . I hope no American patriot will ever lose sight of the essential policy of interdicting in the seas and territories of both Americas, the ferocious and sanguinary contests of Europe . . . I should rejoice to see the fleets of Brazil and the United States ride together as brethren of the same family and have the same interests."

When Monroe was Madison's Secretary of State, and the South American nations were fighting for their independence, Jefferson wrote him, "Every kindness which can be shown the South Americans, every friendly office and aid within the limits of the law of nations, I would extend to them. . . . Interest would wish their independence, and justice makes the wish a duty. They have a right to be free, and we a right to aid them. . . ."

The fruit of this philosophy appeared at Monticello via the post office one day in October, 1823, in Jefferson's eightieth year. Europe was now in control of the nations who had defeated Napoleon and the rulers of Prussia, Austria, Russia, Spain and France had formed a reactionary "Holy Alliance" to maintain their thrones by force. England, aloof from the continent as always, stood outside this new circle of power, watching it warily. When revolution shook South America, the Holy Alliance began plotting to restore Spain's dominion there, and the British government, anxious to maintain the balance of power, revealed the plot to the United States.

The British offered to make a joint declaration with the United States, warning the Holy Alliance to stay out of the Western Hemisphere. The American ambassador had rushed the proposition to President Monroe, and now he sought the advice of his old chief, Jefferson. He wanted to know whether such a joint declaration might entangle America with European politics, whether, in any case, this opportunity might be a justifiable exception and, finally, whether he could trust the English.

Jefferson instantly grasped the significance of the issue. It was, he said, "the most momentous which has ever been offered to my contemplation since that of independence. That made us a nation, this sets our compass and points the course which we are to steer through the ocean of time opening on us." Our main object, Jefferson reiterated, "should surely be, to make our hemisphere that of freedom." Therefore, we should accept by all means, Britain's proposition. It might do the Mother Country some good, too. "By acceding . . . we . . . bring her mighty weight into the scale of free government, and emancipate a continent in one stroke."

In Washington, D.C., Jefferson's Republican convert, John Quincy Adams, was Secretary of State. Together he and Monroe weighed Jefferson's advice and an equally affirmative reply from Madison, and then added to it a fillip of their own. Largely at Adams' urging, Monroe decided to make a declaration warning the Holy Alliance to stay out of the Americas without any formal British support. That way the Holy Alliance could not accuse the United States of plotting against them with England, although it was common knowledge throughout Europe that the English fleet stood ready to back up America's determination. Thus the Monroe Doctrine, as it came to be called, gained added force by warning all European powers that the United States would consider any attempt to "extend their system to any portion of this hemisphere as dangerous to our peace and safety."

VIII

Throughout these same years, Jefferson was constantly bombarded with inquiries from historians who were working on biographies and narratives of the Revolution and the following decades. He answered them as honestly as he could, but after he gave his original library to the Library of Congress, he lacked many official papers and documents and he always carefully warned his correspondents that he was working from memory. He was alarmed by what he accurately foresaw was a preponderance of New England and Federalist prejudice among the historians on his horizon. John Marshall's *Life of Washington*, which pictured the first President as a Federalist hero-saint, tormented by Republican infidels, Jefferson called "a five volume libel."

At the age of seventy-seven he wrote a memoir, now known as his autobiography, but he carried the story only up to the end of the French Revolution. Well before he reached that point, he remarked, "I am tired of talking about myself." But sometime during these retirement years he carefully revised his diary, or *Anas*. This explosive mixture of stories told to him and notes on immediate experiences was especially detailed during his years in Washington's cabinet, and Jefferson clearly intended it to be his refutation of the Federalists.

The finest piece of reminiscence Jefferson wrote, however, was his estimate of Washington. Discussing him with a man who had written an essay on Federalist propaganda in Washington's era, Jefferson said:

I think I knew General Washington intimately and thoroughly; and were I called on to delineate his character, it should be in terms like these.

His mind was great and powerful, without being of the very first order; his penetration strong, though not so acute as that of a Newton, Bacon or Locke; and as far as he saw, no judgment was ever sounder. It was slow in operation, being little aided by invention or imagination, but sure in conclusion. Hence the common remark of his officers, of the advantage he derived from councils of war, where hearing all suggestions, he selected whatever was best. . . . He was incapable of fear, meeting personal dangers with the calmest unconcern. Perhaps the strongest feature in his character was prudence, never acting until every circumstance, every consideration was maturely weighed; refraining if he saw a doubt, but, when once decided, going through with his purpose, whatever obstacles opposed. His integrity was most pure, his justice the most inflexible I have ever known, no motives of interest or consanguinity, of friendship or hatred, being able to bias his decision. He was indeed, in every sense of the words, a wise, a good and a great man.

IX

Not long after the publication of the Monroe Doctrine, Jefferson was writing cheerily to President Monroe. "I shall be among those most rejoiced at seeing Lafayette again." His old friend was returning to his adopted country at the invitation of Congress after thirty-five years in Europe. He was penniless, his great fortune lost in the turmoil of the French Revolution. Tartly, Jefferson added to Monroe, "I hope Congress is prepared to go thro' with their compliment worthily. That they do not mean to invite him merely to dine, that provision will be made for his expences here, which you know he cannot afford, and that they will not send him back empty handed. This would place us under indelible disgrace in Europe." With such prodding, Monroe saw to it that Congress voted Lafayette $200,000 in money and a township of public land in the Louisiana territory.

Lafayette's tour became a triumphant progress up and down the nation, that practically obscured the Presidential election of 1824. High on his list of stops was Monticello. It was a golden day in November when he arrived. A Jefferson grandniece recalled watching the procession of seven carriages come up the mountain, followed by forty or fifty men on horseback. Jefferson, with his daughter Martha, and Dolley and James Madison beside them, waited on the glistening white east portico. Finally the procession appeared through the branches of the willows, the horsemen's gay scarves and glittering spurs flashing in the sunshine. Jefferson walked to the edge of the lawn as Lafayette dismounted from his carriage. For a moment the two old men simply stared at each other, then they tottered forward in a little run, threw their arms about each other and kissed in the French fashion. Tears sprang to the eyes of the hushed encircling spectators. "All was so still," said the grandniece, "that we heard the words distinctly. 'My dear Jefferson. My dear Lafayette.' "

A few months later came a touching letter from John Adams discussing the Presidential election. John Quincy Adams was one of three candidates who split the vote in the hot Presidential race of 1824. The choice of the President was thrown into the House of Representatives. While the country waited in suspense, ex-President Adams wrote to ex-President Jefferson that he hoped "our John" would not be chosen because the close election had created such a turbulent political situation. "I call him our John," Adams said, "because when you was at Cul-de-Sac at Paris, he appeared to me to be almost as much your boy as mine."

A few weeks later John Quincy was chosen President, and Jefferson sent a warm letter of congratulations to Braintree. Adams replied that Jefferson's words had returned him "with rapture to those golden days when Virginia and Massachusetts lived and acted together like a band of brothers." So the two old men, like guardian spirits, joined in looking benevolently down on the republic they had founded.

X

Visitors continued to stream to Monticello. George Ticknor on a second call wrote to his fellow scholar, William H. Prescott, "He

[Jefferson] is now 82 years old, very little altered from what he was ten years ago, very active, lively and happy, riding . . . every day and talking without the least restraint very pleasantly upon all subjects. In politics his interest seems nearly gone . . . but on all matters of literature, philosophy and general interest, he is prompt and even eager. He reads much Greek and Saxon. . . ."

Jefferson continued to correspond with John Adams and other old friends. When Abigail Adams died, her heart-broken husband turned to Jefferson: "While you live, I seem to have a Bank at Montecello [sic] on which I can draw." A dimmer, if not more distant, voice came from across the ocean. Maria Cosway wrote to tell Jefferson the rather sad story of her later days. She had separated from her obnoxious husband and sought solace for a while in a convent. Returning to nurse him in his final illness, she inherited the residue of his considerable fortune. She used the money to set up a school for girls at Lodi, Italy. "Who could have imagined I should have taken up this line? It has afforded me satisfaction unfelt before. . . ." Jefferson replied in warm but somewhat melancholy words, lamenting the death and dispersion of the gay, brilliant coterie they had known in that long-vanished Paris. He expressed delight that she had taken up the "hobby" that had enlivened his old age—the education of the young. To her plaintive sigh—"I long to see you," he replied: "The religion you so sincerely profess tells us that we shall meet again."

Almost every day Jefferson mounted an aging but still high-spirited thoroughbred named Eagle for a one- or two-hour canter. In his eighties, when rheumatism prevented him from reaching the stirrup, he mounted the horse from one of Monticello's terraces. He insisted on riding alone, over the protests of Martha and her daughters, who begged him to take along a servant. Once, fording the Rivanna in flood, Eagle lost his footing on the bank and pitched Jefferson head first into the swirling stream. He managed to catch the pommel of his saddle, and hung onto it until the game old horse reached the opposite bank.

Jefferson might have retained this amazing vigor for a few more years. But the personal world of family and home on which he depended for spiritual sustenance began to disintegrate before his eyes.

First came the misery of watching Anne, the oldest and among the dearest of his granddaughters, suffer the torments of a bad marriage. Her husband, Charles Bankhead, fell deeply in debt, lost his farm and took to drink. He was soon an incorrigible and sometimes violent alcoholic, beating his wife even in her mother's presence, and attacking Thomas Jefferson Randolph on the streets of Charlottesville with "a knife as long as a dirk," stabbing him several times before bystanders intervened. A few weeks later, Martha's husband, Thomas Mann Randolph, caught Bankhead in Monticello, cursing a servant for not bringing him brandy. Randolph's highly inflammable temper went out of control, and he smashed Bankhead over the head with a poker, peeling the skin from his forehead and face and leaving him for dead.

This violence was the prelude for even more serious trouble with Thomas Randolph. The years had erased all traces of that stylish European-educated young man who had won Martha's heart. He dressed like a poor tenant farmer and often drank more than he could hold. More and more he lost what little rein he had on his temper, and "stormed . . . in his big grum voice, in his roughest manner" at Martha, the children, the servants. Martha bore these bitter scenes in silence. Randolph was a somewhat tragic figure. A different wife might have overcome his feelings of inadequacy. But Martha's emotions were hopelessly—and from his viewpoint—inadequately divided between him and Jefferson and long years of association with his father-in-law only sharpened his feeling that he was "a silly bird" among swans.

This inferiority complex was deepened by the steady decline in his own finances. To stave off his creditors, he had permitted his son Jefferson, now a strapping twenty-three-year-old, to assume his debts (which amounted to $33,500) and had deeded his two large farms to him in return. Early in 1825, creditors were pressing young Randolph so hard, he had to sell his father's two farms to save his own property. Bankruptcy meant Randolph lost his right to vote or to hold office in Virginia, a harsh fate for an ex-congressman and Governor.

Jefferson tried to ease the blow by offering Randolph all he had "to the comfortable maintenance of yourself and the family, and to a future provision for them. I have no other use for property." But

Randolph could not bear this final humiliation. He went berserk, accused Thomas Jefferson Randolph of avarice, and Jefferson himself of coldhearted indifference to his plight. He stormed out of Monticello, and took up a hermit's life in a small five-room house at North Milton, several miles away.

Jefferson begged him to return. "Let me beseech you, dear sir . . . to become again a member of the family rather than continue in solitude, brooding over your misfortunes." On the bottom of this letter Randolph scrawled a contemptuous answer, which showed insanity was imminently to be added to his woes. "I never slept a night from Monticello while my wife was there. But I left it early & returned after dark. After my misfortune I wished to avoid the supercilious looks of Mr. Jefferson's various guests. . . ."

To Jefferson's deep distress, Randolph continued his solitary way of life, meanwhile battling fiercely with his son over the details of selling his farms.

As 1826 dawned, an even worse disaster threatened Jefferson—the loss of Monticello, and everything else he owned. For almost ten years he had juggled debt against debt, hoping desperately that the economic situation in Virginia would change for the better. Instead, it kept changing for the worse. Ironically it was the vast new lands that Jefferson had opened to westward migration that were to blame. Between 1810 and 1820, a third of the population of Virginia moved west. Land values in the Old Dominion plunged to the point where plantations were, in Jefferson's mournful words, "sold by the sheriff for one year's rent." The rich new western farmlands glutted the market, and drove prices to unparalleled lows. Year after year, Jefferson had to sell his crops for barely one-third their normal value.

The *coup de grâce* was administered, not by Jefferson himself, but by a friend. Wilson Cary Nicholas, the man he had trusted with the Kentucky Resolutions, and one of Jefferson's most faithful lieutenants in Congress during his Presidential years, cosigned one of Jefferson's loans for $3,000. A few months later Nicholas asked Jefferson to sign a note for him—for $20,000. With some misgivings, Jefferson signed, candidly warning Nicholas that he could not hope to cover such an amount. His old friend assured him that there was nothing to worry about. But Nicholas was balancing an even shakier house of cards than Jefferson. For years he had been investing his capital in land, hoping, with even more optimism than Jefferson, that there would be an upturn. It never came, and one grim day ex-Governor Nicholas followed ex-Governor Randolph into bankruptcy. The holders of the $20,000 note turned ravenously on Jefferson.

The impact of the catastrophic news almost killed Jefferson. He suffered a blockage of the bowels, and for several days his family thought he was dying. But he finally rallied, and he temporarily staved off the financial wolves with a blanket mortgage on Monticello and all his other property. Nicholas' ruin was so total that members of his family hesitated to approach Jefferson. Even his daughter Jane, who had married Thomas Jefferson Randolph, shrank from the confrontation. There was a strong tradition at Monticello that whenever any of the female members of the family returned from a trip, they paid a personal call on Jefferson. A few days after the sad news, Jane returned from a visit home. The poor girl spent half the day wandering about the mansion, unable to find the courage to knock on Jefferson's door. Finally the dinner bell rang. Usually Jefferson did not appear for another half hour, when the second bell was rung. But this time he came out at the first bell, calling, "Has not Jane come?"

She ran to greet him, and instead of his usual "hearty handshake and kiss" Jefferson took her in his arms and gave her a grandfatherly hug. Throughout dinner he talked almost exclusively with her. Never, then or later, did he so much as hint at the disaster her father had brought upon him.

His treatment of Nicholas himself was even more remarkable. On his way to Poplar Forest a few weeks after Nicholas' failure, Jefferson stopped the carriage at the entrance to the ex-Governor's plantation and said to one of his granddaughters: "I ought not to stop; I have not time; but it would be cruel to pass him." He greeted Nicholas as one old friend would meet another and never said a word about their mutual troubles. A few months later, Nicholas paid a visit to his daughter and her husband, who had a house on the edge of the Monticello estate. The ruined man could not bring himself to visit Monticello and face Jefferson in the house that he had all but torn from his grasp.

Jefferson, hearing that Nicholas was in the neighborhood, immediately mounted his horse and rode to greet him. Servants were sent to President Monroe and ex-President Madison and soon the three party chieftains were gathered at Monticello to greet Nicholas as if he was still the head of one of the first families of Virginia, and the administration leader in Congress. Nicholas died a few months later. In the last hours of his life he told his children, with tears of gratitude on his cheeks, that Jefferson had never "by a word, by a look or in any other way" made any allusion to his bankruptcy.

Nicholas' collapse was a blow from which Jefferson's finances never recovered. More and more payments failed to be met and by 1826 the accumulated interest and the debts had soared over $100,000. Total ruin stared Jefferson in the face. In January, 1826, he did not even have enough cash on hand to pay local grocery bills. Frantically he clutched at one last hope. If the legislature would authorize it, he would put his property up for sale at a lottery. He was certain that his name and the value of his lands would clear enough money to pay everyone, and leave a surplus for Martha and the children. He sent his grandson Jefferson pounding to Richmond, to persuade the legislature.

Old friends, such as Joseph Cabell, quickly rallied to his side. Monroe, himself deeply in debt and struggling to save his lands, proved again his fundamental loyalty by dropping everything to lend his support. Dabney Carr, Jr., the son of his old friend, now a Virginia appeals-court justice, lent all his prestige and energy. But the first reaction of the legislature was negative. "The policy of this state, " Jefferson Randolph reported mournfully, "had been against lotteries as immoral, and the first view of the subject was calculated to give alarm."

In a desperate attempt at consolation young Randolph wrote, "I do not anticipate trouble but will not be unprepared to meet it. If you will preserve your health and spirits and not suffer yourself to be affected by it; your grandchildren will be so happy in that, that we shall never think of difficulties nor loss of property as an evil. . . . And if the worst happens we shall among us have aplenty for the comfort of my mother and yourself during your lives: and children that make the poverty of rich men, make the wealth of poor ones."

Jefferson struggled to accept these deeply sincere words but he found it almost impossible. In reply he spoke first of his "mortifica-tion . . . that I had so far over-valued myself as to have counted on [the legislature] with too much confidence. I see in the failure of this hope, a deadly blast of all my peace of mind during my remaining days. You kindly encourage me to keep up my spirits, but oppressed with disease, debility, age and embarrassed affairs this is difficult. For myself, I should not regard a prostration of fortune. But I am overwhelmed at the prospect of the situation in which I may leave my family. My dear and beloved daughter, the cherished companion of my early life and nurse of my age, and her children, rendered as dear to me as if my own, from having lived with me from their cradle, left in a comfortless situation, hold up to me nothing but future gloom. Their affectionate devotion to me (in the unhappy state of mind which your father's misfortunes have brought upon him) . . . makes a willingness to endure life a duty, as long as it can be of any use to them."

Jefferson Randolph was not the only grandson who rallied to Jefferson's aid. Francis Wayles Eppes, Maria's son, wrote a moving letter returning the property Jefferson had deeded to him, as part of his mother's inheritance. "You have been to me ever, an affec-tionate and tender father, and you shall find me ever, a loving and devoted son. What that son would do, I will under all circum-stances." The young man assured Jefferson, "if there be sincerity in human nature," that he did it with "greatest satisfaction," and he would ever remain "as deeply indebted, as though your kind inten-tions had been completely fulfilled."

Meanwhile, Cabell and other friends fought the lottery bill through the legislature. At one point there was talk of granting Jefferson an $80,000 interest-free loan, but the old man, desperate as he was, firmly rejected the idea. He had been well paid for his services to the taxpayers, he said, and he would not accept another cent from them. Finally the lower house passed the lottery bill by a mere four votes. "I blush for my country," Cabell wrote Jefferson, "and am humiliated to think how we shall appear on the pages of history." There was resistance in the Senate too but it finally col-lapsed and the "Jefferson lottery" began selling tickets.

Alas, the sales were catastrophically disappointing, even when Governor John Tyler presided at public meetings. Jefferson must have been touched, however, by learning that two of his old Virginia enemies, John Randolph and John Marshall, were heavy subscribers, Randolph buying $500 worth of tickets. Unfortunately an economic depression coincided with the lottery. "The distress of the money market is great beyond all former example," Jefferson Randolph wrote. "Banks are curtailing and universal distrust prevails. Heavy failures are anticipated. . . ."

In desperation, Jefferson Randolph went north to sell tickets, or to raise money by direct subscription. The direct approach proved to be far more effective than the lottery, which was finally abandoned. New York sent $8,500, Philadelphia $5,000, Baltimore $3,000. Jefferson rejoiced in this outpouring, and in the hope that much more money would follow. "No cent of this," he exclaimed, "is wrung from the taxpayer—it is the pure and unsolicited offering of love." Mercifully, he was spared the bitter truth that this initial burst of generosity was never revived. This meant that Monticello would eventually go under the auctioneer's hammer and would moulder through a hundred years of abuse and decay, before Jefferson lovers of the twentieth century rescued it and restored it to its pristine splendor.

The terrible strain of his financial crisis weakened Jefferson badly. For most of the month of February he was confined to his bed, suffering from an acute form of diarrhea. He sensed he was dying, and began to say his farewells. To James Madison he wrote a particularly touching letter. After discussing his financial problems he broke off and said, "But why afflict you with these details? Indeed, I cannot tell, unless pains are lessened by communication with a friend."

Then he added a last testimonial to their friendship, which had endured, "now half a century. . . . The harmony of our political principles and pursuits have been sources of constant happiness to me through that long period. . . . You have been a pillar of support through life. Take care of me when dead, and be assured that I shall leave with you my last affections."

On the 16th of March he made his will. In it, along with gifts to John Adams and his grandchildren, he gave freedom to five of his Negro slaves. Two were children of Sally Hemings, whom he had trained to support themselves. Blacksmith Joe Fosset, who had run away to Washington, D.C., in 1806, was also freed. Sally was probably dead. Her name had long since vanished from Monticello's farm book.

Thereafter, Jefferson slipped slowly downward, his strength ebbing. In Braintree, Massachusetts, John Adams, ninety, was slipping away at the same gentle pace. Jefferson's mind remained clear and firm. On March 30 he wrote to President John Quincy Adams a detailed letter on the treaties of commerce negotiated by America, in the years after the Revolution. On May 15 he wrote a long letter to the son of Light Horse Harry Lee, who was revising his father's memoirs of the Revolutionary War in the South. Jefferson recalled with amazing detail the frantic days of Arnold's raid and discussed once more the capture and burning of Richmond, in words that hinted of past pain. "Is the surprise of an open and unarmed place, although called a city, and even a capital, so unprecedented as to be a matter of indelible reproach? Which of our own capitals during the same war, was not in possession of the same enemy not merely by surprise and for a day only, but permanently?"

A few days later he was writing to Ellen, married to a Boston Coolidge, a letter full of small news about visiting young grand-nieces and their suitors. "According to appearances they had many nibbles and bites," he said gaily, "but whether the hooks took firm hold of any particular subject or not, is a secret not communicated to me. If not, we shall know it by a return to their angling grounds, for here they fix them until they catch something to their palate."

Late in June, came an invitation from the mayor of Washington to join the citizens of that city in a celebration of the fiftieth anniversary of American independence. Crippled wrists, waning spirit and draining body vanished, as Jefferson picked up his pen to answer this appeal, and the memory of those great days flared in him, one last time. Only he, John Adams and Charles Carroll still survived "that host of worthies," as he called them, "who joined us on that day, in the bold and doubtful election we were to make for our country, between submission or the sword." It would console him deeply to see how "our fellow citizens, after half a century of experience and prosperity, continue to approve the choice we made." But age and disease made his physical presence impossible. He could only send his words.

Then came the last bright flame of that eloquence which had fired the Revolution. "May the day be to the world, what I believe it will be (to some parts sooner, to others later, but finally to all) . . . the palpable truth, that the mass of mankind has not been born with saddles on their backs, nor a favorite few booted and spurred, ready to ride them legitimately, by the grace of God. . . . Let the annual return of this day forever refresh our recollection of these rights, and an undiminished devotion to them."

A few days later, Jefferson was too weak to get out of bed. Yet, over Martha's protests, he talked for several hours with Henry Lee, discussing recent floods on the James River, the future of the university and the imminence of death. Jefferson said he looked forward to it "as a man would to the prospect of being caught in a shower—as an event not to be desired, but not to be feared." Hospitable to the end, he insisted young Lee stay to dinner.

On July 2, he called his family to his bedside. Surrounded by the faces of those he had loved and who had loved him, he spoke to them briefly, urging them all to live honest and truthful lives, in his memory. The youngest grandson, eight-year-old George Wythe Randolph, looked both sad and baffled. With a smile Jefferson turned to his older brother, Jefferson Randolph, and said, "George does not understand what all this means."

Later in the day Jefferson called Martha Randolph to his bedside. He handed her a small casket, in which he had written in his still firm clear hand a very special good-by.

A DEATHBED ADIEU FROM TH. J. TO M. R.
Life's visions are vanished, its dreams are no more
    Dear friend of my bosom, why bathed in tears?
I go to my Father's: I welcome the shore
    Which crowns all my hopes or which buries my cares.
Then farewell, my dear, my lov'd daughter, adieu!
    The last pang of life is in parting from you!
Two seraphs await me long shrouded in death;
    I will bear them your love on my last parting breath.

The two seraphs were, of course, those two golden women so alike in their beauty and their frailty, his wife, Martha, and his daughter, Maria.

Jefferson slept throughout the day on the 3rd of July and awoke about 7 o'clock. His faithful grandson Jefferson Randolph, and

Nicholas Trist, husband of granddaughter Virginia, were by his side. "This is the 4th of July," he said, with evident satisfaction. Thus for the first time he revealed his last wish—to die on the fiftieth anniversary of independence. Is there better proof that those words he had written in Philadelphia fifty years ago had penetrated to the very core of his being, had, in the deepest sense, become his life?

Regretfully they told him that it was still the third and he sank again into sleep. At 9 P.M. the doctor came to give him his medicine and he shook his head. In a calm, distinct voice he said, "No, doctor, nothing more." The medicine was laudanum and without it the dying man became restless. He sat up in bed and leaned forward, as if he was hunched once more over his portable desk, writing the explosive words of youth. "The Committee of Safety must be warned," he said.

"During the night of the 3rd," Nicholas Trist later recalled, "as I sat on the sofa, close to his pillow, my eyes were constantly turning from his face to the clock in the corner, the hands of which, it seemed to me, never would reach the point at which I wished to see them. . . . It wanted yet an hour or more of that moment, when, his head turning toward me, he whispered inquiringly, 'This is the 4th?'" Trist tried to pretend he had not heard Jefferson speak. "This is the 4th?" he repeated. Repugnant as it was for him to deceive Jefferson, Trist nodded assent. "Ah," Jefferson murmured, deeply pleased.

He fell into another restless sleep while Trist, Jefferson Randolph and the others stood noting the minute hand of the watch, "hoping for a few minutes of prolonged life." Their wish was granted. Jefferson's withered chest continued to rise and fall as the clock passed midnight. At 4 A.M. he called for Burwell, one of the slaves whom he had freed in his will. He did not speak again. He ceased to breathe, Jefferson Randolph said, "without a struggle, fifty minutes past meridian [12:50], July 4th, 1826. I closed his eyes with my own hands."

A few hours later, in Braintree, Massachusetts, John Adams joined his old friend in eternity. His last strikingly symbolic words have been quoted over the decades: "Thomas Jefferson—still survives."

As the news of the two deaths spread across the land, all but the most hardened skeptics were silenced by a profound awe. Most people agreed with President John Quincy Adams, who noted it in his diary as another sign that America had a special destiny in the world. Humbly the President—and the nation—stood "in grateful and silent adoration before the Ruler of the Universe."

On July 5, Jefferson was buried beneath the great oak on Monticello's hillside, beside his wife and daughter, and his friend Dabney Carr. The funeral was private. Only a few neighbors came, uninvited, braving a soft summer rain.

On his gravestone he asked his family to chisel the following inscription:

HERE WAS BURIED THOMAS JEFFERSON,
AUTHOR OF THE
DECLARATION
OF
AMERICAN INDEPENDENCE
OF THE
STATUTE OF VIRGINIA
FOR
RELIGIOUS FREEDOM
AND FATHER OF THE
UNIVERSITY OF VIRGINIA

Thus Jefferson, in his last words to the nation, reiterated that first momentous commitment to freedom in 1776. Above him on his mountain, he left another kind of epitaph, Monticello. Here is Jefferson's vision of the purpose of this freedom—a world where science and art are equal and accepting partners in the pursuit of happiness, where mind, heart, eye, hand, are equal sharers in the creation and enjoyment of beauty and truth. Poet Karl Shapiro perhaps said it best in his tribute to Jefferson:

". . . the architecture of your hands
Quiets ambition and revives our skill
And buys our faithlessness."

Jefferson's last and best legacy is his life. By now it should be evident that no real understanding of the man from Monticello can be achieved merely by studying his ideas. It is his life that tells us, often more vividly than his words or his buildings, the many meanings of a reasoned commitment to freedom. As President and Vice President, Secretary of State and ambassador to France, Continental Congressman and Virginia Governor and legislator, Thomas Jefferson lived these meanings to their depths and heights. May this book help renew the illumination of this life in our time.

A JEFFERSON FAMILY TREE

Thomas Jefferson I (d. 1697)
m. Mary Branch

Thomas Jefferson II (c.1677-1731)
m. Mary Field

Peter Jefferson (1707-1757)
m. Jane Randolph

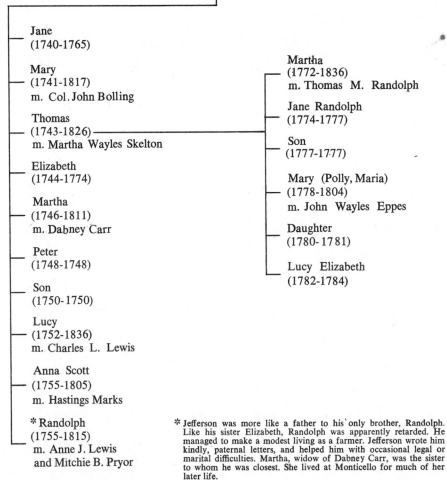

Jane
(1740-1765)

Mary
(1741-1817)
m. Col. John Bolling

Thomas
(1743-1826)
m. Martha Wayles Skelton

Elizabeth
(1744-1774)

Martha
(1746-1811)
m. Dabney Carr

Peter
(1748-1748)

Son
(1750-1750)

Lucy
(1752-1836)
m. Charles L. Lewis

Anna Scott
(1755-1805)
m. Hastings Marks

* Randolph
(1755-1815)
m. Anne J. Lewis
and Mitchie B. Pryor

Martha
(1772-1836)
m. Thomas M. Randolph

Jane Randolph
(1774-1777)

Son
(1777-1777)

Mary (Polly, Maria)
(1778-1804)
m. John Wayles Eppes

Daughter
(1780-1781)

Lucy Elizabeth
(1782-1784)

* Jefferson was more like a father to his only brother, Randolph. Like his sister Elizabeth, Randolph was apparently retarded. He managed to make a modest living as a farmer. Jefferson wrote him kindly, paternal letters, and helped him with occasional legal or marital difficulties. Martha, widow of Dabney Carr, was the sister to whom he was closest. She lived at Monticello for much of her later life.

NOTE ON SOURCES AND METHODS

The primary source for any biographer of Jefferson is, of course, his own letters and other writings. Until recently, these were scattered in manuscript collections around the nation. Jefferson's dream of leaving to biographers a beautifully ordered collection of his papers was destroyed by his bankruptcy. The sale of Monticello dispersed his papers, which were parceled out among several members of the family. Many were lost, others mutilated or at least unwisely altered by well-meaning editors. Now, more than 150 years later, this historical disaster is being repaired by the magnificent new edition of *The Papers of Thomas Jefferson*, edited by Julian P. Boyd, of Princeton University. Seventeen volumes have been issued thus far, bringing Jefferson up to the last years of his ambassadorship in France.

Thereafter the writer must fall back to older editions of Jefferson papers, by no means complete. I have used *The Writings of Thomas Jefferson*, edited by Paul Leicester Ford, and *The Writings of Thomas Jefferson*, edited by Andrew A. Lipscomb and Albert Ellery Bergh, which is more voluminous (twenty volumes) but not so well edited. Equally valuable as a source book is the first of the multi-volumed biographies of Jefferson by Henry S. Randall. Randall, writing in the late 1850's, was able to interview many of Jefferson's surviving grandchildren, and they gave him access to letters which have since disappeared.

Almost as valuable as a source book is Henry Adams' ten-volume history of Jefferson's Presidency. But it is a source which must be used with caution because Adams hated Jefferson with a cold, carefully concealed intellectual passion. He used ridicule and irony, weapons which have become favorites in our era. To him can be traced the widespread belief that Jefferson's Presidency was a failure. Irving Brant, whose multi-volume biography of James Madison impressed this writer enormously, gives incontrovertible evidence of how Adams mistranslated dispatches of foreign ministers to their governments, creating the impression of a bumbling Jefferson and a timid, indecisive Madison.

Still another source of historical hostility to Jefferson is, of course, Americans who have converted Jefferson's controversy with Hamilton into an ideological struggle between conflicting forces which is still going on today. It is, in my opinion, an exercise in futility. I have tried to show, in this book, how in terms of their own times, the radical Jefferson and the conservative Hamilton were in many ways the very reverse of these labels. More important, the controversy has inclined many Americans to forget that both men were Americans, deeply committed to what they believed was the country's best interests. Hamilton is, if anything, a tragic figure who was still developing as a man and as a political thinker when he was struck down by Burr's bullet.

The most useful and illuminating contemporary work on Jefferson is Dumas Malone's *Jefferson and His Time*, three volumes which bring Jefferson up to the eve of his Presidency. Richer in insights into Jefferson's emotional and artistic life are Marie Kimball's three volumes, which bring Jefferson only to the end of his French ambassadorship. Nathan Schachner's 1000-page, two-volume life of Jefferson is consciously iconoclastic at least in intent, but it falls short of being a satisfactory portrayal, on a number of levels. But it does remain the most ambitious effort to see the "emperor" without his clothes.

The length and breadth of Jefferson's career and the complexity of his personality have made the multi-volume approach to his biography almost inevitable. Unfortunately, in our time-conscious era, these works are difficult for anyone but the professional historian to read. At the same time the very complexity of Jefferson's life cries out for reinterpretation in the troubled light of the second half of our uncertain century. This has been my primary motive in attempting the almost impossible task of compressing Jefferson into a single volume.

To supplement written sources, I have drawn on Jefferson manuscript collections, special studies and unpublished theses and dissertations at the Alderman Library of the University of Virginia and at the Massachusetts Historical Society. I made several trips to Monticello and Williamsburg as well as a journey to France, where I visited the Bagatelle, Marly, Fontainebleau, and every other part of the Paris region which still retains any resemblance to the way it looked when Jefferson was America's ambasador and the *ancien régime* was in its last flowering.

For special aspects of Jefferson, there are a number of illuminating books. Fiske Kimball's *Thomas Jefferson: Architect*, published in 1916, restored Jefferson as the father of American architecture. More recent, *Thomas Jefferson: Scientist*, by Edwin T. Martin, is a useful series of essays on this aspect of Jefferson's amazing variety. Helpful in a more eclectic way are *Thomas Jefferson Among the Arts* and *Thomas Jefferson, Humanist*. A new book which I have found especially useful is *The Family Letters of Thomas Jefferson*, beautifully edited by James Adam Bear, Jr., and Edwin Morris Betts. This is the first comprehensive collection of source material on this side of Jefferson's life, and I have drawn heavily on it. Mr. Bear, who is curator of Monticello, was also extremely helpful during my several visits to the mansion.

For special studies of different periods of Jefferson's life, aside from the multi-volume biographies, I found Frank Van der Linden's *The Turning Point* especially helpful. Ably researched and written, it focuses on Jefferson's struggle with Adams and Burr for the Presidency. Among biographies of Jefferson's contemporaries, the two I found most helpful were *John Adams* by Page Smith, which makes a point of contrasting the two men, and Irving Brant's magnificent multi-volume study of Madison already mentioned. Almost as helpful was Adrienne Koch's *Jefferson and Madison: The Great Collaboration*, which in a more condensed but penetrating way examines the highlights of this historic partnership. Julian Boyd's *Number Seven* is an excellent summary of Alexander Hamilton's almost treasonous intrigues with British agents and ambassadors. Louis Sears' *Jefferson and the Embargo* is an excellent antidote to Henry Adams' New England bias on this aspect of Jefferson's Presidency.

As with every historical work, many books which serve no immediate purpose are read, merely for background. Particularly enjoyable is *Jacobin and Junto* by Charles Warren, a delightful study of a Jeffersonian Republican who happened to be the brother of a leading Federalist. It shows that Jefferson's concern about the exploitation of the many by the few was by no means mere political sloganeering. John C. Miller's *Alexander Hamilton* is a model of objective biography which sees Hamilton with all his faults, yet nonetheless finds (deservedly so) much to admire.

Two books which take a decidedly negative stance toward Jefferson are also worth citing. Leonard Levy's *Jefferson and Civil Liberties; The Darker Side* narrates the several occasions when Jefferson supposedly lapsed from his own ideals, in regard to freedom of the press, habeas corpus and similar rights, particularly in the Burr conspiracy and during the embargo. Mr. Levy never seems to ask why Jefferson made these difficult, agonizing decisions. The book is academic in the worst sense of this term. It has no concept, much less appreciation, of the dilemmas and ambiguities involved in the exercise of political power. Daniel Boorstin's *The Lost World of Thomas Jefferson* demonstrates still another danger in writing about Jefferson—it focuses only on his ideas, and ignores his life. Although many of Jefferson's scientific ideas have been superseded by later discoveries, his political life, the story of the way he overcame the divsion within himself which so many men must face, and committed himself to the preservation and building of the American nation is relevant today and will be until the end of time.

Perhaps the most illuminating of these background books is Merrill D. Peterson's *The Jefferson Image in the American Mind*. It tells in fascinating detail the mood swings among politicians and historians toward Jefferson's reputation. He has been claimed or quoted on both sides of almost every controversy in the history of the nation from the era of Andrew Jackson to the days of Franklin D. Roosevelt. Wisely, the book makes no attempt to judge among the claimants. It simply makes clear the enduring power of Jefferson's name.

BIBLIOGRAPHY

Abernethy, Thomas Perkins. *The Burr Conspiracy*. New York: 1959.
Adams, Henry. *History of the United States of America During the Administration of Thomas Jefferson* (10 Vols.). New York: 1889.
Anderson, D. R. *William Branch Giles*. Menasha, Wisc.: 1914.
Axelrad, Jacob. *Philip Freneau, Champion of Democracy*. Boston: 1967.
Bacon, Edmund. *Jefferson at Monticello* (Overseer's Recollections). New York: 1862.
Beard, Charles A. *Economic Origins of Jeffersonian Democracy*. New York: 1927.
Becker, Carl. *The Declaration of Independence*. New York: 1940.
Berman, Eleanor Davidson, D.S.Sc. *Thomas Jefferson Among the Arts*. New York: 1947.
Betts, Edwin Morris, and Bear, James Adam, Jr., editors. *The Family Letters of Thomas Jefferson*. Columbia, Mo.: 1966.
Betts, Edwin Morris, editor. *Thomas Jefferson's Farm Book*. Princeton, N.J.: 1953.
Beveridge, Albert J. *The Life of John Marshall* (4 Vols.). New York: 1916.
Biancolli, Louis. "Thomas Jefferson, Fiddler." *Life*, XXII, April 7, 1947.
Boorstin, Daniel J. *The Lost World of Thomas Jefferson*. New York: 1948.
Bowers, Claude G. *Jefferson and Hamilton—The Struggle for Democracy in America*. Boston: 1925.
———. *Jefferson in Power*. Boston: 1936.
Boyd, Julian P. *Number Seven—Alexander Hamilton's Secret Attempts to Control American Foreign Policy*. Princeton, N.J.: 1964.
———, editor. *The Papers of Thomas Jefferson* (Vols. 1–17). Princeton, N.J.: 1950.
Brant, Irving. *James Madison* (5 Vols.). New York: 1941–61.
Bruckberger, R. L., translated by C. G. Paulding and Virgilia Peterson. *Image of America*. New York: 1959.
Bullock, Helen V. *My Head and My Heart*. New York: 1945.
Burnett, Edmund Cody. *The Continental Congress*. New York: 1941.
Cappon, Lester J., editor. *The Adams-Jefferson Letters* (2 Vols.). Chapel Hill, N.C.: 1959.
Chinard, Gilbert, editor. *The Literary Bible of Thomas Jefferson—His Commonplace Book of Philosophers and Poets*. Baltimore, Md.: 1928.
———. *Thomas Jefferson, the Apostle of Americanism*. Boston: 1937.

Cooke, Jacob E., editor. *Alexander Hamilton—A Profile*. New York: 1967.

Cresson, W. P. *James Monroe*. Chapel Hill, N.C.: 1946.

Cunningham, Noble E., Jr. *The Jeffersonian Republicans in Power*. Chapel Hill, N.C.: 1963.

Dix, John A. *Memoirs*, edited by his son, Morgan Dix. New York: 1883.

Dunbar, Louise Berman. "A Study of Monarchical Tendencies in the United States from 1776 to 1801." Thesis, Graduate School of the University of Illinois, Urbana: 1920. Reprinted from the University of Illinois Studies in the Social Sciences, Vol. X, No. 1, Pp. 1–150.

Eckenrode, H. J. *The Randolphs*. New York: 1946.

Ford, Paul Leicester, editor. *The Writings of Thomas Jefferson* (Vols. I–X). New York: 1897.

Freeman, Douglas Southall. *George Washington* (7 Vols.). New York: 1957.

Gibbs, F. W. *Joseph Priestley*. London: 1965.

Graydon, Alexander. *Memoirs of a Life Chiefly Passed in Pennsylvania Within the Last Sixty Years*. Edinburgh: 1822.

Griswold, Rufus Willmot. *The Republican Court: Or American Society in the Days of Washington*. New York: 1867.

Hunt, Gaillard, editor. *The First Forty Years of Washington Society— The Family Letters of Mrs. Samuel Harrison Smith (Margaret Bayard)*. New York: 1906.

Isaac. *Memoirs of a Monticello Slave*, as dictated to Charles Campbell in the 1840's by one of Thomas Jefferson's slaves. Charlottesville, Va.: 1951.

Johnson, Allen. *Jefferson and His Colleagues*. New York: 1921.

Kimball, Fiske. *Domestic Architecture of the Early American Colonies and of the Early Republic*. New York: 1922.

———. *Thomas Jefferson: Architect*. Boston: 1916.

Kimball, Marie. *Jefferson, The Road to Glory*. New York: 1943.

———. *Jefferson: The Scene of Europe*. New York: 1950.

———. *Jefferson: War and Peace*. New York: 1947.

Koch, Adrienne. *Jefferson and Madison: The Great Collaboration*. New York: 1964.

Lehmann, Carl. *Thomas Jefferson, American Humanist*. New York: 1947.

Levy, Leonard W. *Jefferson and Civil Liberties; The Darker Side*. Cambridge, Mass.: 1963.

Lipscomb, Andrew A., and Bergh, Albert Ellery, editors. *The Writings of Thomas Jefferson* (Vols. I–XX). Washington, D.C.: 1904.

MacPherson, James. *The Poems of Ossian*. New York: 1805.

Malone, Dumas. *Jefferson, The Virginian* (Vol. I of *Jefferson and His Time*). Boston: 1948.

———. *Jefferson and the Rights of Man* (Vol. II of *Jefferson and His Time*). Boston: 1951.

———. *Jefferson and the Ordeal of Liberty* (Vol. III of *Jefferson and His Time*). Boston: 1962.

———. *The Public Life of Thomas Cooper*. New Haven: 1926.

Martin, Edwin T. *Thomas Jefferson: Scientist*. New York: 1952.

Miller, John C. *Alexander Hamilton and the Growth of the New Nation*. New York: 1959.

Miller, John C. *The Federalist Era*. New York: 1960.

Morgan, Edmund S. *Virginians at Home—Family Life in the 18th Century*. Williamsburg, Va.: 1952.

Nock, Albert Jay. *Jefferson*. New York: 1926.

Nye, Russell Blaine. *The Cultural Life of the New Nation*. New York: 1960.

Padover, Saul K. *Jefferson*. New York: 1942.

Parmet, Herbert S., and Hecht, Marie B. *Aaron Burr—Portrait of an Ambitious Man*. New York: 1967.

Peterson, Merrill D. *The Jefferson Image in the American Mind*. New York: 1960.

——, editor. *Thomas Jefferson, A Profile*. New York: 1967.

Randall, Henry S. *The Life of Thomas Jefferson* (3 Vols.). Philadelphia: 1871.

Randolph, Jane C. H. *Thomas Jefferson, Monticello Music*. St. Louis: 1941.

Randolph, Sara N. *The Domestic Life of Thomas Jefferson*. Charlottesville, Va.: 1947.

Rice, Howard C., Jr., editor. Chastellux, Marquis de, *Travels in North America in the Years 1780, 1781, and 1782* (2 Vols.). Chapel Hill, N.C.: 1963.

Robbins, Roland Wells, and Jones, Evan (archeologist who dug out Shadwell): *Hidden America*. New York: 1959.

Roof, Katherine Metcalf. *Colonel William Smith and Lady*. Boston: 1929.

Rosenberger, Francis Coleman, editor. *Jefferson Reader—A Treasury of Writings About Thomas Jefferson*. New York: 1953.

Schachner, Nathan. *Thomas Jefferson* (2 Vols.). New York: 1951.

Sears, Louis Martin. *Jefferson and the Embargo*. Durham, N.C.: 1927.

Smith, Page. *John Adams* (2 Vols.). New York: 1962.

Tolles, Frederick B. *George Logan of Philadelphia*. New York: 1953.

Tucker, George. *Life of Thomas Jefferson*. Philadelphia: 1837.

Van der Linden, Frank. *The Turning Point—Jefferson's Battle for the Presidency*. New York: 1962.

Walters, Raymond, Jr. *Albert Gallatin*. New York: 1957.

Warren, Charles. *Jacobin and Junto—Early American Politics as Viewed in the Diary of Nathaniel Ames, 1758–1822*. Cambridge: 1931.

Watson, Elkanah. *The Memoirs of Elkanah Watson, Men and Times of the Revolution*. New York: 1857.

Wharton, Ann Hollingsworth. *Social Life in the Early Republic*. Philadelphia: 1902.

White, Leonard P. *The Jeffersonians—A Study in Administrative History, 1801–1829*. New York: 1951.

Wilstach, Paul. *Jefferson and Monticello*. New York: 1925.

INDEX

Adair, John, 313
Adams, Abigail, *see* Adams, Mrs. John
Adams, Abigail ("Nabby"), *see* Smith, Mrs. William
Adams, Charles, 263
Adams, John:
  ambassador to England, 130–131
  breach with Jefferson, 184–185
  British constitution praised by, 175
  Burr defended by, 317
  cabinet, 233, 247
  Continental Congress and, 38, 39, 41, 42, 48, 51, 52, 58, 59, 60, 77
  death of, 384
  death of son Charles, 263
  Declaration of Independence and, 52, 57, 58, 61
  "Discourses on Davila," 181, 184–186
  elected President, 229
  election of 1796 and, 226–229
  election of 1800 and, 250–270
  "midnight appointments," 278, 296, 298, 307
  mission to France, 123, 124
  peace negotiations, 117
  Presidency of, 229–270, 274, 278, 290, 296, 298
  reunion with Jefferson, 359–361
  Vice President, 157, 175, 181, 226
  XYZ affair and, 239–240, 250
Adams, Mrs. John (Abigail), 124, 126, 127, 130, 131, 143, 147–148, 257, 306–307, 360, 361
  death of, 375
Adams, John Quincy, 124, 184, 288, 289, 290
  elected President, 374
  embargo (1807) and, 336
  Louisiana Purchase approved by, 304
  President, 385
  Secretary of State, 371
Adams, Samuel, 38, 41, 246
Adams, Thomas, 24, 25, 246
Adet, Pierre, 227–228
Age of Reason, The (Paine), 284
Agricola, 185
Albemarle County, Virginia, 7, 11, 28
  captured British troops imprisoned in, 82
Alexander, Tsar, 333
Alien Act, 241–242, 243, 299
Allen, "Long John," 243
Alston, Joseph, 258, 260, 313
Amati, Nicola, 44
Ambler, Jacquelin, 5–6
Ambler, Mrs. Jacquelin (Rebecca), 4–6, 136, 240
American Philosophical Society, 183, 189, 255
  Jefferson and, 231–232, 324, 350

American Revolution, 76, 77, 78,
    82–91, 100–101
  beginning of, 36–39, 48
  Canada and, 48, 67
  France and, 83
  Spain and, 83
Ames, Fisher, 239, 257, 304
Anglicanism, 74
Annapolis, Maryland, Continental
    Congress moved to, 116
Appointments, political, Jefferson
    and, 297–299, 310
"Aristides," 194
Arnold, Benedict, 88–91, 97
Articles of Confederation, 67, 78,
    117, 167
Artois, Comte d', 134
Aurora, The, 239
"Avenia" (antislavery poem), 322

Bache, Benjamin Franklin, 239,
    243
Bacon, Edmund, 281
Bacon, Francis, 176
Bagatelle, 134
Bailey, Theodorus, 264, 267
Bank of England, 176
Bank of the United States, 176–
    177, 178
  official printer of, 195
  opening of, 186–187
Bankhead, Charles, 376
Bankhead, Mrs. Charles, *see* Ran-
    dolph, Anne
Barbary pirates, 131
Barbé-Marbois, François de, 97–
    98, 114, 303
Bastille, 152
Bayard, James A., 256, 263, 267,
    269
Bear, George, 263
Beckwith, George, 166, 167, 174,
    180
Berlin and Milan Decrees, 333

Bible, Jefferson, 362
"Bill for Establishing Religious
    Freedom," 79, 81, 128
"Bill for the More General Dif-
    fusion of Knowledge," 81, 363
Bill of Rights, Jefferson and the,
    154
Bingham, Anne, 144–146, 187–
    189, 192
Bland, William, 7
Blenheim (Carter estate), 18, 94,
    95
Blennerhassett, Harmon, 317
Bonaparte, Napoleon, 299–304,
    314, 320, 333, 334, 335, 371
Boston Tea Party, 27
Braxton, Carter, 69
Breckinridge, John, 245
Breed's Hill, battle of, 39
Bremo, 326
Brown, Dr., 19
Brutus, 185
Buffon, Georges de, 99, 122, 125,
    232
Bunker Hill, 39
Burgoyne, John, 77
Burr, Aaron, 183, 228
  conspiracy by, 312–320
  duel with Hamilton, 312
  election of 1800 and, 251, 257–
    270
  flight to Europe, 320
  trial of, 317–319
  Vice President, 273, 310–313, 315
Burr, Theodosia, 258
Burwell, Rebecca, *see* Ambler,
    Mrs. Jacquelin
Burwell, William A., 322, 337
Butler, Pierce, 189, 192

Cabell, Joseph, 365, 379, 380
Cabell, Samuel Jordan, 294
Caesar (slave), 95

Caesar, Julius, 176
Callender, James, 279–280, 283, 307, 308
Camden, South Carolina, battle of, 87
Canada, American Revolution and, 48, 67
Capital, national, fight over location of, 171–172
Capitol, U.S.:
 architectural competition for, 173
 construction of, 259
Caractacus (horse), 96
Carr, Dabney (brother-in-law), 8, 12, 22–23, 108, 114
Carr, Mrs. Dabney (sister), 8, 22, 77, 105–106, 107
Carr, Dabney, Jr., 121, 379
Carr, Peter, 25, 121
Carrington, Edward, 318
Carrington, Mrs. Edward, 318
Carroll, Charles, 382
Carter, Landon, 73, 74
Carter, Robert, 33
Carter's Grove (mansion), 13
Cary, Archibald, 37
"Catullus," 194
Central College (Charlottesville), 363
Charleston, South Carolina, captured by British, 86
Charlestown, Massachusetts, 39
Charlottesville, Virginia, 92, 93, 95
Chase, Samuel, 58, 59, 279, 297
Chastellux, Marquis de, 103–104, 125
Chesapeake, U.S.S., 332–335
Chesterfield Courthouse, 90
Church, Angelica, 146
Church of England, 74
City Point, Virginia, 90

Claiborne, William C., 264
Clark, George Rogers, 85, 89, 90
Clark, William, 320–321
Clay, Henry, 367
Clinton, De Witt, 310
Clinton, George, 183, 195, 310
 election of 1800 and, 251
 election of 1808 and, 339
 Vice President, 311, 312, 339
Clinton, Henry, 101
Cobbet, William, 241
Coke, Sir Edward, 5, 55
Committee of Correspondence, 22, 27, 28
Committee of Safety, 31, 47
"Common Sense" (Paine), 48
Concord, battle of, 36
Condorcet, Marquis de, 126
Constitution, U.S., 154
 Hamilton's opinion of, 175
 interpretation of the, 177–178
Constitutional Convention, 154, 168, 175, 177, 178
Continental Congress:
 First, 30–31, 33, 34, 35
 moved to Annapolis, 116
 orders to Washington, 76
 paper money issued by, 84
 peace negotiations, 84, 97, 113–114, 116–117
 Second, 38–72, 74, 77, 78, 113–116
 slavery issue and, 119–120
Cooper, Thomas, 253, 364
Corbin, Alice, 4
Cornwallis, Charles, 87, 91–92, 93, 95–96, 100, 101
Corny, Madame de, 126
Cosway, Maria, 132–143, 144, 146, 375
Cosway, Richard, 132–134, 136, 138, 141, 142
Cotton gin, invention of the, 369
Craik, William, 263

Croswell, Harry, 308
Custis, Martha, *see* Washington, Mrs. George
Custis, Nellie, 190

Dallas, Alexander James, 210
Danquerville, M., 138
Daveiss, Joseph Hamilton, 313
Davies, Wilson, 299
Dayton, Elias, 68
Dayton, Jonathan, 313
Deane, Silas, 71
Dearborn, Henry, 279
Declaration of Independence:
  approved, 60, 67
  draft of, 52–66, 68
  editing of, 60–66
  publication of, 67–68
  signing of, 67, 68
  vote on, 58–60
Democracy, Jefferson's opinion of, 166–167
Democratic-Republicans:
  election of 1800 and, 250
  election of 1808 and, 338–340
Democratic Societies, 224
Demosthenes, 176
Dent, George, 263
Désert de Retz, 136
Dickinson, John, 39, 40, 41, 42, 46, 51, 58–59, 60, 247
"Discourses on Davila," 181, 184–186
District of Columbia, *see* Washington, D.C.
Dorchester, Lord, 166
Dougherty, Joseph, 322–323
Drummond, Mrs., 12, 14
Duane, William, 278
Duer, William, 167, 170, 187, 193
Dunmore, Earl of, 22, 27, 28, 33, 35, 36, 37, 45–46, 47
Du Pont de Nemours, Pierre Samuel, 253

"*e pluribus unum*," 69
Eagle (Jefferson's horse), 375
Easson, John, 299
Eaton, William, 313–314, 315
Edgehill (plantation), 169
Elections, Presidential:
  1796, 226–229
  1800, 250–270
  1804, 308–309
  1808, 338–339
  1824, 374
Electoral College, 228
Elk Hill (plantation), 33, 35, 91, 108
  taken by British, 96
Ellsworth, Oliver, 241
Embargo (1807), 334–338, 340–342
Embuscade (frigate), 206
Encyclopédie Méthodique, 128, 129
Entails, 73, 74, 81
Eppes, Elizabeth, 45, 69, 106, 107, 108, 114, 121, 148, 191
Eppes, Francis, 15, 40, 45, 69, 114
Eppes, Francis Wayles, 380
Eppes, John (Jack), 190, 191, 237–238, 294–296, 349
Eppes, Mrs. John, *see* Jefferson, Maria
Eppington, 237, 238

Faquier, Francis, 86
Farewell Address (Washington), 226
Federalist papers, 169
Federalists, 194, 199, 200, 215, 224, 226, 236–237, 240–241
  election of 1796 and, 226–228
  election of 1800 and, 250–270
Fenno, John, 181, 186, 194, 195
Fithian, Philip, 33
Fleming, William, 7, 93
Forest, The (house), 4, 8–15, 23, 69, 86

Fosset, Joe, 381

Fourth of July, celebration of, 292, 332

Fowey (man-of-war), 36

France, American Revolution and, 83

Franklin, Benjamin:
ambassador to France, 130–131
Continental Congress and, 38, 42, 43, 52
Declaration of Independence and, 52, 57–58, 67
illness, 156, 160
Jefferson's risqué story about, 290–291
mission to France, 71, 123
peace negotiations, 117

Franklin, Temple, 290

Freedom of the press, Jefferson and, 282, 308

French Revolution, 149–153, 157, 181, 184, 253
attitude in U.S. toward, 199–205

Freneau, Peter, 252

Freneau, Philip, 183–184, 193, 194, 195, 199–200, 207–208, 212, 214, 252

Fries (auctioneer), 246

Fulton, Robert, 288, 325

Gadsen, Christopher, 38

Gallatin, Albert, 223, 236, 287
embargo (1807) and, 336
Madison Administration and, 348
Secretary of the Treasury, 278, 298, 299, 326, 336
Yazoo fraud and, 297

Gallatin, Mrs. Albert, 287

Gates, Horatio, 77, 86–87, 103
election of 1800 and, 251

Gazette of the United States, The, 181, 184, 186, 187, 194, 268, 313

Gelston, David, 259

Genet, Edmond, 200–204, 206–215, 224

George III, King (England), 21, 29, 31, 33, 34, 39, 41, 44, 46, 48, 49, 56–57, 68, 153, 166
Jefferson introduced to, 131

George, Lake, 183

Gerry, Elbridge, 232, 235, 252

Giles, William Branch, 192, 241, 224–225, 278

Gilmer, George, 50, 77

Graff, Mr. (bricklayer), 52–53

Grasse, Comte de (François Tilly), 101

Gray, Francis Calley, 351

"Great Claw," 232

Green, Timothy, 260

Greene, Nathanael, 90, 92

Halifax, 48

Hamilton, Alexander, 146
Adam's Administration and, 233, 247–248, 250
Army and, 240
assassination threat, 241
Bank of the United States and, 176–177, 178
Constitutional Convention and, 175, 178
death of, 312
defense of Harry Croswell, 308, 311, 312
duel with Burr, 312
election of 1796 and, 229
election of 1800 and, 250–270
Federalist papers, 169
Gazette of the United States and, 181
Hammond, George, and, 179–181
interpretation of the Constitution, 178
Jay Treaty defended by, 225
Jefferson and, 167–182, 186–189, 193–216, 223

Hamilton, Alexander (*Cont.*)
Louisiana Purchase approved by,
304
Madison's battles with, 225–226
Opposition to Burr, 311–312
"Report on Manufacturers," 193
Secretary of the Treasury, 167–
216, 223–229
war debts of the states and, 169–
172
Hammond, George, 179
Hancock, John, 51, 58, 60, 67, 71
Harpers Ferry, 98
Harrison, Benjamin, 30, 31, 41,
42, 43, 44, 58, 59, 61, 78
Hay, George, 317
Helvetius, Madame, 127
Hemings, Betty, 281
Hemings, James, 128, 192, 281
Hemings, John, 281
Hemings, Sally, 147, 280–282, 381,
382
Henderson, Richard, 73–74
Henry, Patrick, 21–22, 27, 28, 30,
34, 96, 115, 192
appeal to arms, 34–35, 36
Constitution, U.S., and, 154
Continental Congress and, 30, 35
Governor, 82, 84, 85
Hamilton's financial program
opposed by, 177
Hichborn, Benjamin, 261–262
Hills, The (estate), 188
Hiltzheimer, Jacob, 38
Hoban, James, 173
Hogendorp, Gijsbert Karel van,
118, 126
Holy Alliance, 371, 372
Hopkinson, Francis, 116
Houdon, Jean Antoine, statue of
Washington, 129
House of Burgesses, 10, 19, 20–22,
26–30, 35, 36
Hudson *Wasp*, 308

Humboldt, Alexander von, 282,
324, 327
Humphreys, David, 121, 143, 157

Indian Queen Tavern (Philadel-
phia), 251
Indians, American, defended by
Jefferson, 99
Inflation, 84
Irving, George W., 259
Isaac (slave), 221

Jefferson, Jane Randolph (daughter), 25, 27, 45
Jefferson, Lucy Elizabeth (daughter), 87, 89, 90, 104, 121, 126
Jefferson, Maria (daughter), 146–
148, 153–160, 169, 190–191, 237,
285, 293, 358
death of, 305–306
death of daughter of, 249–250
Jefferson, Martha (daughter), 19,
106, 107–108, 114–115, 116,
121–123, 130, 153, 168–169,
191, 194, 219, 237, 243, 285,
293–296, 306, 327–328, 347, 376
marriage to Thomas Randolph,
159–160
Jefferson, Martha (sister), *see*
Carr, Mrs. Dabney
Jefferson, Mary (daughter), 78,
121
Jefferson, Peter (father), 16–17,
18, 24
Jefferson, Mrs. Peter (mother),
47
Jefferson, Thomas:
Adams family and, 124
ambassador to France, 130–156,
160
Ambler family antipathy for,
240
American Philosophical Society
and, 231–232, 324, 350

Jefferson, Thomas (*Cont.*)
architect, 13, 38, 129, 172–173, 325–326, 351, 364–365
autobiography, 372
bachelor days, 6–14
"Bill for Establishing Religious Freedom," 79–81, 128
"Bill for the More General Diffusion of Knowledge," 81, 363
Bill of Rights and, 154
breach with John Adams, 184–185
Burr's conspiracy and, 312–320
Cabinet, 278–279
Callender, James, and, 279–280
campaign of slander against, 279–284, 307–308, 309
Capitol building (Virginia) designed by, 129
Carr family and, 23
celebration of Fourth of July, 292
Chesapeake affair and, 332–333
Committee of Safety and, 47
Constitution, U.S., and, 154
Continental Congress and, 30–31, 34, 35, 38–72, 77, 78, 85, 113–119
correspondence files, 366–367
Cosway, Maria, and, 132–143
county collector of supplies for American soldiers, 76
death of, 384
death of daughter Maria, 305–306
Declaration of Independence and, 52–68
declaration of religious freedom, 79, 81
democracy and, 166
draft of Virginia's constitution, 49–50
education, 21
elected President, 270

election of 1796 and, 226–229
election of 1800 and, 250–270, 338–340
election of 1804 and, 308–309
embargo (1807) and, 334–338, 340–342
estimate of Washington, 372–373
father's death, 17
foreign policy, 300
freedom of the press favored by, 282, 308
French Revolution and, 149–153, 157, 201–206
funeral, 385
gardening and, 14, 24, 25, 326, 347, 352
Genet, Edmond, and, 202, 206–215
George III and, 131
Governor (Virginia), 84–97, 101–103, 107
grandchildren and, 191, 194, 327–331, 354–358, 366
Hamilton and, 167–182, 186–189, 193–216, 223
Hemings, Sally, and, 280–282, 307
Henry, Patrick, and, 21–22
honeymoon, 16–19
hospitality of, 354–355
House of Burgesses and, 10, 20–22, 26–30
humor and, 289–291
in France, 122–155
inaugural address, 270, 274–277
inaugural address, second, 309
inauguration of, 273–277
Indians defended by, 99
informality of, 286–287
inscription on gravestone of, 385
interior decoration and, 33, 191–192
interpretation of the Constitution, 177–178

Jefferson, Thomas (*Cont.*)
inventor, 324–325
Judiciary Act repealed by, 296
Jupiter's death, 249
last message to Congress, 340
law practice, 7, 10, 20, 23
Lewis and Clark expedition, 320–321
library, 219, 222, 244, 350, 352, 359, 372
lineage, 11, 14
literary skills, 37, 54, 98
loneliness of, 189, 293, 294
Louisiana Territory and, 300–305, 309
love of books, 17, 26, 352, 366
love of music, 3, 9
Madison, James, and, 75, 113, 128–129, 154, 156–158, 173, 183, 189–190, 192–193, 196, 208, 211, 230–231, 236, 243, 247, 326, 343, 348–349, 381
Madison's inauguration and, 342–343
marriage, 15–16
Mazzei, Philip, and, 24–25
Memorial (Washington, D.C.), 255
migraine attacks, 47, 126, 168, 338
Missouri Compromise and, 367–368
Monroe, James, and, 87–88, 105, 128, 189–190, 211, 235, 339, 348, 379
mother's death, 47
nailery, 221
Navy and, 299–300
nominated for Governor, 83–84
nominated to go to France, 71–72, 97, 113–114
Notes on Virginia, 98, 103, 106, 118, 254, 282, 290, 303

on brink of insanity, 107–108, 157
opinion of Negroes, 99–100, 369
Paine, Thomas, and, 284–285
paleontology and, 232
parents, 11, 16–17
patronage and, 297–299, 310
peace and, 332
personal finances, 347, 358–359, 377–381
personality of, 3, 42, 115
Philadelphia home of, 191–192
physical description of, 3
piracy and, 131, 300
political appointments and, 297–299
popularity, 305, 340
preamble to the Virginia constitution, 53–54
President, 273–344
public speeches, 35
religion and, 253–255, 356, 361–362
reply to Lord North's "Conciliatory Proposal," 42–43
retirement, 347–386
reunion with John Adams, 359–361
riding and, 15
risqué stories and, 290–291
romance with Rebecca Burwell, 4–6
school system proposed by, 81
science and, 324–325
Secretary of State, 156–161, 165–216, 301
slavery opposed by, 57, 100, 115–116, 119–120, 282, 321–323, 368–370
South America and, 370–371
student days, 4–5, 16, 17, 25
Supreme Court and, 296
tall stories of, 289–290
third term issue and, 338–342

Jefferson, Thomas (*Cont.*)
tour of New York State, 183
treaties and, 120–121
treatment of captured troops, 82–83
tributes to, 344, 385
Tuckahoe and, 16
University of Virginia founded by, 363–366
Vice President, 229–270
Virginia and Kentucky resolutions, 244–245
Virginia constitution and, 115–116
Virginia legislature and, 70–82
Washington, George, and, 114, 156–157, 196, 207, 212–214, 215, 249
White House and, 173, 285–296, 323, 343
wife's death, 106–108
will, 381
XYZ affair and, 239–240
Yazoo fraud and, 297
Jefferson, Mrs. Thomas (Martha):
burial place, 108
Carr family and, 23
children, 19, 25, 77, 78, 87, 104
courtship, 8–12, 14
death of, 106–108
delicate health of, 48, 53, 67, 69–72, 76, 78, 86, 90, 104–106
father's death, 23
honeymoon, 16–19
inheritance, 281
inscription on tombstone of, 108
marriage, 15–16
Monticello and, 18, 19–20, 25, 31–33, 69–70
physical description of, 4
slaves owned by, 23
Jefferson Bible, 362
Johnson, William Samuel, 167
Jouett, Jack, 93

Judiciary Act, 296
Julien, Chef, 288
Jupiter (slave), 3, 11, 15, 48, 221–222
death of, 249

Kennedy, John, 274
Kentucky, 73
Kentucky resolutions, *see* Virginia and Kentucky resolutions
King, Rufus, 367
Kingston, Duchess of, 137
Knox, Henry, 167, 168, 182, 187, 189, 202, 203, 208, 210, 211, 212, 213, 235
Knox, Mrs. Henry, 189
Krumpholtz, Johann Baptiste, 134
Krumpholtz, Julie, 134

Lafayette, Marquis de:
American Revolution and, 90–93, 100, 101
French Revolution and, 149–152, 205
Jefferson and, 97, 123–124, 126, 165
tour of U.S., 373–374
Lansdowne (Bingham's country house), 188
Latrobe, Benjamin H., 291, 325
Lee, Arthur, 124
Lee, Charles, 233
Lee, Francis L., 22
Lee, Henry, 383
Lee, Richard Henry, 22, 34, 40, 41, 42–43, 49, 50, 51, 58, 67, 69, 71, 72, 77
Lemaire, Etienne, 288
L'Enfant, Charles, 172
Leopard (frigate), 332
Lewis, Meriwether, 328
expedition of, 320–321
Jefferson's secretary, 280, 293
Lewis, Warner, 7

Lexington, battle of, 36, 39
Library of Congress, U.S.:
  destroyed by British, 350
  Jefferson's library becomes foundation of, 350
Life of Washington (Marshall), 372
Lincoln, Abraham, 274, 304
Lincoln, Levi, 279, 307
Linn, James, 263, 267
Lispinard, Anthony, 259
Little Sarah (British brigantine), 209–211
Livingston, Edward, 264, 266, 267
Livingston, Robert, 51, 266, 301, 303
  Declaration of Independence and, 52
Livingston, William, 40
Locke, John, 55, 176
Logan (Indian chief), 99
Logan, George, 189, 241, 247, 321, 337
Louis XVI, King (France), 150–153, 199, 200
Louisiana Purchase, 300–303, 314, 316, 320
Louisiana Territory, 300–303, 314
Lyon, Matthew, 243, 246, 252, 267

Maclay, William, 177
Macpherson, James, 26
Madison, James, 75, 81, 86, 128–129, 195
  battles with Hamilton, 225–226
  Cabinet, 348
  Congress and, 216, 220, 236
  Constitutional Convention and, 154
  elected President, 340
  election of 1800 and, 258–259
  election of 1808 and, 338–340
  Federalist papers, 169
  founding of University of Virginia, 363, 364
  Genet affair and, 214
  inauguration of, 342–343
  Jay Treaty denounced by, 225–226, 236
  Jefferson and, 75, 113, 128–129, 154, 156–158, 173, 183, 189–190, 192–193, 196, 208, 211, 230–231, 236, 243, 247, 326, 343, 348–349, 381
  Louisiana Purchase and, 303
  marriage, 224
  opposition to Hamilton's financial program, 176–179, 193–194
  President, 348–349
  quarrel with Hamilton, 169–172, 173
  retirement, 362
  Secretary of State, 278, 280, 286, 287, 298, 300, 302, 303, 326, 335
  tour of New York State, 183
  Virginia and Kentucky resolutions and, 244–245
  Virginia constitution and, 115–116
  Yazoo fraud and, 297
Madison, Mrs. James (Dolley), 224, 236, 279, 287, 343
  inaugural ball instituted by, 343
Madrid (château), 134
Magdalene (British revenue cutter), 36
Maison Carrée, 129, 148
Mandeville, Lady Julia, 9
Mansion House, The, 187–188
Marie-Antoinette, 200
Marly-le-Roi (palace), 135
Marshall, John, 239–240, 381
  antipathy for Jefferson, 317
  Burr's trial and, 317–319
  Chief Justice, 273–274, 278, 317–318
  election of 1800 and, 251, 265

Marshall, John (*Cont.*)
 Life of Washington, 372
 Secretary of State, 248, 261
Martin (slave), 95
Maryland (U.S. warship), 284
Mason, George, 55, 78
Mason, John M., 254
Mazzei, Philip, 24, 83, 234, 254
McHenry, James, 233, 235, 247,
 248
McKean, Thomas, 252, 268, 277,
 308
McLane, Allen, 269
McLeod, Kenneth, 94, 95
Megalonyx, 232
Melbourn, Julius, 369
Merry, Anthony, 286–288, 292,
 312
Merry, Mrs. Anthony, 287, 292,
 293–294
Mifflin, Thomas, 209
Mills, Robert, 326
Minerva, 234
Missouri Compromise, 367–368
Missouri River, 99
Mitchill, Samuel Latham, 288, 290,
 325
Monetary system, U.S., 69, 120
Monroe, James, 87–88, 105, 128,
 143
 ambassador to France, 232, 235,
  237
 American Revolution and, 91,
  101
 Congress and, 216
 election of 1800 and, 259, 268
 election of 1808 and, 338–340,
  348
 envoy extraordinary to France,
  302, 303
 Genet affair and, 214
 Jefferson and, 87–88, 105, 128,
  189–190, 211, 235, 339, 348, 379
 Lafayette and, 373–374

 mission to England, 332
 President, 362, 371–372, 373
 Secretary of State, 348, 371
Monroe Doctrine, 372
Monticello, 18
 autumn at, 70
 captured troops entertained at, 82
 description of, 103–104, 352–354
 development of, 14, 15, 20, 24,
  25, 31, 36, 47, 77, 351
 Lafayette's visit to, 374
 rebuilding of, 222
 routine at, during Jefferson's re-
  tirement, 353–354
 taken by British, 94–95
Montmorin, Comte, 152
Montpelier (estate), 236, 243
Moore, Betsey, *see* Walker, Mrs.
 John
Morris, Gouverneur, 202, 204,
 205, 248, 259, 260, 263, 267–268,
 269, 291
 Louisiana Purchase approved by,
  304
Morris, Lewis, 263, 270
Morris, Robert, 60, 120, 172, 188,
 240
Morris, Mrs. Robert (Mary), 188

Napoleon, *see* Bonaparte, Napo-
 leon
National Gazette, 193, 199, 207
National Intelligencer, 255, 274,
 277, 282
Natural Bridge, 24, 104, 136, 141
Navy, U.S.:
 Adams, John, and, 235, 247
 Jefferson and, 299–300
Negroes, Jefferson's opinion of,
 99–100
Nelson, Thomas, Jr., 47–48, 49,
 101
Nelson, Mrs. Thomas, Jr., 47–48
Nelson, William, 4

New England *Palladium,* 254
Newton, Isaac, 176
Newton, T., Jr., 299
Nicholas, George, 96–97, 103, 245
Nicholas, Jane, *see* Randolph, Mrs.
Thomas Jefferson
Nicholas, Robert Carter, 27, 78, 96, 244
Nicholas, Wilson Cary, 244–245, 363, 377–379
Nicholson, Joseph, 266, 267
North, Lord, 42, 43
Notes on Virginia, 98, 103, 106, 118, 254, 282, 290, 303

Ohio River, 98–99
Ordinance of 1784, 119
Osborne's, 91
Otis, Harrison Gray, 188–189

Pacificus, 211
Page, John, 5, 6, 7, 8, 17, 19, 48, 67, 84, 86, 93, 298
Governor of Virginia, 306
Paine, Thomas, 48, 284–285
"Rights of Man, The," 184
Paleontology, science of, founded by Jefferson, 232
Palladio, Andrea, 13, 14, 351, 364
Pantops Plantation, 237, 238
Parker, John, 299
Patent Office, U.S., 165
Paterson, William, 167, 284
Patronage, Jefferson and, 297–299, 310
Pendleton, Edmund, 49, 50, 67, 69, 70, 74, 75, 78, 84, 247
Petit, Adrien, 128, 135, 148, 192, 221, 228
Philadelphia, Pennsylvania, in 1765, 37–38
Philadelphia Aurora, 258, 278
Philadelphia *Daily American Advertiser,* 226

Philips, William, 83, 90, 91
Philodemus, 185
Philosophes, 126
"Philosophy of Jesus, The," 362
Pichon, André, 302
Pichon, Louis André, 287
Pickering, Timothy, 232, 240, 247, 248, 340, 341
election of 1808 and, 339
embargo (1807) and, 335–336
Pinckney, Charles, 252
Pinckney, Charles Cotesworth, 232, 235, 239
election of 1800 and, 250–251, 257, 260
Pinckney, Thomas, 228, 258
Pinckney, William, 335
mission to England, 332
Pine, Mrs., 191
Piracy, Jefferson and, 131, 300
Pittsburgh *Gazette,* 200
Plumer, William, 285, 304
Poems of Ossian, The, 26
Polygraph, 326
Poplar Forest, 46, 95, 96, 355–356
Porcupine, Peter, *see* Cobbet, William
Portfolio, The, 280
Portsmouth, Virginia, 90
Potter, Suzanna, 4
Prescott, William H., 374
Priestley, Joseph, 253
Primogeniture, 73, 74, 81
Princeton, New Jersey:
battle of, 76
Continental Congress meets in, 116
Prospect Before Us, The (Callender), 279
Publicola, 184, 185
Purdie, Doctor, 299

Raleigh Tavern (Williamsburg), 6, 22, 28, 136

Randolph, Anne (grandchild), 191, 194, 219, 328, 329, 347, 376
Randolph, Benjamin, 38, 45, 52–53, 54
Randolph, Benjamin Franklin (grandson), 327
Randolph, Cornelia Jefferson (granddaughter), 329, 357
Randolph, Mrs. David, 317
Randolph, Edmund, 23, 27, 50, 102
  Attorney General, 167, 178, 180, 182, 194, 202, 203, 208, 210
  Burr's defense attorney, 317
  Secretary of State, 224
Randolph, Ellen (grandchild), 243, 293, 328–330, 352, 353, 354, 356, 357
Randolph, George Wythe, 327, 383
Randolph, James Madison (grandson), 327
Randolph, Jane, see Jefferson, Mrs. Peter
Randolph, John, 23, 44, 46, 295, 296, 316, 321, 337, 348, 349, 381
  election of 1808 and, 338, 339
  Yazoo fraud and, 297
Randolph, Martha Jefferson, 291
Randolph, Meriwether Lewis (grandson), 327
Randolph, Nancy, 4
Randolph, Peyton, 30, 35, 36–37
  death of, 46
Randolph, Thomas Jefferson (grandson), 219, 295, 330–331, 353, 376–377, 378
Randolph, Mrs. Thomas Jefferson (Jane), 378
Randolph, Thomas Mann, 16, 17, 159, 160, 169, 294–296, 327, 358, 376
  Governor of Virginia, 368
Randolph, Thomas Mann, Jr., 159–160, 168–169, 191, 194

Randolph, Mrs. Thomas Mann, Jr., see Jefferson, Martha (daughter)
Randolph, William, 11
Randolph, Mrs. William, 11, 16
Recorder, 280
Reign of Terror, 152
Republican Party:
  election of 1800 and, 250–270
  Jefferson and the, 277–278
Richmond Recorder, 307
Richmond, Virginia:
  American Revolution and, 89, 91
  capital moved to, 87
Riedesel, Baron de, 83
"Rights of Man, The" (Paine), 184
Rittenhouse, David, 189, 231
Rochambeau, Comte de, 101
Rochefoucauld, Comtesse de la, 126
Rochefoucauld, Duke de la, 126, 205
Rodney, Caesar, 38, 59, 60, 258
Roosevelt, Franklin D., 274
Rose, George, 335
Rosewell (Page plantation), 7, 8, 19
Rush, Benjamin, 189, 254, 290, 324, 359–360
Rutledge, Edward, 38, 51, 59, 60
Rutledge, John, 38, 40

Sacajawea (Indian squaw), 320
St. John's Church (Richmond), 34
Saratoga, battle of, 77, 82
Savannah, Georgia, captured by British, 83
Schuyler, Philip, 168, 178, 183
"Scourge," 194
Seal, U.S., 69
Sedgwick, Theodore, 189, 265, 270, 274
Separation of church and state, 75

Shadwell (Jefferson family home), 5, 8, 22, 47, 158
  destroyed by fire, 3, 12, 13, 17
Shapiro, Karl, 385
Shays, Daniel, 155
Sherman, Roger, 52, 57
Shippen, Thomas L., 143–144
Short, William, 121, 127, 129, 205, 298, 324
"Signing of the Declaration of Independence" (Trumbull), 134
Skelton, Bathhurst, 4, 10
Skelton, Martha Wayles, see Jefferson, Mrs. Thomas (Martha)
Skipworth, Robert, 12, 14
Small, William, 36
Smith, Cotton Mather, 254
Smith, Joseph Cotton, 231
Smith, Margaret Bayard, 255–257, 273, 287, 289, 293, 325, 327, 352–354
Smith, Robert, 279
Smith, Samuel, 261–262, 264, 267, 269, 279
Smith, Samuel Harrison, 255–256, 277, 282, 343
Smith, William, 143–144, 298
Smith, Mrs. William (Abigail), 124, 143
"Songs of Selma, The," 26
Sons of St. Tammany, 183, 228, 251
South America, Jefferson's interest in, 370–371
South Carolina, American Revolution and, 86–87
Southall, Dr., 299
Spain, American Revolution and, 83
Staunton, Virginia, 94
Stenton (estate), 189
Sterne, Laurence, 9, 14, 106
Steuben, Johann von, 90
Stiles, Ezra, 361

Suffolk, Virginia, burned by British, 85
Sullivan, James, 309
Sullivan, John, 125
"Summary View of the Rights of British America," 30
Supreme Court, U.S., Jefferson and the, 296

Talleyrand, Charles Maurice, 238–239, 302, 303
Tarleton, Banastre, 86, 93–95, 97
Taylor, John, 242–243
Tenth Amendment (U.S. Constitution), 177
Tesse, Madame de, 126
Thomas, John Chew, 267
Thomson, Charles, 51, 52
Thornton, William, 173
Ticknor, George, 351–352, 366, 374
Tilly, François, see Grasse, Comte de
Todd, Dolley Payne, see Madison, Mrs. James
Transylvania, 73
Treaties, with foreign countries, 120–121
Trenton, battle of, 76
Trist, Nicholas, 384
Tristram Shandy (Sterne), 9, 26, 106
Trumbull, John, 132, 133, 134
Tuckahoe (Randolph estate), 16, 88, 89, 91
Tyler, John, 105, 380

Vancouver Island, 173
Vattel, 203
Venezuela, 298
Virginia:
  American Revolution and, 85, 88–97, 100
  Constitution, 85

Virginia, University of, founding of, 363–366

Virginia and Kentucky resolutions, 244–245

Virginia *Gazette*, 33

Volney, Constantin, 231, 253

Wagner, Jacob, 298

Walker, John (Jack), 7–8, 28, 86

Walker, Mrs. John (Betsey), 7–8, 307

Walker, Thomas, 19, 94

War of 1812, 349

Warren (plantation), 245

Warren, Joseph, 44

Washington, D.C.:
  early days in, 259
  planning for, 172
  sacked by British, 349

Washington, George:
  celebration of birthday of, 292, 310
  Commander-in-Chief, 39, 43, 48, 75–76, 77, 90, 92, 101, 102, 117
  Continental Congress and, 30, 76, 78
  correspondence with Jefferson, 114
  death of, 248
  Declaration of Independence and, 68
  Farewell Address, 226
  Hamilton's bank bill signed by, 178
  health, 166
  Houdon's statue of, 129
  House of Burgesses and, 29
  Jefferson and, 114, 156–157, 196, 207, 212–214, 215, 249
  Jefferson's estimate of, 372–373
  marriage, 10
  Paine, Thomas, and, 284
  President, 154, 156–158, 160–161, 166–216, 223–229, 232, 235, 237
  summoned from retirement, 240

Washington, Mrs. George (Martha), 10, 190, 262

Washington Federalist, The, 313

Waterhouse, Benjamin, 324

Waxhaws Creek, 86

Wayles, John (father-in-law), 10, 14, 15, 19, 33, 281
  death of, 23
  Hemings family and, 281

Wayles, Martha, *see* Jefferson, Mrs. Thomas (Martha)

Wayles, Tabitha (sister-in-law), 12, 14

Wayne, Anthony, 93

Webster, Noah, 234–235, 258

Westham, Virginia, 89

Westover, Virginia, 89

Westward expansion, 85, 119, 321, 377

Whisky Rebellion, 223

White, Mary, *see* Morris, Mrs. Robert

White, Thomas, 188

White House, 259
  design for the, 173
  Jefferson and the, 173, 285–296, 323, 343

Whitesides, Mr. 188

Whitney, Eli, 369

Wildair (Jefferson's horse), 283

Wilkinson, James, 312–320

Williamsburg, Virginia:
  American Revolution and, 90, 100, 101
  in 1765, 37

Willing, Anne, *see* Bingham, Anne

Willing, Elizabeth, *see* Jackson, Mrs. William

Willing, Thomas, 188

Wilson, James, 51, 55

Wolcott, Oliver, 233, 241

Wythe, George, 21, 29, 51, 58, 70–72, 78, 219

XYZ affair, 239–240, 250

Yates, Betsey, 7
Yazoo fraud, 297
York (Negro servant), 320

York, Pennsylvania, 93
Yorktown, Virginia, 100–102
Yrujo, Madame, 287
Yrujo, Marquis de Casa, 287–288

A Note About the Author

Thomas Fleming grew up in Jersey City, N.J., graduated cum laude from Fordham University and from 1958 to 1960 served as executive editor for *Cosmopolitan*. In 1963 he received the Brotherhood Award of the National Conference of Christians and Jews for magazine writing. His first books, *Now We Are Enemies,* an hour-by-hour account of the battle of Bunker Hill, and *Beat The Last Drum*, the story of Yorktown, won him high praise as "the Bruce Catton of the American Revolution," and he followed these successes with three other books on the Revolutionary and Colonial periods. He is one of the few modern writers who is building a reputation in both fiction and non-fiction fields as a significant interpreter of the American past and present. *A Cry of Whiteness, King of the Hill, All Good Men* and *The God of Love*, are all novels dealing with the inner life of the American city. *The New York Times* has said ". . . Mr. Fleming has as intense an interest in his scrofulous wedge of geography as Faulkner had in his."